INTRODUCTION TO THE PROPHETS

Introduction to the Prophets

Paul L. Redditt

WILLIAM B. EERDMANS PUBLISHING COMPANY
GRAND RAPIDS, MICHIGAN / CAMBRIDGE, U.K.

Published 2008 by
Wm. B. Eerdmans Publishing Co.
2140 Oak Industrial Drive N.E., Grand Rapids, Michigan 49505 /
P.O. Box 163, Cambridge CB3 9PU U.K.

Printed in the United States of America

13 12 11 10 09 08   7 6 5 4 3 2 1

Library of Congress Cataloging-in-Publication Data

Redditt, Paul L.
Introduction to the Prophets / Paul L. Redditt.
p.   cm.
Includes bibliographical references and indexes.
ISBN 978-0-8028-2896-5 (pbk.: alk. paper)
1. Bible. O.T. Prophets — Criticism, interpretation, etc.   I. Title.

BS1505.52.R43   2008
224'.061 — dc22

2008016713

www.eerdmans.com

Contents

Abbreviations

Books and Periodicals

AB	Anchor Bible
ABD	*Anchor Bible Dictionary,* ed. David Noel Freedman. 6 vols. New York: Doubleday, 1992.
ANET	*Ancient Near Eastern Texts Relating to the Old Testament,* ed. James B. Pritchard, 3rd ed. Princeton: Princeton University Press, 1969.
AOTC	Abingdon Old Testament Commentaries
ATD	Das Alte Testament Deutsch
AUSS	Andrews University Seminary Studies
BDB	Brown, Francis, S. R. Driver, and Charles A. Briggs, *A Hebrew and English Lexicon of the Old Testament.* Oxford, 1907.
BEATAJ	Beiträge zur Erforschung des Alten Testaments und des Antiken Judentum
BHK	*Biblia Hebraica,* ed. Rudolf Kittel. 3rd ed. Stuttgart, 1937.
BHS	*Biblia Hebraica Stuttgartensia*
BKAT	Biblischer Kommentar, Altes Testament
BZAW	Beihefte zur Zeitschrift für die alttestamentliche Wissenschaft
CBQ	*Catholic Biblical Quarterly*
CC	Continental Commentaries
CurBS	*Currents in Research: Biblical Studies*
DDD	*Dictionary of Deities and Demons in the Bible,* ed. Karel van der Toorn, Bob Becking, and Pieter W. Van der Horst. 2nd ed. Grand Rapids: Wm. B. Eerdmans, 1999.

EDB	*Eerdmans Dictionary of the Bible,* ed. David Noel Freedman, Allen C. Myers, and Astrid B. Beck. Grand Rapids: Wm. B. Eerdmans, 2000.
FOTL	The Forms of the Old Testament Literature
FRLANT	Forschungen zur Religion und Literatur des Alten und Neuen Testaments
GBS	Guides to Biblical Scholarship
HAR	*Hebrew Annual Review*
HDR	Harvard Dissertations in Religion
IB	*The Interpreter's Bible,* ed. George Arthur Buttrick. 12 vols. New York: Abingdon, 1951-57.
ISBE	*International Standard Bible Encyclopedia,* ed. Geoffrey W. Bromiley. 4 vols. Grand Rapids: Wm. B. Eerdmans, 1979-1988.
ITC	International Theological Commentary
JBL	*Journal of Biblical Literature*
JSOTSup	Journal for the Study of the Old Testament Supplement Series
JSPSup	Journal for the Study of the Pseudepigrapha Supplement Series
KAT	Kommentar zum Alten Testament
LHB/OTS	Library of Hebrew Bible/Old Testament Studies
LTQ	*Lexington Theological Quarterly*
LXX	Septuagint (Greek Version of the Bible)
MT	Masoretic Text
NAC	New American Commentary
NCBC	New Century Bible Commentary
NEB	New English Bible
NIB	*The New Interpreter's Bible,* ed. Leander Keck. 12 vols. Nashville: Abingdon, 1994-2004.
NICOT	The New International Commentary on the Old Testament
NIV	New International Version
NIVAC	New International Version Application Commentary
NRSV	New Revised Standard Version
NT	New Testament
OBO	Orbis biblicus et orientalis
OBT	Overtures to Biblical Theology
OT	Old Testament
OTL	Old Testament Library
OTM	Oxford Theological Monographs
REB	Revised English Bible
RevExp	*Review and Expositor*
RSV	Revised Standard Version
SBL	Society of Biblical Literature

SBLDS	Society of Biblical Literature Dissertation Series
SBLSemS	Society of Biblical Literature Semeia Studies
SBLSymS	Society of Biblical Literature Symposium Series
SBT	Studies in Biblical Theology
SHBC	Smyth & Helwys Bible Commentary
TOTC	Tyndale Old Testament Commentaries
TLZ	*Theologische Literaturzeitung*
UUÅ	Uppsala Universitetsårsskrift
VTSup	Supplements to Vetus Testamentum
WBC	Word Biblical Commentary

Ancient Texts

Dead Sea Scrolls

1QIsᵃ	Cave 1 at Qumran: msᵃ of Isaiah
1QpHab	Cave 1 at Qumran: pesher (=Commentary) on Habakkuk
4QXIIᵃ	Cave 4 at Qumran: msᵃ of the Twelve
7Q2	Cave 7 at Qumran: a Greek papyrus of the Letter of Jeremiah
11QMelch	Cave 11 at Qumran: ms of a work named Melchizedek

Philo

Cherubim	*On the Cherubim*
Confusion	*On the Confusion of Tongues*
Heir	*Who Is the Heir*
Names	*On the Change of Names*
Planting	*On Planting*
QG	*Questions and Answers on Genesis*

Josephus

| *Ant.* | *Jewish Antiquities* |
| *J.W.* | *Jewish War* |

Rabbinic Literature

B. Bat.	*Baba Batra*
Pesiq. Rab Kah.	*Pesiqta de Rab Kahana*
Pirqe R. El.	*Pirqe Rabbi Eliezer*
Taʿan.	*Taʿanit* (*y.* designates the Jerusalem Talmud)

Targumic Texts

| *Tg. Ps.-J.* | *Targum Pseudo-Jonathan* |

Preface

The purpose of this book is to introduce college and seminary students — and other interested readers — to the Major and Minor Prophets of the Old Testament. I have tried to write more in a conversational than a scholarly tone, in hopes of sustaining reader interest. I have assumed no appreciable knowledge of the Old Testament on the part of the reader. I hope to equip readers to engage in a profitable reading of the prophets on their own, giving readers the essential information for that reading, including enough information about the methods employed by biblical scholars to enable students to comprehend many of the conclusions of scholars and in turn to draw their own conclusions. My own debt to and dialogue with other scholars are inadequately reflected in the footnotes, which were deliberately kept to a minimum. Still, I must mention Mark J. Boda of McMaster University, James D. Nogalski of Baylor University, and Aaron Schart of the University of Essen, Germany, partners in dialogue about the prophets, especially the Minor Prophets.

This work has been a labor of love on the books of the Old Testament/Hebrew Bible to which I have devoted my scholarly inquiry. The reader has the right to know that I am a believing Christian, and that fact will from time to time influence issues I choose to discuss. That said, I do not think that the Major and Minor Prophets were written specifically to or about people or events of the twenty-first century. They seem, instead, self-evidently to have been written for and to have spoken to the contemporaries of the prophets. Though they occasionally predicted the not-too-distant future, they overwhelmingly spoke to the prophets' own time.

Among the prophets' contemporaries were the scribes/editors who recorded and preserved their words. As the recorded messages took shape, some editors even added to their words in an effort to keep those messages alive and relevant to subsequent generations. The texts as we have them were assembled over the years and rose through the centuries in the estimation of their readers to the level of divinely-inspired scripture. Hence, modern readers would do well to keep these processes in mind when they approach the prophets. Whatever one might think about the inspiration of the prophetic texts, one should include the work of these editors.

I have elected to follow the canonical order in the English Bible rather than that of the Hebrew Bible, which does not treat Lamentations or Daniel as prophetic books, or a reconstructed chronological order, which would begin with Hosea, Amos, and Isaiah and end with Daniel. Nevertheless, I have tried to structure this volume in such a way that readers could take up the various books in chronological order. In particular, students using this book for a college or seminary class should find it relatively easy to follow the treatment of books in any order chosen by the professor. To accomplish this objective, I have occasionally repeated some information or the definitions of terms and have also included a glossary.

I have followed a consistent arrangement in the treatment of each book, the outline of which follows.

Introduction to the Book and Its Times

    Place in the Canon

    Setting (time and place)

    Structure, Integrity, and Authorship

    Main Genres

    Special Issues

Introduction to the Prophet

Basic Themes

Problems Raised by a Study of the Book

Conclusion

Questions for Reflection

For Further Reading (a short annotated reading list)

I owe gratitude and thanks to a host of people. First, I want to thank Allen Myers, Senior Editor at Wm. B. Eerdmans Publishing Co., for inviting me to write this book, and the production staff that helped bring it into being. Additionally, I want to thank Dr. James Crenshaw of Duke University for reading portions of this manuscript for suggestions, Drs. Jeffrey Asher, Sheila Klopfer, Joe Lunceford, and Roger Ward of Georgetown College for reading portions of the book for clarity of expression and for their support, and Dr. Norman Wirzba of Georgetown for his help with the Greek philosopher Plato. Any mistakes that remain are my own. Thanks also go to the administration of Georgetown College and to the members of its Information Technology Service for their support and help. I also want to thank my wife Bonnie for her constant support of my passion for the study of the Hebrew Bible. Finally, I want to thank generations of my students at Otterbein College in Westerville, Ohio (1972-86), at Georgetown College in Georgetown, Kentucky (1986 to the present), and at the Lexington Theological Seminary, Lexington, Kentucky (when I have taught an occasional class there). Among them I want especially to thank my own children Pamela Duenas and Alan Redditt for entering with me into the study of the prophets in classes at Georgetown College. To all these students I dedicate this work, in hopes that more students will be drawn to their own study of Israel's great prophets.

PAUL L. REDDITT
Georgetown, Kentucky

Introduction

When many people hear the word "prophet," they think of someone who predicts the future, perhaps through some kind of hocus-pocus. Jewish and Christian believers typically would not cast the prophets of the Old Testament in such a light, since they rarely accuse the biblical prophets of trickery or magic. Some of them might even ascribe to the biblical prophets direct access to God, allowing them to see what God would do in the future. In doing so, they would not seem to stand far from the biblical prophet Amos, who said: "For the Lord GOD does nothing unless he reveals his secret to his servants the prophets"[1] (3:7). Even that verse, however, does not suggest that God would disclose events hundreds or thousands of years in advance. It speaks rather of God's declaring through a prophet the divine source for imminent punishment for the sins of a city or people.

While predictions of the future appear often in the prophetic books, anticipating God's coming punishment and/or salvation, they do not exhaust the preaching of the prophets of the Old Testament. Much of their recorded proclamations, indeed by far the majority, dealt with explanations of past and present events and exhortations for the people to live righteously, priests to teach properly, and rulers and judges to administer justice fairly. So prominent in the preaching of the prophets are these motifs that some scholars in the mid-twentieth century spoke of the prophets as "Forthtellers" rather than "Foretellers." But that way of speaking seems one-sided as well; hence it is better to speak of the prophets as both

---

1. All Scripture translations are by the author unless otherwise stated.

"Foretellers" and "Forthtellers," servants of God speaking to their own audiences on all kinds of subjects.

Modern readers of the prophets would do well to remember that the books were not written to them, but to ancient Israelites who lived hundreds of years before Jesus. Hence, when the prophet Isaiah spoke to the fearful and stubborn King Ahaz of Judah telling him that God would give a sign (Isa 7:14), that sign (the birth of a son to a young woman) was for Ahaz and his people. Before that child would grow old enough to choose the good instead of the bad, the threat of the kings of Israel and Damascus to overthrow Ahaz would evaporate. When Isa 9:6 announced that "a child has been born for us, a son given to us," the "us" in question was Isaiah and his ancient Israelite audience, not a modern American one. To be sure, the Christian New Testament applied such texts to Jesus, and a Christian reader may want to see in what way that application is valid. The task of the reader of the Old Testament, however, is to understand first what it meant in its Old Testament context. Hence, this book invites its readers to a venture in reading sacred texts in a way that takes those texts seriously and reads them first for their meaning in their own context. Only then will we approach the question of applied meanings in the New Testament and/or for the contemporary reader.

In what follows, this book will first address the basic question "What is a Prophet?" That question has already been broached in these comments, but it will be answered at much more length in Chapter One. Then the book will turn to the Major and Minor Prophets of the Old Testament, studying them in their canonical sequence. Many introductory books take the prophets in chronological order (Amos, Hosea, Isaiah, Micah), and there is considerable merit in doing so. Recent Old Testament scholarship, however, has begun to focus more on the canonical sequence. That focus is especially important in connection with the Minor Prophets, which appear to be connected editorially in ways that a chronological reading misses. The same is no less true, however, for Isaiah, which is typically divided into two or three sections and studied as representative of eighth- and sixth-century prophecy, without ever attending to the book's final form. This book will attempt to accomplish both the historical and canonical readings by taking the books in canonical order and paying attention to historical markers present in each.

To accomplish this task, Section I will examine the so-called "Major Prophets," beginning with a chapter on method in studying the prophetic books, then dedicating two chapters to Isaiah and one each to Jeremiah, Deutero-Jeremianic books including Lamentations, Ezekiel, and Daniel. Section II will dedicate a chapter to discussing the approach to be taken in connection with the Minor Prophets, construed as one book in the Hebrew Bible. Then it will investigate the Twelve in canonical order, three per chapter. This will eliminate very short chapters (e.g., on Obadiah, which contains only 21 verses). Nevertheless, each of those four chapters will begin with attention to the plot of the Book of the Twelve. Finally, the Conclusion will pull together a number of teachings of the prophets for a more synthetic approach, as well as investigate briefly the canonization and ways of reading the prophets. Each chapter, as well as the Conclusion, will end with questions for further reflection about the book(s) discussed and with a brief bibliography for students who wish to read further.

CHAPTER 1

What Is a Prophet?

People called prophets appear in much of the Old Testament. As early as Gen 20:7, God says to Abimelech, king of Gerar, that Abraham is a prophet who would intercede for Abimelech. In Exod 7:1 God tells Moses that Aaron his brother would act as Moses' prophet or spokesman. In Judg 6:8 God sends an unnamed prophet to Israel to explain why the Midianites had overrun them. Prophetesses also appear in these books. Exod 15:20 designates Miriam, Moses' sister, a prophetess, and Judg 4:4 calls Deborah a prophetess. All these people seem to be fulfilling roles that the tradition later came to associate with prophets/prophetesses. Yet another fifteen prophetic figures appear in 1 and 2 Samuel and 1 and 2 Kings, not to mention the so-called "Major and Minor Prophets." What, though, are prophets? What did they do? How did they relate to their audiences, to other institutions and officials in ancient Israel, and to each other? This chapter will seek to answer those questions.

Prophecy in the Ancient Near East

Prophecy was a form of intermediation between God and Israel, but it was not unique to Israel. The ancient Near East knew several similar forms. In-

---

Much of the information in this chapter appeared previously in Paul L. Redditt, "Introduction to Prophetic Literature," *Eerdmans Commentary on the Bible,* ed. James D. G. Dunn and John W. Rogerson (Grand Rapids: Wm. B. Eerdmans, 2003) 482-88.

termediation between the gods and a society could take the form of soul possession, in which a god took over the psyche of a medium. Conversely, it could occur through what is called "soul migration," a state in which someone's soul leaves the body for various purposes. It could also be attained by social and/or psychological conditioning, in which someone became susceptible to seeing or hearing communications from beyond. Sometimes guilds existed to train people as intermediaries. Also texts occasionally speak of divine election or report mystical experiences that lead someone to become an intermediary.[1] A number of texts from the ancient Near East illuminate the world in which OT prophecy was born. A few famous examples follow.

Twenty-eight letters found at Mari, a city in the middle Euphrates valley from the mid-third millennium to its destruction in 1762 B.C.E.,[2] mention prophetic figures, male or female, called *apilu*. These prophets claimed to have received a message from the gods Adad or Dagon and frequently quote what the gods said. Various persons received messages for the king, warning him of danger, instructing him what to do, and promising divine blessings if he followed the directions. For example, one letter to Zimri-Lin, an eighteenth-century king of Mari, warns of a coming revolt and advises him to surround himself with dependable bodyguards. Most texts from Mari dealing with prophets, however, report on the divination of the answer of a god to someone's question brought by the prophet to that deity. Indeed, divination was widespread, though not always associated with prophets.

Egypt also knew of prophets, though they may have been priests as well. They divined by manipulating various objects and interpreting dreams or signs. Occasionally they predicted the future. For example, Pharaoh Thutmose IV (reigned ca. 1412-1403) received a message in a dream telling him to clear the sand away from the Sphinx.[3] The "Prophecy of Nefer-rohu" purports to derive from the court of Snefru (a Fourth-Dynasty pharaoh who ruled ca. 2600), but actually dates to the twentieth century and speaks after the events have occurred. It "predicts" the chaos that would sweep over Egypt at the end of the Old Kingdom and the restitution of order when Amen-em-hep I became king.[4] The narrative is now

---

1. Philip R. Davies and John Rogerson, *The Old Testament World,* 2nd ed. (Louisville: Westminster John Knox, 2006) 167.

2. Dates in this book will be B.C.E. unless otherwise specified.

3. *ANET,* 449.

4. *ANET,* 444-46.

considered to be an example of ancient propaganda in support of the new dynasty, but it reflects the ancient belief that some people at least could "foretell" the future.

An Egyptian narrative from ca. 1100, "The Journey of Wen-Amon to Phoenicia,"[5] is the oldest literary reference to prophets in Canaan. It relates the trip of an official of the temple of the Egyptian god Amon at Karnak to Byblos on the coast of Phoenicia to purchase lumber for a ceremonial barge for the god. He narrates an incident that occurred while an official from Byblos was offering sacrifices to his gods. During the ceremony a god seized one of the attendants, as evidenced by his ecstatic, frenzied behavior. In this frenzy, he directed the Prince of Byblos to conduct business with Wen-Amon. Such frenzied behavior was also attested in eleventh-century Israel by the prophetic group surrounding Samuel and influencing Saul as well (1 Sam 10:5-10; cf. 1 Sam 19:20-24).

Such texts show that Israel emerged in a context where persons could divine the will of the gods and even experience possession by them. It is worth asking, then, whether there are noticeable differences between the prophets from the rest of the ancient world and those from Israel. In a way this whole book will answer that question, but for the moment two general observations are in order. First, the concept of monotheism developed in OT prophetic texts. The Ten Commandments require that Israel worship no other gods than YHWH,[6] but it does not deny their existence. Moses' successor Joshua is reported as saying: "choose this day whom you will serve, whether the gods your ancestors served in the region beyond the River [i.e., Mesopotamia] or the gods of the Amorites in whose land you are living [Canaan]; but as for me and my household, we will serve the LORD" (Josh 24:15). Scholars typically argue that the earliest proponent of monotheism was the exilic (586-539) prophet whose teachings are found in Isaiah 40–55. There is no question that passages in those chapters teach monotheism: e.g., "I am YHWH, and there is no other; besides me there is

---

5. *ANET*, 25-29.

6. The name given by God to Moses (Exod 3:15) consisted of four consonants: YHWH, translated "LORD" by the RSV and NRSV. Jews traditionally refused to pronounce the name, and the Masoretic Text (the MT = the text of the Hebrew Bible produced by Hebrew scholars called Masoretes) supplies the vowels for the divine name Adonai. That combination of consonants and vowel yields the term Jehovah. Scholars usually supply instead an "a" and an "e," vowels one might expect, resulting in the name Yahweh, but those vowels are debated. It seems better, therefore, simply to use the consonants only and thereby avoid the debate.

no God" (Isa 45:5). It seems, however, that the prophet Jeremiah might deserve the honor of being the first. Words placed on his lips sound monotheistic: "Has a nation changed its gods, even though they are no gods?" Jeremiah obviously anticipates a negative answer. Then he continues: "But my people have changed their glory [i.e., YHWH] for something that does not profit" (Jer 2:11).

Second, the prophets insisted that God demands moral behavior. This behavior included sacrificial worship, of course, but it also included fair play and social justice. Indeed, sacrifice without justice was worthless (Isa 1:12-17; Amos 5:21-24). This demand issued from the very nature of God, who was thought to be so concerned with social justice and political affairs that God entered battle on the side of the oppressed, even if in doing so God opposed Israel (Amos 5:14-15, 18-20). Still, the prophets could not finally bring themselves to say that God would totally abandon Israel, but depicted God as holding or pulling back, nowhere more eloquently and poignantly than in Hos 11:8-9:

> How can I give you up, Ephraim?
>   How can I hand you over, O Israel? . . .
> My heart recoils within me:
>   my compassion grows warm and tender.
> I will not execute my fierce anger;
>   I will not turn[7] to destroy Ephraim;
> for I am God and no mortal,
>   the Holy One of Israel in your midst,
>   and I will not come in wrath.

Terms for Prophets

The OT uses three words in particular to designate prophets. The first is the Hebrew word *ro'eh*, which derives from a verb meaning "to see." A *ro'eh* was one who saw things, particularly things that were hidden, usually by inquiring for information from God. Today, a *ro'eh* would probably be called a "diviner," one who can discover things that are hidden. A classic

---

7. The Hebrew text employs the verb *shub*, which generally means to "turn, return, or repent," but may be used adverbially to mean "again." RSV and NRSV translate the word adverbially, but the context seems to require the translation "turn."

OT text about a *ro'eh* is 1 Samuel 9–10. A young man named Saul and his servant search unsuccessfully for the lost donkeys of Saul's father Kish, until finally they seek out Samuel, a *ro'eh*. God had already prepared Samuel for Saul's arrival, however, by informing the seer that Saul was coming, that Kish's lost donkeys had returned home safely, and Samuel was to anoint Saul the first king of Israel.

The means of divination included, among others, the interpretation of dreams (see Jer 23:25-32, which discusses the means in connection with false prophets, though dream interpretation was also considered valid in Daniel 2 and 4 and in Joel 2:28[8]), casting lots (Jonah 1:7), inspecting dissected livers (Ezek 21:21, ascribed here to the king of Babylon, but widespread in the ancient Middle East), necromancy (1 Sam 28:8-25, but always condemned in the OT), and reading the stars (Ezek 32:7; Joel 2:10).[9]

The term *hozeh* derived from a second word meaning "to see," and was used in connection with things a prophet "saw" (cf. Ezek 13:16, 23). The term often denoted visions, as in the case of Balaam's oracles (Num 24:4, 16). Visions could also include auditions, what the prophet heard (Amos 7:1-9). In other cases (e.g., the opening verses of Isaiah, Amos, Micah, and Habakkuk), the term probably referred to the entire revelation received by the prophet.[10]

The third term, *nabi'*, appears frequently as a designation for prophets, particularly in 1 and 2 Samuel, 1 and 2 Kings, Jeremiah, and Ezekiel, less frequently in Isaiah and the Book of the Twelve. The verbal form of the word frequently appeared in connection with speaking or delivering a message, a usage consistent with Claus Westermann's thesis that prophets modeled their phrase "Thus says YHWH" after the style of messengers of kings and with the practice of earlier prophets at Mari.[11] The term came to be preferred over *ro'eh* (1 Sam 9:9), which may have taken on a negative

---

8. Sometimes in the OT, as here, the division of books into chapters and verses differs between the Hebrew and English Bible. All citations in this book will be according to the English Bible.

9. Lester E. Grabbe argues that prophecy is but one type of divination; "Introduction and Overview," *Knowing the End from the Beginning: The Prophetic, the Apocalyptic, and Their Relationships*, ed. Grabbe and Robert D. Haak. JSPSup 46 (London: T. & T. Clark, 2003) 12.

10. G. V. Smith, "Prophet," *ISBE*, 3:986-1004.

11. Claus Westermann, *Basic Forms of Prophetic Speech* (Philadelphia: Westminster, 1967) 98-128.

connotation. Even *nabi'*, however, could be applied to a false prophet (1 Kgs 22:22). In view of these three terms for prophets in the OT, therefore, Lester L. Grabbe is correct to define a prophet quite generally as "a mediator who claims to receive messages directly from a divinity, by various means, and communicates those messages to recipients."[12]

True and False Prophets

Prophets, like most other authorities, disagree at times, and at times those disagreements caused problems for the people of ancient Israel. In such cases, it would have been helpful to be able to distinguish true prophets from false. Accordingly, the book of Deuteronomy gives two criteria for judging whether a prophet is legitimate, and hence to be followed. The first is simple: does the prophet speak in the name of YHWH (Deut 18:20)? In a context of multiple gods for every nation, there were plenty of deities demanding worship. For Israel, however, only YHWH mattered, so prophets speaking on behalf of other gods were to be ignored. So, the first criterion concerns the authority of the god on whose behalf the prophet spoke. The second criterion (Deut 18:22) pertains only to prophets speaking in the name of YHWH: did their predictions come true? This criterion would work well in retrospect, though even there one might find cause for disagreement. For example, the so-called "Second Isaiah" announced that God had chosen Cyrus (founder of the Persian Empire) as his servant to free the Jewish exiles in Babylon. One might agree in retrospect (e.g., in 500 B.C.E., after some of the exiles had returned home) that Cyrus had overthrown Babylon without necessarily having to agree that YHWH the God of Israel was the power behind Cyrus's throne. Indeed, the prophet himself had God say to Cyrus (Isa 45:4):

"I call you by your name; I surname you though you do not know me."

A similar difficulty with this criterion is this: how "right" did a prophet have to be in order to be "right"? 100 percent? 75 percent? 50 percent? The early postexilic prophet Haggai seems to have predicted that Zerubbabel, a man charged by the Persians with rebuilding the temple in

---

12. Lester L. Grabbe, "Prophetic and Apocalyptic: Time for New Definitions — and New Thinking," in Grabbe and Haak, *Knowing the End from the Beginning*, 129.

Jerusalem, would become king. It appears as if Haggai reversed the prediction of Jeremiah that God would send king (Je)Coniah or Jehoiachin into exile, as it were, ripping the signet ring[13] (Coniah) from his right hand and giving it to the Babylonians (Jer 22:24). Haggai declared that God would make Zerubbabel like a signet ring (Hag 2:23). So far as is known, however, Haggai was wrong in that prediction; neither Zerubbabel nor any other postexilic figure ever ascended the throne of David. Did that mean that Haggai was incorrect about other things he said, namely that it was God's will to rebuild the temple and that God would bless the people of Judah if they did? The people who assembled the prophetic books did not seem to think so.

One other problem appears in connection with this second criterion, and that is that it works only in retrospect. It might be fine for people looking back in time to explain what happened, but it would be of no help to people faced with choosing between two conflicting prophets about a decision in the present or near future. The prophet Jeremiah found himself in just that situation. Jeremiah had challenged King Zedekiah not to listen to the official prophets in Jerusalem, who were assuring him that Jerusalem would not fall to the Babylonians, even though in 597 the Babylonians had successfully besieged the city and exacted a heavy toll in wealth and exiles (2 Kgs 24:10-17). As Jeremiah assessed matters, the proper foreign policy for Zedekiah was capitulation to the Babylonians, an assessment he preached from the early days of Zedekiah's reign (597-586) until the sad ending of the city at the hands of the Babylonians in 586 (Jer 27:12-15). In a classic confrontation, another prophet named Hananiah publicly disagreed with Jeremiah, claiming God had sent him a message that God would bring the exiles and stolen temple vessels back to Judah within two years (Jer 28:1-4). Jeremiah responded by saying that one might judge whether a prophet was true or false by what might be called "a rule of thumb": the prophets of old who had turned out to be true prophets had preached doom and gloom (Jer 28:7-9).

One can certainly understand why Jeremiah made this statement. Who, after all, is more likely to have been prophesying for money, someone predicting future good for his benefactors and the country's establishment or someone condemning them for their treatment of the poor? Still, Jere-

---

13. A signet ring was a ring bearing the seal of the king, used to "sign" official documents.

miah's statement does not constitute a third criterion. Words attributed to
Jeremiah himself in the so-called "Book of Consolation" (Jer 30:1–31:40)
promised a new Davidic king (30:9; cf. 30:21), a return from exile (30:10-11;
cf. 31:8), defeat of Israel's political enemies (30:11), the rebuilding of Jerusalem (31:12, 38-40), the reuniting of Israel and Judah (31:9, 15-20), and a new,
unbreakable covenant (31:31-34). Only the return and the rebuilding of Jerusalem actually occurred. Nothing in the book, however, indicates that
any of those promises to the exiles constituted false prophecy; rather, they
seemed crucial to the people who had preserved Jeremiah's preaching. The
same prediction of future blessing is true in other prophetic books, as a
glance at Isa 7:1-17; 9:2-7; and 11:1-9 will show.

An even more disturbing text dealing with false prophets, however, is
one that portrays YHWH as leading prophets astray (1 Kgs 22:19-23). King
Jehoshaphat of Judah and King Ahab of Israel were contemplating war
against Aram (Damascus and its environs). Jehoshaphat asked Ahab to inquire of his prophets whether the war would turn out well for Israel and
Judah. Ahab's prophets immediately gave a rosy prediction, but
Jehoshaphat was prudently cautious and asked if Ahab had any other
prophets. Ahab indeed had one more, Micaiah ben Imlah, but he was out
of favor with the king because, as Ahab put it, "he never prophesies anything good about me, just evil." Jehoshaphat pressed Ahab to consult
Micaiah, which he did. Eventually, Micaiah predicted the downfall of the
Israelite king, much to Ahab's disgust. Micaiah then spoke of a vision he
had seen, in which YHWH was sitting on his throne, with the entire heavenly host present. God was holding council, seeking input about how to
defeat Ahab. Various members of the divine council, referred to as spirits,
offered suggestions. Eventually, one spirit volunteered to be a "lying spirit
in the mouth of all [Ahab's] prophets" (v. 22). Micaiah concluded with this
comment: "So, you see, YHWH put a lying spirit in the mouth of all his
prophets" (v. 23).

This text, like others (e.g., 2 Sam 24:1-9), was groping toward monotheism, with resulting theological problems. In a context of multiple gods,
some can be good while others are bad. Some can favor one course of action while others prefer a different course. When, however, people limit
their gods to one, what do they do about such differences? Here, the narrative postulates various lesser beings offering different courses of action,
and has YHWH choose which proposal to accept. The narrative thus solves
the problem by putting YHWH in charge, but — simultaneously and per-

haps inadvertently — raises an issue about God's character: is YHWH the kind of God who would cause prophets to lie? Still, the narrative holds one last twist: it was not Ahab that was killed in the battle, but Jehoshaphat. Thus, even when God made the call, humans still acted on their own volition, and the outcome was not rigged.

Central and Peripheral Prophets

People in ancient Israel clearly thought there was a class of people called "prophets," who functioned alongside priests and wise men. Jer 18:18 quotes enemies of Jeremiah as saying: ". . . instruction shall not perish from the priest, nor counsel from the wise, nor the word from the prophet." One should not assume, however, that all the prophets in the prophetic corpus held an office. Professional prophets played a significant role in the cultus, particularly in the temple at Jerusalem, to promote the welfare of the people. They spoke the word by delivering the message God had given to them and by interceding with God on behalf of the people.[14] Such prophets almost surely included Isaiah, Haggai, and Zechariah, and *may* have included Joel (cf. 1:1–2:18) and Nahum. Their message would have been reinforced by the authority of their temple office, and in the case of Isaiah by ready access to the king (Isa 7:3-17).[15]

Other OT prophets, however, lived more on the periphery of the cultus, as a few examples will show. Amos, for example, denied that he was a professional prophet or even an apprentice to one (Amos 7:14): "I am no prophet, nor a son [i.e., an apprentice] of a prophet; rather, I am a herdsman, and a dresser of sycamore trees." What is more, Amos was a southerner, from the little town of Tekoa, located 12 miles south of Jerusalem, but he flourished in Israel, from which he was unceremoniously banished (Amos 7:12-15). Jeremiah, on the other hand, was from the north (specifically from Anathoth, which lay just north of the border with Judah, in the

14. Aubrey R. Johnson, *The Cultic Prophet in Ancient Israel*, 2nd ed. (Cardiff: University of Wales Press, 1962) 74.

15. Thomas W. Overholt, in fact, thinks that "In general, . . . prophets were religious intermediaries who functioned at the national level" with ties closer to the monarchy than the cult; "Prophet, Prophecy," *EDB*, 1086. It is probably relevant that the heyday of prophecy was the period of the monarchy, but as mentioned above some prophets even in the eighth century leveled scathing criticism against the monarch and/or the cultus.

tribe of Benjamin) and attempted to work in Judah. Furthermore, he was from the priestly family of Abiathar, a priest who was with David from his outlaw days until his death, but who backed Adonijah instead of Solomon for king and was banished from Jerusalem by Solomon (1 Kgs 2:35). Micah was from the town of Moresheth and railed against the corruption caused by cities. The postexilic prophet Malachi was probably a Levite and thus associated with the Second Temple in Jerusalem,[16] but at a time when the Levites were losing power to the priests.[17] Even Ezekiel, who was a priest from Jerusalem, lived and prophesied in exile, deprived of any contact with the temple in Jerusalem. Likewise, his audience was comprised of exiles in Babylon. Both were peripheral by virtue of their status in Babylon, regardless of their status when they lived in Judah.

Whether a prophet was central or peripheral depended on several factors.[18] In general, one would expect central prophets to be male, to derive their authority from their office, to belong to the upper class, to be on the temple payroll, and to support the status quo. In theory, their followers would include the entire nation, but in practice followers might be more limited to the upper class. By contrast, one would expect peripheral prophets to derive their authority from a charismatic experience, to belong to the lower class, to earn a living from a "profane" occupation (one not associated with the cultus). They might include women. Their followers might well belong to a smaller, perhaps even disadvantaged, group within the society, who found their plan for revitalizing society appealing.

Two features of this paradigm do not seem to fit ancient Israel very well. First, the few women named as prophetesses in the OT did not necessarily belong to the periphery of society. Second, Isaiah reports a call vision (Isa 6:1-13), which might have served to help legitimize him to his audience (cf. Moses' call vision in Exod 3:1–4:23 and Ezekiel's in Ezek 1:4–3:27). It is not wise, therefore, to press all the distinctions in classifying each prophet. Details in the text may point to which distinctions apply to a given prophet.

---

16. Paul L. Redditt, *Haggai, Zechariah, Malachi*. NCBC (Grand Rapids: Wm. B. Eerdmans, 1995) 151-52.

17. Gabriele Boccaccini, *Roots of Rabbinic Judaism: An Intellectual History, From Ezekiel to Daniel* (Grand Rapids: Wm. B. Eerdmans, 2002) 68-72, 87-89.

18. The distinctions made here between central and peripheral prophets come from I. M. Lewis, *Ecstatic Religion* (Baltimore: Penguin, 1971) 100-15, 127-33. He also added gender, but Israel may have been more open to prophetesses than were some other nations.

At times readers can detect a reconstructionist element in the saying of the OT prophets. One excellent example is the temple vision of Ezekiel (Ezek 40:1–42:20, concerning the new temple for Jerusalem), where the prophet offers an idealized new floor plan with great symmetry. In reading such texts, however, a reader would do well to keep in mind a series of questions Douglas A. Knight posed for a reading of the book of Deuteronomy: "Whose text is it? For whom and why was it important to fashion the stories . . . [and] prophetic sayings . . . into their present forms? Who stood to gain? Who had the power to see to the survival of the text?"[19] That is not to say that the prophets or the scribes who recorded/preserved (and even applied and supplemented) their words and deeds were necessarily after power or wealth, but neither, probably, were they objective and dispassionate about the words of the prophets. Sometimes the watchful reader can detect their bent.

Prophets and Their Audiences

It is clear, therefore, that the recognition of people as prophets implies an audience with its own needs and wishes. One community's prophet could be another community's madman (Hos 9:7). One biblical prophet might have a perspective diametrically opposed to that of another. The prophet Nahum, flourishing in the dying days of the cruel and hated Assyrian Empire, could call down God's destruction upon the capital city of Nineveh (Nahum 2–3). The *prophet* Jonah seems to concur, but the *author* of the book of Jonah felt quite differently and portrayed God as One moved to compassion by human repentance. Perhaps it was because that author lived centuries later, long after the sting of Assyrian oppression had subsided. Perhaps it was because in his own context the *author* hoped for generous treatment at the hands of foreign rulers. Hence, God had to correct the *prophet* with the question with which the book ends: "And should I not be concerned about Nineveh, . . . ?" Finally, the preexilic/exilic book of Jeremiah could proclaim the demise of Coniah (Jehoiachin), calling him

19. Douglas A. Knight, "Whose Agony, Whose Ecstasy? The Politics of the Deuteronomic Law," in *Shall Not the Judge of All the Earth Do What Is Right? Studies on the Nature of God in Tribute to James L. Crenshaw,* ed. David Penchansky and Paul L. Redditt (Winona Lake: Eisenbrauns, 2000) 99.

God's signet ring that God would throw away (Jer 22:24-27). By contrast, the postexilic temple prophet Haggai (Hag 2:23) proclaimed that God would make Zerubbabel his new signet ring. New or different circumstances sometimes called for a new word.

People often think that prophecy died out after Malachi, who flourished between 515 (the year of the completion of the rebuilding of the temple in Jerusalem) and 456 (the coming of Ezra to Jerusalem). They sometimes point to Zech 13:2-6 as evidence. Actually, however, that text is evidence that prophecy continued on. To be sure, Zechariah 9–14 may well date from well into the Persian period, perhaps before the time of Nehemiah,[20] though scholars often put it later. The point is, however, that the text blames contemporary prophets for lying or idolatry but reckons with their continuance. From the perspective of the author of Zech 13:2-6, prophets should be ashamed of themselves for their behavior. That scolding and promise of punishment, however, do not prove prophets ceased to function. What the text really points out is that its author did not accept contemporary prophets, and did not think God accepted them either. Differently stated, the author did not belong to their audience and did not accept the message and/or agenda of the prophets of his day. Neither, by the way, did he think much of the royal family (Zech 12:10–13:1) or the leaders he called the "shepherds" (10:1-3a; 11:4-17; 13:7-9). Prophecy may have been pushed one way or another in the postexilic period, but it did not die out. Indeed, it carried on into NT times, when it flourished among Christians.

Prophets, Kings, Wise Men, and Priests

How did the prophets relate to the other identifiable office holders in ancient Israel: kings, wise men, and priests? With respect to kings, it is clear that the careers of most, though by no means all, of the so-called "writing prophets" fell during the period of the divided monarchy, particularly between the mid-eighth and early-sixth centuries, i.e., between the time of Amos (ca 760) and the fall of the temple (586). In the books of 1 and 2 Samuel and 1 and 2 Kings, however, prophets anoint, correct, advise, condemn, and praise the monarchs, beginning with Nathan's remonstrance of David for his sin with Bathsheba (2 Sam 12:1-10). Moreover, King Ahab calls Elijah

---

20. Redditt, *Haggai, Zechariah, Malachi*, 94-100.

"you troubler of Israel" (1 Kgs 18:17), and complains of Micaiah ben Imlah that he "never prophesies anything good about me, just evil" (1 Kgs 22:8). The central prophet Isaiah was in a position to criticize Ahaz (Isa 7:13-17). King Jehoiakim could shred the written oracles of Jeremiah and throw them on a brazier to warm his hands (Jer 36:23), but Jehoiakim's brother, King Zedekiah, was reduced to bringing Jeremiah from prison to the palace to consult with him (Jer 37:16-21). Clearly, the prophets' right of royal review depended on who the king was and whether he cared to face the prophet. Still, a king might be criticized openly by a prophet, even in a sanctuary sponsored by a king, regardless of the king's wishes (Amos 7:11). Probably the most negative prophet vis-à-vis the kings was Hosea, who perhaps considered the whole institution God's punishment upon Israel (13:10-11):

> Where is your king now, that he may save you?
>> (Where) in all your cities are your rulers
>> Of whom you said "Give me a king and rulers"?
> I gave you a king in my anger,
>> And I took him away in my wrath.

(It should be admitted that some scholars see this text as a repudiation of one particular king, not the monarchy. Even so, the words are scathing.) On the other hand, a pro-monarchical editor added several passages to prophetic collections (Hos 3:5aβ; Amos 9:11-12; Mic 5:2-5a; Zech 9:1-10), and perhaps Hab 3:12-14 already contained one.

Whether that editor should be called a "prophet" might be debated. He might be thought of as part of the movement of the wise.[21] Katrina J. A. Larkin has argued that a type of wisdom stands behind the use of citations that is so prominent in Zechariah 9–14.[22] Even the earlier prophet Amos seems to have borrowed the formula "For three transgressions of . . . , yea for four . . ." from wisdom circles. Thus, while prophets and wise men can be distinguished in idealized descriptions, in real life they seem to have overlapped, and biblical prophets (cf. Amos) sometimes borrowed from them as they did from others in their society.

---

21. That movement most likely was responsible for the book of Daniel in its present form. Cf. the depiction of Daniel as a wise man able to outdo the wise men in Babylon and the references to the "wise" in Dan 12:3, 10.

22. Katrina J. A. Larkin, *The Eschatology of Second Zechariah: A Study of the Formation of a Mantological Wisdom Anthology* (Kampen: Kok Pharos, 1994) 30-49.

Prophets and priests coexisted during the period of the monarchy. The previously mentioned text (Amos 7:11) and other passages where prophets criticized priests (Isa 28:7; Hos 4:9; Mal 1:6-13) give the impression that the two groups were unalterably opposed. In some cases, however, the prophets criticized other prophets at the same time (Jer 23:11; Ezek 7:26; Jer 4:9 adds the princes for good measure). Also, prophets and priests sometimes served at the same temple (e.g., Isaiah in Jerusalem), and Jeremiah, Ezekiel, and probably Joel were priests. Malachi apparently was a Levite (see above). Further, the temple was rebuilt under the urging of the prophets Haggai and Zechariah. The priests gained exclusive control of the second temple, so that Aubrey R. Johnson surmised that they reduced prophets to the rank of temple singers.[23] Gabriele Boccaccini thinks the postexilic Zadokites made a prophet out of Moses and used him to legitimize their own takeover of religious life with Aaron as their real hero.[24]

Prophecy as Literature

In light of these developments, then, it seems clear that the sayings of various prophets were preserved, copied, edited, combined, and canonized by scribes, who passed on a more-or-less fixed set of writings to the rabbis.[25] At times these scribes left identifiable traces of their work. For example, Hos 14:9 not so humbly notes that "those who are wise" understood the works of God in the history of Israel, implying that the scribes and attentive readers would not repeat the mistakes of past generations. Presumably those "wise ones" (or scribes) collected — and modified — the sayings of the particular prophets named in the OT because those prophets had turned out to be correct, at least essentially, in their assessment of their own days and could be "updated" to speak to new days. In other words, the scribes saw in those prophets' messages the key to the future. In that sense they were *foretellers* for the scribes.

---

23. Johnson, *The Cultic Prophet in Ancient Israel*, 75.
24. Boccaccini, *Roots of Rabbinic Judaism*, 88.
25. Philip R. Davies, *Scribes and Schools: The Canonization of the Hebrew Scriptures* (Louisville: Westminster John Knox, 1998) 33-35.

Prophets Known and Anonymous

The issue of unnamed scribes' contributing to the prophetic corpus needs further explication. In the books of Joshua, Judges, 1 and 2 Samuel, and 1 and 2 Kings, prophets interact with various leaders and predict certain events. In some cases (over twenty in the books of Kings) their fulfillment is duly noted (e.g., the revolt of Jeroboam against the Davidic monarchy, predicted in 1 Kgs 11:26-39 and fulfilled in 12:20-24). Many of these prophets are known by name, but not all. In some cases (e.g., Judg 6:8) an anonymous prophet is said to have spoken to the people. In the Major and Minor Prophets of the Bible, however, everything is attributed to the prophet whose name the writing carries. Modern critical scholars are convinced, however, that those books contain a significant amount of data from other persons, namely, editors and others whose prophecies were added without acknowledgment. Those additions include materials such as superscriptions at the beginnings of books (e.g., Isa 1:1), sections of books (e.g., Zech 9:1), or single chapters (e.g., Hab 3:1-19); descriptions of events (e.g., Jer 7:1-15//26:1-24); summaries of sermons (e.g., Jon 3:4); and even "updates" of prophetic messages to apply them to new situations (Hos 1:7). Sometimes information imbedded in the additions will make clear that they are secondary to the prophet. Amos 9:11-15 is one such example. Scholars have often seen it as an addition because it predicts salvation when the rest of the book predicts doom. A prophet of doom, however, could predict salvation beyond punishment. What makes it clear that Amos 9:11-15 derived from somebody after the prophet himself is what it presupposes: the fall of the Davidic monarchy. Verse 11 does not predict the fall, but looks back on it and predicts its restoration. The prophet Amos flourished about 760 B.C.E., and the Davidic monarchy fell to the Babylonians in 586. Hence, Amos 9:11-15 was written nearly 200 years after the career of Amos.

The book of Isaiah contains such disparate material that many scholars advocate distinguishing First Isaiah from hypothetical Second and Third Isaiahs. The same holds true for Zechariah. No one means literally that three different people named Isaiah or Zechariah had their sayings assembled into the respective collections. Rather, the names indicate unknown authors whose comparatively lengthy sayings were added to the collections of well-known, earlier prophets. Many additions, however, are smaller in content — like Amos 9:11-15. Sometimes it is possible to trace several additions by a common hand, but often a reader must simply reckon with the probable presence of one or more unknown "prophets" in a given work.

Some modern readers reject the idea of additions to the sayings of the prophets, on the grounds that such additions would constitute plagiarism. There are two problems with their objection. First, it brings a modern, idealized concept of authorship to bear on ancient authorship. Apparently people were not concerned much about plagiarism until books could be mass produced by printing, so that authors could earn money from their intellectual output. In modern times to "steal" someone's words could amount to stealing some of that person's income or at least reputation. Hence, in today's world plagiarism is not only considered unethical, but also illegal. In the ancient world no such prohibitions applied to the work of writers. Besides, there is a real sense in which what they were doing was the opposite of plagiarism. In plagiarism one passes off the work of another author as one's own; in ancient prophecy the later prophets/redactors/scribes were attributing their work to someone else. They were more comparable to ghost writers or presidential speech writers than deceivers.

The second problem with this objection is that it fails to acknowledge the crucial role that editors and other others play in a published work. Editors correct everything from spelling to grammar to errors of fact and perception. This very book is the product of a host of people, not just the one whose name appears as the author.

Summary

This chapter has attempted to answer the question "What is a prophet?" It has done so in a variety of ways. First, it noted the existence of prophets in some of the cultures surrounding Israel, but showed that the prophets of Israel distinguished themselves from those prophets by developing the concept of monotheism and by contending that an ongoing relationship with God depended on proper moral action on the part of Israel's people. Next, the chapter explained three terms applied to prophets: the *ro'eh* was a diviner, the *hozeh* a seer, and the *nabi'* a messenger. The latter term came to be preferred in the Hebrew Bible. Not all prophets were to be believed, however; some were false. The distinction in Deuteronomy probably served the Israelite community: (1) a true prophet must speak in the name of YHWH, and (2) his message must come true. It seems not to have been necessary that a prophet's words come true to the last detail, but they had to come true enough to be convincing. Jeremiah added a "rule of thumb" to the effect that true prophets were more likely than false prophets to say what the audience did not want to hear. Prophets might or might not have been connected with a major worship center, but their status as central or peripheral did not determine or preclude their inclusion in the prophetic canon. Their status did, however, affect who listened to them. Central prophets spoke to the whole nation, at least in theory, while peripheral prophets spoke to smaller groups within the culture. At least some preexilic prophets seem to have had access to the king, though their relationship may have been rocky. Some in the canon not only were associated with the temple, but were priests themselves. Even so, priests and kings alike could be the objects of prophetic critique. At times prophets also seem to have borrowed from members of the wisdom circle in old Israel, and eventually the sayings of the prophets came into the possession of scribes for collection, preservation, and canonization. In that process the words of unknown prophets seem to have been attached to the messages of the prophets whose names stand at the heads of the collections.

Questions for Reflection

1. What difference does it make, if any, that prophets flourished in other nations besides Israel? Why do you think so?
2. What is at issue in our understanding of God and of ancient Israel in the prophetic insistence that God demanded social justice from the people of Israel?
3. What do you think of the means of divination employed by some prophets? Do some seem more reliable than others to you? Why or why not?
4. How much of what a prophet said had to be correct for the prophet to be judged a "true" prophet?
5. What motives might have influenced the prophets' messages? What motives might have influenced the preservation of their messages? What motives might influence our reading of those messages?
6. What is at issue for our understanding of the nature of God in Micaiah ben Imlah's vision in which God sent a lying spirit on some prophets?
7. Could a prophet be a proper patriot and oppose the policies of his king?
8. What do you think of the scholarly view that editors added their own words and those of other unknown prophets to the messages of prophets known by name?

For Further Reading

Brueggemann, Walter. *The Prophetic Imagination.* Rev. ed. Minneapolis: Fortress, 2001. A brief study of the prophets as people advocating basic changes in human society.

Gitay, Yehoshua, ed. *Prophecy and Prophets: The Diversity of Contemporary Issues in Scholarship.* SBLSemS. Atlanta: Scholars, 1997. A collection of articles by eight scholars discussing most of the issues raised in this chapter.

Rad, Gerhard von. *Old Testament Theology,* Vol. 2. New York: Harper and Brothers, 1965. Part One (pp. 3-125) discusses questions preliminary to a study of the prophets and their theology.

Scott, R. B. Y. *The Relevance of the Prophets: An Introduction to the Old Testament Prophets and Their Message.* Rev. ed. New York: Macmillan, 1968. Treats issues such as the theology of the prophets, their view of history, their view of the social order of Israel, and their relevance to contemporary readers.

The Major Prophets

Isaiah, Jeremiah, Lamentations, Ezekiel, Daniel

The title "Major Prophets" is used to designate the three prophetic books Isaiah, Jeremiah, and Ezekiel, plus the poetic collection Lamentations, and the apocalypse Daniel. Roman Catholic Bibles also place the Deutero-Jeremianic books Baruch and — as its last chapter — the Letter of Jeremiah after Lamentations. The title distinguishes these books from the so-called "Minor Prophets," Hosea through Malachi, called the Book of the Twelve in the Masoretic Text (MT). The distinction is based partly on length, in that each of the books of Isaiah, Jeremiah, and Ezekiel is approximately as long as the Book of the Twelve. Neither Lamentations nor Daniel is considered a prophetic book in the Hebrew Bible, appearing instead among the *Kethubim*[1] (or Writings), the third and final part of the Hebrew Bible. Their inclusion among the Major Prophets in Christian Bibles requires explanation. Lamentations is included presumably on the basis of the (erroneous) tradition that Jeremiah wrote it, so despite its brevity it follows Jeremiah among the Major Prophets. In the Septuagint (LXX), Baruch and the Letter of Jeremiah follow Lamentations. They were accepted into the Roman Catholic canon, and will be discussed in the chapter on Lamentations. Daniel, which is about as long as Hosea or Zechariah, was placed after Ezekiel, because the seer Daniel is said to have flourished into the reign of the Persian king Darius, who ruled years later than the time of Ezekiel. The Roman Catholic version of Daniel is somewhat longer than the Protestant version. The additional materials will be discussed briefly.

---

1. *Kethubim* is a Hebrew word transliterated into English. Other Hebrew words will be used from time to time.

CHAPTER 2

Approach to the Major Prophets

An acquaintance of mine tells students in his seminary classes: "The Bible[1] is not a self-interpreting book." That sentence reminds the students that the Bible comes with no instructions on how to read it. Moreover, the Old Testament is the product of people who lived thousands of years ago in the Middle East (what people today sometimes call West Asia or Southwest Asia). It was written by a few of those people for some of their own contemporaries. None of it was written for twenty-first-century readers in the West — or even for twenty-first-century inhabitants of Israel. My friend's sentence also implies that readers employ reading strategies, though often — maybe even usually — without recognizing they are doing so. An obvious example of nonawareness of reading strategies is the comment "I don't interpret the Bible; I just take it literally, as it is." This sentence overlooks the fact that taking a text "literally" is itself a reading strategy.

1. We would do well to remember that the word "Bible" comes from the Greek word *biblia,* which means "books." We think of the Bible as a collection, bound within a single cover. That means of reproducing the Bible did not come into vogue for Christians before the fourth century c.e. The rabbis who settled on the books in the Hebrew Bible did not make their selections before the end of the first Christian century, and the Masoretes, the rabbis who copied the texts and added vowels to the words of the Hebrew Bible, worked from the sixth to the tenth century. The Dead Sea Scrolls were all on *scrolls,* not in books. A text the length of Genesis or Jeremiah required a scroll about as long as was convenient to handle. It is not clear how early scribes copied the Hebrew Bible into books, but the oldest known codex containing the prophets dates from 895 c.e. Before the production of such books, one might have access to only a single scroll with only a small part of the Hebrew Bible.

One difficulty with that particular reading strategy is that much literature is not intended literally. If I said, "My wife is like a red, red rose," most
readers would understand that I was not describing her physical appearance, but making some kind of metaphorical comment. Poetry is inevitably not just literal, even when it has a literal referent. Prose too is crammed
with nonliteral words or phrases: e.g., "sunset," "He let me down," or "She
blew up in anger." Parables, though often apparently prose, not poetry, are
always metaphorical too. Hence, Sunday School teachers have told children for years that a parable "is an earthly story with a heavenly meaning."
Precisely! Parables are about something more than they appear to be
about, and it is up to the reader to figure out what.

Even prose, however, is susceptible to varying interpretations, particularly narratives. Amy Johnson Frykholm observes that a story "invites
multiplicity. A story is multisided and reflexive. It mirrors back onto its
reader and creates a prism of stories inside of only one."[2] In other words,
readers interpret narratives in light of their own experiences, values, and
perspectives. In addition, readers typically participate in one or more communities or contexts that mediate meanings, leading readers to accept,
moderate, and/or reject narratives in whole or in part.

Moreover, unlike listeners who are present when a speaker says something, readers must provide a context for what is said. One example of the
problem inherent in that necessity will suffice. Consider this example,
please. "The young woman smiled at him when he entered the room. She
turned down the sheet, and patted the bed for him to get in." I had in mind
a mother in her small son's room, putting him to bed. I suspect some readers at least have a very different scenario in mind.

Part of what the modern reader may need to supply for sayings and
narratives alike is the historical setting. The opening verses of Haggai 1
read as follows:

1 In the second year of Darius the king, in the sixth month, on the first
day of the month, the word of YHWH came by the hand of Haggai the
prophet to Zerubbabel, the son of Shealtiel, governor of Judah, and to
Joshua son of Jehozadak, the high priest: 2 Thus says YHWH Sĕbaoth,
"This people says 'The time has not come to build the house of

2. Amy Johnson Frykholm, *Rapture Culture: Left Behind in Evangelical America* (Oxford: Oxford University Press, 2004) 182.

YHWH.'" 3 Then the word of YHWH came into being through the hand
of Haggai the prophet: 4 "Is it the time for you yourselves to live in
roofed houses, while this house [lies] in ruins?"

Even though v. 1 provides the setting for the narrative, and vv. 2-4 repeat
God's injunction to Haggai along with the opening question Haggai was to
ask his audience, this passage will seem obscure to the reader who cannot
supply the historical context.

That context is the second year of the reign of King Darius I, emperor of
Persia. He had come to the throne after a power struggle in 521. In those un-
settled days, Haggai heard God telling him to urge the rebuilding of the temple in Jerusalem. It helps a reader to know that according to Deuteronomy 12
there was to be only one sanctuary to God in Israel, and according to tradition that sanctuary was the temple in the capital city of Jerusalem. Unfortunately, King Nebuchadnezzar, the great founding king of the so-called "Neo-
Babylonian Empire" (which existed from 605 to 539), had destroyed that
temple in 586 (cf. 2 Kgs 25:1-21). The temple lay in ruins until the Persians
overthrew the Babylonians in 539, whereupon King Cyrus allowed Jews who
wished to return to Jerusalem to rebuild the temple. The first person charged
with that responsibility was named Sheshbazzar (Ezra 1:1-4), but he seems
not to have completed his assignment. The temple remained in ruins down
to the time of Haggai in 520. He urged the people of Jerusalem to finish the
rebuilding project, which they did in the year 515 (Ezra 5:1–6:15).

Against this background, Hag 1:1-4 makes sense: God commanded
Haggai to urge the people in Judah and Jerusalem to finish the rebuilding
project. It is important to note, however, that the previous paragraph is a
historical reconstruction based on three different passages of Scripture and
some familiarity with the broader scope of history in the Fertile Crescent in
the seventh and sixth centuries. Even so, there are holes in the reconstruction. Who exactly were Sheshbazzar and Zerubbabel? What was their relation to each other, if any? When did Zerubbabel come to Jerusalem, and under what Persian king? What exactly was the condition of Jerusalem when
Haggai spoke? For example, the word translated "roofed" above is often
translated "paneled." Were the people Haggai addressed living in luxurious
"paneled" houses, or had they just managed to get their own houses under
roof before the prophet challenged them to work on the temple?

This business of reconstructing the context out of which a text arose
and/or in view of which a text is to be interpreted can be risky, but the in-

terpreter has little option.³ Another professor-acquaintance of mine states the matter this way: a text without a context is pretext for whatever we want to make of it. Without a context, the interpreter will most likely read the passage in light of the interpreter's own context and situation. That mistake is not too likely in Hag 1:1-4, but consider Isa 9:6, which reads: "a child is born to us, a son is given to us, and the government will be upon his shoulders." Who is designated by the word "us" in that verse? One person certainly is Isaiah himself. When people use the first person singular or plural, they are necessarily including themselves. Apparently, then, Isaiah was speaking of someone in his own time (ca. 735), whom Isaiah expected to become the ruler of Judah. That person presumably was the crown prince of Judah. It is a stretch to see how twenty-first-century c.e. readers could share the same king, so the word "us" originally would not include us twenty-first-century people. It is also a stretch to see how Isaiah could have had Jesus in mind, since he was born over 700 years later, though many Christians read the verse that way.

Another text often understood in light of the reader's own context, but also in this case in light of subsequent reuse in the Bible, is Isa 7:14, which reads: "Therefore, YHWH himself will give to you (plural) a sign: 'behold, the young woman with child; she will bring forth a son, and she will call his name Immanuel.'" Most Christian readers have assumed that the young woman is Mary and the son is Jesus, but Isaiah was speaking to Ahaz, his king. It is by no means the case that Isaiah was speaking to him of events that would take place centuries after the king's death. Attention to the context of 7:14 shows, instead, that the son Immanuel was to be a sign to Ahaz and his entourage. Before *that* son could grow old enough to discern good from bad, the siege Jerusalem was undergoing (mentioned in 7:1) would come to an end. The child was to be a sign that God would be with Ahaz and the people of Jerusalem; hence, his name: God *(el)* with *(imma)* us *(nu)*. The book of Matthew, however, applies that text to Jesus. We can understand the appropriation of the Isaianic passage as follows: if that son born in eighth-century Jerusalem, whoever he might have been,

---

3. Actually, in places, the task of determining the historical setting of prophetic messages is compounded by the work of later editors, who — in an attempt to make texts speak to their own later audiences — may have stripped some messages of dates and place names precisely so that postexilic readers would read the texts in light of their own day. By doing so they grant modern readers the right to apply texts to their own situation. Even so, modern readers should recognize that the texts were not written to, about, or for them.

could signify to Isaiah and Ahaz the presence of God among God's people in the eighth century, the evangelist had grounds for claiming that the son Jesus signified God's presence among God's people in the first century (cf. Matt 1:23). The reader of the Bible, however, needs to be aware of both contexts. Otherwise the reader may conflate the two, as readers have done for centuries, and claim that the prophet Isaiah predicted the virgin birth of Jesus seven centuries before it happened.

(By the way, the Hebrew word in Isaiah translated "young woman" is ʿ*almah*. The word for "virgin" is *bethulah*. An ʿ*almah* might have been a virgin, of course, but the word itself does not signify that any more than the English phrase "young woman" does. For whatever reason, however, when the book of Isaiah was translated into Greek, the interpreters used the Greek word for virgin, *parthenos*. That translation fit the evangelist's purposes even better than the Hebrew original, paving the way for him to deny that Mary and Joseph had had sexual relations.)

It should be clear by now that reading involves paying attention to the nature of the literature one is reading and formulating reading strategies appropriate to that nature. The pages that follow will describe briefly the types of reading strategies or "methods" scholars use in reading a text. These methods do not typically attempt to point to a modern application, but focus instead on understanding the text itself.[4] For purposes of this discussion, methods will be classified under two types: (1) older methods focusing on history and (2) newer methods focusing on anthropology and literature or adopting a particular ideological perspective.

Historical Methods of Study

The number of methods used in biblical study has exploded since the mid-1960s. Before then, scholars had developed several methods that focused either on the words themselves or on the historical milieu out of which they arose. Those methods were divided into "lower criticism," called text criticism, and several types of "higher criticism," consisting of source criticism, form criticism, tradition history, redaction criticism, and historical criticism (a term which doubled as a designation for all five of these last-mentioned

---

4. The issue of application is separate, but application is aided by an appropriate understanding of any text.

methods). Beginning in the mid- to late 1960s, scholars began turning to other disciplines to learn other methods. These included rhetorical criticism (including intertextuality), canonical criticism, social-scientific criticism, structural criticism, narrative criticism, reader criticism, deconstructive criticism, and ideological criticism (reading the text from black, feminist, and third world perspectives). Entire books have been dedicated to describing these methods collectively (see For Further Reading) and individually. It will be possible here, therefore, only to sketch these methods, but they will appear later in this book as they impinge on the prophetic books.

Text Criticism

Text criticism is the most basic and necessary tool at the OT scholar's command. It is simply the attempt to reconstruct as far as possible the best wording for problematic biblical texts. Over years of transmission, some texts seem to have been corrupted. It is easy to see how. If scribes copied from one text to another, their eye may have skipped a word or line or repeated a word or two. Bad handwriting or misspellings might have led to different guesses as to the correct word by different copyists. Scribes who copied by ear may have misunderstood what they heard. A scribe may have left out a phrase or sentence and stuck it in a margin, from which it was reintroduced into the text in the wrong place by another scribe. Or scribes may have deliberately changed a text to correct it.

An example of text criticism at work may be found in connection with Isa 26:19. The verse seems to predict the resurrection of the righteous dead, in contrast with v. 14, which says essentially that dead people stay dead. Verse 19 reads:

> Your [i.e., God's] dead ones will live [plural verb],
>   my corpse will rise [plural verb],
> Wake up and shout for joy, all you that dwell [in] dust,
>   for the dew of light is your [God's] dew,
>   and you [God] will cause it to fall [upon] the land of the shades.

The second line has a singular subject (corpse) and a plural verb. It is possible, of course, that the writer simply made a grammatical error, or that the text suffered in transmission, so scholars routinely emend the text to read "their corpses." Hans Wildberger, however, suggests that the text originally contained a double verb and read "Your dead ones will live and rise." He suggests that a later scribe wrote the Hebrew for "my corpse" in the margin in anticipation that he would be included in the resurrection. A later copyist then inserted the addition in the body of the text. He did not, however, change the verb to agree in number with the singular noun (my corpse) that had now become its subject.[5]

Both suggestions attempt to clear up the difficulty in the text. Which one a reader chooses, if either, may depend on other issues. For example, if one believes the text predicts the future physical resurrection of all righteous persons, then one may choose the emendation that reads "their corpses." If, however, one thinks the "resurrection" in view might be a national resurrection such as is found in Ezekiel's vision[6] of the dry bones (interpreted in Ezek 37:12 as a return of the exiles to Israel from Babylon), then one might be more inclined to accept Wildberger's solution. Even so, if Wildberger is correct, the scribe that inserted "my corpse" certainly understood the text as a prediction of individual, physical resurrection.

All scholars who work from the Hebrew text have to use text criticism one way or another, since in places the Hebrew is unintelligible. Indeed, the Masoretes[7] developed their own set of textual readings. When confronted with a text that was impossible to read or had an offensive meaning, they copied the flawed text anyway (called the *kethib,* meaning "it is written"). In the margin then they supplied their own reading (called the *qere,* meaning "to be read"). In view of this necessary and venerable use, text criticism is widely accepted and sometimes is referred to as "lower criticism," in contrast with the remaining methods, which are referred to as "higher criticism." Traditional scholars have sometimes been reluctant to use some or any of the latter.

---

5. Hans Wildberger, *Isaiah 13-27.* CC (Minneapolis: Fortress, 1991) 536.

6. A vision is a narrative genre reporting on an "altered state of consciousness in which extrasensory audiovisual experiences, usually revelatory in character, are perceived in private by individuals, often prophets or seers"; David E. Aune, "Vision," *ISBE,* 4:993. Visions are easier to identify when they report on things not normally discernible, e.g., God (Ezek 1:26-28) or the color of objects at night (Zech 1:8). Sometimes, however, the only way to recognize a vision is that the Bible identifies it as such.

7. The Masoretes were Jewish scholars who codified the Hebrew text — called the Masoretic Text — between 600 and 1000 C.E. They also devised a system of vowels, accentuation, and other pointers for reading the consonantal text.

Source Criticism

Source criticism begins with the observation that texts sometimes contradict each other, at least apparently (contrast who incited David to take a census in 2 Sam 24:1 and in 1 Chr 21:1), or that they repeat a story essentially (cf. the two versions of the call of Moses in Exod 3:1–4:23 and 6:2–7:1). Two versions of the same narrative are called doublets (cf. the two-fold explanation of the naming of Isaac, which means "laughter" in Gen 17:17-19 and 18:9-15); three are referred to as triplets (cf. the threefold attempt to pass off the wife of a patriarch as his sister in Gen 12:10-20; 20:1-18; 26:1-11). Other times, scholars think they detect two or more different literary styles within a book. (Contrast the repetitive style and the use of the name *elohim* [translated "God"] for God in Gen 1:1–2:4a with the simple style and the use of the divine name YHWH *elohim* in 2:4b-25, not to mention the obvious differences in the sequence of creation in the two accounts.) Or notice the difference in the number of animals God told Noah to take on board the ark: a pair of every kind of animal in Gen 6:19-20, but one pair of unclean and seven pairs of clean animals only four verses later in 7:2.)

Scholars often try to explain such difficulties by postulating the existence of two or more written sources behind such texts, particularly three (or more) behind Genesis. Books in the prophetic corpus sometimes exhibit the same phenomenon. The book of Isaiah, for example, repeats a section of 2 Kings (Isaiah 36–39 // 2 Kgs 18:13–20:21). Even though Isaiah omits 2 Kgs 18:14-16 and adds the material in Isa 38:9-20, the style is that of 2 Kings, not Isaiah. Moreover, in Isaiah 1–39, one reads about the prophet Isaiah and other persons and events from the eighth century in Israel, including references to the reigning Assyrian Empire. When readers move to Isaiah 40, however, they never again for the rest of the book encounter one person or event from the eighth century. Instead, Isaiah 40–55 appears to be addressed to Judeans living in exile in Babylon (after the fall of Jerusalem in 586) and to predict its downfall at the hands of the rising Persian emperor Cyrus the Great, who defeated the Babylonians in 539. Further, Isaiah 56–66 in places seems to have in view the destroyed temple (e.g., Isa 63:18) and at other times its restitution (e.g., Isa 56:3-8; 62:1-12). If so, it would contain voices from the years either side of 515, when the rebuilding of the Jerusalem temple was completed. It would appear then that at least four different hands can be found in the book of

Isaiah: Isaiah the prophet in places in chs. 1–35; the same hand as that of the author of 2 Kings in chs. 36–39; the hand of an unknown prophet in exile anticipating the return of the exiles to Judah in chs. 40–55; and the hand or hands behind chs. 56–66. Most scholars comfortable with this method also see a major break between Zechariah 8 and 9 (and perhaps 11 and 12 as well), and they may also see a number of hands behind most of the prophetic books.

Form Criticism

The next method of study, form criticism, began with the recognition that given types or genres of literature typically follow a similar structure and typically arise from a specific setting in life. When we read the words "Once upon a time, . . ." we know to expect a "fairy tale." Also, we expect to read nursery rhymes to our children at bedtime; we do not expect the President of the United States to recite a few at the State of the Union Address (except perhaps for dramatic effect). It seems also to have been the case that prophets often expressed themselves in specific genres of speech, each with its own common structure and similar content. Hence, in form criticism scholars attempt to identify genres that show a similar structure, a similar content, and a typical setting in life in which they arose and/or perhaps from which they were borrowed. By doing so, the reader — like the ancient Israelite — at once anticipates the basic thrust of what the prophet is about to say and a typical framework for understanding it. (A person may hear a nursery rhyme in a variety of settings, but recognizing that one is hearing a nursery rhyme clues in the listener/reader to the nature of the genre. Presumably, the listener would not mistake "Twinkle, twinkle, little star" for an astronomer's report.)

These genres may be either poetry or prose. Poetic types include genres as diverse as hymns, love songs, and proverbs, while prose types include such genres as genealogies, lists, and laws. Prophetic books likewise include both poetic sayings and prose narratives and sermons. The main types utilized in each prophetic book will be discussed in place, but a couple of examples are appropriate here. Claus Westermann identified the primary type(s) of prophetic speech as judgment against individuals or the nation of Israel. These judgments are often introduced by the "messenger formula," "Thus says YHWH." Westermann thinks that the formula derived from the common practice of people sending messengers as emissaries to speak on their behalf to others.[8] When prophets introduced their message "Thus says YHWH," therefore, they were following an established practice that would be familiar to their audience. The audience would recognize their implicit claim to be spokespersons for God, who was the ultimate source of their warnings.

Another prophetic genre is the admonition, a type of prophetic speech similar to laws and to proverbial instruction since they all employ imperatives and prohibitions. A typical admonition may be found in Amos 5:14-15:

14 Seek good and not evil, that you may live, and it will be thus:
    YHWH, God of hosts, will be with you, just as you have claimed.
15 Hate evil and love good, and establish justice in the gate;
    perhaps YHWH, God of hosts, will be gracious to the remnant
        of Joseph.

Prophets were typically skillful speakers, however, perfectly capable of manipulating their audience and content for maximum effect. If prophets called people to worship, members of their audience might reasonably expect them to say something like this:

Come to [the temple at] Bethel and sacrifice, to Gilgal and
    multiply sacrifices;
    Bring your sacrifices every morning, your tithes every year.

A quick glance at Amos 4:4, however, will show a dramatic and sarcastic twist:

Come to Bethel and *transgress,* to Gilgal and multiply *transgressions;*
    Bring your sacrifices every morning, your tithes every third day.

By manipulating or tweaking what people would expect him to say, Amos was claiming that the very attempt of unscrupulous worshippers to offer sacrifices was itself a transgression. He increased the sarcasm by telling them that if they brought their tithe every third day, they still could not buy off God. For Amos, sacrifice at the altar combined with a tightfisted

8. Claus Westermann, *Basic Forms of Prophetic Speech* (Philadelphia: Westminster, 1967) 100-15.

attitude toward the poor distorted God's instructions to help the poor and would result in God's rejection of the worshippers and their sacrifices.[9]

Tradition History

The direction of source and form criticism was to splinter texts into smaller and smaller units, often in an attempt to get "back" to the words of an original writer or prophet. With the rise of tradition history, however, scholars began to seek larger units to piece together for interpretation. Perhaps one of the most familiar of such studies was that of Martin Noth, who argued that the first five books of the OT were comprised of five previously independent collections of traditions dealing with the patriarchs, the exodus, the wandering in the wilderness, the conquest, and the giving of the law.[10] These themes were joined together following an old confession of faith found in Deut 26:5-9:

> 5 My father was a wandering Aramean, and he went down to Egypt and sojourned there with a few people, and there he became a great, powerful, and numerous nation. 6 But the Egyptians treated us badly; they made us suffer, and they gave us hard labor. 7 Then we cried out to YHWH, the God of our fathers, and YHWH heard our voice, and he saw our misery and our oppression. 8 So, YHWH brought us out from Egypt with a mighty hand and an outstretched arm, with great fear, and with signs and with wonders. 9 Then he brought us to this place, and he gave to us this land, flowing with milk and honey.

Another way scholars trace a tradition is to observe its reappearance in later literature. An excellent example is the reuse of the exodus traditions in Isa 43:16-17; 51:10; 52:11-12, as well as references to the wandering in the wilderness in 43:19-20; 49:9-10; 51:11; 55:12-13. Westermann observes that "The place which Deutero-Isaiah gives to the Exodus is so conspicuous

9. This book will include a discussion of the genres in each of the Major and Minor Prophets. Names of the forms or genres will follow the nomenclature proposed by W. Eugene March, "Prophecy," in *Old Testament Form Criticism*, ed. John H. Hayes, 141-77 (San Antonio: Trinity University Press, 1974).

10. Martin Noth, *Überlieferungsgeschichte des Pentateuch* (Stuttgart: Kohlhammer, 1948); trans. *A History of Pentateuchal Traditions* (Englewood Cliffs: Prentice-Hall, 1972).

that all the other events in Israel's history recede into the background."[11]
Such use of old traditions has recently become widely noticed under the
general heading of "intertextuality," which will be discussed later in connection with canonical criticism.

Redaction Criticism

In NT scholarship, a development similar to the one in OT studies took
place. Form critics, for example, had sought the words of Jesus behind the
work of the evangelists, and eschewed the framework of the gospels. Redaction critics, however, began to value what the form critics had abandoned, i.e., the work of the redactors (editors), and became interested in
the theology of the final (or main) redactor of each gospel. So, for example, Hans Conzelmann studied the theology of the evangelist responsible
for the gospel of Luke.[12]

Redaction critics seek to understand the theology and purpose(s) of
the main redactor (and maybe others too) of a book as disclosed by the arrangement of traditions and by differences between the redactor's perspective (visible through introductory, concluding, or other comments) and
those of the redactor's sources. For example, the narrative of the rise of the
monarchy in Israel in 1 and 2 Samuel is colored by the narrative of the people's rejection of Samuel's sons as judges in 1 Samuel 8. That narrative is
told to portray monarchy in a bad light; kings take people's possessions in
taxes, their sons for soldiers, their daughters as concubines or wives (1 Sam
8:11-17). Hence, the people of Israel would be better off without a king. Besides God was already their king; they did not need another. Nevertheless,
the author/redactor of Samuel and Kings also had to create a place for the
Davidic dynasty, which held sway for centuries. He did so by including an
account of the rise of David, culminating in the narrative of God's promising David an abiding dynasty, providing, of course, that his descendants
obeyed God (2 Samuel 7). The narrative of the rise of the monarchy in ancient Israel is framed by those two episodes: the one pointing to the evils of
monarchy, the other to its place in God's workings with Israel.

The prophetic speeches collected in Joel offer another interesting

---

11. Claus Westermann, *Isaiah 40–66.* OTL (Philadelphia: Westminster, 1969) 22.
12. Hans Conzelmann, *The Theology of St. Luke* (New York: Harper & Row, 1960).

study in redaction. The first half of the collection (Joel 1:1–2:17) contains varying types of prophetic speech. It opens (in 1:1-4) with what is probably a redactional introduction that names the prophet (1:1), calls upon people to hear what follows and anticipates the language of 2:2 that nothing similar had ever happened before (1:2), directs that the message be passed on (1:3), and introduces the motif of destruction (1:4). In other words, these four verses prepare the reader for the contents of 1:5–2:17 and probably stem from the hand of a redactor.

Next comes a twofold warning to the people of Judah (1:5-7, 8-12), followed by a call for a fast (1:13-14). Chapter 1 concludes with a lament (1:15-20), which is followed by another call to fast and a lament (2:1-11). The following passage (2:12-17) responds to 2:1-11, hoping for a reversal of the catastrophe predicted in ch. 1. In all these verses, the prophet (presumably Joel) appears to be associated with the cult and admonishes the priests to call a solemn assembly for the purpose of public, communal confession. The passage concludes with another call to fast (2:15-17) that repeats (in v. 15) part of the previous calls to fast (in 2:1 and 1:14). (This technique of returning to the starting point is a redactional device called an "inclusion.")

Beginning with 2:18, however, the collection assumes a basically different tone, one in which YHWH blesses the people in fulfillment of the hope expressed in 2:12-17. This is the kind of difference on which redactors fasten. If one does so, one will note that 2:18-27 carefully predicts the reversal of the calamities predicted in 1:4-20 and 2:17.

2:19a	reverses 1:10b (Grain, wine, and oil predicted to fail)
2:19b	reverses 2:17 ("Make not your heritage a reproach")
2:20	reverses the fortunes of Israel, but has no clear antecedent
2:22a	reverses 1:18 (Beasts groan, are perplexed and dismayed)
2:22b	reverses 1:7 (Fig tree and vines are destroyed)
2:23	reverses 1:20a (Water is dried up)
2:24	reverses 1:10b (Grain, wine, and oil predicted to fail)
2:25	reverses 1:4 and perhaps alludes to 1:5-7 and 2:11
2:26	reverses 1:16 (Food is cut off)
2:26-27	reverses 2:17b (Israel is a reproach)[13]

13. Paul L. Redditt, "The Book of Joel and Peripheral Prophecy," *CBQ* 48 (1986) 228.

There is more, however. What follows in Joel 2:28–3:21 continues in the same positive vein, with 2:28-32 possibly being the latest part of the collection (following the addition of 2:18-27 and 3:1-21). In any case, it appears to be the product of someone not connected with the temple, and not even part of the power structure. The prophet's vision of God's pouring God's charisma on all the people, sons and daughters, old and young, and even slaves (vv. 28-29) is the hope of those out of power, not of the ensconced elite.

As it has developed, redaction criticism has sometimes been yoked with another newer method, social-scientific criticism (see below), in an attempt to describe the differing social milieus out of which a given text arose. In connection with Joel 2:28–3:21, then, it is possible to suggest that followers of the prophet Joel, himself a cult prophet, moved or were shoved more and more to the periphery of Judean society, and as they were displaced they updated their master's message with one that expressed the hopes of people outside the power structure.[14]

Historical Criticism

The last of the older methods is called historical criticism, a term sometimes applied collectively to source, form, and redaction criticism and to tradition *history* as well as this method, because all of them work historically. More narrowly construed, however, historical criticism seeks to uncover the historical background for biblical texts and sometimes to determine whether biblical narratives are even historically likely. (It is this second function that has caused many traditional believers, scholars or not, to reject historical criticism.) The discussion of Hag 1:1-4 at the beginning of this chapter can double as an example of the function of illuminating the historical background of text. The narrative of Jonah will provide

---

14. Redditt, "The Book of Joel and Peripheral Prophecy," 229, 232-33. Let the reader be aware that not all socio-redactional critics would agree with this assessment of Joel. Marvin A. Sweeney argues for a more unified redaction of the book and a redactor from the Zadokite priesthood; "The Priesthood and the Proto-apocalyptic Reading of Prophetic and Pentateuchal Texts," in *Knowing the End from the Beginning: The Prophetic, the Apocalyptic, and Their Relationships*, ed. Lester L. Grabbe and Robert D. Haak. JSPSup 46 (London: T. & T. Clark, 2003) 168-70. We are both working from the same observations, but drawing different inferences. Unfortunately, the use of the same methods does not always produce the same results.

an example of the second function. It was set in the reign of Jeroboam II, king of the northern kingdom of Israel from 786 to 746 (cf. 2 Kgs 14:25, which mentions Jonah). The narrative recounts both the rebellion of the prophet against God's command to go preach to the inhabitants of Nineveh, the capital of the Assyrian Empire, and the prophet's eventual mission there. The incident that changed the prophet's mind, of course, was his being swallowed by a great fish and living in its belly three days and three nights (Jon 1:17).

Historical critics employ the criteria of other historians as they write. Typically, historians work critically (not accepting contradictions at face value), are concerned with natural causality (not the interference of God), and may well employ the principle of analogy (things that cannot happen now did not happen in the past). In any case, the sheer improbability of a person's living three whole days inside a fish strikes historical critics as evidence that Jonah is not a piece of historical writing.[15] This example points to another issue as well. Scholars often suggest that readers should determine the nature of their literature before attempting to ascertain its historicity. The point is well taken. Who would demand historical accuracy in a narrative that begins "Once upon a time"? Sometimes, however, it is details within a narrative that show that it is not an attempt at history writing.

Finally, we should also remember that the attempt to describe exactly what happened and to do so by the use of more-or-less rigorous social-scientific criteria is a product of the modern period. Biblical authors were unencumbered by our canons of historicity and quite likely would have seen no point in such a view. They often told narratives precisely for their educative value and would have seen nothing wrong with making sure the reader saw that point, even by putting appropriate sentiments in the mouths of characters in the narrative (cf. the speeches in Isa 36:4-20).

An example of where historical criticism both illuminates the background of a text and calls its historicity into question is Daniel 11. Scholars have long recognized that 11:2-20 constitutes a thinly-veiled tracing of the history of Judah from the end of the Persian period down through the reign of Seleucus IV, ruler of the eastern or Asian portion of Alexander the Great's empire. The Seleucids collectively were called the king of the north

---

15. That conclusion is debatable, of course. Moreover, one should note that Bible students who think the story is historically improbable might nevertheless think it is a short story that teaches valid theological lessons.

in Daniel 11. Seleucus IV was succeeded by Antiochus IV, whose reign is the subject of 11:21-45. Verses 21-39 continue tracing the history, but in vv. 40-45 the seer predicts that Ptolemy (the ruler of Egypt, called the king of the south) would provoke another battle with Antiochus, who would respond by fighting his way south, with Judean casualties numbering in the tens of thousands. After defeating the Egyptians, Antiochus would attempt to return home to defeat enemies near Persia, only to meet his death in Judah "between the sea (= the Mediterranean) and the beautiful mountain" (= Jerusalem). None of these events discussed in vv. 40-45 occurred. A historical critic would explain the anomaly by suggesting that the actual author of Daniel lived ca. 165, just before the death of Antiochus IV in his own homeland, wrote in vv. 2-39 about things that had already transpired, but did so from the perspective of the earlier sage Daniel,[16] and then in vv. 40-45 engaged in genuine prophecy, predicting the demise of Antiochus. In all fairness to the author, he got that right; he just missed the details of how Antiochus would die.

•   •

EXCURSUS
A Brief Historical Background for the Study of the Prophets

It should be clear by this point that a reader needs to know at least the broad contours of Israelite history in order to place prophets in their proper historical context. Consequently, I will try to situate each prophet and/or section of a prophet book in its own context. It might be useful, however, to survey the sweep of Israelite history from the eighth to the second centuries, i.e., during the period of the Major and Minor Prophets. To get a running start on that survey, I will begin with the reign of David.

David was elected king of Judah around 1000 and, seven years later, of the northern tribes that had earlier followed Saul. He died about 961 and was succeeded by one of his sons, Solomon, who reigned until about 923. Judah accepted Solomon's son Rehoboam I as successor, but leaders of the northern tribes wanted to negotiate some relief from Solomon's taxes and other measures. When Rehoboam refused, the northern tribes seceded,

---

16. See the discussion of pseudonymity in Chapter 8 on Daniel.

electing a man named Jeroboam I as king, and the two little kingdoms began a period of co-existence. Soon, however, the Assyrians extended their hegemony from Mesopotamia into the Levant (the countries bordering on the eastern shore of the Mediterranean Sea) and eventually into Egypt. Their power waxed and waned, but often involved the payment of tribute by the vassal kingdoms. The prophets Amos, Hosea, Isaiah, and Micah flourished during the Assyrian period. Perhaps the most disastrous event during those years was the Assyrian defeat of Samaria and the reduction of Israel into a province of Assyria in 722. After three centuries of Assyrian dominance, the Babylonians under Nabopolassar (beginning about 626) and Nebuchadnezzar (in 605) conquered Assyria and established the so-called Neo-Babylonian Empire. The prophets Nahum, Habakkuk, and Zephaniah flourished during that period, and Jeremiah began his career.

Conditions under Babylon did not differ significantly from those under Assyria, so that Judah twice withheld tribute and twice the Babylonians successfully besieged Jerusalem (598 and 587), the second time destroying the city and its temple. The prophet Jeremiah remained active that long, and the book of Lamentations looks back on the fall of the city. The prophet Obadiah also reflected on the loss and future restoration of the city. Thousands of upper class Judeans and people with skills valued by the Babylonians went into exile in Babylon.[17] Among them were the prophet Ezekiel and (probably) the anonymous prophet whose messages are contained in Isaiah 40–55, typically called Second Isaiah by scholars.

The Babylonian conquerors were themselves conquered by the Persians, led by Cyrus the Great in 539. In the ensuing years, even a century or more, Judeans returned to Judah. Hopes for a renewed monarchy (cf. Haggai and Zechariah) proved futile, but hopes for a rebuilt temple and a functioning priesthood were realized. The messages found in Isaiah 56–66, often attributed to a "Third Isaiah," illuminate the Persian period. The prophets Joel and Malachi also flourished then, and the narrative of the prophet Jonah probably arose at that time, though it was set during the Assyrian period.

The nemesis of the Persians was the Greeks under Alexander the Great. He wrested the Levant from Persian control in 332 while en route to Egypt. Alexander died in 323, and his four generals divided up his empire

---

17. The term "exile" refers to Judeans forced to live outside Palestine, while the term "Diaspora" refers to those who did so even though they could return home.

among them. Daniel 11 chronicles the events of the Greek period down to 165 that affected Jerusalem and the group of pious scribes responsible for that book. In brief, the Ptolemies, who gained control of the Egyptian part of Alexander's empire, controlled Judah until 198. Then the Seleucids took control, eventually causing a revolt led by Judas Maccabeus, with which the group behind the book of Daniel seems to have been out of sympathy. Over the next century or so, Judah experienced some periods of relative freedom from the Greeks, ultimately losing it to the Romans.

•   •

Newer Methods of Study

Scholars are aware of the shortcomings of the various methods discussed thus far, and have tried to keep their limitations in mind as they use them. Since the mid-1960s, scholars have turned to other disciplines (e.g., anthropology and the study of literature) for newer methods. Also, aware that all methods have presuppositions, some scholars have adopted particular perspectives (e.g., third world, African-American, and feminist) from which to read the Bible. We will now turn to discuss these newer methods. The first two, rhetorical and canonical criticism, can be seen as outgrowths of the historical methods we have just been examining.

Rhetorical Criticism

As a *modern* tool of OT studies, rhetorical criticism began with James Muilenburg's presidential address at the Society of Biblical Literature in 1968, entitled "Form Criticism and Beyond." In that address, Muilenburg lamented the splintering of texts in form criticism and suggested that attention to rhetoric would help Bible students avoid chopping the text into supposedly unrelated bites.[18] Rhetoric, of course, was a subject of study as far back as the Greeks and Romans and continues in contemporary literary study. Essentially, rhetoric may be defined as the art of speaking or writing well. It may be practiced for literary artistry and/or for persuasive

18. James Muilenburg, "Form Criticism and Beyond," *JBL* 87 (1969) 1-18.

effect. Rhetorical criticism, then, is the study of the literary effectiveness of a text. It looks for devices that authors use in effective speech or literature (e.g., repetitions and patterns) and authors' choice of words (or their diction). Muilenburg called attention to ring compositions or inclusion devices (where the author returns to the starting point), parallelism in structure, repetitions of key words at the beginning of lines, strophes, and even the use of defining particles (such as "because," "behold," and "therefore"). Not every instance of such small features as particles is structurally or rhetorically significant, but some are.

An example of repetition with great rhetorical effect may be found in Isa 5:25b, which reads: "For all this his [God's] anger is not turned away, and his hand is raised up still." This phrase appears in a description of God's punishment of the people of Judah, signaling that there was more to come. Its appearance there foreshadows its further appearance four chapters later in 9:12b, 17b, 21b; and then in 10:4b. In those verses it serves as a refrain, interpreting what has happened to Judah and predicting further punishment. Its repetition drives home the message like a pile driver.

Two other rhetorical devices are the inclusion device (also called *inclusio*) and the chiasmus, both of which return to their point of departure, thus providing a sense of completeness. An example is Psalm 8, which begins and ends with the same affirmation: "O YHWH our Lord, how majestic is your name in all the earth." An example in prophetic literature may be found in Joel 1:8-13. There the prophet calls upon someone to *lament* (v. 8) because "The grain offering and the drink offering are cut off from the house of YHWH" (v. 9). Toward the end of that section the prophet gives directions for a fast (v. 13):

> Put on sackcloth and lament, O you priests,
>   Wail, O you who are ministers of the altar;
> Come, spend the night in sackcloth,
>   You who are ministers of my God,
> For there is withheld from the house of your God
>   Grain offering and drink offering.

The passage then ends with a command to the priests to "sanctify a fast" where the priests and others would *lament* (v. 14).

A chiasmus is similar in that a text returns to its starting point, but it does so by retracing its steps backwards. It might look like this:

A · B · C
C′ · B′ · A′

The following is an example taken from Jonah 1:3, as translated word for word by Phyllis Trible:[19]

A And/but-arose Jonah to-flee to-Tarshish
   from-the-presence-of YHWH
    B and-he-went-down to-Joppa
      C and-he-found a-ship
        D returning (to) Tarshish
      C′ and-he-paid her-fare
    B′ and-he-went-down in-it
A′ to-return with-them to-Tarshish from-the-presence-of YHWH.

In this case the entire verse reverses itself in line "D," which has no corresponding phrase.

One aspect of rhetorical criticism that started receiving much more attention in the 1980s is called intertextuality. Intertextuality may be defined as "interconnections among texts." Types of intertextuality include quotations of or allusions to other texts and the use of catchwords, themes or motifs, and framing devices. Intertextuality may occur consciously, as when Jer 26:18 specifically refers to and quotes Mic 3:12 ("Zion shall be plowed like a field"), or perhaps subconsciously when words or phrases from a familiar context are repeated in another. In this book, the issue of intertextuality will come to the foreground especially in connection with the Book of the Twelve or Minor Prophets.

Canonical Criticism

If Muilenburg was concerned with seeing the integrity of passages, and redaction criticism was interested often in the theology of whole books or segments of books, canonical criticism carried these concerns one step further to argue that the focus of interpretation ought to be on the final,

---

19. Phyllis Trible, *Rhetorical Criticism: Context, Method, and the Book of Jonah.* GBS (Minneapolis: Fortress, 1994) 129.

canonical shape of a book. Brevard S. Childs argues that canonical criticism in the OT should focus on the Masoretic Text (MT) of the Hebrew Bible. Its consonantal text (not including the vowel points) was stabilized by about the end of the first century c.e. It was, in fact, the only Hebrew text to be stabilized, and it continued in use through history as the vehicle of the "whole canon of Hebrew scripture."[20] This method also will stand relatively to the forefront in this volume, particularly in connection with the Minor Prophets, which will treated as one book as in the MT. Even so, the use of canonical criticism does not preclude the use of source, form, or redactional criticism, though it does insist on dealing with the text as a completed whole.

Social-Scientific Criticism

The next two methods draw upon social sciences, especially anthropology. Since archaeology is a social science, and because scholars have long employed the insights of archaeologists in understanding biblical texts, social-science criticism is not new. It did, however, take a turn in the late 1960s when biblical scholars turned explicitly to the work of cultural anthropologists and of sociologists to derive models by which to interpret biblical texts. In doing so, one analyzes the OT under the categories a cultural anthropologist might employ: e.g., marriage rules and rites, kinship systems, ways of making a living, order and social structure, conflict and war, and religion. One can also test[21] anthropological theories or models against OT texts to see what light such theories might shed on those texts.

20. Brevard S. Childs, *Introduction to the Old Testament as Scripture* (Philadelphia: Fortress, 1979) 97. The whole volume views the OT from that perspective. Childs does not question the validity of the previous methods of biblical study, but he does insist that the object of OT study is the book in that stabilized form, not individual passages deemed the "original" version of what prophets and others said, laid out like a dissected frog in a biology lab (my analogy).

21. In doing so, one should attempt not to superimpose models on the text. Cf. the discussion of central and peripheral prophets in Chapter 1. There I noted that one would expect charismatic calls among peripheral prophets, authenticating their status. In the Old Testament, however, the temple prophet Isaiah as well as the priests Jeremiah and Ezekiel reported call visions. Of course, both Jeremiah and Ezekiel were peripheral in some sense as well. Still, the point here is that the model indicates what one might expect and signals in this case where Israel may have differed.

The tribal arrangement of ancient Israel, for example, has been interpreted in light of other societies with an agrarian basis. One brief description of that society during what is typically called the period of the judges (ca. 1200-1000 B.C.E.) reads as follows.

> As an economy, the new society was grounded in highland agriculture dependent on a mix of crops and herds nurtured by a scattered populace spread over broken terrain and encountering diversified ecological niches with particular subsistence demands. As a polity, the new society was able to practice tributary-free agricultural and pastoral production. The situation obtained for some two centuries because Israel was able to stay free of domination by other states and also to refrain from developing an Israelite state.[22]

In simple terms this description says that the Israelites made their living as independent herdsmen and farmers, not sharecroppers, and did not have to pay heavy taxes to a central government because there was none.

Employing insights from anthropology sometimes allows a reader to interpret even a whole book in a consistent manner. The book of Daniel, for example, contains two basic types of narratives: court narratives (chs. 1, 3, 4, 5, and 6) and visions (chs. 8-12). Two narratives (chs. 2 and 7) combine elements of both. Focusing on the court narratives, one may hypothesize a group of Jewish scribes living in Babylon or elsewhere in the Persian or Greek Empires hoping to succeed as servants in a foreign court. They collect and remember a number of narratives about scribes that do succeed, usually because they remain faithful to their Jewish faith. Eventually, however, the fortunes of some such scribes in Jerusalem turn sour during the reign of Antiochus IV Epiphanes. Their group becomes apocalyptic, telling narratives of God's imminent intervention on behalf of the "wise" (2:12-28; 12:3, 10), the "people of the saints of the Most High" (7:18, 27). In this understanding of Daniel, it is the change in the social status of the group behind the group that gives rise to the collecting and eventual disseminating of the whole range of narratives.[23]

22. Norman K. Gottwald, "Sociology of Ancient Israel," *ABD* 6:83.
23. Paul L. Redditt, *Daniel.* NCBC (Sheffield: Sheffield Academic, 1999) 20-34.

Structural Criticism

Structural criticism, a particular form of social-scientific criticism, originated from — among other places — the thinking of Claude Levi-Strauss, a twentieth-century French anthropologist who recognized that humans think in polarities. Simply put, one does not understand "hot" without understanding its opposite "cold." Texts, moreover, are meaningful only insofar as readers recognize similarities and distinguish differences. The method that grew out of his observations is called "structural" exegesis because it seeks interrelations or structures built on similarities and differences. Such structures include everything from "letters, syllables, words, their denotations, . . . their connotations . . . — to larger features such as sentences, paragraphs, parts; characters, actions, situations, subplots, and plots; metaphors and other figures, allusions to other texts, figurative units, and the like."[24] Examples of structure on this level would include those Robert G. Culley assembled under the heading of "Examples Where Intervention Comes as Help": Elisha makes bad water good to drink (2 Kgs 2:19-22), Elisha makes poisoned stew good to eat (2 Kgs 4:38-41), Moses makes bitter water sweet (Exod 15:22-27), Elisha recovers an axe-head lost in the Jordan (2 Kgs 6:1-7), and Elijah brings a dead boy back to life (1 Kgs 17:17-24).[25]

A structural approach to Jonah, for example, might distinguish a narrative program (God, the subject, tries to conjoin Jonah to his will) and its anti-program narrative (Jonah, the anti-subject, refusing the role of subject).[26] Following this structure, in the narrative program God directs Jo-

24. Daniel Patte, "Structural Criticism," in *To Each Its Own Meaning: An Introduction to Biblical Criticisms and Their Application,* ed. Steven L. McKenzie and Stephen R. Haynes, rev. ed. (Louisville: Westminster John Knox, 1999) 183. For a discussion of the underlying philosophy, see Brian W. Kovacs, "Philosophical Foundations for Structuralism," in *Narrative Syntax: Translations and Reviews,* ed. John Dominic Crossan. Semeia 10 (Missoula: Scholars, 1978) 85-105. Kovacs argues that the presuppositions of structuralism are such that it resists being considered simply one method among many. Since it claims to identify deep structures of thinking, it must, Kovacs says, take priority. Other methods may supplement it, but none may stand as its equal.

25. Robert C. Culley, *Studies in the Structure of Hebrew Narrative* (Philadelphia: Fortress, 1976) 72-91.

26. Centre pour l'Analyse du Discourse Religieux, "An Approach to the Book of Jonah," in *Perspectives on Old Testament Narrative,* ed. Robert C. Culley. Semeia 15 (Missoula: Scholars, 1979) 85.

nah to go east to Nineveh to preach to its inhabitants. In the anti-program, Jonah refuses, and goes west to Tarshish instead. Jonah has misconstrued YHWH as the land-bound God of Israel only; YHWH also turns out to be God of the sea as well. In the narrative program, Jonah travels to Nineveh, where he delivers God's message (Jonah 3:4): "[There are] yet forty days before Nineveh is overthrown." The people of Nineveh repent with such gusto that even the king repents in sackcloth and the animals are made to fast. In the anti-program, however, Jonah is incensed that the people have repented, that God has forgiven them and has decided not to destroy them. Jonah even explains/complains to God (and the reader) that he knew the nature of God was to forgive and wanted no part in the salvation of the city, hence his flight to Tarshish. Perhaps he was even annoyed because his prediction did not come true, casting doubt on his future-telling abilities.[27] In the anti-program, Jonah settles down to await God's punishment of the city. In the narrative program, God makes a plant grow overnight to shade the angry prophet. Then the next night God makes a worm to destroy the plant God had just made. In the anti-program Jonah sulks at this final insult. In the program narrative, however, God confronts the prophet. Was Jonah justified in being angry about the demise of the plant, which he had neither planted nor tended? The prophet insists he was justified. The book ends on a question, the final note in the program narrative: is God not, therefore, justified in God's concern for the great city Nineveh, which God had made? The reader is left to answer the question and in so doing to choose between the program narrative and the anti-program narrative.

Narrative Criticism

This reading of Jonah perhaps already has bled over into narrative criticism, so it will be appropriate to turn there next. Indeed, the line between narrative criticism and reader criticism is pretty fluid too, so there is room for debate about the lines drawn here between various methods. For simplicity's sake, however, I will treat narrative criticism as an outgrowth of older studies that emphasized such features of narrative as setting (the time and place something occurred), plot (complication, climax, denoue-

---

27. Probably a reader would not be wrong in seeing this part of the anti-program as comedic, even farcical.

ment), characters, tone (the author's attitude), and point of view (first or third person, limited or omniscient). It also took note of rhetoric, including features or devices such as irony and foreshadowing. Narrative plots traditionally have been described as comic, in which the action ascends or ends on a positive note, or as tragedy, in which the action descends or ends on a negative note. To be sure, plots can do both along the way, but usually one or the other wins out in the end. Further, subcategories of narratives (e.g., folk narratives, rituals, or cosmogonies) may exhibit their own peculiarities. In a fable, for example, animals and perhaps even inanimate objects are endowed with human characteristics.

In the prophetic literature of the OT, one encounters a number of narrative genres: reports of visions, reports of symbolic acts, prophetic legends, and biographical sketches, sometimes joined together over several chapters as in Jeremiah 26–28, 36–45. One also discovers scholars speaking of the "plot" of prophetic oracles or even of the plot of the Book of the Twelve. Paul R. House, for example, argues that the plot of the Twelve is essentially comedic, starting as it does with the doomsayers Hosea and Amos and ending with the more upbeat postexilic prophets Haggai through Malachi.[28] Since at least the rise of form criticism, scholars also have paid attention to the oral nature of much prophetic literature, including such rhetorical devices as alliteration, rhyme, wordplay, and repetition.

Isaiah 24–27 will provide a satisfactory choice to illustrate a narrative analysis of a prophetic collection. The four chapters probably formed a separate collection secondarily inserted into the book of Isaiah, a working hypothesis that might meet objection from some scholars. Even so, the majority would treat these chapters as a more-or-less self-contained collection of originally disparate materials, including prophecies of disaster and salvation, an expression of woe, several songs, an allegory, and the like. Despite its title "the Isaiah apocalypse," it is neither from the hand of Isaiah nor an apocalypse. It has sometimes been called "proto-apocalyptic," a designation which also has its detractors, but which points to its similarities to later apocalypses.

Since plot inevitably deals with time, I will describe its plot temporally. It opens on a note of impending doom (Isa 24:1-23a), which gives way in a half verse (24:23b) to God's self-manifestation in Zion. Next, the chapters depict a future upswing, in which two songs (25:1-5; 26:1-6) surround a

28. Paul R. House, *The Unity of the Twelve.* JSOTSup 97 (Sheffield: Almond, 1990).

brief passage combining a depiction of the eschatological banquet on Zion (25:6-8), with two short pieces contrasting the bright future of Zion (25:9-10a) with the future punishment of Moab (25:10b-12). Turning back to the present, it portrays present difficulties that will eventuate in God's rescue of the faith (26:7-21). It concludes (27:1-13) with a series of short sayings portraying once again the ultimate victory of God and elevation of Israel. Even here, though, one part (27:7-11) of the concluding chapter focuses on something Israel must do to experience the new day: correct worship practices at the altar. This plot is essentially comedic, though much of the passage sounds gloomy, even in the closing chapter. Perhaps it should be called a double plot since it builds twice to a positive outcome.

Reader Criticism

Reader criticism developed alongside narrative and structural exegesis. It recognizes that readers themselves participate in the making of meaning in texts. At times it has gone so far as to say that readers alone make the meaning, but that version of this method is open to the criticism that texts may not legitimately be made to say *anything* the reader wants them to say. For example, it would not be legitimate to read the sentence above "readers themselves participate in the making of meaning in texts" and say that it means that readers have no role in determining what a text means.

Moreover, instead of pursuing the intention of the original author, some reader-critical studies refer to various authors and readers of/in a text. There were the real flesh-and-blood authors and original flesh-and-blood readers. At times one even spots narrators and audiences within a text, as for example in Ezek 11:24-25, where the text suddenly mentions the audience to whom Ezekiel related his vision. Reader critics also note that all texts imply an author and audience. Those implied authors are the flesh-and-blood authors once removed, the authors as they attempt to portray themselves; and the implied readers are the readers as the authors want them to be, seeing and buying into what the real authors want them to accept.[29] Certainly, then, it is true that a text implies more than one level

---

29. Robert M. Fowler, "Who Is 'the Reader' in Reader Response Criticism?" in *Reader Response Approaches to Biblical and Secular Texts,* ed. Robert Detweiler. Semeia 31 (Decatur: Scholars, 1985) 10-11.

of author and reader. Still, sociological studies are often interested in the nature of the persons or group by whom and for whom a text or several texts are produced and preserved. While these concerns might not be identical with those of the Reader, they are at least quite similar.

In OT studies, however, reader critics do insist that merely "discovering" the historical (or sociological) background for a text and doing other things like analyzing its grammar do not result necessarily in opening a text for modern readers or the church. I think in past generations this distinction was made in terms of "exegesis" (determining what the text meant in its original context) and "interpretation" or "hermeneutics" (determining what the text means to the modern reader). Reader critics want to combine these tasks into a more seamless reading.

Edgar W. Conrad offers a reader-oriented approach to the Book of the Twelve.[30] He argues that information for reading was encoded in biblical books, information that a Model Author could have reasonably expected a Model Reader to understand. He offers an example. The book of Isaiah opens (1:1) with the phrase "the vision of Isaiah, son of Amoz," whereas the book of Jeremiah opens by calling what follows "the words of Jeremiah" and Amos by speaking of "the words of Amos." The book of Ezekiel opens (1:1) with a Hebrew word translated "and it happened." Conrad notes that both Jeremiah and Amos are associated with nonprophet groups, the priests of Anathoth and the shepherds of Tekoa, respectively. Hence, their "words" are not designated as having come in a vision, whereas those of the prophet Isaiah were. Ezekiel, another unconventional prophet (he was also a priest), and Jonah both flourished in a foreign country. Information about them simply comes in a form appropriate for a narrative.

These verses do not, of course, exhaust what a reader critic would want to say, nor even what Conrad said in the article I am drawing on, but they do offer the possibility that the opening words of a book in the Major and Minor Prophets might clue the perceptive reader in exactly the same way that the opening line of a narrative that runs "Once upon a time" clues a Model Reader today about the nature of the literature to follow. Equally as important to the reader critic, it does so to anyone aware of the clue without recourse to what comes after. What follows in the prophetic col-

---

30. Edgar W. Conrad, "Forming the Twelve and Forming Canon," in *Thematic Threads in the Book of the Twelve,* ed. Paul L. Redditt and Aaron Schart. BZAW 325 (Berlin: de Gruyter, 2003) 90-103.

lections will confirm (or perhaps deny) the clue provided by the opening designation of contents.

Deconstructive Criticism

Deconstructive criticism may be seen as a development along the lines of reader criticism in that it focuses on the written text itself as the locus of meaning. What is distinctive about deconstructive criticism, however, is its insistence on several characteristics of literature:

> its incompleteness, that is, the way in which the hearer or reader has to fill in the picture that is suggested by speech or writing; its enclosure within itself, that is, the way in which the immediate connection of words is not with "reality," but with other words in a pattern that gives them meaning; and the unfixed flowing quality of language, that is, the way in which meanings are continually being enlarged or shifted as a reader moves through a text.[31]

One of the leading figures in deconstructionism is the French thinker Jacques Derrida. His essay on the Tower of Babel (Gen 11:1-9) will illustrate the emphasis on language itself in deconstructionism. Derrida understands that passage as being in some sense the primal narrative, the narrative of the birth of narrative, myth, and the making of figures of speech. For Derrida, then, the narrative seems to be other than one might think: less a fall narrative or a narrative about transformation of culture; more a study in the making of meaning in words, speech, and literature. Above all, however, it is about the incompleteness and inadequacy of language.[32] Humans never can fully communicate with others; their efforts always come up against a gap, perhaps even a chasm, they cannot cross with total success.

Peter D. Miscall offers a deconstructionist reading of Isaiah, which I will summarize here to provide an idea of how a deconstructionist might work.[33]

---

31. William A. Beardslee, "Poststructuralist Criticism," in McKenzie and Haynes, *To Each Its Own Meaning*, 253.

32. Jacques Derrida, "Des Tours de Babel," in *Poststructuralism as Exegesis*, ed. David Jobling and Stephen D. Moore. Semeia 54 (Atlanta: Scholars, 1992) 3-34.

33. Peter D. Miscall, "Isaiah: The Labyrinth of Images," in Jobling and Moore, *Poststructuralism as Exegesis*, 103-21.

Miscall finds a number of themes in the book: light, words, good light, evil darkness, fire, water, dryness, sun and shade, smelting, and idol. All of these themes (and more) comprise a labyrinth, intersecting at various junctures. In following a labyrinth, Miscall notes, one does not reach a set entrance, center, or exit. Similarly, in a deconstructionist reading one does not arrive at a previously determined meaning. The reading, rather, is directed by the reader. "(T)he reader decides which textual threads to pick up and follow, how far to follow each one and whether to tie them all together at some end or center or just leave them lying on the page."[34] Thus, the reader *contributes* to a text's meaning, but does not *determine* its meaning.

In connection with the last of his themes, Miscall discusses idols and idolmaking in Isa 44:9-20. He comments that "The idolmaker . . . cuts down a tree and uses part of it for heating and for cooking; the other part he makes into an idol, a carefully crafted image, that he falls down before and worships. One way to avoid such idolatry is to burn the part of the tree used in the idol and simply never make it."[35] Miscall continues with this observation about the prophet: he "fashions not with tree and wood but with words and images. He must turn them into counsel and strength that can stand forever. But words and images in words can also turn into idols, into crafted images and figures that are wooden and stony, that are fixed and cannot move."[36] The reader must take care not to absolutize any given reading and thus make such an idol.

Ideological Criticism

Aware that all methods bear their own presuppositions, and thus are not neutral, scholars have proposed a variety of ideological readings. In formerly colonial areas, readings began to emerge that looked especially fondly on the book of Exodus with its emancipation of the ancient Israelites from slavery in Egypt. In the 1960s, with the rise of the Black Power movement, African Americans made the same move. In the ensuing years others have proposed feminist readings or readings that support particular minorities in the West or the third world in general. Collectively, such

34. Miscall, "Isaiah," 107.
35. Miscall, "Isaiah," 117.
36. Miscall, "Isaiah," 117.

readings can be called "liberationist." These readings may on the one hand point to places where the Bible seems compatible with the views of liberationist readers, but on the other hand these readings may criticize the Bible for its own "failures" in perpetuating male domination or other matters to which the scholars are sensitive.

An example of such a reading may be made in connection with Hosea 1–4. In the narrative of Hosea's marriage (Hosea 1–3), the northern kingdom of Israel is compared to the adulterous wife of Hosea. The language is unflinching:

> YHWH told Hosea, "Go, take to yourself a wife of whoredom, and beget children of whoredom, for the land commits great whoredom by turning away from YHWH." (Hos 1:2)

Feminist readers (who are not necessarily women) might well object to the use of the phrase "whoredom." Why "whoredom"? Why not "adultery"? Why use the female epithet "whore" for the objects of Hosea's (and God's) wrath? Why not call them something more neutral in gender or even call them by a masculine term? Why symbolize the general condition of idolatry with a term normally used of women? Does not such a term perpetuate antiwomen stereotypes and feelings? If one responds that Hosea did so because he was going to cast God in the husband's role, feminist readers might well challenge that stereotype as well. Is God male? No. God is neither female nor male. It is humans that are gendered beings.

Hosea himself apparently recognizes the tension in the term "whore" as applied to those who commit idolatry. In Hos 4:14 he has God say:

> I will not punish your daughters when they play the whore,
>   nor your daughters-in-law when they commit adultery;
> for they [masculine plural = the men] turn aside to prostitutes,
>   and they sacrifice with temple prostitutes,
>   so that a people without understanding is ruined.

At least here the prophet makes it clear that the women are less to blame than the men, but that concession raises even more starkly the issue of why use a female-gendered term at all.

A Combination of Methods

With ideological criticism, our review of the primary methods of biblical studies is complete. There has been no effort to explain the methods fully, only to indicate the variety of tools available to the reader to aid in the task of understanding the Bible. All these methods yield insights; they are not necessarily in opposition to each other. Some work better on one passage than on another. This book will employ a combination of methods in pursuing its task of introducing the Major and Minor Prophets.[37]

Questions for Reflection

1. Which of these methods seem most compatible to you? Why? Do any of them seem incompatible with your view of the Bible? Why or why not?
2. Why should one even bother with any of these methods? Can't one simply read the Bible for what one can derive from it at face value? What if any advantage do you see in attempting to use some or all of these methods?
3. Text criticism is also called "lower criticism" and is often acceptable to traditional scholars who have no sympathy for any of the other methods. Why do you think that is?
4. Does employing some or all of these methods reduce the Bible to "just another piece of literature"?

For Further Reading

Gunn, David M., and Danna Nolan Fewell. *Narrative in the Hebrew Bible.* Oxford Bible Series. Oxford: Oxford University Press, 1993. A treatment of how to read biblical narratives, with special attention to specific texts including the book of Jonah (ch. 6).

Habel, Norman C. *Literary Criticism of the Old Testament.* GBS. Philadelphia: Fortress, 1971. A discussion of the rise of the method called *source criticism* in this chapter, along with several examples of how to use it.

---

37. The proponents of structural, reader, and deconstructionist exegesis might well object that their methods are substantially incompatible with the others, or at least must be primary. Since I am not prepared to grant them priority, I will make less use of those methods. Still, I hope at times to demonstrate further their usefulness.

Lance, H. Darrell. *The Old Testament and the Archaeologist.* GBS. Philadelphia: Fortress, 1981. A discussion of the methods of biblical archaeology, including reports on excavating Solomonic sites as examples of how archaeologists work.

McCarter, P. Kyle. *Textual Criticism: Recovering the Text of the Old Testament.* GBS. Philadelphia: Fortress, 1986. A description of the problems that have arisen in OT texts and a discussion of how the method works.

McKenzie, Stephen L., and Stephen R. Haynes. *To Each Its Own Meaning: Biblical Criticisms and Their Application.* Rev. ed. Louisville: Westminster John Knox, 1999. An excellent overview of the various methods of biblical study.

Petersen, David L., and Harold Kent Richards. *Interpreting Hebrew Poetry.* GBS. Minneapolis: Fortress, 1992. A discussion of parallelism, meter and rhythm, and poetic style, combined with an analysis of three poetic texts, including Isa 5:1-7.

Powell, Mark Allan. *What Is Narrative Criticism?* GBS. Minneapolis: Fortress, 1990. A discussion of various ways of reading narratives (Structuralism, Rhetorical Criticism. Reader-Response Criticism, and Narrative Criticism), with a discussion of such topics as point of view, irony, symbolism, plot, characters, and setting, based on texts from the New Testament.

Trible, Phyllis. *Rhetorical Criticism.* GBS. Minneapolis: Fortress, 1994. A description of the rise and development of rhetorical criticism, with a study of the book of Jonah showing how it is used.

Tucker, Gene M. *Form Criticism of the Old Testament.* GBS. Philadelphia: Fortress, 1971. A brief introduction to the history of the methods, with a description of the main genres of Old Testament literature and examples of how it works. Pp. 54-77 discuss prophetic passages.

CHAPTER 3

Isaiah 1–39

Prophecy was not new in the eighth century in Israel. According to the OT, it had been around in some form since the time of the judges (cf. Judg 6:8). The exploits of the great ninth-century prophets Elijah, Micaiah ben Imlah, and Elisha, plus other unnamed prophets, fill thirteen chapters in 1 and 2 Kings. Prophecy did, however, undergo a new development beginning in the eighth century. People started collecting the sayings of the prophets, including sayings without attached narratives, and recording them in writing[1] (hence the name "Writing Prophets" for the Major and Minor Prophets). The earlier prophets mentioned in Joshua — Kings are known as much or more for what they did, and their sayings are attached to narratives. The practice of recording messages primarily arose in connection with Amos (the earliest of the writing prophets), whose sayings comprise all but a few verses of the collection associated with his name. The only narrative in that collection describes an encounter with a priest in Bethel, during which the priest ordered him to leave Israel and return to his home in Judah (Amos 7:10-17). The writing prophets eventually included the other eleven Minor Prophets as well as the Major Prophets.

One of the larger collections was associated with the prophet Isaiah. By no means, however, did all of the sayings derive from the eighth-century

---

1. Writing seems to have blossomed in Judah in the late eighth century, as evidenced by archaeological finds, as a part of the process of urbanization. It is no coincidence that the "writing prophets" date from this time and later. For a readable discussion of this process in ancient Judah, see F. E. Peters, *The Voice, the Word, the Books* (Princeton: Princeton University Press, 2007) 94-101.

prophet Isaiah of Jerusalem. We have already noted in the discussion of source criticism in Chapter 2 that the book of Isaiah also includes sayings from the exilic and postexilic periods. For convenience' sake, therefore, this chapter will deal only with Isaiah 1–39; Chapter 4 will take up Isaiah 40–66.

Introduction to the Book and Its Times

The book of Isaiah is well known to readers of the NT, which cites Isaiah more than any other OT book except Deuteronomy. A number of these citations apply the predictions and other messages to Jesus, though — as we shall see — it is doubtful Isaiah had Jesus in view. It is also known for its teachings, particularly the ideas of monotheism and the remnant (the idea that after God punished Israel God would save part of the people). As mentioned above, critical scholars think the book appeared over a period of more than 200 years, not simply during the lifetime of the prophet for whom it is named. We shall turn first to consider other matters associated with the book itself before focusing our attention on its teachings.

The Place of the Book in the Canon

In the MT the book of Isaiah stands at the beginning of the Latter Prophets. It did not always stand there. In the rabbinic work *B. Bat.* 14b (ca. 180 C.E.), we find this list of the *Nebiim* (Prophets): Joshua through Kings, as in modern Bibles, but then the Latter Prophets in the sequence Jeremiah, Ezekiel, Isaiah, and the Twelve. One explanation for this sequence is that 2 Kings ended with the destruction of Jerusalem, a theme at the heart of Jeremiah's message and Ezekiel's too. Isaiah would then end the three on a note of promise. It might simply be, however, that the books were arranged in order of approximate descending length, since Jeremiah is the longest and the Twelve the shortest. The Greek Bible, the Septuagint (abbreviated LXX), by contrast, places the Book of the Twelve first, then Isaiah, Jeremiah, Ezekiel. Modern English Bibles divide Isaiah, Jeremiah, and Ezekiel from the Book of the Twelve (which possibly were called the Minor Prophets because in general they are short), and add Lamentations and Daniel as Major Prophets (even though Lamentations contains only five chapters and Daniel only twelve). The MT contains Isaiah, Jeremiah, and

Ezekiel, in what looks like chronological order. The Book of the Twelve (our Minor Prophets) also is arranged more or less in chronological order. This volume, however, will follow the sequence of the Major Prophets of the English Bible, since it is based on that text.

The Setting for the Book

The setting for much of Isaiah 1–39 and the ostensible setting for the entire book is Jerusalem in the eighth century. The prophet addresses the wider Assyrian world, including the northern kingdom of Israel, the petty kingdoms surrounding Israel/Judah, and the greater powers of Egypt and imperial Assyria. In Isaiah 1–39 the prophet Isaiah and other people and events appear throughout, though not in every chapter. In the rest of the book, however, neither Isaiah, nor other eighth-century persons, nor any eighth-century events are mentioned again. Isaiah 40–55 instead addresses people and conditions in Babylon during the exile (586 to 539). The only person mentioned by name there is Cyrus, the king of the Persians who led his army to capture Babylon in 539. The chapters mock Babylonian gods, not Canaanite or Assyrian gods. Just as suddenly, in Isaiah 56-66 the focus switches back to Jerusalem and its temple, addressing both instead of exiles, and promising future rebuilding and glory. It would appear that Isaiah 56-66 addresses the circumstances and hopes of the early Persian period in Judah (± 500).

The Integrity and Authorship of the Book

This complicated setting begs for an answer. Why would one eighth-century prophet speaking to his own trouble-filled time spend roughly forty percent of his space addressing events that did not transpire for 200 or more years later, and which, presumably, his audience could not understand without prophetic discernment of their own? Turning their attention to this question, source critics posited three basic hands or groups behind the book of Isaiah. The first hand is that of Isaiah of Jerusalem, who was responsible for much, though not all of Isaiah 1–39.[2] The second, in Isaiah 40–

---

2. Scholars debate that issue too. Most find a different hand in the so-called Isaiah Apocalypse (Isaiah 24-27) and the hand of the author of Kings in the account of the invasion

55, is the hand of an exile in Babylon with his fellow Judeans about the time Cyrus began his attack on the Babylonian Empire (*ca.* 550). He had suffered with his people and announced their return to Jerusalem, if they would just trust God. The third hand — or group of hands — seems to reflect the conditions in Jerusalem soon after the exiles began returning. That prophet anticipated God's restoration of Jerusalem after the exile. Critical scholars call these latter two writers or groups Second (or Deutero-) Isaiah and Third (or Trito-) Isaiah. Such scholars are opposed by traditional scholars, who usually think one man, the eighth-century prophet Isaiah, wrote the entire book. They propose that under inspiration by God Isaiah saw centuries into the future and accurately predicted what would happen. They may also deny that Isaiah 56-66 presupposed the postexilic period, and offer a reading of those chapters against the backdrop of the eighth century.

How should one evaluate these views? The simplest way is by assessing their strengths and weaknesses. First, with respect to the critical view that there were multiple Isaiahs, we may say that it answers well the question of why different parts of the book seem both to presuppose and address conditions of the exile in Babylon and later: namely, those parts were written by and to people living through those conditions. Negatively, however, we may say that it does not answer why or how materials from such different times wound up in the same book. (Scholars have talked in the past about a school of disciples of Isaiah that lasted through the exile; today they are more likely to speak of the activity of scribes in collecting, preserving, editing, and promulgating such composite works.)

With respect to the traditional view that Isaiah of Jerusalem wrote the entire book, we may say that it addresses supremely well the weakness of the critical theory: these chapters are all on the same scroll because they were all written by the same man during his lifetime. Negatively, however, we may say that it leaves unanswered why God would reveal information perhaps more than 200 years before it was needed. Still less does it explain why anyone would have bothered to preserve such information. To see the force of this weakness, the reader might imagine this scenario. Suppose during a State of the Union Address in deeply troubled times the President

---

of Sennacherib (Isaiah 36-39), which it copies substantially. Passages like Isa 2:2-4 and 4:2-6 predicting a new age seem incongruous in the message of Isaiah, which was gloomy to say the least. Quite possibly the hands of redactors (editors) who stitched the passages together appear as well.

of the United States began talking about people no one had heard of and addressing Americans being held captive far away when none was known to be in captivity. We would question what was going on. Whom was he talking about and why? What about us?

Rightly or wrongly, source critics and most other critical scholars since the early nineteenth century have concluded that three (or more) hands stand behind this book. One of the methods of source criticism is a study of style. The book of Isaiah offers an excellent opportunity to see how source critics worked. While they discerned a similar vocabulary and the use of some themes throughout, they also thought they discovered differences. Their results and my assessment of their work will be presented in the following excursus.

•   •

EXCURSUS
STYLE IN THE BOOK OF ISAIAH

The issue of style in Isaiah is complex. Two sections in particular will highlight the problem. (1) Isaiah 24–27, the "Isaiah Apocalypse," is a mixed bag of poetry and prose, difficult to assess in terms of style, except for one hand. It appears to be a highly repetitive, sometimes rough, prose hand at work throughout the four chapters, perhaps comprising close to half the verses. I attribute that style to an editor, who pulled the chapters together.[3] The poetry tied together by this repetitive prose is often full of repeated sounds and other literary touches. (2) Isaiah 36–39 repeats almost all of 2 Kgs 18:13–20:19 (except 18:14-16). The narrative in Isaiah adds the material found in 38:9-20, much of which is identified as an independent document (which, by the way, is poetic). See below for further discussion.

The larger issue of the style of the prophet Isaiah within chs. 1–39 — as distinct from the style(s) of chs. 40–55 and chs. 56–66 — is likewise complicated. Perhaps the classic description of their styles was prepared by S. R. Driver.[4] Driver provides a list of ten words or forms of expression

3. Paul L. Redditt, "Isaiah 24–27: A Form Critical Analysis" (unpublished Ph.D. dissertation, Vanderbilt University, 1972).

4. S. R. Driver, *An Introduction to the Literature of the Old Testament* (Cleveland: World, 1956) 230-44; repr. of *An Introduction to the Literature of the Old Testament* (New York: Scribner's, 1897).

used *repeatedly* in chs. 40–66, but never in chs. 1–39. He gives another nine that appear once or twice in chs. 1–39 — without any special force — that are used in chs. 40–66 with special nuances. He lists three other features of chs. 40–66: the duplications of words, which occurs fifteen times in 40–66, but only 3 times in 1–39; the habit of repeating these words in adjacent clauses; and differences in the structure of sentences, especially with the relative particle omitted more often in 40–66 than in 1–39. Driver describes Isaiah's poetry as picturesque and impressive in its imagery. He deems it full of "grandeur and beauty of conception, wealth of imagination, vividness of illustration, compressed energy and splendour of diction."[5] He calls it "chaste and dignified," and says "the language is choice, but devoid of all artificiality or stiffness; every sentence is compact and forcible; the rhythm is stately. . . ."[6] It is never diffuse, never monotonous.

This way of analyzing Isaiah's style has been challenged by traditional scholars. They object that critical scholars limit Isaiah to only part of the material ascribed to him, describe that style, and then try to hold the rest of the book to that standard. The point is well taken; what they describe *is* the way one works when making arguments about style. One isolates materials with the highest likelihood of authenticity on various grounds and uses them as the criterion (stylistically and in terms of content, setting, etc.) to determine the authenticity of more problematic texts. Still, traditional scholars can point to *similarities* between chs. 1–39 and 40–66 and use those similarities as evidence of common authorship. Critical scholars typically object that many of these examples derive from exilic or postexilic materials within chs. 1–39; e.g., chs. 24–27, 34–35. G. L. Robinson and R. K. Harrison offer a typical summary of the word agreements between chs. 1–39 and 40–66.[7]

Verbal Agreements

40:5; 58:14 . . . . 1:20	56:8 . . . . 11:12
43:13 . . . . 14:27	61:2; 63:4 . . . . 34:8
45:11; 60:21. . . . . 19:25; 29:23	65:25. . . . . 11:9
51:11. . . . . 35:10	

---

5. Driver, *Introduction*, 228.
6. Driver, *Introduction*, 228.
7. G. L. Robinson and R. K. Harrison, "Isaiah," *ISBE* 2:896.

Similarities in Thought or Figure

40:3f.; 49:11 . . . . 35:8-10	54:7f. 26:20
41:17f.; 43:19. . . . . 35:6f.	55:12. . . . . 14:8; 32:15; 35:1f.
42:1; 61:1 . . . . 11:2	56:7 . . . . 2:2
42:7. . . . . 9:2 (MT 9:1)	56:8 . . . . 11:12
42:13 . . . . 31:4	56:12. . . . . 22:13
42:18-20; 43:8. . . . . 6:9	59:3 . . . . 1:15
43:13 . . . . 14:27	59:11. . . . . 38:14
43:24. . . . . 1:14	60:13. . . . . 35:2
43:26. . . . . 1:14-19	60:18 . . . . 26:1
45:9; 64:8 (MT 64:7) . . 29:16	60:21 . . . . 11:1
45:15 . . . . 8:17	61:8 . . . . 1:11, 13
47:3. . . . . 3:17; 20:4	62:10 . . . . 11:12
47:10 . . . . 29:15; 30:1	63:17. . . . . 6:10
49:2. . . . . 11:4	65:3; 66:17. . . . . . . 1:29
49:26. . . . . 9:20 (MT 9:19)	65:19. . . . . 35:10
51:4 . . . . 2:3	65:25. . . . . 11:6
51:9 . . . . 27:1	66:16 . . . . 27:1
53:2 . . . . 11:1, 10	

On the whole, however, these data ignore many differences and fail to support the view that Isaiah 40–66 derived from the same hand(s) as Isaiah 1–39.

Obviously this issue is not cut and dried. One makes such decisions based on the evidence. Perhaps, then, it might be worth noting that the book contains no headings after 13:1 that ascribe materials to Isaiah. Are we to assume that it all was? Maybe, maybe not. In any case, in what follows in this chapter we will look at Isaiah 1–39, saving Isaiah 40–66 for the next chapter. Such a procedure will permit preserving the apparent chronology of the book. Nevertheless, an effort will be made to present the book as a whole in this chapter and the next.

•   •

The Structure of Isaiah 1–39

Normally in this volume, the structure of a book will be discussed in connection with its integrity and authorship. The answers to those latter questions were so important to the issue of the structure of Isaiah, however, that a discussion of its structure needed to be postponed until now.[8] In macro terms the structure of Isaiah as a whole is twofold: doom (chs. 1–39) and hope (chs. 40–66). That structure, however, obscures a multitude of nuances, not the least of which is that chs. 1–39 contain a great deal of hope, while chs. 40–66 contain a great deal of doom. For reasons I have already given, however, we will examine only Isaiah 1–39 in this chapter.

The first three sections of Isaiah 1–39 form a progression for the most part:

> Isaiah 1–12: largely prophecies of doom against Jerusalem and Judah;
> Isaiah 13–23: mostly prophecies of doom against foreign nations; and
> Isaiah 24–27: many prophecies of doom against the whole earth.

(I will outline more fully the first and third of these sections in the discussion of the themes of Isaiah 1–39.) It is more difficult to discern a broad pattern behind chs. 28–39. Four distinct sections appear:

> Isaiah 28–32: mostly prophecies of doom against Jerusalem and Judah again;
> Isaiah 33: a prophetic liturgy;
> Isaiah 34–35: contrast of the futures of Judah and Edom;
> Isaiah 36-39: a narrative of possibly the last major event in the career of the prophet, the saving of the city of Jerusalem during the siege by Sennacherib.

Main Genres in Isaiah 1–39

Form critics have also been busy on Isaiah, isolating a number of different genres. Marvin A. Sweeney, for example, identifies 97 genres, some of which overlap.[9] This volume does not refine the categories so extensively, and space does not permit attention to them all. We shall examine only the

8. Even that statement might well be challenged by canonical or reader critics, who might argue that their readings make the discussion of authorship and integrity mute. It will be necessary to come to grips with the canonical shape of the book, but that discussion will occur at the end of this and the next chapters.

9. Marvin A. Sweeney, *Isaiah 1–39 with an Introduction to Prophetic Literature.* FOTL XVI (Grand Rapids: Wm. B. Eerdmans, 1996); list and descriptions on pp. 512-44.

main genres, beginning with one of the earliest texts, Isaiah 6. It is often identified as a call vision. Such visions typically include a manifestation of God, a confession of inadequacy by the prophet, God's rejection of the prophet's inadequacy, and God's commissioning the prophet. Call visions often focus on the mouth of the prophet. Moses protested that he could not speak well (Exod 4:10-16); God touched the mouth of Jeremiah (Jer 1:9); and Ezekiel ate the scroll containing God's message (Ezek 2:9–3:3). Recently, scholars have wondered whether Isaiah 6 fits this pattern. They have described it as a "commission account," focusing on YHWH's sending Isaiah forth as a prophet.[10]

The book of Isaiah contains a number of other genres we will see repeatedly in prophetic literature. These include prophecies of salvation (Isa 7:7-9); woe oracles (e.g., 1:4; 5:8-24); admonitions or commands to do something (1:16-17); disputation speeches, i.e., arguments between the prophet and opponents (8:16-22); and trial speeches (e.g., 3:13-15 or 17). The book contains prophecies of judgment against individuals (e.g., 22:16-24) and the people at large (e.g., 30:9-14). It also contains a whole section of prophecies against foreign nations (much of chs. 13–23). The collection named for Amos among the Minor Prophets opens with nearly two chapters of such prophecies, and Jeremiah (cf. chs. 46–51) and Ezekiel (cf. chs. 25–32) have them too. Probably these sayings were rarely if ever delivered personally to the foreigners. Instead they may have been efforts to sway kings or public opinion by denouncing the policies of other countries that looked enticing to the people and kings of Judah or Israel.

One of the most remarkable prophetic genres is the report of a symbolic act (Isa 20:1-6). In this genre God instructs the prophet to take some public action and then explain its meaning. In Isaiah 20, for example, God instructs Isaiah to remove his outer garment and sandals (presumably leaving the prophet wearing a loin cloth) and walk around in public. When a crowd forms to see what the prophet is up to, he explains that his dress and behavior are a sign to the people of Egypt and Ethiopia that they would soon go into exile for not defending the city of Ashdod against Assyria.

The book of Isaiah, like many others, draws genres from the worship

---

10. Sweeney, *Isaiah 1–39*, 132-36. Brevard S. Childs finds elements of both a call vision and a commissioning vision; *Isaiah*. OTL (Louisville: Westminster John Knox, 2001) 52-53. Joseph Blenkinsopp calls it a "throne room vision"; *Isaiah 1–39*. AB 19 (New York: Doubleday, 2000) 222.

of God at the temple. In the section discussing the campaign of Assyria against Judah (chs. 36–39), we find two genres at home in the Psalter: the complaint and the song of thanksgiving. In a complaint worshippers make their case for divine action and implore God to rescue them from their difficult straits. Isaiah 37:16-20 is a perfect example. King Hezekiah has received a letter from the messengers of Sennacherib, the king of Assyria, threatening to attack Jerusalem. Hezekiah goes to the temple and offers a prayer/lament, begging God to rescue Jerusalem and the temple. Part of his lament is to remind God that the Assyrians were polytheists. By contrast, Isa 38:10-20 records Hezekiah's song of thanksgiving when he recovered from sickness. He reminds God (and, hence, himself) that he had been near death and thanks God for rescuing him.

The book of Isaiah puts four more genres to especially good effect. The first is announcements. Isaiah 7:14-17 is a birth announcement used in a narrative about the refusal of King Ahaz to trust God in the face of a siege by two neighbors, Israel and Damascus. Isaiah 9:6-7 appears to be a specific kind of birth announcement: one heralding the birth of a crown prince. Sweeney classifies Isa 11:1-10 as an announcement of a royal savior. (See the discussion of royal figures below.) The second genre is the liturgy, sometimes called the "prophetic liturgy." It is a composite genre made up of a variety of smaller units of diverse genres. Isaiah 33 is comprised of a reproach (v. 1-2), a request for delivery (vv. 2-6), a congregational lament (vv. 7-9), a promise of God to respond (vv. 10-12), God's promise of victory to those who live uprightly (vv. 13-16, which includes a brief entrance liturgy in vv. 14b-16, typically used at the gate of the temple), a celebration of the kingship of God manifested in rescuing Jerusalem (vv. 17-22), and a promise of forgiveness for the sins of the people (vv. 23-24). The third genre is the dirge, a funeral song, which a later prophet in the book of Isaiah uses mockingly over the death of the king of Babylon (14:4-23). The last is the allegory, which may be described as a narrative that presents a series of metaphors. An example is 5:1-7, a song about a vineyard. Its owner lavished on it everything possible to make it bear "champagne" quality grapes, only to harvest wild grapes too bitter to use (vv. 1-4). The owner condemns the vineyard to return to its earlier state (vv. 5-6). Then (v. 7) the prophet allegorizes the song, equating the owner with God, the vineyard with Israel, and the vines with the people of Israel.

One last genre, the *massa'*, warrants mentioning. It is "a prophetic discourse in which the prophet attempts to explain how YHWH's actions are

manifested in the realm of human affairs."[11] These pronouncements analyze past and present events in order to draw conclusions about YHWH's
actions and intentions. The word *massa'* appears four times in Isaiah: 13:1;
14:28; 15:1; and 30:6, each time in a superscription to a short saying. In 13:1
the saying concerned Babylon, so presumably it came from the late
preexilic period or, more likely, the exilic period (despite its appearance in
Isaiah 1-39). The prophet has heard news, perhaps about threats to the
Babylonian Empire after the death of Nebuchadnezzar, and interprets the
meaning of those threats to the exiles: God is sending an army (the Persians?) to crush Babylon.

A Special Issue in Isaiah 1–39

Two passages in the book of Isaiah read largely identical to passages elsewhere in the OT. The first is Isa 2:2-4, which is nearly identical to Mic 4:1-3.
There are four possible explanations: Isaiah borrowed from Micah; Micah
borrowed from Isaiah; the two borrowed from a third text; or both books
passed through the same hand or related hands during their transmission.
The fact that Mic 4:4 seems to resonate with the sixth-century text Zech
3:10 suggests that the Mican passage came to its present form at the same
time as or even after Zech 3:10, but later than did Isa 2:2-4. This modification eliminates the first option, but the other three remain open, with either of the last two seeming more likely.

The second passage (Isaiah 36–39) is much longer. It reads for the
most part the same as 2 Kgs 18:13–20:19, with two major differences.
(1) There is nothing in 2 Kings like Isa 38:9-20, and (2) there is nothing in
Isaiah 36 like 2 Kgs 18:14-16. The style of the passages resembles that of
2 Kings, so there is widespread agreement that during the course of the
growth of Isaiah the narrative from 2 Kings was borrowed. It is easy to see
why. The narrative shows Isaiah as a key player in Judah's response to the
invasion of Sennacherib.[12] The priority of 2 Kings is shown by what Isaiah
36 omits: three verses (2 Kgs 18:14-16) that admit King Hezekiah sued

---

11. Sweeney, *Isaiah 1–39*, 534.

12. Blenkinsopp argues that these chapters, along with ch. 7 and 20:1-6, under the influence of the so-called Deuteronomistic school (responsible for Deuteronomy, Joshua, Judges,
Samuel, Kings, and parts of Jeremiah), are fairly late, and attempt to make Isaiah over into a
prophet as that school understood prophets; *Isaiah 1–39*, 458-61.

Sennacherib for peace, paying him dearly for sparing the city. In Sennacherib's own annals, he brags that he made Hezekiah a prisoner in his royal residence and exacted heavy tribute.[13] In other words, Sennacherib's account and 2 Kgs 18:14-16 agree. One is permitted to conclude, then, that the original narrative contained vv. 14-16. As the story stands in 2 Kings, it adds an additional lengthy narrative, perhaps in two versions, reporting on subsequent actions, in which Sennacherib's army was defeated. A redactor of Isaiah had at his disposal this longer version of the narrative in 2 Kings. The verses about Hezekiah's paying tribute were unimportant to him, so he excluded them. He appears to have been a fan of Hezekiah, who thought highly of the king, maybe more highly than the redactor at work in 2 Kings.[14] He had at his disposal a prayer he thought Hezekiah had (or should have) offered, and inserted that prayer at a dramatic place in the narrative.

What these passages show is that at times OT books were written or revised with an eye on other OT books. This is another piece of the accumulating evidence that the book of Isaiah was not written entirely during the lifetime of the prophet. At this juncture, we should remember that ancients did not necessarily share our view of authorship. To ascribe one's views to a figure one admired was probably intended not only to gain an audience for one's views but to pay honor to the earlier figure that inspired one's writing. Doing so was, then, the opposite of plagiarism, and kept alive and updated the past worthy — in this case, Isaiah — for future generations. In short, Isaiah's rootedness in the eighth century B.C.E. was remembered, his words were preserved, and his insights kept alive for new situations in new times. A voice from the past, thus, spoke over and over to new situations meeting new needs.

Introduction to the Prophet

Who was this prophet, whose figure loomed so large during his lifetime and continued to grow for centuries after his death? His name was

---

13. See the "Prism of Sennacherib," most easily available in *ANET*, 287-88.

14. The author of 1 and 2 Chronicles clearly thought so, for in 2 Chronicles 29–30 he ascribed to Hezekiah a reformation like that of Josiah in 2 Kings 22–23. The Chronicler also omitted any reference to Hezekiah's paying tribute to Sennacherib.

Yeshayah, which meant "Salvation of Yah." His message, however, was often one of doom, though he saw a new day, through an obedient monarchy, beyond that doom. He appears to have lived in Jerusalem in the eighth century and flourished there as a prophet.

We know little about Isaiah's private life except perhaps that he was married to a prophetess. At least we should probably hope so, since in 8:3 he says that he "went" to the prophetess, and she conceived and bore a son. The child received the remarkable name Maher-shalal-hash-baz, which means something like "speedy spoil, hasty prey."[15] The emphasis on speed coincides with Isaiah's message in ch. 8, namely that a threat by northern Israel and Damascus against King Ahaz and Jerusalem would disappear quickly. Apparently Isaiah already had a son named Shear-jashub, which means "A Remnant Will Return," whom he took with him at God's direction when he confronted King Ahaz over that threat. As we shall see, Isaiah predicted the birth of another child, to be called Immanuel, though whose child that would be is not clear. It is possible that the child was Isaiah's, but may well have been the king's or someone else's.

Isaiah's public career probably began with his commissioning to be a prophet, recorded in a vision in Isaiah 6.[16] That call seems to have been prompted by the death of King Uzziah, whose long reign (783-742), combined with a reduction in Assyrian power for about the same time frame, had allowed prosperity among the small upper class in Jerusalem and Judah.[17] Uzziah's death had been preceded by the rise of Tiglath-pileser (745-727) to the throne in Assyria, a man determined to strengthen Assyrian influence. The transition period between rulers is always fraught with ten-

---

15. The prophet Hosea gave his children similar names. We do not know if the names were simply part of the literature, or whether the names were real. Names in ancient Israel often were derived from physical characteristics, from unusual occurrences at the time of their birth, or from other family members.

16. Blenkinsopp argues, contra most scholars, that Isaiah 6 constitutes a "throne room vision" that commissioned the prophet "for a specific political mission in connection with the threat of a Syrian-Samaritan invasion in or about the year 734"; *Isaiah 1–39,* 223-24. In so arguing, Blenkinsopp is working from the widely-accepted view that Isaiah 6–8 formed an early unit (perhaps the first "edition" of Isaiah). At the same time he is disregarding the date in the incipit introducing the passage: "the year that king Uzziah died" (i.e., 742). It seems doubtful to me that the connection of Isaiah 6 with the following two chapters precludes separating Isaiah 6–8 and treating Isaiah 6 as a call, an event in its own right.

17. Estimates typically put the upper class at 5 percent of the population or less at that time.

sion; that between Uzziah and Jotham was especially so, in view of the more aggressive behavior of Assyria. The vision seems to have been set inside the temple. In that vision Isaiah "saw" God sitting above the holy of holies, the innermost portion of the temple. If Isaiah was indeed physically located inside the temple, he would most likely have already been an official of some sort there. In the vision, God commissions the prophet to the thankless task of preaching to the people, despite the foreseeable outcome that his preaching would drive the people away from the prophet and God. It is no wonder Isaiah cries out "How long, O Lord?" The answer is, "As long as there is any one left to hear." Isaiah did not have God's permission to give up on Israel before God did.

It is important to understand the nature of God's commission to Isaiah. Isaiah 6:9 is pessimistic, perhaps even sarcastic. The prophet is to tell the people to keep listening but not really hear, to keep looking but not really see. That sentence is actually a condemnation of their refusal, perhaps even inability, to hear a message from God. If, indeed, God did not want the people to hear, there was an easier way to guarantee that: not send a prophet at all. God warns Isaiah of the overall outcome of his ministry: people would ignore him. Still, God commands Isaiah to make the effort. Perhaps the effort bore some fruit. The book of Isaiah develops the theme of the remnant, the idea that some people would survive.

Isaiah seems to have functioned as a prophet associated with the temple in Jerusalem. He is seen having audiences with kings Ahaz (in ch. 7) and Hezekiah (in chs. 36–39). Neither 2 Kings nor Isaiah mentions any contact with Jotham, coregent for a number of years with his leprous father Uzziah (2 Kgs 15:5) and king in his own right from 742 to 735. Jotham was succeeded by his twenty-year-old son Ahaz, who was on the throne during the hostilities with northern Israel and Damascus beginning in 734. 2 Kings 16:2 says he reigned 16 years. Hezekiah came to the throne about 725, perhaps as a coregent with Ahaz the last six years of his reign. 2 Kings 18:2 says Hezekiah ruled twenty-nine years (until 697). He was the king when Sennacherib invaded in 701; therefore Isaiah's public career lasted until then at least.[18]

18. The dates of the kings of Judah in the eighth century are debated, so the sketch offered above may be off somewhat. The American archaeologist and OT scholar William F. Albright is associated with the theory that Sennacherib invaded twice, the second time in view in Isaiah 36–39, with the result that he thinks Hezekiah ruled until 687. That theory has wider acceptance in the United States than in Europe. It is not accepted in this book.

Basic Themes in Isaiah 1–39

Isaiah 1–39 constitutes a rich tapestry of theological themes, not all deriving from the eighth century. We will examine seven before turning our attention to Isaiah 40–66. These themes include: (1) justice in human affairs, (2) punishment for sin, (3) the rejection of sacrifice, (4) hope through savior figures, (5) the idea of the remnant and the restoration of Jerusalem and Judah, (6) God's power over Assyria (and other foreign powers), and (7) proto-apocalyptic eschatology, particularly in chs. 24–27. In conclusion, we will offer a retrospective reading of Isaiah 1–39 as a prelude to Isaiah 40-66. Before looking at the first five of these themes, it will be helpful to outline Isaiah 1–12, chapters that emphasize those themes.

Isaiah 1–5 **Introduced by a superscription**[19]
naming Isaiah as the seer.
1:1-31 A collection of messages condemning Judah and Jerusalem
2:1–4:6 The pride and punishment, restoration and elevation of Judah
5:1-7 An allegory of Israel's relationship to God
5:8-30 Six reproaches of Israel and a prediction of invasion

Isaiah 6–8 **An Apparent First Collection.**
Opened with an incipit beginning Isaiah's call vision.
6:1-13 Isaiah's call vision
7:1-25 The insolence of Ahaz and the promise of Immanuel
8:1-15 The promise of *Maher-shalal-hash-baz*
8:16-22 Instructions to bind and seal a scroll (Isaiah 6–8?)

Isaiah 9–12 **Hope for Judah; doom for Assyria.**
No special marker opening the section.
9:1-7 The messianic king
9:8–10:4 Four passages condemning the northern kingdom of Israel
10:5-19 The punishment of Assyria
10:20-27a The hope of a remnant
10:27b-34 God's halting the advance of Assyria

---

19. A superscription is a heading for a chapter, section of a book, or a whole book that introduces the author and/or contents of what follows. An incipit is the opening words of a narrative or narrative book.

11:1-16 The messianic king and his kingdom
12:1-6 A song of deliverance and a song of thanksgiving

Justice in Human Affairs

Isaiah 1:1-31 is a composition that puts together sayings from different periods in the prophet's life. The opening verses condemn and warn the people about God's punishment for their behavior. Next it turns to the issue of sacrifices, saying God was tired of burnt offerings without justice. The linchpin of the piece, therefore, turns out to be justice, so that is where we will start.

What is justice? For Isaiah, the issue is not theoretical, but practical. He specifies three components in 1:1-17. First, to be just one must "rescue the oppressed." In our culture powerful people often take advantage of those without power. So it was in ancient Israel as well. Deuteronomy has several pieces of legislation to speak to this issue. Israelites were not to charge interest on charitable loans to other Israelites (Deut 23:19). Wealthy persons were not to bribe judges (16:18-20). People loaning money were not to barge uninvited into homes of people to get what they were going to hold in security for a loan (24:10-13) or to take a necessity from a widow as security (24:17). They were to pay daily workers their wages at the end of the day, not hold them until later (24:14). These laws require compassion and even charity to the poor, and they stand as evidence that some people with means in ancient Judah took advantage of their power over their neighbors. Isaiah required making efforts to relieve poor people from such burdens.

Likewise, a just person was to "defend the orphan." It was (and still is) too easy to take advantage of orphans, children who by definition have no adult to stand up for them against the "system." Widows also were vulnerable. To a considerable extent females depended on their fathers during their childhood, their husbands when they married, and their children if they outlived their husbands. What about the woman who had no man to look out for her? (We should note here that sometimes the Bible adds resident aliens to the list of those needing "justice.")

What these people often had in common was a lack of money and, hence, a lack of political and interpersonal clout. Isaiah maintains that the way a society treats such people serves as a kind of litmus test to determine whether the society (and particularly its political and social leadership) is just. If the poor could get a fair shake, if they have a decent shot at the goods of the society, then the society could consider itself "just." Isaiah thought his own society had failed the test.

One example of the structure of ancient Israelite society that was open for abuse was the relationship between the urban rich and the peasants in the surrounding towns. Ancient Israel was a peasant society, which means simply that peasants were farmers tied to the land on which they were born. Traditionally, the land would be passed down from generation to generation and not sold outside the family. We may suppose that over time large families might divide land until the farms were too small to support a family, but high death rates and some migration perhaps kept that eventuality from destroying the system. We might also imagine that property might be merged through marriage. Clearly, though, the real threat was that land might pass out of the hands of the family into the hands of more wealthy people. Such exchanges presumably were not always fair, at least not in the eyes of those who lost ownership of their lands. Nor were they always fair in the eyes of Isaiah. Hence, he issued this scathing denunciation: "Woe unto the ones adding house to house. They join field to field until there is no space [for anyone else]. You live for yourselves in the midst of the field" (Isa 5:8). Apparently, Isaiah saw some people who were gobbling up everything in sight, regardless of the consequences to others. Interestingly enough, he did not accuse them of breaking human laws and threaten them with human justice. Instead, he accused them of breaking God's laws and threatened them with divine punishment.

Punishment for Sin

This brings us then to the second theme of Isaiah, punishment for sin (wrongdoings against God). In Isaiah 1 the punishment takes the form of an invading army. Verses 5-6 speak of a frightful beating administered on Judah. Verses 7-8 make it clear that an army has devastated the land (cf. also v. 20). The description is such that many commentators think Isaiah had in view the invasion of Sennacherib in 701, which reduced the land to shambles, leaving Jerusalem standing "like a booth in a vineyard." To understand that phrase, one needs to know a little about vineyards. In ancient Israel, when harvest time came, people would erect small huts in the vineyards and stay in them overnight throughout the harvest season. They would pick the grapes, carry them to the winepress, and squeeze out the juice. After the harvest, the vines would turn brown, and the huts or booths would age over the winter. The once-green vineyards would be bleak, with only a flimsy shelter left standing. Such was the appearance of Judah, with Jerusalem as the "booth."

Isaiah proclaims God's punishment for mistreating the poor, as we saw earlier. Sin could also take the form of idolatry (1:29; 2:8, 18, 20; 10:10-11; 31:6-7), from which the people of Judah were to repent (2:5; 31:6-7). To be sure, Isaiah was by no means convinced the people would repent (see ch. 6), but he calls them to do so just the same. Isaiah also condemns as sinful the people's failure to depend on God (7:10-13; 9:13-17). For such sins, Isaiah delivers a series of descriptions of God's punishment, all ending with the same refrain: "Despite all this, [God's] anger has not turned away, and his hand is outstretched still [in punishment]" (5:25; 9:12, 17, 21; 10:4). Later prophetic voices continue this motif of punishment. Isaiah 22:10-11, for example, looks back from the perspective of the exilic period on a broken and defeated Jerusalem.

The Rejection of Sacrifice

Before leaving Isaiah 1, we should note that vv. 24-25 explicitly promise God's punishment of those who took advantage of the poor (vv. 21-23). In the face of such behavior, God rejected the very sacrifices, assemblies, and Sabbath-keeping (vv. 11-14) God had commanded them to observe in the Ten Commandments and in early law codes like Exod 23:10-19 and 34:11-28. How should one understand such language? It is possible, of course, that Isaiah simply gave up on the sacrificial system. That does not seem likely, however, because he offered nothing in its place. Accordingly, it would seem better to assume Isaiah was opposed to sacrifice by the members of his audience who had not repented of their behavior toward the poor. Those people either saw no wrong in what they were doing or else they were trying to buy off God. The former alternative seems the more likely, but either would have been offensive.

Hope through Savior Figures

Isaiah anticipates three savior figures in chs. 7–9. The first (Immanuel) appears in 7:1-16, though the figure in that chapter is a sign of God's protection, not someone who would act to rescue Israel. This text has become controversial, not so much for what it says as for how the Gospel of Matthew uses it. This text received brief attention in Chapter 2 above as an example of the reuse of a biblical passage by a later author. Here it will receive a more thorough discussion.

The background of the chapter emerges from the narrative of the chapter itself. The setting is Jerusalem, specifically the king's palace, in 734-733. King Pekah of Israel and King Rezin of Aram (Syria) plan to withhold tribute from the Assyrians. They pressure King Ahaz of Judah to join their revolt, even besieging Jerusalem and threatening to replace Ahaz with their own puppet, the son of a man named Tabeel.

The action begins with God's directing Isaiah to take his son *Shear-jashub* ("A Remnant Will Return") to meet Ahaz near a water conduit. (Perhaps the king had gone there to view the besieging army at the foot of the hill on which Jerusalem stood.) Isaiah is to tell the king not to worry about the Syro-Israelite threat (vv. 3-9). God further directs Ahaz (presumably through Isaiah) to name his sign, whatever it would take to convince Ahaz to remain aloof from the Syro-Israelite coalition (vv. 10-11). Ahaz refuses, saying: "I will not ask; I will not assay[20] God." Isaiah responds angrily (v. 13): "Listen up, O house of David. Is it not enough for you to try the patience of humans that you must try the patience of my God?"

Regardless of whether Ahaz wanted a sign from God, he would get one (v. 14). Isaiah responds: "Therefore, YHWH himself will give to you (plural) a sign: 'behold the young woman with child; she will bring forth a son, and she will call his name Immanuel.'" It is not clear whom the plural pronoun includes, but this much is clear: it includes King Ahaz. Presumably it includes others around him, perhaps his (otherwise unmentioned) advisors, who had closed his mind against sitting out the siege. Perhaps it in-

---

20. The verb *nasah* often means "prove" or "tempt." To refuse to tempt God would be a good thing. Here, it perhaps means "assay" (the second meaning given in BDB, 650). To assay something is to analyze or to judge the worth of something. In that sense, Ahaz refused even to accept the possibility that God would intervene to save him and Judah. Isaiah's angry response makes a great deal of sense in view of such a refusal.

cludes his family. Perhaps it just includes others who accompanied the king that day.

The young woman is not identified. It is unlikely that it is someone who just happened by; still less is it likely that Isaiah is speaking of someone who is not even present (e.g., Mary the mother of Jesus). Nor is it the case that Isaiah identifies the woman as a virgin. In Chapter 2 we saw that the Hebrew word in Isaiah translated "young woman" is 'almah. The word for "virgin" is *bethulah*. An 'almah might have been a virgin, of course, but the word itself does not signify her virginity any more than does the English phrase "young woman." Further, the text itself demands that the woman under discussion is someone present at the time with Isaiah, Shear-jashub, and Ahaz. Verses 15-16 state that the son would be someone the king would watch grow up. At a minimum, the child would live in the vicinity of Ahaz, and might even have been his son.

The young woman would name her son *Immanu'el*. The name is a composite of two words and a pronoun in the form of a suffix. The word *Imma* is the preposition "with." The syllable *nu* is a pronominal suffix meaning "us." The word *'el* is a noun meaning "God." So, the name Immanuel means "God with us" or even "God [is] with us." The son would be a sign to Ahaz and others, no matter how unwilling the king was to have a sign or trust in God, that God would be with Ahaz and his people. Before he would grow old enough to choose among foods, the threat posed by Syria and Israel would disappear.

Immanuel is mentioned again in Isa 8:8, quite enigmatically. Verses 1-4 narrate the birth of Isaiah's second son Maher-shalal-hash-baz ("speedy spoil, hasty prey"). In v. 4 God makes a promise similar to the one made in connection with Immanuel in 7:14: before the infant learned how to call for his father or mother, the threat would disappear. Verse 8 then addresses Immanuel. Do the two verses refer to the same person, given the similarity of the promises? Similarity is not necessarily identity, so Maher-shalal-hash-baz is not necessarily Immanuel. Rather, he seems to be a second sign of the outcome of the siege of Jerusalem. If Immanuel is a sign of God's presence, Isaiah's son is a sign of the brevity of the siege.

The next savior figure appears in 9:2-7, only this time he is expected to act. Many scholars consider the text exilic or postexilic because of its similarity to Second Isaiah's use of the symbols of darkness and light. That is by no means a necessary conclusion, but the meaning of the passage is pretty much the same either way. It looks back on oppression and warfare, perhaps at the hands of the Assyrians, perhaps the later Babylonians. It celebrates the birth of a son on whom governmental authority already rests. That sounds like a crown prince, and if so would date the song prior to the fall of the Davidic dynasty in 586. A number of scholars go so far as to say the son was Hezekiah, though that is by no means certain either.

We may leave open the identity of the prince, and focus instead on what was said about him. Verse 6 gives him four titles: Wonderful Counselor, Godlike Warrior, Abiding Father, and Peaceful Prince. Suffice it to say, these are not ordinary titles for a ruler. They express a profound hope in and for the Davidic king. Isaiah or whoever penned these words saw a new day for Israel through the medium of an obedient monarch. He *should be* a counselor whose wisdom and judgment would inspire wonder, a warrior[21] who would win victories over every foe, a long-lived father to the people (who would wish for a short reign of a perfect king?), and a peacemaking prince. This prince would assume the throne of David and rule the kingdom with justice *'ad-'olam*, "from this time on indefinitely." The preposition *'ad* means "unto," and the noun *'olam* designated a long duration of time, in the past or the future. Hebrew could form compounds such as *'olam 'ad-'olam*, meaning something like "age to age," but it probably could not designate something as eternal. So Isaiah 9 articulates hope for a perfect king, though not one who was divine in our sense of the term.

The final figure appears in Isa 11:1-9. Some scholars think this passage also is exilic or postexilic, but again that is not a necessary conclusion. It too might have derived from the period of the monarchy. Regardless, it envisions a shoot (a technical term for the king). He would be "from the stump of Jesse," the father of David. God would grant him three sets of "spirits," or abilities. We might call them "gifts." They would include (1) wisdom and understanding, (2) counsel and might, and (3) knowledge and the fear of God. The overlap with Isaiah 9 is clear. Isaiah 11:4 also emphasizes righteous justice in his caring for the poor and disadvantaged of his society. The passage ends, however, with a beautiful picture of the land if the king managed to rule justly (vv. 6-9; cf. more briefly in 65:25).

---

21. The idea of a "divine" or "godlike" warrior was widespread in the ancient Near East. The term probably did not mean that the king would be divine, though ancient kings often thought they ruled under divine favor. Certainly the narratives about the choice of David as king (esp. 1 Sam 16:1-13) would suggest that ancient Israel thought of David and his dynasty as God's choice to rule Israel, and Ps 2:7 designates the Davidic ruler as God's "son" — by adoption. Such ideas did not make ancient rulers "divine" in the sense that they were gods.

6 The wolf will sojourn with the lamb, and the leopard with the goat.
   The calf and the lion and the yearling will stretch out together,
   and the little child will lead them.
7 The cow and the bear will feed together, and their little ones
      will stretch out,
   and the lion will eat straw like the ox.
8 The infant will play near the hole of an asp,
   and the young child will stick his hand into the den of a viper.
9 They will neither hurt nor destroy on all of my holy mountain,
   for the earth will be full of the knowledge of the LORD,
   like the waters covering the seas.

This idyllic scene reverses the loss of paradise after the sin of Adam and Eve. It depicts nature at peace with humanity and itself. While it does not consider such things as the explosion of the rabbit population if their predators quit eating them, it does state the principle of nonviolence in crystal clear terms.[22] That is worth our remembering.

The Remnant and the Restoration of Jerusalem and Judah

The idea of a remnant appears already in Isa 1:9 in the forlorn statement that "Except that YHWH of hosts left some of us as survivors, we would have become like Sodom, we would have ceased to exist like Gomorrah." In this verse, the "remnant" is simply people in Judah whom God rescued in grace from the Assyrian army. The idea is used again in 10:20-23. There the remnant is no longer survivors in Judah, but exiles sent away by an unnamed enemy. That enemy could have been Assyria once again, but many scholars see an exilic hand at work here. The concept had taken on moral overtones. Verse 21 uses the name of Isaiah's son Shear-jashub: "a remnant will return" to God. The word *jashub* ("return") also means "turn" and "repent," so the idea seems to be that exiles would repent of their sins, turn to God, and return to their homeland. Isaiah 4:2-3 says much the same thing.

The idea of the restoration of Judah and Jerusalem is presented in

22. Donald E. Gowan, *Eschatology in the Old Testament,* 2nd ed. (Edinburgh: T. & T. Clark, 2000) 104. According to Gowan, the prophet was concerned about violence of any sort, not about ecological balance.

other ways as well. For example, 11:11-16 envisions the return of exiles from Babylon in the east, from the Aegean seacoast in the west, and from Egypt and Ethiopia in the south. Isaiah 14:1-2 depicts the nations returning Israel to its home. Isaiah 29:1-4 anticipates the restoration of festivals to Jerusalem, and 32:1-8 portrays an idyllic monarchy once more. All such hopes, however, depend on something else: God's power over the other countries.

God's Power over Assyria (and Other Foreign Powers)

Probably the classic text in which Isaiah speaks of God's control over other humans is 10:5-19 (cf. 14:24-27). There, the prophet has God describe the Assyrian king as the "rod" in God's hand, by which God would punish Israel. The problem with human-administered justice, however, is that humans often get carried away. Isaiah had to admit that Assyria had gone far beyond the bounds of anything Israel/Judah actually deserved. As a consequence God would have to punish Assyria next for its excesses. A later prophet pushed that message to the next empire. In Isaiah 13–14, a passage explicitly labeled as "the *massaʾ* concerning Babylon that Isaiah son of Amoz saw" (13:1), the later prophet "updated" his worthy predecessor, indicating that God would send the army of the Medes to punish Babylon for its excesses in punishing Assyria. (The Second Isaiah saw that role being carried out by Cyrus.)

The theme of God's punishment of foreign nations became so important to those transmitting the traditions about Isaiah that they assembled eleven chapters (13–23) focused largely on that motif. Nations to be punished included Babylon (chs. 13; 14:4-32; 21:1-10), Moab (chs. 15–16), Damascus (17:1-6), Egypt and Ethiopia (chs. 18–19), Edom (21:11-12), Arabia (21:13-17), and Sidon (23:1-18). Further, the postexilic composition in chs. 34–35 contrasts the future restoration of Israel with the future punishment of Edom. As mentioned at the outset of this chapter, these pronouncements most likely were rarely delivered personally to the foreigners. Instead they may have been efforts to sway kings or public opinion by denouncing the policies of other countries that looked enticing to leaders in Judah or Israel.

Proto-Apocalyptic Eschatology

The final theme in Isaiah is eschatology. The term itself is derived from two Greek words: *eschaton* (meaning "end" or "last") and *logos* (meaning "word," and by extension "doctrine"). In Christian theology, the term typically refers to the second coming of Jesus, resurrection, judgment, and the afterlife. Old Testament scholars use the term more broadly to designate a future radical change for the better instigated by God. The term "apocalypse" designates a genre of revelatory narrative offering an imminent, sometimes violent, sometimes otherworldly eschatology.

Isaiah 24–27 is often referred to as the Isaiah Apocalypse, though it has long been recognized that the chapters neither derive from Isaiah nor constitute an apocalypse. The name now simply recognizes that the passage appears in the book bearing the name Isaiah and is enough *like* an apocalypse to so designate it. Many scholars prefer the designation "proto-apocalypse," but even that term perhaps betrays a view of the history and nature of the genre that is too restrictive. Still, the term does recognize many similarities between these chapters and works that are apocalypses. So, if one does not push the designation too far, it may prove helpful.

The structure of these chapters has been debated, but the following outline will make clear their major demarcations.

> 24:1-20 Proclamation of world cataclysm
>> 24:1-13 Desolation of nature and of human efforts
>> 24:14-16 Shouts of glee versus pining over treachery
>> 24:17-20 Images of final destruction
> 24:21–26:6 Liturgy of salvation and punishment
>> 24:21-23 God's victory over enemies and reign on Mount Zion
>> 25:1-5 The destruction of the old world order
>> 25:6-10a God's reign on Mount Zion and elevation of Israel
>> 25:10b-12 God's punishment of Moab
>> 26:1-6 Celebration in Jerusalem of God's victory
> 26:7-21 Israel's present and future contrasted
> 27:1-13 Israel's future before God
>> 27:1 God's defeat of cosmic (and thus also human) opponents

27:2-6 An allegory of Israel's turning to God (based on Isa 5:1-7)

27:7-11 Tasks for Israel to perform to usher in the new day

27:12-13 The return of the exiles to Judah

A full discussion of the genre "apocalypse" must await the treatment of the book of Daniel, which is an apocalypse, at least the last half of it. It will suffice here to note that, like Isaiah 24–27, apocalypses expect an imminent (and often violent) end of the present world order, delivered directly by God and not by a surrogate like the Assyrians or Babylonians. They may also depict a new world order, which Isaiah 24–27 does in the form of a restored Israel. These chapters appear to be exilic.[23] The chapters never mention kings or priests, though they are concerned with Jerusalem (24:23; 25:6-10a; 26:2) and apparently with its altar and temple (27:7-11). The haughty city of 25:1-5 and 26:5-6 functions as a foil to the Jerusalem the prophet knows or longs for. The author wants the temple, or at least its altar, restored and purified and those outside the land to return home. He awaits God's intervention to bring about those conditions.

A Problem Raised by a Study of Isaiah 1–39

One problem — at least for Christian readers — raised by a critical study of Isaiah is the relationship of the savior figures to Jesus. The issue is created by Matthew's statement (in Matt 1:23) that the birth of Jesus fulfilled what Isaiah said in Isa 7:14. In the previous chapter of this volume, however, we saw that the evangelist was claiming that Jesus signified God's presence among God's people in the first century C.E., just as Isaiah thought Immanuel had in the eighth century B.C.E. The complicating factor is that the LXX translated the Hebrew word *'almah* ("young

---

23. Dan G. Johnson argues that 24:1-20 was written in 587 on the eve of the fall of Jerusalem; that 24:12–27:1 was added when an exilic prophet expected Babylon to fall; and that 27:2-13 was added later in the exilic period, when the author developed his view that the triumph of God would reach fruition with the restoration of Israel; *From Chaos to Restoration: An Integrative Reading of Isaiah 24–27*. JSOTSup 61 (Sheffield: JSOT, 1988) 16-17. One may accept Johnson's date and still question whether the "city" referred to 25:2 and 26:5, 6 really is Babylon, a conclusion that seems doubtful to me. Cf. Paul L. Redditt, "Once Again, the City in Isaiah 24–27," *HAR* 10 (1986) 317-35.

woman")[24] with the Greek word *parthenos* ("virgin"). English translators naturally translate *parthenos* in Matthew as "virgin," but they have often translated '*almah* in Isa 7:14 the same way.

Once that (mis)reading of Isa 7:14 is established in the minds of Christian readers, the statement that "a son is born to us" in Isa 9:6 is also taken as a reference to Jesus, despite the fact that Jesus never took the throne of David (v. 7). The fact that the word "us" must have included the speaker Isaiah seems to escape notice. Partly again the problem lies in English translations. In particular, the title '*el gibbor* (typically translated "Mighty God") seals the issue. What other human than Jesus would the Bible call "God," people ask. As mentioned above, however, the title '*el gibbor* referred to a mighty warrior, one perhaps with godlike fighting ability, but not God. The shoot from Jesse in Isa 11:1-9, nevertheless, is simply assumed to be Jesus, the descendent of Jesse through David. There is nothing about vv. 1-5 to suggest the earthly Jesus, but the description of the perfect kingdom that follows in vv. 6-9 might seem to invite application to Jesus' millennial reign.

What we have are three texts that make perfectly good sense as follows: the first as narrative about a child about to be born and who will serve as a sign to King Ahaz, and the remaining two as texts expressing the hope that future kings of Judah would be perfect. Many Christians, however, project the NT on them and read them as references to Jesus. If, however, Christians read them in the context of eighth-century Israel, they may use these texts to build bridges between the OT and the NT without distorting their OT meanings. Matthew used Isaiah 7 to indicate that Jesus represented "God with us," and Christians may affirm that without dismissing its original meaning. Isaiah 9 and 11 may serve as two indicators of the kind of messiah some Jews in the first century C.E. were longing for. Jesus, however, apparently eschewed building a political kingdom in favor of a spiritual one.

Conclusion

It remains in conclusion to offer a wholistic reading of Isaiah 1–39 in anticipation of Isaiah 40–66. Isaiah 1–39 has turned out to be a collage of texts

---

24. BDB, 761, defines the word as follows: "young woman (ripe sexually; maid or newly married)."

from preexilic and exilic periods (with possibly a few texts from the Persian period).The first two sections (chs. 1–12, 13–23) have superscriptions attributing their contents, or at least a portion of them, to eighth-century Isaiah of Jerusalem. Isaiah 36-39 shows the prophet at work with a king late in his career, just as Isaiah 7 shows him at work with a king early in his career. One might infer, therefore, that Isaiah 1–39 took its shape during or soon after the exile (586-539). If so, one purpose for the book would seem to be to explain that the disaster that befell Jerusalem in 586 was not God's fault, but the fault of the people. In fact, God had gone out of God's way to send the great and elegant prophet Isaiah to warn Jerusalem and Judah. Indeed, Isaiah was even said to have named Judah's conqueror (Babylon; cf. chs. 13–14) and predicted the conqueror's overthrow. That overthrow was anticipated by the description of the overthrow of the Mesopotamian power Assyria in the time of Isaiah.

The reader of the Isaiah scroll was prepared, therefore, to unroll the remaining columns and see how that prediction would turn out. What the reader discovers is another collage, but one divided into two parts: chs. 40–55 discussing the exile and directing the exiles (the new remnant) to prepare for the new exodus to Israel, and chs. 56–66 detailing the struggle to rebuild the new Israel in its old homeland. The whole book (chs. 1–39 and 40–66) is held together by the overall plan of Doom and Hope. It is held together also by repeated themes, such as the repetition of 11:6-9 in briefer form in 65:25 and by the use of the theme of the remnant. It is time, therefore, for us too to unroll the next part of the scroll.

Questions for Reflection

1. How do you settle the issue of how many authors stand behind the book of Isaiah? What do you make of the argument from style?
2. Based on Isaiah's view of justice, do you think that our country maintains a just society? Why or why not?
3. How do you understand Isaiah's attack on the sacrificial system? Did Isaiah want to abolish it, or did he have some other aim in mind? Defend either answer.
4. Do you think God ever uses one nation to punish another? Why or why not? If you think God uses nations that way, can you suggest examples?
5. Do you think Isaiah 7, 9, and 11 had Jesus in view? Why or why not?

For Further Reading

Blenkinsopp, Joseph. *Isaiah*. AB 19–19B. 3 vols. New York: Doubleday, 2000-
    2003. A translation, introduction, notes on the Hebrew text and com-
    ments by a leading American OT scholar.
Childs, Brevard S. *Isaiah*. OTL. Louisville: Westminster John Knox, 2001. A ca-
    nonical reading of the text by the scholar who prompted the method of
    focusing on the MT as it stands as the text to discuss in OT studies.
————. *Isaiah and the Assyrian Crisis*. SBT, 2nd ser. 3. London: SCM, 1967. A
    study of the threat to Judah and Assyria posed by Assyria in 701.
Clements, R. E. *Isaiah 1–39*. NCBC. Grand Rapids: Wm. B. Eerdmans, 1980. A
    critically aware, balanced commentary on Isaiah by a widely respected
    British scholar.
Conrad, Edgar W. *Reading Isaiah*. OBT. Minneapolis: Fortress, 1991. A study of
    Isaiah from the perspective of reader criticism, illustrating that method's
    focus on structure, the implied reader, and the implied author.
Johnson, Dan G. *From Chaos to Restoration: An Integrative Reading of Isaiah
    24–27*. JSOTSup 61. Sheffield: JSOT, 1988. An imaginative reading of these
    chapters attempting to discern behind them an exilic setting for the hope
    they express.
Kaiser, Otto. *Isaiah 1–12; Isaiah 13–39*. OTL. Philadelphia: Westminster, 1972-74.
    A detailed form-critical commentary with careful study of the work of
    redactors. Translation of ATD 17–18.
Sweeney, Marvin A. *Isaiah 1–39 with an Introduction to Prophetic Literature*.
    FOTL 16. Grand Rapids: Wm. B. Eerdmans, 1996. A study of 97 genres plus
    15 formulas employed in the book of Isaiah.

CHAPTER 4

Isaiah 40–66

The study of Isaiah 1–39 revealed that a major time break occurs at the end of Isaiah 39. After that point, neither Isaiah nor any other person or event from the eighth century is mentioned. Stylistic and theological differences also distinguish Isaiah 1–39 from the remainder of the book. These differences have led scholars to speak of multiple "Isaiahs" and to divide the book between chs. 39 and 40 (and between 55 and 56 as well). Still, the entire book stands under the name Isaiah, even if much was added anonymously. Thus it will not do justice to the book to treat Isaiah 40–66 in isolation from 1–39. In what follows the major sections of Isaiah will be treated individually, but redactional features that tie the entire corpus together will also be studied.

The Setting of Isaiah 40–55 and 56–66

The only person to be named explicitly in Isaiah 40–66 is Cyrus (44:28; 45:1), a Persian who led a revolt against the Medes, a group of people who lived northeast of the Babylonian Empire and in the first half of the sixth century B.C.E. ruled everything from eastern Turkey through Persia. By 550, however, Cyrus had rebelled successfully against the Medes. He then moved across northern Mesopotamia and attacked Lydia in 547/6. What Cyrus did next is not clear, but in the summer of 539 he attacked Babylonia, taking Babylon in October without a fight. Isaiah 40–55 predicts but does not describe that fall.[1] It would appear, therefore, that Isaiah 40–55 dates from the period between 550 and 539 and arose in Babylon.[2]

Isaiah 56–66, however, deals with Jerusalem and Judah again, but after the destruction of the temple by the Babylonians (63:18-19; 64:10-11). It anticipates God's re-creating Jerusalem (65:18-19; 66:6) and even pictures foreign laborers rebuilding its walls (60:10). It is possible, however, that the earlier messages in Third Isaiah arose before the exiles began returning in 538. Others, however, arose before the rebuilding of the temple between 520 and 515, and a few texts seem to speak of a temple flourishing in Jerusalem once more (56:5-7; 66:6). If so, the time for at least a part of Isaiah 56–66 is the years after 515. The location of this writing is Jerusalem.

Regardless, we shall proceed with our study of Isaiah 40–66 in two steps, noting their (editorial?) overlap. At the same time, however, we need to recall Brevard Childs's view that Third Isaiah cites and alludes to Second Isaiah to such an extent that those passages "serve to call attention to Second Isaiah as an authoritative warrant and offer support for [Third Isaiah's] continuing use of the same material."[3] Joseph Blenkinsopp, despite some disagreement with Childs, finds seven concepts that chs. 40–55 and 56–66 share: comfort to Israel; a *via sacra* back home (made into a metaphor in 56–66); the coming of God (with power) to rescue Israel; the glory of God; the creator God; the complex of justice, righteousness, salvation; and the servant and the servants of God.[4] However, he also notes a heavy reliance of Third Isaiah on Jeremiah 1–12 pertaining to themes concerning Jerusalem: as a bride (Jer 2:2, 32; cf. Isa 61:10; 62:4-5), a faithless wife with children (Jer 2:9; 3:20-22; cf. Isa 57:3-13), a whore (Jer 4:30-31; cf. Isa 57:3), as engaged in an exhausting pursuit of strangers (Jer 2:25, 33-37; cf. Isa 57:10), and shedding innocent blood (Jer 2:34; cf. Isa 57:5; 59:3).[5] Moreover, Blenkinsopp thinks that the Deuteronomistic editors behind Deuteronomy, Joshua, Judges, Samuel, Kings, and parts of Jeremiah exhibit striking

1. See Isa 41:25 and particularly 43:14. The reader may recall that in chs. 13-14 an exilic redactor "updated" the traditions about Isaiah, indicating that God would send the army of the Medes to punish Babylon for its excesses in punishing Assyria. The Second Isaiah saw that role being fulfilled by Persia instead.

2. For a brief discussion of exilic life in Babylon, see Chapter Seven, "Ezekiel: The Setting of the Book."

3. Brevard S. Childs, *Isaiah*. OTL (Louisville: Westminster John Knox, 2001) 442.

4. Joseph Blenkinsopp, *Isaiah 56–66*. AB 19B (New York: Doubleday, 2003) 31-34.

5. Blenkinsopp, *Isaiah 56–66*, 78.

similarities to Second and Third Isaiah, particularly in the shared emphasis on the incomparability of YHWH.[6] These parallels suggest that in the early Persian period individuals or small groups of scribes drew on the same motifs in their editing process; indeed, different texts may have passed through the hands of the same or some of the same scribes en route to their final form. Still, unlike a few of the collections in the Book of the Twelve, Third Isaiah shows no interest in the restoration of the monarchy.

Major Changes in Prophetic Eschatology During and After the Exile

The destruction of Jerusalem and the exile of its leading citizens (2 Kings 24–25; Jer 52:28-30) brought about social and political changes (decimating the population and ending the monarchy) and theological changes too. Nowhere were those theological changes more obvious than in connection with prophetic eschatology. Georg Fohrer traces five basic changes that came about in exilic and postexilic prophecy, beginning with Second Isaiah. They include: (1) the destruction of the world kingdoms; (2) the redemption and freeing of Israel as the saved community, cleansed and assembled in Jerusalem; (3) the establishment of wonderful, paradisiacal living conditions for the holy community; (4) the immanent assumption of rulership by YHWH or his messiah; and (5) the conversion of the nations or their remnant. The foundation of this eschatology was the belief that in the future God would bless Israel; the present was the time when the great reversal was beginning to be visible to the discerning.[7] This new eschatology stands at the heart of the hope for the future of both Second and Third Isaiah.

Introduction to the Book and Its Times

We have seen that Isaiah 40–66 is a complicated double collection of prophetic messages from the late exilic and early Persian periods, situated and focused on the one hand (chs. 40–55) in Babylonia and on the other hand

---

6. Joseph Blenkinsopp, *Isaiah 40–55*. AB 19A (New York: Doubleday, 2002) esp. 51-54.

7. Georg Fohrer, "Die Struktur der alttestamentlichen Eschatologie," *TLZ* 85 (1960) 403-6.

(chs. 56–66) in Jerusalem. It completes the work of the eighth-century prophet Isaiah and those who collected, edited, and updated his sayings.

The Integrity and Authorship of Isaiah 40–55 and 56–66

Is it nevertheless likely that one hand stands behind all of Isaiah 40–66? Traditional scholars, of course, answer in the affirmative and consider Isaiah of Jerusalem to be that author. Though critical scholars have divided over the issue,[8] they typically are less convinced. Claus Westermann thinks that Second Isaiah was a prophet living in Babylon and Third Isaiah was his disciple living in Jerusalem between 539 and 521.[9] Klaus Baltzer is no longer sure of the sequence, arguing that Isaiah 60–62 appears possibly to be older than, say, Isa 52:7-10. He thinks that the tone of Third Isaiah toward foreigners is more hostile than Second Isaiah's and that the two express different attitudes toward the cult.[10] Blenkinsopp allows the possibility that Second Isaiah was written in Neo-Babylonian Judah, though not necessarily in Jerusalem, but ultimately concludes in favor of a Babylonian origin.[11] We will adopt the view that the two parts (40–55 and 56–66) derive from different hands, whose works were brought together editorially, irrespective of any master-disciple relationship. In other words, there may well have been no *single* hand behind either collection. Where the prophets lived will not substantially affect the understanding of the texts, since what is important is whom they addressed.

We should also note that a few scholars have argued that Isaiah 35 and/ or 36–39 belong in some way to Isaiah 40–66. We have already seen in our study of Isaiah 1–39, however, that chs. 36–39 round off the career of the eighth-century prophet and also prepare for what follows. We will not pursue that issue further. Isaiah 35 seems so integrally connected to Isaiah 34, contrasting the fates of Edom and Judah, that the two chapters should be seen as one composition. Isaiah 35:5-8 may serve well as an introduction to Second Isaiah, and it may share the sentiments of and even depend on

---

8. See William Holladay, "Was Trito-Isaiah Really Deutero-Isaiah After All?" in *Writing and Reading the Scroll of Isaiah: Studies of an Interpretive Tradition,* ed. Craig C. Broyles and Craig A. Evans, 193-217. VTSup 70 (Leiden: Brill, 1997)

9. Claus Westermann, *Isaiah 40–66.* OTL (Philadelphia: Westminster, 1969) 27.

10. Klaus Baltzer, *Deutero-Isaiah.* Hermeneia (Minneapolis: Fortress, 2001) 2.

11. Blenkinsopp, *Isaiah 40–55,* 104.

Third Isaiah as Blenkinsopp argues, but it does seem to have been part of Isaiah 1–39.[12]

The Structure of Isaiah 40–55 and 56–66

Baltzer analyzes Isaiah 40-55 as a work in six "acts," plus a prologue and epilogue. His overall structure is as follows:

> Prologue: 40:1-31 "In Heaven as on Earth"
> Act I. 41:1–42:13 The Beginning of What Is to Come
> Act II. 42:14–44:23 Jacob/Israel (Again) YHWH's Servant
> Act III. 44:24–45:25 The Sovereignty of God and Earthly Rule
> Act IV. 46:1–49:13 The Downfall of Babylon
> Act V. 49:14–52:10 The Rise of Zion/Jerusalem out of Deepest Humiliation
> Act VI. 52:11–54:17 Salvation for the Servant of God — Salvation for Zion/Jerusalem
> Epilogue: 55:1-13 Festival of the Pilgrimage to "the Holy City"[13]

The major movements in this structure are three: (1) explanation of the exile: chs. 40–45; (2) the downfall of Babylon: chs. 46:1–49:13; and (3) anticipation of the return home: chs. 49:14–55:13.

Isaiah 56–66 forms the conclusion to Isaiah, not simply an add-on corpus. Many scholars argue that chs. 60–62 form the core of this work, leaving 56–59 and 63–66 as the other two major sections. Chapters 59 and 63–64 constitute communal laments, and part of ch. 56 and all of ch. 66 form a prologue and epilogue. The resulting structure looks like this.

> 56:1-8 Prologue: Salvation to all, including foreigners and eunuchs
>
> 56:9–58:14 Condemnation, repentance, and compassion as true worship
>
> > 56:9-12 Condemnation of Israel's leaders (called "shepherds")
> >
> > 57:1-13 Condemnation of idolatry and an invitation (v. 13) to take refuge in God

---

12. Blenkinsopp, *Isaiah 40–55*, 54.
13. Baltzer, *Deutero-Isaiah*, viii-xv.

57:14-21 Proclamation of God's turning to Israel

58:1-14 Call to compassion as true worship

59:1-21 Lament: Israel's sins have prevented God's mercy

60:1–62:12 The Glory of God's new day

60:1-22 Jerusalem's glorious restoration

61:1-11 The Servant's mission to Zion (cf. the Servant in chs. 40–55)

62:1-12 The glory of God's people

63:1–64:12 A lament of the people, introduced by a song about God's vengeance

65:1-25 God's response to the lament

66:1-24 Epilogue: The New Jerusalem and the New Creation (cf. 11:6-9; 65:17, 25)

Main Genres in Isaiah 40–55 and 56–66

What genres of literature did the prophets behind Isaiah 40–55 and 56–66 employ in building their works? Some of the most-used genres were discussed in connection with Isaiah 1–39. The emphasis here will be on other genres in Isaiah 40–66. The following discussion draws upon Westermann's lengthy delineation.[14] The most characteristic genre for Second Isaiah is the promise of salvation (cf. 41:8-13, 14-16; 43:1-4, 5-7; 44:1-5). It is a variation on the earlier prophecy of salvation with distinctive emphases. Introduced by the words "Fear not," it is an elaboration of a priestly assurance of salvation communicated to a penitent individual in an individual lament. It concludes with an explanation of why God chooses to act. A similar genre is what Westermann calls the *proclamation* of salvation (cf. 41:17-20; 42:14-17; 43:16-21; and 49:7-12). It is directed at the community as a whole, usually refers to a lament ceremony, and does not begin "Fear not." It may well be combined with a disputation speech (cf. 51:9–52:3).

Other genres appear as well, including songs celebrating God (cf. 40:12-17, 18-24, 25-26) and trial speeches (43:22-28; 50:1-2). Westermann

14. Westermann, *Isaiah 40–66*, 11-21 and 296-308.

also argues that the Servant[15] songs (42:1-4; 49:1-6; 50:4-11; 52:13–53:12) form a separate strand, written by the Servant himself, except for the fourth.[16] They do not, however, form a distinct genre. In our discussion of the Suffering Servant below, we will examine each for its genre, discovering two that resemble call visions, a third that is lament, and a fourth that is a song of thanksgiving.

In his discussion of the structure and composition of Isaiah 56–66, Westermann points again to the proclamation of salvation (esp. in chs. 60–62, as well as 57:14-20; 65:16b-25; and 66:6-16). Not everything in Third Isaiah is so upbeat, however. Isaiah 59 and 63–64 are "genuine" community laments, i.e., songs actually sung in worship, not simply facsimiles written by a prophet.[17] One also encounters admonitions (58:1-12) and words of judgment against foreign nations (cf. 63:1-6). Finally, Westermann points to "apocalyptic additions" (cf. 60:19-20; 65:17, 25; and 66:20, 22-24). These verses do contain motifs common in later apocalypses, but it is doubtful that they belong to separate genres from the verses around them. That is so even if Westermann is correct that the verses are additions to their contexts, which is also debatable.

Special Issues in Isaiah 40–55 and 56–66

One special issue in Isaiah 40-55 is its re-use of creation and exodus motifs. The concept of creation appears already in Isa 40:12-22. The author raises three verses (vv. 12-14) of rhetorical questions about creation. Who (other than God) measured out the water and marked off the heavens? The obvious answer to us is "No one, God did it." That answer was obvious to Sec-

---

15. For purposes of clarity I will capitalize the word Servant only when it applies to the so-called Suffering Servant in Second Isaiah.

16. Westermann, *Isaiah 40–66*, 20.

17. One may question whether that distinction is as absolute as Westermann wants to make it. A number of prophetic collections contain hymnic and other liturgical genres. These include, e.g., three hymn fragments in Amos (4:13; 5:8-9; 9:5-6) and the concluding hymn that constitutes Habakkuk 3. In a penetrating essay, Erhard S. Gerstenberger suggests that some prophetic books may have passed through the hands of singers; "Psalms in the Book of the Twelve: How Misplaced Are They?" in *Thematic Threads in the Book of the Twelve*, ed. Paul L. Redditt and Aaron Schart, 72-89. BZAW 325 (Berlin: de Gruyter, 2003). Elsewhere within the Isaiah corpus, Isaiah 24–27 contains songs in 25:1-5; 26:1-6; and 27:2-5(6).

ond Isaiah too, but not necessarily to the Jews in exile and not at all obvious to the Babylonians, who had their own creator-god. The prophet's second question (v. 13) entertained the possibility that another divinity directed YHWH's creative work. The implied answer, however, was "No one advised God." The third question pondered whether God had another divinity to teach God such things as justice and what we might call human psychology. The tone of the questions makes clear the same negative answer. Verses 18-20 insist that God is incomparable, and vv. 21-22 emphasize that God created the universe.

Buried in this teaching about creation is the remarkable verse Isa 45:6b-7, which reads as follows.

> 6b I am YHWH, there is no other god, 7 forming light and creating darkness, making wholeness and creating calamity. I, YHWH, am doing all these things.

The verse employs two pairs of opposites: light and darkness, wholeness and calamity. In Hebraic thinking such opposites are not polarities, but the ends of continua. It is the writer's way of saying, "That includes everything from A to Z." So, to say that God created light and dark meant that God included all shades, not just the extremes. The same is true for wholeness and calamity. These observations mean, of course, that 45:7 meant God created everything. In doing so, the prophet seems to move beyond the theology of Gen 1:1–2:4a, in which God starts with darkness and creates light.[18] Here God is said to have created both — and everything in between. This verse is as close as the OT comes to expressing the idea of *creation ex nihilo,* creation from nothing.

This prophet also re-uses the motif of the exodus in Isa 55:12. He has God call the people to "Go out in joy, be led back in peace." The first exodus had been from Egypt (cf. 51:10); the second would be from Babylon (cf. 51:11). A more extended use of the motif appears in Isa 43:2-3. God promises to be with the people when they pass through waters, rivers, and fires. At first, it might appear as if 43:2 simply has in mind dangers, i.e., fire and waters. It follows directly upon the re-use of creation language in v. 1, however, and continues in v. 3 with a reference to God's giving Egypt for Israel's

---

18. I remember an OT professor in seminary saying, "If someone had pushed the author of Genesis 1 by asking where the primal darkness came from, he probably would have answered that God made it too. However, no one seems to have pushed him."

refuge. Thus, v. 2 also turns out to have the exodus under Moses in view. The re-use of creation and exodus motifs (not to mention Noah in 54:9) makes it clear that Second Isaiah was drawing upon images from what eventually became the Torah of the Hebrew Bible.

A different sort of issue emerges in connection with Isaiah 56–66, and that is the connection between those chapters and Haggai and Zechariah. In the discussion of the date of Third Isaiah, we saw that part of it arose before the rebuilding of the temple between 520 and 515. That would make the prophet(s) responsible for Third Isaiah contemporaneous with Haggai and Zechariah. Those prophets unabashedly supported the returning exiles under the Davidic prince Zerubbabel and the priest Jeshua in their efforts to rebuild the temple. An account of that rebuilding project appears in Ezra 1–6, also told from the perspective of the repatriated exiles. Perhaps the same is true of Isaiah 56–66, though some scholars think possibly those chapters derived from the hand of a person or persons not affiliated with the returning exiles.

Paul D. Hanson argued that the later addition Zechariah 9–14 was the product of "the same visionary tradition . . . found in Third Isaiah."[19] That specific claim has not maintained a wide following lately, but it still points in the right direction. Judah in the Persian period was a tiny, splintered community. There was, of course, a priestly class in charge of the temple. That class may well have come back from Babylon, pushed aside whoever was in charge of the altar during the exile,[20] and took over under Persian authority, leading and benefiting from the rebuilding of the temple. It seems, though, that several factions opposed that group — some opponents with a differing political agenda, some with a more socio-religious agenda. (See Chapter 13 on Haggai, Zechariah, Malachi for a fuller discussion.)

What all this means for our consideration of Isaiah 56-66 is that people contemporary with its rise might have seen it as sectarian. Differently put, time would tell whether people "out of step" with the view of controlling parties had a share of the truth as well. In any such situation, it be-

19. Paul D. Hanson, *The Dawn of Apocalyptic* (Philadelphia: Fortress, 1975) 286.
20. Jeremiah 41:5 speaks of 80 men from Shechem, Shiloh, and Samaria (all important northern cities) arriving in Jerusalem to offer sacrifices about three months after Jerusalem fell to Babylonia. Apparently the altar was still in use, despite the destruction of the temple. A functioning altar would require a functioning priesthood. There is every reason to suppose that sacrifice continued there throughout the period of the exile (cf. Zech 7:1-3 and 8:18-19).

hooves people to listen to dissenting voices. Had someone in postexilic Judah not listened, these eleven chapters might well have been lost. What may well have saved them was their unabashed depiction of a glorious new day for Jerusalem.

Introduction to the Prophet Behind Isaiah 40–55

We turn now to focus on the figure(s) behind Isaiah 40–55 and the emphases of those chapters. If the "prophet" responsible for chs. 40–55 is not Isaiah of Jerusalem, who was it? Indeed, was that prophet actually several people? The answers to these questions must be teased out of the material indirectly. We have already seen that the chapters address people exiled in Babylon, commanding them on God's behalf to keep the faith and to be ready to flee from Babylon (48:20). God was about to take them back to Jerusalem in a "second" exodus (40:1-11). The author(s) appear(s) to have been in Babylon during the exile, though that is not actually stated in the book. Nor would we expect it to be, necessarily. Second Isaiah was attached to the work of Isaiah of Jerusalem, thereby borrowing his identity.

Was Second Isaiah a figure who went through severe suffering and/or difficulties? That is possible, because the chapters contain four songs about a Servant whose suffering is described or alluded to in all of them (42:2-4; 49:4 [7]; 50:6; and 52:14 + 53:3-11). We do not know, unfortunately, how much — if any — of Second Isaiah was written by the prophet who spoke in the first person in 49:1-6 and 50:4-11. We shall look at the Servant as the last of four themes in Second Isaiah. It does appear, however, that at least two hands (the Servant's and one or several more) stand behind Isaiah 40–55. For the sake of simplicity, though, I shall simply continue to speak of Second Isaiah.

Basic Emphases in Isaiah 40–55

At the risk of paying too scant attention to these important chapters, we will examine only four of their major emphases. Like other prophets, Second Isaiah had to explain the exile. What had gone wrong? In the eighth century, Hezekiah had repented and God had forgiven and spared Judah. God did not, however, spare Judah in the early sixth century. Why not?

What theological implications did the fall of Jerusalem and its temple have? Was God unable to protect God's own people, city, or temple against the Babylonians and their gods? Was there hope for the future beyond the exile? Second Isaiah answered all these questions. The book also contains four songs about an enigmatic figure, a man who apparently suffered deeply and whose career perhaps paralleled and exemplified the experience of Israel in exile. Second Isaiah simply called him "the Servant."

Explanation for the Exile

Second Isaiah attributes the fall of Jerusalem to Babylon and the destruction of the temple to Israel's penchant for sinning (43:14-28). In vv. 14-21 the prophet promises restoration, and in vv. 22-28 he reflects on the cause of the destruction in the first place. Israel had not called on God (v. 22) and had not offered sacrifices — at least not properly (vv. 23-24). Instead of sacrifices they had presented iniquities to God (v. 24). We hear overtones of the recriminations of Isaiah of Jerusalem in Isaiah 1. Indeed, vv. 26-28 take the form of a trial speech, in which God tries and convicts the people for sinning and the "interpreters" (prophets?) for misinterpreting God's will. Hence, God had delivered Judah to Babylon. Babylon and its gods were no more than the instruments with which God would punish Judah.

The exiles would surely have objected that whatever they did would have been less sinful than what their polytheistic captors had done. After all, the Babylonians did not even number YHWH as a god in their pantheon. For his part Second Isaiah agrees that Israel had been punished double for its sins (40:2), but would not agree that they were without fault and did not deserve what had happened to them. Still less would he agree that the Babylonian gods were more powerful. Indeed, he denies that they were gods at all (45:5).

Monotheism

With this denial of other gods Second Isaiah articulates monotheism. Scholars typically say that Second Isaiah was the first to do so, though it is possible Jeremiah was the first (Jer 2:10-11). Regardless, the topic invites further exploration.

Humans entertain a variety of views of the divine. Polytheism may be defined as belief in and worship of many gods. In such systems, the gods typically are conceived of as responsible for various natural phenomena (e.g., sun, rain, fertility) and human endeavors (e.g., war). They may also be conceived as existing in some kind of hierarchy, usually headed by one high, remote god. In Indian religions, and perhaps others, polytheism seems to have given way to the idea that all the gods participated in something more basic; we would probably call it "divinity." Some scholars name this view henotheism, thus emphasizing a "oneness" behind the many. Ultimately, Indian religions developed the idea that all is one (a view called monism). Old Testament thinking developed along different lines. Early on (the OT says beginning with Abraham), Israel thought that its god YHWH was the only being deserving of Israel's worship. Second Isaiah made the crucial step to monotheism, with its insistence on belief in and worship of one God, combined with the denial of the existence of all other gods.

Isaiah 45:5-8 announces the uniqueness of YHWH. Verse 5, in fact, proclaims monotheism in its starkest form: "I am YHWH, there is no other; besides me there is no other god." Monotheism is a logical, but not necessarily inevitable inference from the credo in Deut 6:4: "Hear, O Israel; YHWH our God, YHWH is one." That confession emphasizes that for Israel, there were no other gods. The Canaanites, Egyptians, Assyrians, and others had a pantheon of gods. Not so Israel; Israel had but one God, the God of Abraham, Isaac, and Jacob. Second Isaiah takes the confession one step further: there is no god but YHWH. The rest were mere pretenders.

Israel had, of course, long believed that YHWH created the world, and monotheism is a logical extension of that belief too. The step from confessing that the creator-god is the only god is longer than it looks to us. Many nations believed their gods created the world without drawing the conclusion of monotheism. Their creation myths spoke of a variety of gods and goddesses, not all of whom were involved. Unlike those nations, Israel drew the inference that their God YHWH was the only God, and Second Isaiah was one of the first to do so. What is more, YHWH the God of Israel was about to act on behalf of Israel. God's action would not only free Israel, but also testify to the nations (including Babylonia with its horde of divinities) that they should recognize the God of Israel (45:6).

Isaiah 46:1-13 adds another dimension to Second Isaiah's view of God. It follows that if YHWH is the sole god, YHWH was superior to the hundreds of divinities the Babylonians worshipped. Hence, Second Isaiah imagines Marduk (Bel), the chief god of Babylon, and Nebo (Marduk's son) bowing down to YHWH (v. 1a). One mark of the superiority of YHWH over the Babylonian gods was that God announced in advance through the prophets what God was going to do (v. 10). Second Isaiah also seems to have drawn upon his audience's familiarity with such events as the Babylonian New Year ceremony, when images of Babylonian deities were paraded through the streets on carts or other conveyances. This practice gave the prophet the opportunity to ridicule Babylonian religion (vv. 1b, 3-7; cf. 40:18-20). He says, in effect, that the Babylonians had made their own gods, who were so weak they had to be carried about by their worshippers. YHWH, by contrast, was carried about by no one, but is the one who carried Israel (46:4).

The Babylonians or even exiled Jews might have objected that the images were not the deities themselves, but only representations of those deities. To the prophet, however, the distinction between a nonexistent god and an image representing that nonexistent god is not a distinction worth making. Hence, the prophet has great fun ridiculing the Babylonian gods, pointing out their impotence, and contrasting them with the powerful YHWH who created the world (cf. 41:21-29; 44:9-20). YHWH could even create YHWH's Israel, destroy it, and create it again (46:13). God's salvation was near, even if the exiles did not see it coming and many no longer even believed God could save them (49:14).

Hope for the Future

The third basic theme of Second Isaiah is his hope for the future. As we noted at the outset of this chapter, Fohrer traces five basic changes that came about in postexilic prophecy. In Second Isaiah they include: (1) the destruction (41:25-29; 44:24–45:4) and humiliation of Babylon (47:1-15); (2) the redemption and freeing of Israel as the saved community (40:2-5; 55:12-13), cleansed and assembled in Jerusalem (40:9-11); (3) the establishment of wonderful, paradisiacal living conditions for that holy community (54:1-3, 11-14; cf. the elaboration in 65:17-25); (4) YHWH's immanent assumption of rulership (52:7) led by God's Davidic messiah (55:3-4); and (5) the conversion of the nations or their remnant (55:5). It does not appear that Second Isaiah speaks of the reunification of Israel and Judah, at least not explicitly. He refers often to Jacob/Israel, but seems to have in view Judah. He never mentions a northern tribe or the northern capital, Samaria.

We will note five texts that build this scenario. The agent of God's salvation would be Cyrus the Great, the Persian king. To be sure, Cyrus was a foreign king rather than a Davidic king. He did not even recognize that God was using him (45:4). Nevertheless, according to Second Isaiah God chose to use Cyrus, and even called him God's "anointed" (or "messiah"). God could save Israel any way God chose.

The salvation of Israel would be accompanied by the humiliation of Babylon (47:1-15). The Babylonians had thought there was no power besides their own, but they would realize that there was no power besides YHWH's (v. 8). They had trusted in their wisdom (v. 10), which was immense. (They had developed great art and architecture, math, astronomy, astrology, medicine, and a number of sciences.) None of that wisdom would help them before God. Rather (v. 14), God would burn Babylon as a fire burns stubble.

Isaiah 54:1-8 portrays the transformation of Israel as a widow, all of whose children had been slaughtered. God tells her, however, to weep no more, but to enlarge her tent. Then in a stunning change of images, the prophet compares God to a husband wronged by his wife, but now ready to take her back and produce offspring with her (vv. 3-8). Preexilic prophets were loath to use such images of God, since one of the most important Canaanite gods was Baal, god of fertility. Fertility rites soliciting the help of fertility gods threatened the worship of YHWH in preexilic Judah. Exilic Isaiah, however, dared to use such language in addressing exilic Israel, perhaps either for shock effect or because he saw no further danger in such talk.

It is now appropriate to turn to the prophet's opening announcement of comfort that God was about to send the exiles home (40:1-11). His basic thesis is that Israel had suffered double what it deserved (v. 2). Verse 3 reports the sound of a heavenly voice ordering the building of a super highway across the Arabian Desert from Babylon to Jerusalem, one-way only. The mountains are to be leveled and used to fill in the valleys; the rough places in the road are to be made smooth (v. 4). This highway is not to follow the accepted way around the Fertile Crescent; instead it is to run straight across the desert (v. 3). Such language is poetic, not literal, of course, but it communicates truth better as a consequence of its daring ideas and exciting expression. In v. 9 Second Isaiah personifies Mount Zion as a herald who proclaims to the cities of Judah that salvation is coming. Also in 52:7 a messenger carries the good news to Zion/Jerusalem that salvation is coming. The news is so beautiful that even the feet of the person carrying that news are beautiful to the hearers. (Isaiah 43:14-21 also presents this return home in another figure, as a new exodus.)

What, then, is Israel to do as it awaits the new day? The prophet's answer is straightforward (48:20-22). The exiles are to remain faithful and prepare to leave Babylon (again overtones of the exodus) for Zion as soon as God makes the travel arrangements.

The Role of the Suffering Servant

The fourth major emphasis is the Suffering Servant. The Hebrew word *'ebed* ("servant") appears twenty times in eighteen different verses in Isaiah 40–55 (see chart below). In four of those cases (41:8; 44:1, 21a; 45:4), the Servant is explicitly identified as Jacob/Israel, and 44:2 substitutes the name Jeshurun for Israel (cf. Deut 32:15, where Jeshurun is used in synonymous parallelism with Jacob). Two cases (Isa 41:9; 44:21b) simply continue the previous verse, where the Servant is identified as Jacob/Israel. Another verse (42:19) mentions the Servant twice, the first time in parallelism with God's messenger. That text clearly plays on the references to blind and deaf Israel, to whom God sent Isaiah (see 6:9-10). God gave the Servant God's teachings, but the blind and deaf recipients were robbed and plundered (42:22), a reference to the fall of Jerusalem. Verse 24 makes clear the identity of the Servant: Jacob/Israel in exile. In two more verses (43:10 and 48:20), the context shows that the Servant is the exilic community. In sum, all ten of these verses are best seen as referring to the exiles.

One other verse (44:26) employs the word "servant" in parallelism with "messengers." A few ancient versions read "servant" as a plural, indicating an identification of the two figures. The singular noun in the Hebrew text itself, however, might suggest that the Servant was numbered among the prophets. Since the word "servant" is explained by the appositive "Jacob/Israel" just six verses later (45:4), connecting the Servant to messengers/prophets in 44:26 distinguishes the two usages. Hence, 44:26 represents more limited meaning than "exiles."

Seven (42:1; 49:3, 5, 6; 50:10; 52:13; 53:11) of the remaining eight occurrences appear in or next to the "Suffering Servant" poems (marked SS and numbered in the chart below). What is the situation with regard to these passages? Is the Servant they speak of the exiles or a prophetic figure, individual or collective? The third song (50:4-11) seems clearest, so we will start with it. It describes the work of the Servant as that of a teacher, someone who has been abused rather than obeyed by his fellow Israelites. With this passage in mind, we will take up the remaining songs in sequence.

In the first song (42:1-4) also, there is no identification of the Servant as Israel/Jacob. God presents the Servant, indicating that the Servant will bring forth justice. It is not clear to whom God speaks in vv. 5-9. In v. 6 God says that God had called someone and made him "a covenant to the people, a light to the nations," a phrase that 49:6 (in the second Servant poem) repeats. Verse 7 picks up language from Isaiah's call vision, but here (unlike 42:19) the addressee is not blind and is not equated with Jacob/Israel as the Servant was in 42:24. His mission, in fact, is to "bring out the prisoners from the dungeon" (42:7). If these verses have the Servant in view, they would appear to mean that the Servant would be instrumental in God's rescuing the exiles from Babylon. Thus, even if one extends the song through v. 6 or v. 7, or v. 9 with Baltzer,[21] there is still no warrant for saying the Servant is Israel or some other collective group. Blenkinsopp sides with those scholars who think the Servant in this verse only was Cyrus, but he is never specifically identified as such in the text.[22] Nor is it clear that Cyrus was as peaceful a man as this verse makes out the Servant to be.

The second song (Isa 49:1-6) is trickier, or at least v. 3 is. In that verse God addresses the Servant, calling him Israel. That might seem to settle the issue, except that vv. 5 and 6 say that the Servant will be God's messenger to Jacob/Israel. It is difficult to see how Israel could be a messenger to restore the survivors of Israel (49:6). How, then, might one understand v. 3? Westermann simply takes the word "servant" as a gloss, an early interpretation of the text, which is possible.[23] Childs offers a different reading. He speaks of a "predicative" force to the sentence: "You are my servant; *you* are now Israel."[24] As of that moment, the Servant became the new Israel, the

---

21. Baltzer, *Deutero-Isaiah*, 124-37.
22. Blenkinsopp, *Isaiah 40–55*, 209-12.
23. Westermann, *Isaiah 40–66*, 208-9.
24. Childs, *Isaiah*, 384.

harbinger of Israel to come. Moreover, he has a message for the old Israel. In other words, God gives the Servant the name Israel, just as God did for Jacob in Gen 32:28. The opening verses sound like a description of the experiences of an individual: he was in his mother's womb; God made his mouth like a sharp sword; God gave him the name Israel.

The final song is 52:13–53:12. There one finds no reference to Jacob/Israel, but one does find language that seems best understood as referring to an individual. In 53:8, a voice says that the Servant was stricken for the sins of "my people." The Masoretes suggested reading "his people" (cf. 1QIsᵃ, a scroll of Isaiah among the Dead Sea Scrolls), and *BHS* suggests reading the two words as one, resulting in a word we may translate "for their sins." Certainty on this text is impossible, but the Servant seems to be a single person who suffered for the nation, not the nation itself. The earlier mention of the Servant (52:13) must refer to the same person.

A final mention of the Servant appears in 49:7, where the NRSV translates the Hebrew word *'ebed* as "slave" instead of "servant," apparently in an attempt to distinguish the servant there from the Servant of the Servant Songs. We should note, however, the closeness of language between 49:7 on the one hand and 52:15 and 53:3 on the other. Childs comments that 49:7 "follows the same pattern of the [S]ervant's humiliation and abuse, his ultimate recognition by kings and rulers, and his final vindication by God"[25] as in 52:13–53:12. Moreover, 49:8 picks up language from 42:6, where the Servant is an individual. It would appear, therefore, that 49:7, 8-11 constitutes a redactor's work tying the second Servant Song (49:1-6) to its context. The redactor saw the work of the Servant as instrumental in the exiles' return to Jerusalem and Judah (49:8-11).

The results of this survey can be depicted in the table on page 98, which shows the salient points of this discussion. It is possible now to read the four Servant Songs with understanding. In doing so, it will be helpful to focus on three issues: the genre of each song, the task of the Servant in each, and the office or person in ancient Israel typically associated with each task.

The first song appears in 42:1-4(9). Where it ends is uncertain, but that uncertainty will not substantially affect its meaning. In terms of its genre, it resembles in some ways a call vision, except that vv. 1-4 refer to God's imbuing the Servant with God's charisma in the past. It is perhaps better to

---

25. Childs, *Isaiah*, 386.

The "Servant" in Second Isaiah

Text	Designates Prophet(s)	Designates Israel	Comments
41:8		X	Israel/Jacob called "servant"
41:9		X	Continues the thought from v. 8
42:1 (SS 1)	X		V. 7 distinguishes the Servant from the exiles
42:19 (twice)		X	Allusion to disobedient Israel in v. 24
43:10		X	Servant = the exiles
44:1		X	Jacob/Israel
44:2		X	Jacob/Jeshurun (= Israel)
44:21a		X	Jacob/Israel
44:21b		X	Mentions only Israel, but continues v. 21a
44:26	X		Servant//prophets
45:4		X	Jacob/Israel
48:20		X	Jacob only, but the verse addresses exiles
49:3 (SS 2)	X		Alludes to call vision
49:5 (SS 2)	X		Call vision
49:6 (SS 2)	X		Call vision
49:7	X		Ties SS 2 to its context
50:10 (SS 3)	X		Servant distinguished from Israel
52:13 (SS 4)	X		Servant suffers in vv. 14-15
53:11 (SS 4)	X		Servant suffers for the exiles

agree with Baltzer that this text reads like a presentation of God's servant. References to his call validate the presentation. If the text includes vv. 5-7, God is there addressing the Servant instead of the people. The specific point that God had called the Servant as a light to the nations appears also in 49:6, which we saw earlier is best understood as an addition. Regardless, both verses speak of the Servant, not of Israel.

What is the function of this Servant? The answer comes in 42:4, "to establish justice in the land/earth." One office associated closely with establishing justice in ancient Israel was the monarchy. Another would be that of judge. Baltzer points to one specific judge, Moses, who was also responsible for conducting Israel out of Egypt during the exodus. He thinks the Servant is being depicted as a new Moses.[26] We might also notice that v. 9 speaks of God's revealing new (hidden) truth to the Servant to declare, the function of a prophet. While certainty is impossible, it is clear that Second Isaiah is pointing to someone especially chosen by God for service to Israel and beyond. This multiplicity of offices ascribed to the Servant will appear again.

The second song appears in Isa 49:1-6. Written in the first person singular, it has overtones of Jeremiah's call vision (Isa 49:1, 5, 6 // Jer 1:5). The function of the Servant is to be a light to Israel and the nations. Call visions are associated with prophets. Other first person passages may belong to this same voice: 48:16 and 50:4-11, the third Servant Song. That song is an individual lament, rather reminiscent of the "Confessions of Jeremiah."[27] The song contains expressions of confidence in God that almost invite reading the passage as a song of thanksgiving, and it concludes with an indictment of the exiles for failing to follow his teachings. Clearly then, his function is to teach, an act that was the responsibility of priests and prophets.

The fourth and last song extends from 52:13 to 53:12. Like the first song (42:1-4?), it is about, not by, the Servant. Like the first song, it describes his past suffering, though in much more detail. Its genre resembles the song of thanksgiving, except that even when it speaks in the first person it is not the one who suffered who speaks but his fellow exiles and God. The functions of the Servant are twofold (53:12). The first is to bear sins, a role associated with animals sacrificed at an altar. The second is to make intercession, a role associated with prophets, the specialists in intercession. As in other songs, the role of the Servant is broader than any one office. He seems to represent much (all?) that was salvific in ancient Israel. Although it appears in 53:8-9 that he died, that language is probably metaphorical. Verse 10 only says he was "crushed with pain," which is not the same as saying he died.

---

26. Baltzer, *Deutero-Isaiah*, 128-30.

27. It is possible that the second and third Servant Songs simply constitute traditional songs or borrow from such, but the language is individual and personal, and 49:3-4 receives a response in vv. 5-6. It seems better, then, to take the two songs autobiographically as the creations of a single exile, whose ministry had cost him dearly.

A Problem Raised by a Study of Isaiah 40–55

One crucial problem raised by a study of Isaiah 40–55 is the identity of the Servant. This is not a new problem. The NT narrative of Philip's encounter with the Ethiopian eunuch (Acts 8:26-39) points to the problem. When Philip finds him, the eunuch is reading Isa 53:7-8. Philip asks him, "Do you understand what you are reading?" The eunuch answers: "How can I unless someone guides me? . . . About whom . . . does the prophet say this, about himself or someone else?" (Acts 8:30-31, 34 NRSV). Philip, of course, applies the passage to Jesus; some early Jews applied it to Israel. Various scholars have made suggestions of their own. We shall examine the most prominent of the suggestions.

A typical Jewish reading, and one adopted by a number of Christians as well, is that the Servant is Israel itself. As we have seen, one must concede that in places in Second Isaiah Israel *is* called God's servant. Still, the problem is that in the songs the Servant is called to be a light to Israel (49:6) and the nations and the exiles are called to hear the Servant (50:10). It does not appear, then, that a simple equation of Israel and the Servant is possible. A second possibility is that the Servant is Second Isaiah. The problem with this view is that the Servant poems themselves differ in that two are in the first person singular, while the other two speak of the Servant in the third person. A fourth suggestion is that the Servant is Jeremiah, and we have seen connections between the call visions and laments of Jeremiah and the Servant. Still, the exiles had not been fans of Jeremiah when they were in Judah, and there is no reason to suppose that they thought much about him years later in Babylon. Nor is there any indication that Jeremiah lived in Babylon. Another suggestion is that the Servant is Cyrus, who is mentioned in Second Isaiah. Cyrus, however, was a victor, not a victim. Finally, the typical Christian interpretation is that the Servant is Jesus, but here is another instance where people read the NT (e.g., Matt 12:15-21; Acts 8:30-34) back into the Old. A reading of the Servant poems in their context gives the impression that the texts are talking about a contemporary whom the exiles knew, not an unknown figure who would not come for centuries. The most we can say about the Servant, then, is that he appears to have been an exile, who conceived of himself as a prophet, and whose life and teachings stirred Second Isaiah to see him as someone whose mission paralleled Israel's and cost the Servant dearly.

What then might one say about the NT's appropriation of the figure? It appears to be another case of the authors of the NT using figures from the OT to explain the significance of Jesus. Whomever Second Isaiah had in mind as the Servant, the NT saw Jesus, especially in his death, as that Servant and more. Donald Gowan addresses this issue with a personal note: "As for Isaiah 53, it is my position that Jesus was indeed the fulfillment of those words, but the words themselves do not take the form of a prediction and they originally had nothing to do with Messiah."[28] If I may expand Gowan's comment slightly, I would say that it is permissible to speak of Jesus' fulfilling the Servant Songs in one way or another, even those that are not predictions. It is important, however, for Christians to realize that when we do so we (like the NT) are *applying* the songs, not *interpreting* them.

Introduction to the Prophet(s) Behind Isaiah 56–66

If it was difficult to say anything concrete about Second Isaiah, it is even more so about Third Isaiah. In places (esp. chs. 60–62) the writer(s) employ a style similar to Second Isaiah, but in other cases they deviate from that style. Scholars, therefore, often simply speak of a "school" of writers responsible for the messages assembled here. Still, one can say a few things about that "school." It was located in Jerusalem, and it earnestly hoped for a new and better day, the one predicted by Second Isaiah. Like Second Isaiah, these chapters speak of the exile as double the punishment Judah deserved (61:7) and promise a double reward in recompense. Like Second Isaiah, Third Isaiah uses creation (65:17) and exodus language (63:11-12). Like Isaiah and Second Isaiah, it refers to God as the Holy One of Israel (60:9).[29] Like Second Isaiah, it ventures to speak of God's marriage to Israel (62:5). It is open to foreign converts and others that the OT banished from the temple (56:3-8) but shares the OT's antipathy to Edom and perhaps other enemies of Judah (63:1-6). In 61:1 the speaker seems to allude to the Servant Song found in 50:4-11, to assume the role himself, and to promise restitution to his own group in Jerusalem.

Interestingly, the collection does not mention a new David (Second

---

28. Donald E. Gowan, *Eschatology in the Old Testament,* 2nd ed. (Edinburgh: T. & T. Clark, 2000) 38.

29. The phrase rarely appears outside Isaiah. See 2 Kgs 19:22//Isa 37:23, plus Pss 71:22; 78:41; and 89:18. A similar phrase "The Holy One *in* Israel" appears in Ezek 39:7.

Isaiah mentions him only once), even though Haggai and Zechariah preach that the Davidic prince Zerubbabel would rebuild the temple and Hag 2:20-23 finger him as the new ruler. Micah 4–5, quite possibly from the same time period, reveals great hopes for a new David as well.[30] Jerusalem itself would be a crown of glory and royal diadem in God's hand (Isa 62:3). Perhaps the persons who speak in Third Isaiah returned with someone other than Zerubbabel (e.g., Sheshbazzar; cf. Ezra 1:8; 5:14-16) and were not as excited as Haggai and Zechariah. Perhaps, they had given up hope for a new king and built their hopes around a theocracy. That might account for the twofold mention of Moses (63:11 and 12), though in an obvious reference to the dividing of the waters in the exodus, not as a law-giver.

Basic Emphases in Isaiah 56–66

The structure of Third Isaiah bears repeating here.

> 56:1-8 Prologue: Salvation to all, including foreigners and eunuchs
> 56:9–58:14 Condemnation, repentance, and compassion as true worship
> 59:1-21 Lament: Israel's sins have prevented God's mercy
> 60:1–62:12 The Glory of God's new day
> 63:1–64:12 A Lament of the people, introduced by a song about God's vengeance
> 65:1-25 God's response to the lament
> 66:1-24 Epilogue: The New Jerusalem and the New Creation (cf. 11:6-9; 65:17, 25)

Stripped down, the structure consists of a prologue (56:1-8), doom (i.e., God's condemnation of sinners; 56:9–57:13), hope (60:1–62:12), and an epilogue (66:1-24). That structure looks simple, and perhaps therein lies the problem: life is sometimes messy, not simple. Maybe things did not go as the group behind Third Isaiah thought they should. The laments perhaps register complaints at the pace of the restoration, with chs. 60–62 serving as the response to the first lament and ch. 65 as the response to the second.

---

30. See Paul L. Redditt, "The King in the Book of the Twelve," in *Tradition in Transition*, ed. Mark J. Boda and Michael H. Floyd. LHB/OTS (London: T. & T. Clark, forthcoming).

The first lament bemoans injustice within the early postexilic community, and the second lament the continuing desolation of the country in the early decades of Persian rule. In that reading God's response is that God is willing to restore Judah, but Judah had not turned to God. When the people repented, God would turn Judah into paradise (65:25). We shall examine in more detail three basic emphases used in building this structure.

Condemnation of Leaders for a Lack of Compassion

In the opening verses of Third Isaiah's condemnation of Judah (56:9-12), he laments blind sentinels, mauling dogs, and clueless shepherds. The first and last sound like metaphors for groups that were supposed to guarantee the welfare of people, but failed. The silent dogs turn out to be not watchdogs protecting the people, but attack dogs with ravenous appetites: i.e., people taking advantage of their neighbors. Third Isaiah portrays the leaders as complacent in their own positions and anxious to end their work day early and go drink wine. They care little for those they are supposed to protect. The Hebrew text of 57:7-13 is uncertain in places, so it is not clear whether they are accused of sexual misconduct and idolatry as well. The NRSV translates 57:12, "I will concede your righteousness and your works, but they will not help you." If that translation is correct, their sin is not blatant. It is more a matter of failing to fear God and stand up for God (or God's people) than actively doing wrong. Moreover, God would not continue to be angry (57:16). If they would "loose the bonds of injustice," "let the oppressed go free," "share [their] bread with the hungry, and bring the homeless into [their] house," clothe the naked (58:6-7), and keep the Sabbath (58:13) — a means of making and preserving community — they would find God helping them.

Control of the Temple

Hanson argued that behind Third Isaiah lay a struggle for control over the temple between Zadokite priests returning from the exile and Levitical priests who had maintained the altar during the exile.[31] According to him,

---

31. Hanson, *The Dawn of Apocalyptic*, 86-95.

this conflict left its mark on Third Isaiah in two passages in particular: 63:7–64:11 and ch. 65. Regardless of whether Hanson is correct about these verses, it does seem clear that the reality of early Persian-period Judah was quite different from the picture Second Isaiah had painted. The national boundaries were small (concentrated around Jerusalem and no more than about 30 miles in diameter anywhere), and the returnees were few. The agenda of those repatriates included rebuilding the temple, restoring the importance of Jerusalem, and for some reuniting north and south and re-establishing the monarchy. None of those things happened immediately, not even the rebuilding of the temple. That task was completed between 520 and 516. Further, divisions separated the people, including repatriates separated from those who had never been in exile and repatriated groups separated from one another. Haggai, Zechariah 1-8, and Ezra give testimony to the differences among the population in the last two decades of the sixth century. The struggle over control of the temple probably began at once with a struggle over control of the rebuilding of the temple. So, Hanson has pointed toward a proper understanding of life in Judah in that period, regardless of whether a Levitical group in opposition to a Zadokite group stood behind Third Isaiah. If anything, the various groups were probably more numerous even than Hanson suggested.[32]

Hope for the Future

Fohrer does not include Third Isaiah among the eschatological texts he studies (Second Isaiah, Haggai, Zechariah 1–8, Zechariah 9–12, Joel, and Isaiah 24–27). Still, Third Isaiah does employ most of the themes of postexilic eschatology, including (1) the destruction of Edom (63:1-6) and punishment of God's enemies (66:6); (2) Israel as the saved community, cleansed and assembled in Jerusalem (chs. 60–62; 65:13-25; 66:6-13); (3) the establishment of wonderful, paradisiacal living conditions for the holy community (65:17-25; 66:22-23); and (4) the conversion of the nations or their remnant (56:3-8; 60:10-11; 66:18-24). Third Isaiah does not speak of

32. Hanson himself said much the same thing at a special session on the book *Passion, Vitality, and Foment: The Dynamics of Second Temple Judaism*, ed. Lamontte M. Luker (Harrisburg: Trinity Press International, 2001), at the 2003 annual meeting of the Society of Biblical Literature.

the immanent assumption of rulership by YHWH or God's messiah; nor does he speak of the reunification of Israel and Judah, at least not explicitly. He refers to Israel six times, but never as the northern kingdom. He never mentions a northern tribe or the northern capital, Samaria. What he does over and over is contrast his own present situation in which the wicked prosper and the righteous suffer with the future when the situations of those two groups are reversed.

A Problem Raised by a Study of Isaiah 56–66

This study of Isaiah 56–66 has also pointed out the issue of exclusivity in these chapters. Despite its inclusiveness about foreigners in 56:3-8 and 66:18-24, the book also contains what can only be called a gory description of God's returning from butchering Edom (63:1-6). Their particular wrongdoing seems to have been watching, perhaps egging on the Babylonians in the sack of Jerusalem, and maybe even helping themselves to some of the loot. Still, the predicted divine punishment seems a generation late and excessively violent. Perhaps, with Babylon defeated and the Persians not attacking, Third Isaiah could take aim on a nearer enemy. This problem will surface again in connection with Obadiah in the Minor Prophets (see Chapter 11).

Reading Isaiah 1–66

Mention has already been made of several places where Third Isaiah employs themes used in Second Isaiah: understanding the exile as double the punishment Judah deserved; the use of creation and exodus language; references to God as the Holy One of Israel; and references to God's marriage to Israel. Such examples could be extended, and a quick way of doing so is to look at Childs's tables showing the relationship of Isaiah 65 and 66 to Isaiah 40 (and to 1:1–2:4 as well).[33] Childs's work is typical of canonical and rhetorical criticism. Finding parallels or allusions is something of an art as well as a science, but such studies can be very helpful in accounting for the form of texts long or short.

33. Childs, *Isaiah*, 543-44.

Intertextuality between Isaiah 65–66 and Isaiah 40

65:1	God's presence manifested: Here am I.	40:9	Behold your God
66:15	God comes in fire for judgment	40:10	God comes with might; with God's reward
65:16	Israel's former troubles are forgotten, hidden from God's eyes	40:2	Israel's warfare is ended and iniquity pardoned
66:13	God comforts God's people	40:1	Comfort, comfort my people
65:18	Gladness and joy for Jerusalem	40:9	Jerusalem, herald of good tidings
65:10	Sharon, a pasture for flocks	40:11	God feeds God's flock like a shepherd
66:18-19	God's glory among the nations	40:5	God's glory revealed to all flesh

These chapters open and close the second part of Isaiah, the part which makes no reference to Isaiah and appears to be added. It is precisely in the opening and closing of chapters or books that one might reasonably expect to find the hand of an author or a redactor trying to create a new work from an older one. Childs does not claim that the wording is the same in these parallels, but that the concepts are. They create something of an inclusion device around the whole section. If so, what about Isaiah 1–66? Is there a similar inclusion around the whole book? Childs answers affirmatively, again with seven parallel themes.

Intertextuality between Isaiah 65–66 and Isaiah 1

65:2	God spreads out God's hands to a rebellious people	1:2	Sons I reared, they rebelled against me
65:3	A people who provoke God	1:4	The whole head is sick, utterly estranged
65:3	They corruptly sacrifice in gardens	1:29	You will blush for the gardens
65:6	God will repay into their bosom	1:5	Why will you continue to be smitten?
65:8	I will not destroy them all	1:9	If [YHWH] had not left a remnant, then they would have become like Sodom

65:15	God's servants will be called by a different name	1:26	You will be called the city of righteousness
66:18-20	All nations will come to my holy mountain	2:1-4	Let us go up to the mountain of YHWH

Some parallels may strike readers as more apt than others, but the more parallels one finds convincing, the more one is driven to conclude that the beginning and end of the whole book of Isaiah and each of its halves were edited in light of the other (perhaps quite late, perhaps earlier in its transmission).[34]

Summary

Isaiah 40–66 begins with the people of Judah in exile in Babylon (chs. 40–55) and sees them back home to Jerusalem (chs. 56–66) in accordance with the promise of God in 40:1-11. The book comes full circle from Isaiah of eighth-century Jerusalem to Isaiah of sixth-century Jerusalem. Both parts of the book portray God's relentless concern for God's people and God's desire that the people seek God.

Questions for Reflection

1. How would a message of hope play in the Western Hemisphere? Would different groups have different, even potentially conflicting hopes? What implications might a message of hope for the disadvantaged have for the advantaged? If Second or Third Isaiah visited us today, what might either condemn and why?
2. In a modern culture permeated by scientific views of creation, what relevance — if any — does the idea of *creatio ex nihilo* have?
3. How does the Servant relate to Jesus, if at all?
4. If God is one, what might one think about the God(s) of other faiths than Christianity and Judaism?

---

34. Even Blenkinsopp, who otherwise disagrees about connections between Isaiah 1–39 and 40–66, agrees that at least 1:27-31 and 66:17-24 show such correspondences; *Isaiah 56–66*, 35.

5. How convincing are Childs's parallels between Isaiah 40 and 66 and between Isaiah 1 and 66? Are such analyses helpful? Why or why not?

For Further Reading

Baltzer, Klaus. *Deutero-Isaiah*. Hermeneia. Minneapolis: Fortress, 2001. A lengthy, critical study of Isaiah 40–55 by a leading OT scholar of Germany, describing Second Isaiah as a drama in six acts.

Blenkinsopp, Joseph. *Isaiah 40–55*. AB 19A. New York: Doubleday, 2002. *Isaiah 56–66*. AB 19B. New York: Doubleday, 2003. A translation of the Hebrew text of Second and Third Isaiah, respectively, with introductions and comments.

Childs, Brevard S. *Isaiah*. OTL. Louisville: Westminster John Knox, 2001. A canonical reading of the text by the scholar who prompted the method of canonical criticism in OT studies.

Conrad, Edgar W. *Reading Isaiah*. OBT 27. Minneapolis: Fortress, 1991. A study of Isaiah from the perspective of reader criticism, illustrating that method's focus on structure, the implied reader, and the implied author.

Hanson, Paul D. *The Dawn of Apocalyptic*. Philadelphia: Fortress, 1975. A revision of Hanson's Harvard Ph.D. dissertation, the book broke new ground on Second and Third Isaiah with its discussion of the social background of Third Isaiah, Zechariah 9–14, and other literature. Hanson distinguishes a hierocratic from an apocalyptic group in early Persian Judah.

Westermann, Claus. *Isaiah 40–66*. OTL. Philadelphia: Westminster, 1969. A portrayal of Isaiah 40–66 as the work of an exilic prophet in Babylon and his disciple back in Jerusalem.

Whybray, R. N. *Isaiah 40–66*. NCBC. Excellent, readable critical commentary by a respected British OT scholar. It contains an excellent and readable discussion of genres.

CHAPTER 5

Jeremiah

The book of Jeremiah, the longest of the Latter Prophets, is remarkable for the information it provides about the prophet for whom it is named. A reader should bear in mind, however, that the narratives (and sermons too, for that matter) come through the hands of someone other than the prophet, in this case one or more writers with an affinity for the theology of the book of Deuteronomy. The book paints a portrait of a fiery, but moody, spokesperson for God, one whose mouth got him in trouble with his contemporaries and even got him arrested for treason.

Introduction to the Book and Its Times

Our typical procedure is to begin with an introduction to the book and its times, before investigating what can be known about the prophet. Here we must also see what we can discern about those who preserved his teachings and the narratives about him. Then we shall examine the message of the book.

The Place of the Book in the Canon

In the MT the book of Jeremiah stands after the book of Isaiah and before Ezekiel among the Latter Prophets. In the rabbinic work *B. Bat.* 14b (ca. 180 C.E.), however, we find this sequence: Jeremiah, Ezekiel, Isaiah, and the

Twelve. That sequence reflects the relative length of the four in descending order, a system of arrangement used often in the ancient world. In the LXX Jeremiah is followed by Baruch, Lamentations, and the Letter of Jeremiah, three deutero-jeremianic books that receive their own chapter in this study.

The Setting for the Book

Jeremiah the prophet flourished in Jerusalem in the last several decades leading up to the exile. Narratives about his career are set in places as diverse as a gate to the temple (Jer 7:1-34; 26:1-24), a prison (chs. 32–33), and the king's chamber (37:17-21). After the fall of Jerusalem a group of nobles took him with them to Tahpanhes in Egypt (43:7-13). The book also contains a letter it says was written by Jeremiah to the exiles in Babylon (ch. 29).

The dates for Jeremiah's ministry are debated. The superscription (1:1-3, specifically v. 2) places the start of his career in the thirteenth year of the reign of Josiah (ca. 627 B.C.E.). The traditional understanding is that he began to prophesy before the reform of Josiah recorded in 2 Kgs 22:3–23:25, dated in Josiah's seventeenth year. After the reform took effect Jeremiah fell silent, only to resume preaching early in the career of King Jehoiakim (609-598). The third phase of Jeremiah's career came during the reign of Zedekiah, the last king of Judah. James Philip Hyatt dissented, arguing that no sermon of Jeremiah can be confidently dated before the reign of Jehoiakim. He suggested that the thirteenth year of Josiah's reign was actually the year of the prophet's birth.[1] One can only say "Perhaps." Such a reading of vv. 1-5 is not obvious. The typical scholarly suggestion that Jeremiah was born around 650 is only a guess as well. The truth is that the book does not supply the time of his birth. It does appear, however, that the redactor(s) of Jeremiah wanted the reader to assume that Jeremiah flourished under Josiah and supported his reform. That suggestion is a key to understanding who the redactor(s) might be.

---

1. James Philip Hyatt, "The Book of Jeremiah: Introduction," *IB* 5 (1956) 779. Hyatt argues further that Jeremiah did not support Josiah's reforms, but actually opposed some of them. Hyatt is followed by William L. Holladay, *Jeremiah 1*. Hermeneia (Philadelphia: Fortress, 1986) 1. Both scholars point to the reference in 1:5 to the mother's womb as evidence that Jeremiah's birth date was adopted by the redactor(s) of Jeremiah as the beginning of his prophetic career.

The Structure, Integrity and Authorship of the Book

The structure of the book of Jeremiah has proven illusive, and no one can be said to have solved it satisfactorily. Joel Rosenberg has offered as good an overview as any. He sees the structure of the book as follows.

Symmetrical Literary Pattern in Jeremiah

A   Historical headnote (1:1-3)

   B   Commission (1:10)

      C   "Prophet to the nations" theme introduced (1:5-10)

         D   Doom for Israel; poetic oracles mostly (chs. 1–10)

            E   Prophet cut off from Anathoth; prose mostly (chs. 11–28)

               F   Optimistic prophecies; renewal of Israel. Prose brackets a poetic center (chs. 29–31).

            E′   Prophet returns to Anathoth; prose mostly (chs. 32–45)

         D′   Doom for the nations; mostly poetic oracles (chs. 46–51)

      C′   "Prophet to the nation" theme culminates (chs. 50–51)

   B′   Prophet's concluding message (51:59-64)

A′   Historical Appendix (ch. 52)[2]

Like most such patterns this one may be accused of being arbitrary, as Rosenberg himself admits, especially in connection with the B/B′ pair. Still, there is much to commend it. Starting in the middle, it highlights the optimistic chapters in the middle and nicely handles such pairings as doom for Israel/doom for the nations.

Jack R. Lundbom accounts for the present shape of the book by proposing an original scroll prepared in 605 (Jeremiah 1–20), supplemented by a series of additions: "The King and Prophet Appendix" (chs. 21–23), collections of narrative prose (chs. 24–29, 34–36, and 37–44; describing Jeremiah's final sufferings), a "Book of Restoration" (chs. 30–33), and oracles against foreign nations (chs. 46–51). The book ends with a historical appendix (ch. 52), functioning somewhat like Isaiah 36–39 and like those chapters heavily dependent on the book of Kings. In this arrangement,

---

2. Joel Rosenberg, "Jeremiah and Ezekiel," in *The Literary Guide to the Bible*, ed. Robert Alter and Frank Kermode (Cambridge, MA: Harvard University Press, 1987) 190-91.

Lundbom notes, chronology is a factor, but it is not slavishly followed.[3] Chapters 1–20 date earlier in the prophet's career, and chs. 39–44 describe the end of his career. Those chapters are followed by messages against foreign nations (chs. 46–51) and a historical superscription (ch. 52) that does not even mention the prophet. By contrast one may note the analysis of John Bright, who spoke of three collections (1:1–25:13a; chs. 30–31, if not 33; and chs. 46–51) supplemented by biographical narratives between the sections (chs. 26–29 and 34–45). For Bright, however, the real organizing principle was topical.[4]

These analyses are different, focusing on different data, but are not necessarily incompatible. The text could have arisen through time as described by Lundbom or Bright employing (consciously or unconsciously) the indicators described by Rosenberg. There is no way to know whether any is correct. Such is the difficulty of trying to understand ancient texts. All views, however, have the merit that they draw upon and illuminate data within the text.

Scholars typically question both the integrity and authenticity of the book. For one thing, it contains different types of materials, which are often considered sources. One such "source" is poetic sermons. A second is third-person narratives about the prophet's career, and a third is prose sermons.[5] Both of these last two "sources" employ a style very similar to that of Deuteronomy and the Former Prophets, which are themselves often referred to as the Deuteronomistic History because of their stylistic similarities to Deuteronomy. These similarities might suggest that the book of Jeremiah was written and edited by the same people as the Former Prophets,[6] but they might simply point to a dominant style (perhaps taught by scribes in Jerusalem) of the seventh and sixth centuries. For purposes of this study, the prose materials will not be divided. The number of hands behind them will also be left open.

The number of sources aside, another issue is their nature. Scholars divide quite significantly on this point. On the one hand many scholars

3. Jack R. Lundbom, *Jeremiah 1–20*. AB 21A (New York: Doubleday, 1999) 92-101.

4. John Bright, *Jeremiah*. AB 21 (Garden City: Doubleday, 1965) LVI-LIX.

5. The difference between these last two proposed sources may be seen by comparing 7:1-15 with 26:1-24. The former text goes more into detail about the sermon, while the latter situates the sermon within a narrative context.

6. See, e.g., Walter Brueggemann, *A Commentary on Jeremiah: Exile and Homecoming* (Grand Rapids: Wm. B. Eerdmans, 1998) x.

take the book at face value, finding therein the authentic voice of the prophet, especially in the poetic sections, but also in passages like the Temple Sermon (7:1-15; 26:4-6) and the laments, often called the "Confessions of Jeremiah" (11:18–12:6; 15:10-21; 17:14-18; 18:18-23; 20:7-13; and 20:14-18). The prose sermons are held to be essentially accurate portrayals of the prophet's preaching, though filtered through the style of a scribe (Baruch?), and the prose accounts of the prophet's career are held to be contemporaneous with the prophet's life. Thus, these scholars see the book as the product of the prophet and his "biographers" over a period of four decades (627-587) or so.

Other scholars argue that the material is inauthentic, even the poetic sermons, and reflects an idealized Jeremiah invented by exilic and postexilic writers. Ernst W. Nicholson and Robert P. Carroll are two such scholars. Nicholson emphasizes that the prose materials were the reflections of exilic, Deuteronomic editors, who applied the prophet's message to the period after his life.[7] Carroll compares the Jeremiah of the prophetic book to the Jesus of the Gospels and suggests that no reader should accept anything uncritically as depicting the "historical" Jeremiah. The Jeremiah in the text is Jeremiah as his editors wanted him to be seen.[8] Carroll opposes reading texts like the Confessions as genuine prayers of the prophet giving insight into the prophet's inner thoughts. Regardless of which side one takes in this debate, the only Jeremiah accessible to the reader is the one depicted in this book. We shall discuss that depiction in the section "Introduction to the Prophet."

We may still inquire about where the tradition-bearers lived and redacted the book. The first and most obvious answer is Jerusalem. At some point they almost surely lived there, knew the city, and knew the prophets and officials flourishing there. There is no reason to suppose that they invented Jeremiah, though that is possible. Probably all of the people that appear in the narratives of the book were real people. The tradition-bearers might not have always remained in Jerusalem, however. If not, did they go to Babylon? Maybe; latter traditions placed Baruch there. Still, there is nothing in the book that requires the residence of tradition-bearers in Babylon, and there are no accounts of Jeremiah's going there.

---

7. Ernst W. Nicholson, *Preaching to the Exiles: A Study of the Prose Tradition in the Book of Jeremiah* (Oxford: Blackwell, 1970).

8. Robert P. Carroll, *Jeremiah*. OTL (Philadelphia: Westminster, 1986) 55-64.

There is, however, a narrative of Jeremiah's going to Egypt after the deportation of Zedekiah and the assassination of the Babylonian-appointed governor Gedaliah (chs. 41–44). This account is followed a short chapter later — in the MT anyway — by denunciations of Egypt (ch. 46). Also, the final chapter of the book (52) recounts the fall of Jerusalem in words principally drawn from 2 Kgs 24:18–25:30, but does not repeat the much shorter narrative in 2 Kgs 25:22-26 about the death of Gedaliah already discussed in Jeremiah 40–41. Jeremiah 52:30 instead mentions a third successful siege of Jerusalem in the twenty-third year of Nebuchadnezzar (ca. 580), a defeat not mentioned in 2 Kings 25.[9] That battle was apparently of no interest to the exiles in Babylon, who were more interested in the freeing of King Jehoiachin from prison.[10] The battle was, however, of much interest to the tradition-bearers of Jeremiah, betraying their interest in Judah after the second deportation. All of this material suggests that they were connected in some way to the Judeans who went to Egypt, and this battle proved their wisdom in fleeing to Egypt. It also suggests that Jeremiah was their prophetic hero, just as the priest Ezekiel became a hero to at least some of those who went to Babylon. The theological kinship of the Jeremianic tradition-bearers to Deuteronomy shows they were heavily influenced by its theology. It is possible, though not necessary, that they were related to the group responsible for assembling the Former Prophets.

The fact that Jer 52:31-34 repeats 2 Kgs 25:27-30 about the elevation of Jehoiachin shows that the book of Jeremiah was not completed until after the year that event took place, namely 560. The book anticipates an end to the exile (after 70 years; see 25:11-12; 29:10) but does not describe it. This observation suggests that the editing of the book was finished before 539, when — according to 2 Chr 36:23 and Ezra 1:1-3 — Cyrus, the Persian king and conqueror of Babylon, granted Judeans permission to leave for Jerusalem. If so, the work, which presumably began during the lifetime of the prophet and traced his career in Egypt after 586, attained its basic shape and contents by 539 at the hands of scribes like Baruch.[11] Even so, it seems

9. The first two sieges had been in 597 and 586.

10. The "elevation of King Jehoiachin in exile" meant that if the exiles were ever allowed to return to Jerusalem the king would be free to accompany them. See Rainer Albertz, *Die Exilszeit: 6. Jahrhundert v. Chr.* Biblische Enzyklopädie 7 (Stuttgart: Kohlhammer, 2001) 95.

11. Carroll, *Jeremiah*, 68, argues that the date of 539 is not as secure as most scholars think it is, but grants its plausibility. He thinks there was a post-539 recension. That is possible, of course, and there are texts that seem to date from later (e.g., 23:1-8). It seems prefera-

nevertheless to have continued attracting modifications and additions (e.g., 23:1-8) later in the Persian period.

Main Genres in the Book

The book of Jeremiah contains a kaleidoscope of literary genres, both poetic and prosaic. Poetic genres, which are more prevalent in the first half of the book, begin with a call vision (1:4-10), extended by means of a prose account of God's commissioning the prophet. Poetic genres also include a marvelously-crafted indictment against Israel (ch. 2) that takes the form of a historical review of God's dealings with Israel from the exodus to the time of Jeremiah. It ends with a view to the future when God would punish Judah as severely as God had punished Israel by means of Assyria. Another genre is the extended rhetorical question (3:1-2, 4-5), turned into a prophecy of disaster by means of the transition word "therefore" and a statement of the punishment Judah had already received from God: drought (3:3).[12] Jeremiah also employs an admonition (3:12-14), in which God demands the repentance (turning from sin) of the people of Judah. Jeremiah 4 contains a vision (vv. 23-26) of the dissolution of the world and a return to the primal chaos (the earth was "waste and void"; cf. Gen 1:2). Jeremiah 5:1-9 has aspects of a dialogue between God and the prophet. The very next pericope (5:10-17) begins as a command to someone to go through the vine rows of Judah and destroy them, presumably with fire. As the passage develops, it is the prophet's message that will burn the people (5:14) but not destroy them. Jeremiah 6:22-26 is a typical prophecy of disaster, followed (vv. 27-30) by an explanation that God has made Jeremiah into a silversmith to refine Judah of its dross. A one-verse poetic lament appears in 7:29, a hymn in celebration of God's creative work in 10:12-16, self curses in 20:14-18, and a proverb in 31:29. Jeremiah 22:13-17 constitutes a poetic woe oracle, which also employs a rhetorical question (v. 15) and an accusation against King Jehoiachin (v. 17). Almost surprising, in view of this list of genres of judgment, was the extended

---

ble, however, to think in terms of 539 as the latest date for the basic redaction. The 70-year prophecy of Jeremiah mentioned in 2 Chr 36:21 and Ezra 1:1 appears in works possibly best dated in the fourth century, though some scholars would prefer the fifth or the third.

12. Cf. 8:4-17, which also employs an indictment.

collection of oracles of salvation in Jeremiah 30 and 31, often called the "Book of Consolation."

The last major poetic genre in Jeremiah is the individual lament (11:18–12:6; 15:10-21; 17:14-18; 18:18-23; 20:7-13; 20:14-18), one of the widest-used genres in the Psalter. In Jeremiah they are often called his "Confessions." They also contain some secondary prose. A full-blown lament begins with a brief introduction ("O YHWH"), moves to a complaint about how things are going and perhaps a condemnation of one's enemies, then offers a petition for God to rectify matters, issues an expression of trust, and perhaps even expresses adoration or praise. It may even contain a promise to God to do certain things (e.g., offer a sacrifice) if God grants the request. In Jeremiah, God responds three times to the prophet's laments in 11:21-23; 12:5-6; and 15:19-21.

The book also contains extensive prose accounts, especially in chs. 17–29; 32–45; and 51:59–52:34. Most of this material is biographical narrative about the prophet, including such genres as a description and interpretation of symbolic acts (18:1-12; 19:1-15; 20:1-6; 27:1–28:17; 32:1-44) and accounts of his confrontations with kings (21:1-10; chs. 34–38) and of the fall of Jerusalem (chs. 39–43 and 52). Other prose material includes the incomparable Temple Sermon (7:1-15 and 26:1-24).

Lundbom argues that these sometimes short passages are shaped into collections around themes. A list of his themes will illustrate his point. He names them "People of a Forgotten Covenant (2:1–4:4)"; "Covenant Curses for a Covenant People (4:5–10:25)"; "A Prophet Persecuted, Rejected, and Cursed (11:1–20:18)"; "On Kings and Prophets (21:1–23:40)"; "Prepare for a Life in Exile (24:1–29:32)"; "The Book of Restoration (30:1–33:26)"; "False Covenants, True Covenants (34:1–36:32)"; "Behold the Man" (37:1–40:6)"; "Turn and Take Your Journey — to Egypt! (40:7–44:30)"; "Baruch's Colophon (45:1-5)"; "Oracles to the Foreign Nations (46:1–51:64)"; and "Postscript (52:1-34)."[13]

A Special Issue in the Book

The most striking special issue in the study of Jeremiah is the difference between the MT and the LXX. Simply stated, the LXX is much shorter

---

13. Lundbom, *Jeremiah 1–20; Jeremiah 21–36*. AB 21B (New York: Doubleday, 2001); *Jeremiah 37–52*. AB 21C (New York: Doubleday, 2004).

than the MT (about one-eighth), lacking a number of passages (e.g., 33:14-26),[14] and locates the "oracles against the nations" in a different place. Stylistic features that make the LXX shorter include (1) fewer redactional introductions to units of texts, (2) fewer uses of the phrase "oracle of YHWH," and (3) hardly any occurrences of the epithet "the prophet" in connection with the name Jeremiah.[15] These differences are not likely attributable to the work of the translators, since the LXX tends to be expansive, not reductive. The best explanation seems to be that the LXX was translated from an edition that came earlier than the MT. An argument in favor of this conclusion is the difference in placement (and sequencing) of the "oracles against the nations." In Isaiah and Ezekiel such oracles come toward the middle of the book (Isaiah 13–23 and Ezekiel 25–32), in connection with the "oracles of doom" as they do in the LXX of Jeremiah (following 25:14).[16] By contrast, in the MT of Jeremiah they come almost at the end (chs. 46–51).

Introduction to the Prophet

The name Jeremiah is a compound concluding with the first syllable of YHWH, but the whole name is almost indecipherable today. One suggestion is that it means "YHWH shoots or throws"; others are "YHWH loosens," "YHWH lifts up or exalts," or even "YHWH may found."

Much is said about Jeremiah's life, but some scholars today distrust the information, arguing that the framers of the book shaped the traditions to depict the prophet as they wanted us to see him. That is, of course, possible; we do not know. What we can do, however, is describe the prophet portrayed in the book. That is the prophet accessible to us.

We are told (1:1) that he was the son of a priest named Hilkiah, who belonged to the priests of Anathoth (a town about two miles northeast of Jerusalem). That might mean that Jeremiah was a descendant of the priest Abiathar, who was associated with David during his years of fleeing from

14. Jeremiah 33:14-26 sounds remarkably like passages in the Book of the Twelve, esp. in Zechariah 1–8, as well as 2 Sam 7. It is typically dated in the postexilic period, even as late as 400. This is not the only text apparently interpolated from outside Jeremiah in the MT. It seems to show familiarity with the emerging larger canon.

15. Carroll, *Jeremiah*, 50.

16. Verses 15-29 appear in the LXX as 32:1-24.

Saul. Abiathar sided with Adonijah, not Solomon, in the days before David named his successor. After the ascension of Solomon, Abiathar fled to Anathoth. While the family may have descended from the Levitical priest Eli, it was probably not part of the power structure in Jerusalem. At any rate the book of Jeremiah portrays its hero as a critic of the Jerusalemite priesthood. One other unusual feature of his personal life is that he did not marry — at the command of God (16:2).

The dates of his public career are uncertain, but the book seems to want to portray him as an advocate of the reforms of Josiah ca. 621 (see 2 Kgs 23:4-15, 19-24), since the superscript says he began his career during the reign of Josiah (Jer 1:2). The prophet's praise of Josiah nested in an attack on Jehoiakim (22:15b-16) points in the same direction. By contrast, ch. 22 has the prophet predict the exiles of Shallum (also known in the OT as Jehoahaz) and Coniah or Jehoiachin. Jeremiah's opposition to Jehoiakim was so consistent that the king burned a scroll containing a written copy of some of his messages to the city (ch. 36).

Further, Jeremiah 7 and 26 highlight his tension with — even antagonism toward — Jerusalem in a sermon in which Jeremiah threatened the temple in Jerusalem with divine destruction. In turn he was threatened with death for preaching it. The latter part of his career was played out against the backdrop of the three sieges of Jerusalem by Nebuchadnezzar. Jeremiah is portrayed as advocating surrender to the Babylonians, whom he proclaimed the instrument of God's punishment of Judah. For this stance he was arrested and imprisoned for treason. When Jerusalem fell and Gedaliah was assassinated, Jeremiah along with Baruch was taken to Egypt. Jeremiah denounced his captors for taking him there. His career ended some time after 585, some forty years after the reforms of Josiah.

Basic Emphases in Jeremiah

A book as long and rich as Jeremiah commands far more study than the few pages available here, so the scope of these remarks must be severely limited. We shall examine only nine emphases.

Jeremiah's Prophetic Call

Jeremiah's call to be a prophet appears at the opening of the book (1:4-10), as is also the case with Ezekiel's call (Ezekiel 1–3).[17] It opens with God's announcement to Jeremiah that God had chosen him to be a prophet before Jeremiah was even born. That statement does not mean that Jeremiah had no say in the matter. He could have refused. Nor does it mean that his career as a prophet began at his birth. All it means is that God wanted Jeremiah to be a prophet.

To whom was Jeremiah called to prophesy? The answer is "the nations." The most obvious nation was his own, Judah. Overwhelmingly that is the nation to whom he prophesied. The passage already alerts the reader, however, that Jeremiah would prophesy to others as well. Those named in the text are Egypt (ch. 46), Philistia (ch. 47), Moab (ch. 48), Ammon (49:1-6), Edom (49:7-22), Damascus (49:23-27), the Arabs of Kedar and Hazor (49:28-33), Elam (49:34-39), and Babylon, called the Chaldeans (chs. 50–51).

As is typical in call visions, Jeremiah offers a protest: he is too young (1:6). But God will hear nothing of that objection. Then God touches Jeremiah's mouth (1:9), thus anointing it for God's work. The first part of that work is to pluck up, pull down, destroy, and overthrow, but the second part is to build and plant. As seems to be the case with humans and human institutions, sometimes, before learning or changes can come about, the "old ways" must be eliminated. Often that elimination only comes about when they prove ineffective. So God commissions Jeremiah to preach, but warns him that he will face opposition. Jeremiah is not to heed his contemporaries; he is their hope, but only if he remains true to his call. Of course, as the book unfolds, Jeremiah is faithful to his role, but Judah does not heed his message and pays dearly. So does Jeremiah; this business of being a true prophet of God is not easy.

The First Monotheist in the Hebrew Bible?

What does the Jeremiah of the book say about God? He claims that God selected Israel in the wilderness and cared for the nation with utmost fidel-

---

17. The report of Isaiah's call came only in the sixth chapter. Many scholars think, however, that the original Isaiah scroll contained only chs. 6-8. If so, the description of the prophet's call came first in that scroll, and later editions placed materials in front of it.

ity (2:1-3). Israel, however, disobeyed beginning as soon as it entered Canaan (vv. 7-8). Nor apparently was it doing any better in Jeremiah's day, so God was prepared to punish Israel for its infidelity (vv. 9-19). One verse in this indictment is striking, however, and requires closer scrutiny. Verse 11a reads: "Has a nation changed its gods, even though they are not gods?" What is the view of Israel's God regarding the gods of surrounding nations? Is it monotheistic?

Scholars typically say that monotheism emerged in the MT in Second Isaiah, specifically in Isa 41:23-24; 43:10; and 44:6. Monotheism may be defined as belief in and worship of one God, combined with the denial of the existence of all other gods. Does Jer 2:11a pass this test? It seems to. Jeremiah's point seems to be that the other nations worship a multitude of gods that are not genuine. Only Israel's God would qualify. Nevertheless, God's people had forsaken the worship of the one and only God to worship things worshipped by other peoples, even though those things "were not gods." Unless one wants to ascribe 2:11a to a postexilic editor, one should call Jeremiah the first monotheist in the Hebrew Bible.

The Temple Sermon and Reaction to It

The third theme requiring attention is the famous sermon that 7:1-15 and 26:1-24 report. Chapter 7 opens a collection extending through ch. 20 that many scholars ascribe to the reign of Jehoiakim, even though the king is not mentioned in these chapters. God tells Jeremiah to stand in the gate way of the temple. This location may have been the entrance to the inner court (26:2), within which the temple itself stood. Regardless, it was a prominent place. The sermon he is to deliver has three main points, each including a messenger formula: "(thus) says the LORD." The first (in 7:3-7) is the command for the people to amend their ways. Second (vv. 8-11), Jeremiah asks whether God's temple has become a den of robbers.[18] The prophet thinks it had. Third (vv. 12-15) the prophet commands the people to take an object lesson from the temple that once stood at Shiloh, the temple where Eli was priest. It was perhaps destroyed by the Philistines when they captured and destroyed the city in the eleventh century (1 Sam 4:10-

---

18. A "den of robbers" would be a place where robbers could retreat after gathering their illicit gain.

11), though the Bible does not actually say so. Jeremiah 7:12-14, however, implies as much. The object lesson is simple: the people need God, but God does not need them.

The sermon is summarized in 26:2-5, with the reaction to it narrated in vv. 6-24. Briefly stated, a mob forms and cries for Jeremiah's death. Officials intervene and put Jeremiah on trial, presumably for treason. At the trial, Jeremiah contends that he is simply exercising his prophetic role, and people in the crowd cite a precedent. Micah of Moresheth (specifically called a prophet) had prophesied equally negative thoughts about conditions in Jerusalem in the eighth century, but was not put to death. Instead, the people from King Hezekiah down had repented and God spared the city. The crowd warns that they are about to bring God's wrath on themselves. The result of the trial is that Jeremiah is spared. Lest the reader misunderstand the seriousness of the threat to Jeremiah, however, the narrator adds the case of another prophet who spoke in words "exactly like those of Jeremiah" (v. 20). He fled to Egypt in fear, was arrested and returned to Jerusalem, where he was executed (v. 23). Despite nearly losing his life, Jeremiah continued predicting the overthrow of Jerusalem (cf. chs. 27–28, 32–39). The text portrays Jeremiah's voice as unwelcome and the prophet as lonely.

The "Confessions" of Jeremiah

The book of Jeremiah contains a series of individual laments that scholars often call the "Confessions" of Jeremiah (11:18–12:6; 15:10-21; 17:14-18; 18:18-23; 20:7-13; 20:14-18). That they originated with Jeremiah himself is now contested, but they purport to. Kathleen M. O'Connor argues that the use of the personal voice in the confessions "do[es] not provide evidence of a petulant and disturbed personality. Instead, the personal voice is a weapon in his battle for acceptance as a true prophet of Yahweh. . . . The confessions served a public function in the original life setting of the prophet."[19]

If, however, the usual view that these laments depict Jeremiah as "petulant and disturbed" is correct, it is not immediately obvious why sympathetic admirers would portray the prophet as someone so angry with God

---

19. Kathleen M. O'Connor, *The Confessions of Jeremiah: Their Interpretation and Role in Chapters 1–25*. SBLDS 94 (Atlanta: Scholars, 1988) 3.

as to be in danger of loosing his prophetic calling. Jeremiah 15:19-21 repeats many of the themes/motifs of the call vision, as if God were re-commissioning the prophet. O'Connor argues that the sharp changes in the prophet's mood ". . . can be explained by the confessions' literary form, the psalm of individual lament." Regardless, these prayers point to the role of doubt in religious experience.

Too often people think that doubt is the opposite of believing, and sometimes doubts do drive people to despair of the adequacy of their religion. Such an outcome is not necessary, however, since doubt may serve the greater good of driving someone past pat answers to more satisfying answers. Doubt takes seriously the religious belief or structure under attack *and* the pertinence of the opposition. Such grappling may lead to deeper faith. Certainly the Jeremiah depicted in the book named for him challenged much of official religion in his day. It would not be unusual for him to have second thoughts about whether he was correct to do so. He certainly paid a severe personal price for his opposition when he was imprisoned. The first confession (esp. the prose insertion in 11:21-23) suggests that Jeremiah's own priestly family had turned against him and threatened to kill him. That too is certainly believable if — as seems possible — Jeremiah was causing them professional embarrassment.

The View of the Prophets

Jeremiah 27–28 narrates a prolonged encounter between Jeremiah and other prophets, the sanctioned prophets of Jerusalem. Jeremiah performs the public symbolic act of wearing a yoke on his neck as a sign that Edom, Moab, Ammon, Tyre, Sidon, and Judah would all be sent into exile in Babylon if they refuse to submit to its yoke (27:1-22). In response a prophet named Hananiah announces that God had told him God would break the yoke of Babylon within two years. Then Hananiah breaks the yoke Jeremiah is wearing (28:1-11). Jeremiah makes no immediate response, but some time later God tells him to inform Hananiah that although he has broken Jeremiah's wooden yoke he has only forged an iron one for himself. Jeremiah denounces Hananiah as a self-appointed prophet, who would soon die, which he does (28:12-17). Jeremiah 23:9-40 contains a number of other messages condemning false prophets. In particular, Jeremiah says that they have not stood in the council of God to learn what God has in mind to do as Jeremiah has (23:22). Elsewhere he charges the prophets with saying what the people want to hear, not what God sends the prophets to say (14:11-16). The genuine prophets in the past, Jeremiah insists, had predicted punishment for sin. The burden of proof is on the prophet who predicts peace in Jeremiah's day (28:7-9).

The View of Judah's Last Kings

The messages against the kings of Judah, including but not limited to those collected in 22:10-30, probably were embarrassing to the royal family and seem to have been viewed as treasonous as well. The exception is Josiah, who is praised in 22:15b-16. His first son Shallum (also called Jehoahaz in the OT) ruled only a short time, while Pharaoh Neco of Egypt who had installed him as king did battle in Assyria. As Neco returned to Egypt, he took Shallum with him and replaced Shallum with his brother Jehoiakim. Jeremiah dismisses Shallum with a command to the people not to weep or moan for him.

Jehoiakim was a different matter. During his reign (609-587) he and Jeremiah opposed each other. The woe oracle in 22:13-17 denounces the king for his use of corvee labor to build a royal palace and for other cases of taking advantage of the poor. Verse 19 delivers the insulting prediction that the king would not be buried upon his death, but dragged outside the city gates and thrown down the hillside like a dead animal. There is little wonder that Jehoiakim would cut up and burn a transcription of the prophet's messages (ch. 36).

Jehoiakim rebelled against Nebuchadnezzar in 600 B.C.E. Two years later in December the Babylonian king besieged the city. During that siege Jehoiakim died. His eighteen-year-old son Coniah or Jeconiah (also called Jehoiachin) replaced him while the city sued for peace. Despite the brevity of his reign (a few months), Coniah also drew the ire of Jeremiah, who predicted the king's banishment to a foreign country (22:28). A prose oath placed on the lips of YHWH (vv. 24-26) explains that God would rid Jerusalem of the man and his descendants:

"As I live," oracle of YHWH, "even if Coniah, son of Jehoiakim king of Judah were the signet ring on my right hand, even from there I would tear you off and give you into the hands of those who are seeking your life, indeed into the hands of Nebuchadnezzar, king of Babylonia, yea into the hands of the Chaldeans. I will throw you and the mother who bore you into another land where you were not born; and you shall die there."[20]

The final king to reign during Jeremiah's career was Zedekiah, a son of Josiah and the uncle of Coniah. He repeated the folly of Jehoiakim and revolted against Nebuchadnezzar, which resulted not only in a siege of Jerusalem, but the destruction of the temple and the end of the Judean monarchy. Jeremiah's message under Zedekiah was to surrender, a message that led to the prophet's arrest and imprisonment.

Advice to Surrender

In these confrontations, Jeremiah determined that the Babylonians (also referred to as the "foe from the north")[21] were the instrument God would use to punish the people of Judah for their worship of other gods and their failure to keep God's commandments. Once Babylon had besieged Jerusalem the first time and deported a number of its leading citizens (including King Jehoiachin), there should have been no doubt about their power and willingness to use it.

Some prophets, nevertheless, seem not to have been convinced. The previously-mentioned Hananiah predicted that God would break the hold of the Babylonians within two years and return to Jerusalem King Jehoiachin and the vessels from the temple (28:3-4). That expectation seems to have spread among the exiles too, causing Jeremiah to send them a letter (29:1-23) telling them to settle in, build houses, plant vineyards, marry, and pray for the welfare of the city of Babylon. Their welfare, he told the exiles, was bound up with the welfare of Babylon, and its hege-

---

20. Haggai 2:23 reverses this threat for the Davidic prince Zerubbabel. See the discussion in Chapter Thirteen below.

21. See 1:13-14; 5:15-17; 6:1-5; 10:22; 13:20; 25:9. At times these verses speak of nations — plural, so the prophet might not have known who he thought would invade — perhaps an argument for the authenticity of these texts. Jeremiah 16:15; 23:8; and 31:8 have Babylon in view also, but as the place from which God would rescue God's people, i.e., after the exile. These appear to have been later texts. Further, 25:26 has several northern nations in view, not just Babylon.

mony would last seventy years (29:5-7, 10). That figure should be taken as an approximation. Ezekiel 4:6 sets Judah's exile at forty years. Both seem to mean, however, that none of the exiles should expect to live to return to Judah. The whole tenor of Jer 29:3-7 points that direction.

All that activity, however, was but the beginning of an ongoing dispute between the prophet and the power structure. Zedekiah likewise authorized a revolt against Nebuchadnezzar. When the latter besieged the city a second time, Jeremiah predicted Babylon's victory and Zedekiah's exile to Babylon (32:1-5). When the Egyptians under Pharaoh Hophra came in early 588 to break the siege, the Babylonians lifted it long enough to drive away the Egyptians. During that time Jeremiah decided to go home to conduct family business, but he was arrested for treason and imprisoned (37:11–40:6). Eventually Zedekiah sent for Jeremiah and asked him if he had a word from YHWH. Jeremiah told him that Babylon would send him into exile for not surrendering to the Babylonians. The king kept Jeremiah under house arrest to protect him. Eventually, Zedekiah relented to pressure and transferred Jeremiah to the control of his enemies at court. He was taken from there and put in a cistern, where he nearly died (38:1-7). Ebed-melech, a palace eunuch from Ethiopia, reported Jeremiah's condition to Zedekiah, who dispatched him to rescue the prophet from those who wished to kill him (38:8-13). Soon the king summoned Jeremiah for another audience. Jeremiah repeated his threat and requested that Zedekiah free him. Instead, the king put Jeremiah under house arrest again, where he remained until Jerusalem fell to the Babylonians (38:14-28).

Jeremiah remained there until the fall of Jerusalem, when he was taken to Ramah with other inhabitants of the city (39:1-17). The Babylonians then released him, apparently considering him a friend. Jeremiah declined their offer to go to Babylon (40:1-6) and remained in Jerusalem, still preaching submission to the Babylonians until one of the Judean warlords took him to Egypt with him and his companions (43:1-7). It is worth asking how much of this devastation could have been avoided and at what price if Zedekiah had heeded the prophet's word.

Truth and Treason

The career of Jeremiah illustrates the problem inherent in royally-sponsored religion. The king of Judah was a patron of the temple. That building served as the royal chapel and (after Josiah's reform) claimed to be the one legitimate sanctuary in all Judah, thus appropriating for itself the demands for one sanctuary in Deuteronomy 12.[22] The book of Jeremiah approves of that appropriation and portrays the prophet also approving it (Jer 7:14). The difficulty arose, however, when the prophet attacked the royal house and the priests for idolatry in the temple and other heinous sins (e.g., human sacrifice at a sanctuary at Topheth; 7:30-31). When he also predicted the overthrow of the royal house by a pagan king, he seemed to his compatriots to have gone too far. The truth as Jeremiah saw it required him to act in ways that others found treasonous. The truth as they saw matters required them to silence the prophet.

Hope for the Future

The destruction of Jerusalem and its temple surely must have seemed like doomsday to most of Jeremiah's countrymen. It also would have provided Jeremiah a chance to say "I told you," but the book contains no record of that. Indeed, the book records words of hope for the future attributed to the prophet (30:1–31:40 or 30:1–33:26). Not all predated the fall, and some of these sayings appear to be among the latest in the book and the chance of authenticity for any seems suspect. Scholars have dubbed these chapters the "Book of Consolation."

The predictions of hope are introduced by a "letter to the exiles" in 29:1-32. As we have already seen, the letter (1) repudiates the claim by some prophets resident in Babylon that the exile would end soon, and (2) predicts an eventual end of Babylonian hegemony in "seventy years." If the exiles repented, God would return their descendents to Judah. In the ensuing four chapters a number of typical hopes are attributed to Jeremiah. The first of these hopes is set during the siege of Jerusalem, when Jeremiah purchased a piece of land behind the enemy lines belonging to an uncle, lest it fall into the hands of someone outside the family. This action was to serve as a sign that in the future Judeans would buy and sell their land freely once more (32:1-44). Next, God would restore the fortunes of God's people (30:18-24) by bringing them home (30:10-11; 31:7-9) and rebuilding their cities, especially Jerusalem (30:18; 31:38; 32:36-37; 33:4-11). The northern

22. Such claims are absent in the eighth-century prophets.

kingdom of Israel would be included (31:2-6, 15-22). God would raise up a new Davidic king (33:14-26) and a new Levitical priesthood (33:18, 21-22).

Perhaps the most remarkable promise for the future, however, was the promise of a new covenant. In general, the authors of the Hebrew Bible understood Israel to be related to God through covenants, beginning with Abraham (Gen 12:1-9; 15:1-21; 17:1-27) and the other patriarchs (Isaac in Gen 26:2-5; Jacob/Israel in Gen 28:10-17; 32:24-32). The stipulations of that covenant were worked out in detail in Exodus through Numbers, which Deuteronomy presented anew.[23] God also made a covenant with David (2 Sam 7:1-29), which Jer 33:14-26 sees as continuing in the future, though presumably not through Coniah/Jehoiachin (see 22:28). The covenant that Jeremiah announces, however, is a new covenant, one which is explicitly contrasted with the old covenant given by God to Moses on Mount Sinai (Jer 31:31-34).

Jeremiah draws three contrasts between the two covenants, which prove the superiority of the new over the old. First, the old covenant was breakable; Israel had proved that over and over. The new covenant would be unbreakable. How so? How could a covenant be ironclad? Our question leads to the second contrast. The old covenant was external, written on stone.[24] The new covenant would be internal, written on the heart. But how could that be? The answer came in the third contrast. Whereas the old covenant had been mediated through Moses, the new covenant would be mediated by God directly to the people, whether individually or collectively.

What would that new covenant require? Jeremiah 31 does not say, and perhaps the authors of the book never tried to work it out. Still, based on texts we have already seen, it might be possible to infer some of the stipulations. First and most importantly, it would call for worship of God exclusively (Jeremiah 2 and 7). Second, it would call for people to treat others as God commanded (justly, with no stealing, murdering, committing adultery, or lying; cf. 7:6, 9). Kings would guarantee justice (22:15). Prophets would speak for God, not Baal (2:8b), and tell the truth rather than saying what people wanted to hear (2:8; 5:31). Priests would give correct instruc-

---

23. Many scholars of the Pentateuch think that the Sinai material in Exodus to Numbers was still being codified well into the Persian period, i.e., as late or later than when Jeremiah was completed. Would that make the "new covenant" in Jeremiah a competitor?

24. One may recall here the narrative of Moses' throwing down and breaking tablets of stone with an inscribed set of the Ten Commandments in a fit of anger over Israel's idolatry (Exod 32:19), but there is no way to prove Jeremiah had that text in view.

tion (2:8a; 5:31). It might even be tempting to say that the new covenant would be without sacrifice, since Jeremiah denies that God commanded sacrifice in the wilderness (7:22), but what Jeremiah objects to is sacrifice without repentance and justice. Besides, 33:18 says that "the Levitical priests will not lack a man to offer burnt offerings[25] in [God's] presence."

The Christian New Testament takes its name from the distinction made in 31:31-34, and Heb 8:8-12 quotes those verses in arguing that Jesus had mediated a superior covenant. Even the book of Hebrews, however, does not dismiss sacrifice, but argues that God made the perfect sacrifice in Jesus (Heb 10:1-14). Nothing in Jeremiah suggests that *God* offers a sacrifice. In the book of Jeremiah that function still falls to the Levites.

A Problem Raised by a Study of Jeremiah

A moral problem is raised by the conduct of Jeremiah that has not yet been addressed. At the conclusion to a secret meeting between Jeremiah and Zedekiah, during which Jeremiah counseled the king to surrender to the Babylonians (38:17-18), Zedekiah confesses that he fears officials would ask Jeremiah what the two of them had talked about. The king tells Jeremiah to say simply that Jeremiah had begged for his freedom, and not to mention that the king had asked Jeremiah for advice about the Babylonian siege (vv. 24-26). The officials do question Jeremiah about the meeting, and Jeremiah tells them exactly what the king commanded him to say (v. 27).

The moral issue is this: did Jeremiah lie? A lie may be defined as making a statement one believes to be untrue with the intent to deceive. By that definition Jeremiah seems to have told a lie. If so, was he justified in doing so? Some ethicists argue that no lie could be justified. Immanuel Kant thought that conduct which cannot be universalized may not be considered ethical. In other words, in making ethical decisions one should "suppose everybody did it." If everyone lied, chaos would result. From that perspective, Jeremiah should have simply told the truth. The king, however, thought death would result from Jeremiah's telling the truth, and perhaps the prophet agreed. Does it matter whose death might eventuate? Would it be permissible for Jeremiah to lie to save his own life, but not the life of the

---

25. In this kind of offering, the entire carcass of the animal was burned. It was offered to atone for sins.

king? Or the reverse? Would it have been permissible for Jeremiah to lie to save the king's life, but not his own? Should Jeremiah simply have refused to answer?

Interestingly, the biblical writer unflinchingly says Jeremiah did what he was told. Did that remove the responsibility from Jeremiah? Are people morally responsible for what they do under duress or compulsion, or does culpability enter only when one acts on one's own volition? This is a touchy issue, and one of continuing concern today. Is it sufficient simply to "follow orders"? International courts trying Nazis after World War II said "No."

Summary

The book of Jeremiah paints the portrait of a prophet who flourished in Jerusalem over the last four decades of the Judean kingdom, praising Josiah for his religious reforms and his sense of justice but opposing Josiah's three sons (Shallum/Jehoahaz, Jehoiakim, Zedekiah) and one grandson (Coniah/Jehoiachin) in their exercise of kingship and condemning Jehoiakim. Jeremiah blamed prophets and priests for leading the people astray and the people for turning their backs on God. He preached that Babylon would defeat Judah because its people had turned away from God, a message his contemporaries probably found treasonous. That predicted outcome would be their just deserts for having turned from the one true God of Israel and worshipping the (nonexistent) gods of their neighbors. They had no one but themselves to blame for their downfall. Still, punishment would not be God's final word for Judah — or northern Israel either, for that matter. God would restore them under a Davidic king, a Levitical priesthood, and a new covenant.

Questions for Reflection

1. How important do you think it is, and why, whether the book accurately reports on the Jeremiah of history?
2. What is the role of doubt in religious experience, if any? How does the experience of Jeremiah portrayed in the "Confessions" illuminate that issue?
3. When and/or to what extent do you think Jeremiah's predictions of doom and hope came true?

4. Did Jeremiah lie to the officials about the subject of his audience with King
    Zedekiah in ch. 38? If so, was he justified in doing so? Would one ever be justi-
    fied in telling a lie?

For Further Reading

Brueggemann, Walter. *A Commentary on Jeremiah: Exile and Homecoming.*
    Grand Rapids: Wm. B. Eerdmans, 1998. A commentary combining socio-
    logical and literary approaches to Jeremiah with a theological interpreta-
    tion of its message.
Carroll, Robert P. *Jeremiah.* OTL. Philadelphia: Westminster, 1986. An exten-
    sive commentary investigating the nature of the literature and concluding
    that the work was a postexilic presentation of the prophet as its editors
    wanted him to be seen.
Holladay, William L. *Jeremiah 1; Jeremiah 2.* 2 vols. Hermeneia. Minneapolis:
    Fortress, 1986-89. Thorough commentary on the book of Jeremiah, with
    notes on the Hebrew text, the structure, forms, and setting of passages,
    and an interpretation of each.
Jones, Douglas Rawlinson. *Jeremiah.* NCBC. Grand Rapids: Wm. B. Eerdmans,
    1992. Based on the RSV, but aware of the Hebrew text, containing verse-
    by-verse exegesis, this commentary is more positive than many about our
    knowledge of the historical Jeremiah.
Lundbom, Jack R. *Jeremiah 1-20; 21-36; 37-52.* AB 21A-C. New York: Doubleday,
    1999-2004. A new Anchor Bible commentary on Jeremiah, offering a
    translation, introduction, notes on the Hebrew text, and comments.
    Strong emphasis on rhetorical criticism.
Nicholson, E. W. *Preaching to the Exiles: A Study of the Prose Tradition in the
    Book of Jeremiah.* Oxford: Blackwell, 1970. Argues that preachers in the
    Deuteronomic school used Jeremianic traditions with a free hand in re-
    interpreting the prophet for the postexilic period.
O'Connor, Kathleen M. *The Confessions of Jeremiah: Their Interpretation and
    Role in Chapters 1–25.* SBLDS 94. Atlanta: Scholars, 1988. An exegetical
    study of the "Confessions" of Jeremiah that argues these texts functioned
    publicly and prophetically to defend Jeremiah from charges of false
    prophecy.
Thompson, J. A. *The Book of Jeremiah.* NICOT. Grand Rapids: Wm. B. Eerd-
    mans, 1980. Features an introduction to the book, exploring the author-

ship, date, purpose, structure, and theology of the book. Thompson offers his own translation of the text and verse-by-verse commentary employing modern methods of biblical study.

CHAPTER 6

Lamentations and Other
Deutero-Jeremianic Literature

The influence of Jeremiah during and after the exile was pronounced in some circles. If the book that bears his name contained later materials ascribed to him, such ascriptions continued on after the close of that book. In this chapter we shall examine several such writings: Lamentations, Baruch, and the Letter of Jeremiah, which appears in the Vulgate as the sixth chapter of Baruch.

LAMENTATIONS

The book of Lamentations is a collection of five songs about the destruction of Jerusalem by the Babylonians and the fall of the monarchy in 586 B.C.E. It opens by personifying Jerusalem as a forlorn widow, who not only suffers in her loss but also remembers better years and feels the loss the more keenly because of it. The book does not envision the restoration of Jerusalem but hopes for it, and it ends with the author pondering whether restoration will come at all.

Introduction to the Book and Its Times

The Place of the Book in the Canon

In English Bibles Lamentations follows Jeremiah. That place in the canon is derived from the LXX, in which the books of Baruch, Lamentations, and the Letter of Jeremiah stand between Jeremiah and Ezekiel. Since Protestants do not accord Baruch[1] or the Letter of Jeremiah similar inspiration, both fell away in Protestant versions of the OT. In the MT, Lamentations belongs to the Five *Megilloth* or Scrolls (Ruth, Song of Songs, Ecclesiastes, Lamentations, and Esther) and takes its place among the *Kethubim* (the writings with which the MT ends).

The Setting for the Book

The book of Lamentations focuses on Jerusalem and what happened to it at the hands of the Babylonians in 586. It is among the earliest canonical reflections on the fall of Jerusalem, giving every indication that its author(s) witnessed the events the book deplores. 2 Kings, 2 Chronicles, and Jeremiah all relate the events associated with that catastrophe too and draw their own theological inferences. So does Lamentations. It blames the people as a whole for rebelling against God (Lam 3:42; cf. 5:16b) and the prophets and priests for their part in the sins that led to the destruction of the city and the shedding of the blood of the righteous therein by the Babylonians (4:13).[2] It also condemns the king for infractions not named (2:6). The Edomites, who failed Jerusalem somehow at the time of its fall, come in for their share of the blame as well (4:22). One verse (4:20) highlights the depths of its author's commitment to Jerusalem and the monarchy. Though not absolving the king of guilt in the fall of Jerusalem, the verse speaks of the king as "the breath of our nostrils, YHWH's messiah." The phrase suggests that for its author the monarchy was as essential to Judah's life as breath to a human life.

1. Baruch was Jeremiah's scribe in the book of Jeremiah, hence the placing of the book of Baruch next to that of Jeremiah.

2. The language of 4:13 is difficult, but one can hardly assume it to imply that the priests and prophets were murderers. It is usually understood to mean that because of their sin or because they failed to warn people of Jerusalem against sinning the city was destroyed. I take it to suggest that priests and prophets were involved in the sinfulness of the leaders of the people, with the result that the few righteous people who lived in the city were caught up in a destruction they did not deserve.

The Structure, Integrity, and Authorship of the Book

The book of Lamentations consists of five communal laments (see the discussion of the main genre below) over the fall of Jerusalem.

> Chapter 1 pictures Jerusalem as a widow, mourning her loss, and calling on other nations and on God for pity.
>
> Chapter 2 mourns *God's* destruction of the temple, its environs, and the inhabitants of the city.
>
> Chapter 3 includes a psalm of personal distress (vv. 1-18), an expression of hope for the future (vv. 19-51), and a prayer for vindication (vv. 52-66).
>
> Chapter 4 describes the siege and capture of Jerusalem and places the blame on the sins of the prophets and priests.
>
> Chapter 5 describes the resultant bad times, invokes God's rescue, and ponders God's refusal.

Chapters 1–4 take the form of alphabetical acrostics. In such poetry, the first word of the first line begins with the letter *'aleph,* the first word in the second line with the letter *beth,* and so forth through the alphabet. Since there are twenty-two letters in the Hebrew alphabet, a full alphabetical acrostic would run twenty-two lines (cf. chs. 1, 2, and 4).[3] Lamentations 3 is a triple acrostic, the first three verses beginning with an *'aleph* and continuing through the alphabet, for a total of sixty-six lines/verses. The last chapter of Lamentations, though not an acrostic beyond line 4, also runs twenty-two verses.

What is to be gained by the use of so contrived a genre as an alphabetical acrostic? The simplest answer is "a sense of completeness." When one has gone from A to Z (as we would say), one has covered the subject. That Lamentations does it four times increases the sense that all has been said that can be said about its subject: the fall of Jerusalem. Anything else needs to be left to God. It is perhaps significant that the fifth chapter breaks the mold after the fourth Hebrew letter *daleth* (d). The chapter brings the work to a conclusion on a note of uncertainty (5:20-22).

---

3. We should note that in Lamentations 1 the typical alphabetical order is maintained, in which the sixteenth letter, *'ayin,* precedes the letter *pe.* (Cf. Pss 119: 121-136, where the Hebrew letters are supplied in many English translations.) That order is followed also in Psalms 111 and 112. In Lamentations 2, 3, and 4 the two letters are reversed.

20 Why have you forgotten us unto perpetuity?
  Why have you forsaken us for so many days?
21 Turn us back to you yourself, O YHWH,
    that we may return;
    renew our days as of old,
22 unless you have totally rejected us;
    [unless] you are angry with us beyond measure.

The RSV went so far as to translate v. 22 as questions:

Or hast thou utterly rejected us?
  Art thou exceedingly angry with us?

The point seems clear; the author of Lamentations 5, looking at the ruins of Jerusalem, wonders whether God had given up on Judah. Lamentations 5 itself does not answer that question, but the author of 3:31-33 did not think so and ended the triple acrostic with a typical plea for intervention. Ezekiel, Isaiah 40–66, and Haggai-Zechariah-Malachi sided with that author. Even so, the book of Lamentations itself ends on a note of uncertainty, exhibiting a sense of desertion by humans and by God.[4]

As far as authorship is concerned, the book is anonymous. Tradition ascribed it to Jeremiah, a tradition that probably led to its placement after the book of Jeremiah. The tradition was perhaps based on 2 Chr 35:25, which reads: "Jeremiah also wailed over Josiah." Since Lamentations itself nowhere mentions Josiah, let alone his death at the hands of Pharaoh Neco (2 Kgs 23:29), but laments the fall of Jerusalem, it can hardly be Jeremiah's lament over the dead king. Even so, Lam 4:20, which laments Babylon's deposing the king (Zedekiah), does not lament his death. Whether all five chapters come from the same hand is unclear. Chapter 5 differs from the others not only in that it drops the alphabetical acrostic, but differs in meter as well. A reader critic might dismiss the whole issue of authorship and simply note that the book presents a variety of voices, including a main (male) speaker, the city itself (in chs. 1 and 3), and people in the city (4:15), but God never answers.

4. Norman K. Gottwald, *Studies in the Book of Lamentations,* 2nd ed. SBT 14 (London: SCM, 1962) 52.

The Main Genre in the Book

All five chapters take the form of communal laments.[5] Scholars divide over a more precise designation. Hans-Joachim Kraus calls all five "laments over the ruined sanctuary," which reminds us of their subject matter,[6] while Renate Brandscheidt classifies Lamentations 3 as a legal complaint of the innocent sufferer and the other four as complaints actualizing divine judgment.[7] We may leave aside such precise distinctions of genre and simply recall that laments typically call God's attention to problems, build the case on behalf of the petitioners, and invoke God's intervention.

Special Features Connected with the Study of the Book

The first special feature connected with the book of Lamentations is the meter or rhythm of the laments. While most poetry in the OT has balanced lines with three or four accented syllables in each half line, Lamentations follows a pattern scholars call "Qinah meter." In that pattern, the first half-line has three accents, the second two. Of more importance for readers of English Bibles is that the first half-line is typically the independent thought, the second the dependent thought.[8]

The second special feature is the use of Lamentations in worship. During the Talmudic period (ca. 200-600 C.E.), Lamentations was read privately (*Ta'an.* 30a). After that it came to be read by Jews and Christians alike in public worship. Jews read it on the ninth day of the month of Ab (the fourth month of the Jewish year, usually covering parts of July and August). They did so in services commemorating the fall of Jerusalem. Christian lectionaries often list it for reading at services the last three days of Holy Week. The book's concentration clearly made it appropriate for Jews in remembering the fall of Jerusalem both to the Babylonians and to

5. Some verses address God in the first person singular, but all five laments address God in the first person plural. Generally speaking, form critics classify laments that use both the singular and the plural as communal laments.

6. Hans-Joachim Kraus, *Klagelieder (Threni)*. BKAT 20 (Neukirchen-Vluyn: Neukirchener, 1968) 8-13.

7. Renate Brandscheidt, *Das Buch der Klagelieder*. Geistliche Schriftlesung, Altes Testament 10 (Düsseldorf: Patmos, 1988).

8. Adele Berlin, *Lamentations*. OTL (Louisville: Westminster John Knox, 2002) 2.

the Romans. The death of Jesus in Jerusalem made it suitable for Christian reading during Holy Week.

Basic Emphases in Lamentations

The five laments in this book touch on a variety of topics in connection with explaining and bewailing the fall of Jerusalem. We shall examine four here: the portrayal of Jerusalem as a widow, as a persecuted but penitent sinner, the agony of its defeat at the hands of the Babylonians, and doubt about its future.

Jerusalem the Widow/Wife

The opening lament (1:2-3) personifies Jerusalem as a widow, weeping through the night over her losses. In 5:3 her inhabitants speak of her as their mother. Adele Berlin notes that widows connote the unprotected and disadvantaged, thus projecting a sociological image, not a sexual one. Her children (inhabitants) have gone into exile (1:3), and pilgrims no longer crowd the roads to her desolated temple (1:4). Her defenders (pointing to males and husbands) have failed, and her foes have become her master. In v. 8, however, the image changes. She has sinned grievously, and she is paying dearly. She is depicted as a wife, who has committed adultery.[9] Worst of all, she remembers her former glory, when she herself was a princess (1:7). All she can do is implore God to redress her losses.

Jerusalem the Persecuted Penitent

The third lament (Lam 3:1-18) echoes the complaints of Job (e.g., Job 7:5, 18; 9:34; 16:9; 19:8, 10) and other passages about suffering. This image is gendered as well. As Berlin expresses the matter, "The men suffer in a typically masculine way — they lose power and physical prowess. . . . Chapter 3 is especially vivid in this regard, with its military imagery and its physical brutality. Men also suffer a loss of their role as protector of the family."[10]

9. Berlin, *Lamentations,* 7-8.
10. Berlin, *Lamentations,* 9.

It is significant that the lament attributes both good and bad to YHWH (Lam 3:38), though the "bad" in view here seems to be punishment for sin, not undeserved misfortune. On the one hand, people in Jerusalem had sinned and deserved their punishment. On the other hand, the lamenter is confident of ultimate restoration by God (vv. 22-25, 32-33, 55-66). He is walking a tightrope, recognizing that God had to punish sinners within Jerusalem (v. 42), but insisting that when the people repented (vv. 40-42) God would restore them (vv. 46-66).

The Agony of Defeat

Lamentations contains numerous descriptions of the destruction of the city (e.g., 1:3-6, 10-11; 2:5-10; 4:1-11, 16-19; 5:1-6). These descriptions are substantiated by excavations that lead archaeologists to conclude the whole city experienced destruction.[11] Lamentations pictures its inhabitants searching and begging for food (1:11), its elders sitting on the ground in sackcloth, suffering in silence (2:10), and even its women eating their offspring (2:20). Here the mother image is not symbolic, but real. Their condition is dreadful: instead of being real mothers and feeding their children, they consume them.[12] Compounding the shame and horrors of the city's destruction was the fate of its neighbors. The Edomites had been spared and looked on smugly (4:21), but the day of their punishment would come (4:22). Even those two verses show how badly things were going; the suffering of the city's inhabitants was ameliorated, if at all, only by spite.

Doubt about the Future of Jerusalem

Almost as an afterthought, the concluding verses of Lamentations entertain the possibility that this time Jerusalem and Judah had pushed God too far, that this time they had destroyed their covenant with God. The speaker ponders whether God would indeed redeem God's people again (5:20-22). The city had been destroyed, its temple profaned, and its last king carried

11. Obviously the existence of a major, modern city on the site makes thorough excavation impossible.
12. Berlin, *Lamentations*, 9.

off into exile with numerous other Judeans. One thing was clear: the city did not have the resources to right itself; restitution — if and when it came — would be the work of God.

A Problem Raised by a Study of Lamentations

Lying just beneath the surface of Lamentations is a haunting question: does God keep God's promises? Israel believed that it was God's own people, chosen out of all the nations as God's own (Gen 12:1-9; cf. Deut 7:7-10). The monarchy claimed, and many Judeans seem to have agreed, that God had chosen David and his descendants as the sole, rightful rulers of Judah (2 Samuel 7), and the book of Lamentations seems to accept that view. Now, all of that appeared lost. The speakers did not seem to question whether God *could* keep God's promises, but the closing verses question whether God *would* keep those promises.

Perhaps another way to frame the question is whether there are circumstances under which God would be justified in not keeping promises. Neither the covenant with Abram (Gen 12:2-3, 7) nor with David (2 Sam 7:8-16) mentions grounds for God's terminating either covenant, though the Mosaic covenant is full of stipulations for Israel to obey. Disobeying those laws often brought punishment, but not the severing of the covenant. Even the celebrated case where God threatened to destroy the people and start over with Moses (Exod 32:7-10) ends with Moses persuading God not to do so (32:11-14). Even if God had, Moses himself was a member of that nation, so it would have continued on. The book of Deuteronomy threatens Israel that if it disobeyed God it would lose its land (Deut 28:20-68), but that passage does not threaten Israel with the loss of its covenant relationship with God.

Perhaps we should remember two points. First, Lamentations does not actually say God did abandon Israel; an author only wondered in the book's last verses — in the face of the destruction of Jerusalem — whether God had abandoned it, or would. Second, nowhere does the OT say God would do so. In other words, it leaves its reader squarely on the hot seat: God at times has reason to break God's covenants or promises; it is only the nature of God that offers the answer whether God will break those covenants/promises. A wise course of action would be not to push God.

Summary

The book of Lamentations contains five laments that describe the fall of Jerusalem to Babylon, express the agony the people feel for their loss, and ponder their future with God. The authors are quite convinced that Israel deserved the punishment it received. The future lay in God's hands.

THE BOOK OF BARUCH

Baruch, the son of Neriah, is known to readers of Jeremiah as a secretary of the prophet who appears in Jeremiah 32, 36, 43 and 45.[13] A famous account in Jeremiah 36 has Jeremiah dictate his messages to Baruch, who then reads them in public. They are eventually read to King Jehoiakim by a man named Jehudi. The king shows his utter contempt for the prophet and his prophecies by cutting them off the scroll, two or three columns at a time, as Jehudi reads them. Jehoiakim then throws the shreds onto a brazier to burn so he can warm his hands on a cold day. Jeremiah 43:3 records a different occasion on which other men, upset by the preaching of Jeremiah, accuse Baruch of inciting Jeremiah against them. In that text one might infer that Jeremiah was the spokesman for Baruch rather than Baruch's being the scribe for Jeremiah, but this is the only such place the text reads that way. It is possible, instead, that Jeremiah used Baruch because he was a well-known scribe. Either way, Baruch's abiding fame as a scribe was secured by his mention in the book of Jeremiah, and the book of Baruch builds on that relationship.

Introduction to the Book and Its Times

The Setting of the Book

The book purports to be the work of Baruch, which he wrote in exile in Babylon "in the fifth year, on the seventh day of the month at the time the Babylonians captured Jerusalem and burned it with fire." This would have

---

13. Interestingly enough, Jer 51:59 mentions Seriah, son of Neriah as a scribe used by Jeremiah. He and Baruch were apparently brothers. Perhaps Jeremiah used others too.

been in the year 586. The book claims it was prepared to read to Jeconiah, the king of Judah who was taken to Babylon in the first deportation in 597. The sixth chapter, also known as the Letter of Jeremiah, has its own superscription and appears originally to have been an independent work. It will be treated separately below.

The Structure, Integrity, and Authorship of the Book

The book of Baruch consists of two halves roughly equal in length: the first (Bar 1:1–3:8) in prose, the second (3:9–5:9) in poetry. Each half also consists of two parts. The prose first half contains an introduction and narrative about the writing and subsequent reading of the book (1:1-14) and a prayer of confession (1:15–3:8). The poetic second half contains a salute to wisdom (3:9–4:4) and a series of admonitions (4:5–5:9). The first half of the book fits better with the claim that it was a letter written by Baruch to Jeconiah than does the latter half, though scribes were associated with wisdom literature.

According to 1:1, Baruch, the son of Neriah, the secretary of Jeremiah the prophet, wrote the book, but that ascription is probably not correct. There is no biblical evidence that Baruch went to Babylon, though a tradition to that effect did develop. Instead, Jer 43:6-7 says he accompanied Jeremiah to Egypt. In addition, the author makes a historical error unthinkable for a sixth-century exile. In Bar 1:2 he dates the book "in the fifth year," presumably the fifth year after the destruction of Jerusalem in 587/6, but 1:8 shows remarkable confusion with its talk about returning temple vessels to Jerusalem during the life of Nebuchadnezzar (d. 562). Ezra 5:14-15 specifically attributes that act to Sheshbazzar at the end of the exile. Also Bar 1:11-12 treats Belshazzar as Nebuchadnezzar's son (as does Daniel 5), when in fact he was the son of Nabonidus, the last king of Babylon (556-539). So, it seems likely that the author of the book of Baruch lived some time after the sixth century, and his identity is lost to posterity. It is probable that the book is the product of several authors, because its mixed contents suggest it was compiled from various sources and edited into one piece.

When it was written is not certain either. If — as scholars used to argue — the poetic half, whole or in part, was written in Greek, that would likely place at least the editing of the book subsequent to the acquisition of Judah by Alexander the Great in 332. That view, however, has been contested recently, and it seems likely that the book was originally written in

Hebrew in its entirety. Scholars often maintain that 1:15–3:8 utilizes Daniel 9, written ca. 165, but the confession in Baruch is considerably longer than the one in Daniel 9, which itself draws on typical prayers perhaps available to the author of Baruch as well. That author does, however, seem to know and use the wisdom poem from Job 28 and the equation of torah and wisdom known elsewhere first in Sir 24:23. This last mentioned text points to a date for Baruch ca. 200 B.C.E. or later.

The ascription of the book to the scribe Baruch in Babylon does, however, suggest a plausible place and community for its origin. It is obviously an edited compilation of shorter pieces, and scribes are nothing if not editors and compilers. Furthermore, the book — at least its opening — takes the point of view of someone outside of Palestine, in Babylon to be specific. It even makes the bold move of claiming that Baruch was there and implies that he, not Sheshbazzar, returned the silver vessels taken by Nebuchadnezzar from the temple to their rightful place (1:1-9). Who else besides a group of pious scribes living in Babylon would nurse the tradition that Baruch went there or suggest that he was the benefactor of the temple?

The Main Genres in the Book

The book begins as a narrative (1:1-14), but then switches to other genres. Also within its first half one finds a penitential prayer confessing the guilt of the people (1:15–2:10) and a prayer for forgiveness (2:11–3:8). The second half of the book opens with a song of praise over the wisdom expounded in Torah (3:9–4:4), with overtones of Job 28 in 3:15. Next (4:5-29) comes a lament over the fall of Jerusalem in a way similar to Lamentations. Finally (4:30–5:9), the book contains a promise of salvation similar to those in Second Isaiah, opening with the signature command "Fear not." In some manuscripts the book concludes with another letter, purportedly by Jeremiah to the exiles in Babylon. That letter seems to have been attached secondarily to Baruch.

A Special Issue concerning the Book

A special issue alluded to above is the language in which the book was written. It was preserved in Greek, of course, as part of the LXX. It exists also in three Latin versions, one of which Jerome used in the Vulgate. In addition, there are Syriac, Coptic, and Ethiopic versions, reflecting the book's popularity in Orthodox churches. Still, a good case can be made that it was originally written in Hebrew, though only a few such fragments remain — at Qumran. A study of vocabulary, syntax, and style suggests that 1:1–3:8 are a translation from Hebrew. That seems likely for 3:9–4:4 and even more probable for 4:5–5:9, based on odd Greek phrasings that suggest (mis)translations from Hebrew.[14]

Basic Emphases in Baruch

The genres contained in the book suggest the basic emphases. The opening narrative (1:1-14) exhibits a concern for Jerusalem and the temple, even for Judeans in Babylon. The narrative depicts them as loyal to the temple and its services from the time of the exile on. The following confession of guilt (1:15–2:10) and prayer for forgiveness (2:11–3:8), with its explicit reference to Moses (2:28), exhibit an attitude of dependence on and trust in God to protect the faithful, even while living in the Diaspora. The combination of wisdom with torah (in 3:9–4:4) sets out a defense of the inherited religious beliefs and practices that the author wishes to offer over against the claims of Greek culture. Once again the text emphasizes that Israel's misfortune was a sign of its own moral failings, not the weakness of God. The final sections (4:5–5:9) hold out hope for members of the Diaspora to return home.

A Problem Raised by a Study of Baruch

One question raised by a study of Baruch is that of canonicity. Christians have long held that the book is canonical, with only Protestants dissenting. Nor do Jews accept its canonicity. This issue is even more pointed than with the so-called "additions" to Daniel (chs. 3, 13 and 14), where at least the other chapters are accepted by Jews and Christians — Protestant, Cath-

---

14. See Odil Hannes Steck, *Das apokryphe Baruchbuch: Studien zu Rezeption und Konzentration "kanonischer" Überlieferung.* FRLANT 160 (Göttingen: Vandenhoeck & Ruprecht, 1993) 249-53, 139, 203-4.

olic, and Orthodox. Even so, the thought expressed in the chapter on Daniel also applies here. The determination of what constitutes books with the power to point people to God is one that humans may well answer differently. What inspires one person, congregation, or religious body may leave another uninspired. Contents of the canon are perceived and adopted, not handed down by God.

Summary

The book of Baruch was a composite of traditions set in Babylon, but designed to encourage Israelites everywhere that God, not the Greek conquerors, was still in charge of their destiny even though Israel's moral failures led to the exile.

THE LETTER OF JEREMIAH

The sixth chapter of Baruch in Roman Catholic Bibles is a letter ostensibly written by Jeremiah to exiles en route to Babylon after the fall of Jerusalem to Nebuchadnezzar, king of Babylon. Its obvious biblical parallel is Jeremiah 29, in which the prophet addresses Judeans already there, warning them to prepare for a long exile. The Letter of Jeremiah, however, purports to warn the deportees while en route of the temptation to commit idolatry once they arrived in Babylonia. Though originally an independent document, most likely written in Hebrew or Aramaic, a fragment of it is attested in the first-century B.C.E. Greek papyrus 7Q2 from Qumran. The Letter was attached to Baruch, however, as early as some manuscripts of the Old Latin translation.[15] When Jerome translated the Vulgate (around the turn of the fifth century C.E.), he used such a manuscript and the connection between the two documents was solidified.

---

15. "Old Latin" is a designation for Latin translations of the Bible, which began perhaps as early as 180 C.E. See Arthur Vööbus, "Versions: Latin," *ISBE,* 4:969-74.

Introduction to the Book and Its Times

The setting for the book has already been mentioned: Jeremiah wrote from Jerusalem in 586 to the exiles about temptations they would face in Babylon. Its structure includes an introduction (vv. 1-7) and ten warnings against idolatry, each ending with some kind of denial of the reality of the gods of the Babylonians. Given its brevity (73 verses) and single subject, its unity is not an issue. The author appears to have been someone conversant with biblical polemics against idolatry such as Deut 4:27-28; Isa 44:9-20; Jer 10:1-16; and Pss 115:4; 135:15-18.[16] The book's main genre is logical argument, building the case that idolatry is illogical and useless.

The Basic Emphasis of the Letter of Jeremiah

The Letter is a "pamphlet concerning the groundlessness of fear of idols, [which were] equated with their images."[17] This combination is an old trick, widely attested in the prophets. The idea was to show the lack of intelligence, power, mobility, etc. of molten or carved images as proof of the lack of the same by the gods they represented. A devotee of those gods might well have protested that the images only represented the gods and were useful only as what we would call "visual aids" to worship. Ancient peoples knew perfectly well that the images were made by humans and could not possibly be real gods, but a number of authors of the Hebrew Bible seemed to have thought that the distinction between a false god and an image of that false god was irrelevant. They frequently, therefore, had a good time ridiculing other people for "worshipping" those images.

A Problem Raised by a Study of the Letter of Jeremiah

This pamphlet does raise the question of whether the use of images in religious worship is necessarily idolatrous. One must recall in this connection that the Second Commandment forbade making graven or carved images (Exod 20:4-5) and bowing down to them, and another law (Exod 34:17)

---

16. Otto Kaiser, *The Old Testament Apocrypha* (Peabody: Hendrickson, 2004) 63.
17. Kaiser, *The Old Testament Apocrypha*, 62.

forbade making molten images. Christians, however, have routinely used two- and three-dimensional figures as aids in worship, and sometimes attach great power or at least significance to those figures. Are they wrong to do so? I do not think so.

Perhaps we would do well to ask what the commandments warned ancient Israel against. The answer seems to be "worshipping anything but God." Images of other gods obviously functioned to direct worship toward those gods, but it is that worship which is idolatrous. The biblical injunctions may also serve to remind us that we should take care in how we think about God. We ought not symbolize God by things that are beneath us, but we can only express/depict God in terms of that which we know here on earth. Thus, however we depict — or conceive of — God may best be done in terms of the perfection of that which we recognize as best. Perhaps *our* temptation is to absolutize the ways we *think* about God. If we think of God as father, husband, or king, which the Bible certainly does, we need to be constantly on guard lest we divinize masculinity and suppose that God really is male. Surely what we really mean is that there are ways in which God relates to us that resemble but perfect the ways that fathers, husbands, and kings relate to children, wives, and subjects. Unless we want to try to conceive of God as the absence of any and all points of similarity to the human and earthly, we will depict God in earthly ways.

Summary

The Letter of Jeremiah is a 73-verse pamphlet that attacks the worship of anything but God, the God revealed in the Hebrew Bible.

Questions for Reflection

1. Does God punish whole populations for sins and failures of their religious and political leaders? Why or why not? Do leaders sometimes sin or simply make mistakes that have serious, adverse effects on people? Are unintended consequences always the result of sin? If not, what are some examples from biblical or modern times of such consequences? What actions or events get blamed on God that might have some other explanation?

2. Are there national behaviors for which Western peoples or nations should re-pent? If so, what are some?
3. Does God ever just give up on people? What reasons can you give for your an-swer?
4. What view of prophecy seems to underlie Baruch's presentation of Jere-miah's predicting what the exiles in Babylon would face? What would you add to that view in constructing your own view of biblical prophecy?

For Further Reading

Berlin, Adele. *Lamentations*. OTL. Louisville: Westminster John Knox, 2002. Emphasizes literary and gendered insights without eschewing historical and form criticism.

Gottwald, Norman K. *Studies in the Book of Lamentations*. 2nd ed. SBT 14. London: SCM, 1962. A collection of six studies on the acrostic, the type of literature to which Lamentations belongs, and the theology and signifi-cance of the book.

Hillers, Delbert R. *Lamentations*. AB 7A. Garden City: Doubleday, 1972. New translation, introduction, and commentary on the Hebrew text of Lam-entations.

Kaiser, Otto. *The Old Testament Apocrypha: An Introduction*. Peabody: Hen-drickson, 2004. Chapter 4 offers a brief introduction to both Baruch and the Letter of Jeremiah.

Provan, Iain W. *Lamentations*. NCBC. Grand Rapids: Wm. B. Eerdmans, 1991. A critically aware, balanced, and readable commentary on Lamentations by a widely-respected OT scholar.

CHAPTER 7

Ezekiel

Ezekiel was a priest taken from Jerusalem to Babylon as an exile along with King Jehoiachin in 597 B.C.E. in the first deportation. His career seems to have lasted from the fifth year after that event (1:2) until at least the twenty-seventh year (29:17). Whatever his status might have been in Jerusalem (the book calls him a priest in 1:3), he lived as a peripheral functionary in Babylon, given his status as an exile. He spoke to the exiles with him in Babylon, though most of what he said dealt with the fall of Jerusalem and his vision of its restoration. The book that bears his name opens with a vision of God (Ezekiel 1–3), moves on to anticipate the fall of Jerusalem and the destruction of the temple (chs. 8–11), explains why God had punished God's people (ch. 20), and predicts a new day for Israel with a new temple (chs. 40–48).

Introduction to the Book and Its Times

The Place of the Book in the Canon

In the MT Ezekiel follows Isaiah and Jeremiah and precedes the Book of the Twelve. In the rabbinic work *B. Bat.* 14b (ca. 180 C.E.), Ezekiel stands second, behind Jeremiah, and precedes Isaiah and the Twelve. In the LXX it stands between the deutero-jeremianic books (Baruch, Lamentations, and the Letter of Jeremiah) and the book of Daniel.

The Setting of the Book

The time frame for the book is between approximately 593 (the fifth year after the deportation of Jehoiachin mentioned in 1:2) and 571 (the latest date supplied; cf. 29:17). The first place to be mentioned was "the land of the Chaldeans," Babylonia. Babylon, of course, was its capital. Situated on the Euphrates River roughly 50 miles from modern-day Baghdad, it was a splendid walled city with a great culture, including a high degree of scientific achievement. From the second millennium on, Babylonians developed mathematics (including quadratic equations and a lunar calendar), astronomy, astrology, rudimentary medicine, and knowledge of some chemicals and herbs.

Babylonian religion too was highly developed, but was polytheistic. At the head of its pantheon were three gods. The first was Anu, who was so high above humans they had little contact with him. Next to him was his powerful son Marduk, the chief god of Babylon. The third was Ea, the god of water and wisdom. Following these three were the sun-god Shamash, the moon-god Sin, and the goddess of war and love, Ishtar. The remaining gods ranked beneath these six, with the city of Babylon containing temples to forty-three different divinities.

Archaeologists have uncovered remains of houses in and around Babylon. Country homes surrounding the city were often set in irrigated gardens, but houses within towns were crowded together and made of mud brick. Almost all had an open courtyard in the middle. Roofs were made of palm wood and covered with reeds and leaves. Stairs leading from the courtyards provided access to the roofs.

Ezekiel specifies that he "was among the exiles beside the Chebar River" (1:1). Archaeologists have, in fact, discovered some Hebrew names among Babylonian records, and the Chebar (technically a canal) is mentioned in two fifth-century texts that locate it near the ancient city of Nippur,[1] which lay some 93 miles southwest of Babylon. In the third and

---

1. Ezekiel 3:15 mentions Tel-abib, which means "Hill of Ears," as in ears of barley. Abib is also the name of the month (roughly March/April) in which the Passover and Exodus are said to have occurred and in which the feast of Passover is observed. Walther Zimmerli suggests that the site's name may have been taken from a Babylonian phrase meaning "hill of the flood" that designated an uninhabited mound of an old city. He also suggests that Tel-abib probably lay near Chebar/Nippur; *Ezekiel 1*. Hermeneia (Philadelphia: Fortress, 1979) 139.

second millennia B.C.E., it was the site of important Babylonian priests at a temple to Enlil, who represented the atmosphere, wind, and storm and who ruled over the assembly of the gods. Archaeologists have discovered thousands of ancient texts at Nippur, including economic documents (e.g., bills of sale, wills, records of court decisions), historical documents, and even lexical lists. The find also included more than 4000 tablets containing myths, hymns, epic poems, laments, and proverbs, texts important in understanding Babylonian religion.[2] The city waned in importance over time, however, and scholars speculate that the Babylonians might have settled Jews (and perhaps others) in the ancient city as a way to repopulate it.

Nevertheless, 1:1 suggests that communal religious life was possible in Tel-abib. Still, the exiles were forced to live in the land of Babylonia, aware that they were foreign and subservient. Their anger could boil over in thoughts like those in Psalm 137, where some exiles longed for brutal revenge.

The other place that plays a major role in the book was Jerusalem. Several of Ezekiel's reports of visions depict the city as full of sin and deserving of God's impending punishment. The prophet's message comes across, therefore, as a "tale of two cities," a tale of punishment for Babylon/Babylonia and for Jerusalem, but ultimately of salvation for the latter.

The Structure, Integrity, and Authorship of the Book

At least three features lend structure to the book of Ezekiel. The first is the pattern predictions of doom (against Judah in chs. 4–24 and against foreign nations in chs. 25–32) followed by predictions of hope (chs. 33–48), both preceded by Ezekiel's call vision and commissioning (chs. 1–3). The second feature is a series of three visions termed "visions of God." The first was the call vision in ch. 1. The second appears in chs. 8–11, which repeat phrases from the opening vision and depict God's leaving the temple (11:22-23). The third is the lengthy vision of the future temple with which the book closes (chs. 40–48), in which God returns to the temple (43:1-5).[3]

The last structural feature is the series of dates usually giving the day, month, and year in fifteen passages.

---

2. Paul W. Gaebelein, Jr., "Nippur," *ISBE*, 3:541-43.
3. One should note that 33:1-9 contains language echoing Ezekiel's call vision.

Passage	Day	Month	Year
1:1	5	4	30
1:2–3:15	5	4	5
3:16-27 or 3:16–5:17[4]	12	4	5
8:1-11:25	5	6	6
20:1-49	10	5	7
24:1-27	10	10	9
26:1-21	1	?	11
29:1-16	12	10	10
29:17-21	1	1	27
30:20-26	7	1	11
31:1-18	1	3	11
32:1-16	1	12	12
32:17-32	15	?	12
33:21-22	5	10	12
40:1–48:35	10	?	25

A glance at the dates shows that they follow chronological order with but two anomalies. The first (1:1-3) is the opening date, which specifies "the thirtieth year." Verse 1 is in the first person singular, whereas vv. 2-3 are in the third person. Since v. 4 resumes a first person narrative, it would appear that it originally followed v. 1, and that vv. 2-3 were added. Their apparent function is to identify the "thirtieth year" (of Ezekiel's life?) mentioned in v. 1 with the fifth year of the exile of King Jehoiachin in v. 2. Beginning with 8:1 the remaining dates seem to have the beginning of the exile in view. That conclusion is established by the date given in 33:21, which states that Jerusalem had just fallen. To be sure, that date probably should read "eleventh" year not twelfth,[5] since Jerusalem fell in 586. Regardless, the chronology began with the year Jehoiachin (and Ezekiel) went to Babylon in exile and was anchored by the reference to the fall of Jerusalem.

The second anomaly is the dates in 29:1, 17 and possibly 30:20 (unless the missing number in the date for Ezekiel 26 was higher than 1), since they move from the eleventh year to the tenth, then the twenty-seventh, and fi-

4. This passage does not contain the full formula day, month, and year; it merely states that the vision occurred seven days later than the formula in 1:2–3:15.

5. Victor R. Gold, "Ezekiel," *The Oxford Annotated Bible* (New York: Oxford, 1991) 1043, n. on 33:21-22.

nally back to the eleventh. Obviously something disturbed the chronological arrangement which obtained otherwise. What overrode it was the sequence of doom versus Judah (chs. 1–24) — doom versus foreign nations (chs. 25–32) — hope (chs. 33–48). The predictions of doom in ch. 29 were moved out of historical sequence to accommodate that scheme. Whatever the redactional history of the book of Ezekiel, that sequence — once attained — remained firm.

The integrity of the book was seriously challenged during the twentieth century. Scholars pointed to unevenness in the text and concluded that the text went through a succession of revisions, either by Ezekiel himself or a school associated with him. One need look no further than Ezek 1:4-28 to see an example of this type of work. Walther Zimmerli analyses that vision as follows. According to him the first part of the vision originally consisted of 1:4-5, 6b, 11b, to which v. 6a was added as a gloss. Verses 7-11a entered as an addition concerned with the faces of the creatures, except that v. 9a reveals itself as a still later gloss. Verse 12 came later too, as did vv. 13-14. Likewise vv. 15-21 reveal themselves to be a series of secondary expansions. Verse 22, however, belonged to the original vision, but was secondarily expanded by a series of additions in vv. 23-25. Finally, vv. 26-28 conclude the original vision, except that v. 27a was a gloss.[6]

Though Zimmerli's analysis focused on details within the text, such as variations in the gender in suffixes, more recent scholars have been less willing to divide up the text and plead for a more unified composition, though not necessarily one author. Margaret Odell says simply that "The book of Ezekiel reflects a degree of literary coherence unmatched in the canon of biblical prophets."[7] Accordingly, we shall approach Ezekiel as a unified work. How much derived from the hand(s) of one or more editors and how much from Ezekiel himself may remain open, but his persona looms over the book. The use of first person singular narratives, descriptions of prophetic actions, and occasional personal notes (like the death of his wife) leave the impression that the prophet wrote much of the work.

6. Zimmerli, *Ezekiel 1*, 100-6.
7. Margaret S. Odell, *Ezekiel.* SHBC (Macon: Smyth & Helwys, 2005) 1.

Main Genres of the Book

The first genre one encounters in Ezekiel is the vision. Visions appear in ch. 1 (in connection with Ezekiel's call), chs. 8–11 (in connection with Ezekiel's justification for the fall of Jerusalem), ch. 37 (the "dry bones" vision, anticipating Judah's return to Canaan), and chs. 40–48 (concerning the new temple and environs and God's return). That is a total of 14 chapters in whole or part and constitutes the largest amount of vision material of any book or collection among the prophets. By way of comparison we note that Daniel 8–12 reports visions, as does Zechariah 1–6, though other genres also appear in Zechariah 1, 2, and 6. Otherwise, visions are fairly scarce in the Hebrew Bible. Isaiah's commissioning vision and the visions of Zechariah appear in connection with the temple, as do all the visions in Ezekiel except the vision of the dry bones.

It is probably a safe guess that the seeing of visions was a practice approved by temple officials from the eighth through the sixth centuries, and the visions may have had to conform to certain standards. The depiction of God's returning to the temple in 43:2-5 precedes the giving of a long series of laws about its use, its altar, festivals, and property in 43:6–46:24, material that would be equally at home as a law code in the Pentateuch.

The most important vision is that of storm theophany in 1:4-28a (cf. 1 Kgs 22:19-23; Ps 18:7-15; Isa 6:1-13).[8] YHWH is seated on a throne in heaven, surrounded by thick clouds, lightning, and brilliance. The prophet couches his language in similes. He describes heaven as "something like a dome" and the throne of God as "something like a throne" that consisted of "something like a sapphire." God's own appearance was "something that seemed like a human form." In addition, the prophet mentions "something like gleaming amber" above something that "looked like loins." The prophet was no literalist; he pushed his language as hard as he could to describe the indescribable. Readers of Ezekiel and the rest of the Bible would do well to recognize that all talk about God employs metaphorical language.

Possibly the best-known vision is that of the dry bones in 37:1-14. In that vision "the hand of God" guides Ezekiel to a valley full of bones. God asks the prophet whether the bones could live again. In Israelite culture the presumed answer would have been in the negative, but Ezekiel defers to God. God commands the prophet to prophesy to the bones, which he does.

8. Odell, *Ezekiel,* 18-21.

The bones come together as skeletons once more and then take on sinews and skin. Again at God's command Ezekiel prophesies to the *ruah,* a Hebrew word meaning "breath, wind, spirit." He commands it to come from the four winds and blow or breathe on the bones, which then came alive. What does this vision mean? Ezekiel himself interprets it, saying that the bones that come to life are the nation Israel, which will return to Judah. In other words, the vision employs the image of *individual* resurrection, but uses it to predict a *national* resurrection, the return of the exiles. It is not clear what Ezekiel might have said about individual resurrection.

A second genre is the report of symbolic actions. In Ezekiel 4–5, the prophet sets up a brick to represent a city, in particular Jerusalem, then places toy siege implements around it to depict the siege of the city. Next God tells him to lie on his left side for 390 days to depict the punishment of Samaria (which fell to the Assyrians in 722) for the same number of years. Then, God says for the prophet to lie on his right side for 40 days to depict the punishment of Jerusalem for that number of years.

Three comments are in order. (1) Playing with war toys is strange behavior for an adult prophet. (2) The numbers do not seem to correlate with any improvement of affairs for either Israel or Judah. If one subtracts 390 from 722, one arrives at 332, about the time Alexander the Great took control of the Levant from the Persians. It is difficult to see that as an improvement, and even more difficult to imagine that Ezekiel had that specific outcome in mind. If one subtracts 40 from 586, the resulting date of 546 is still in the Babylonian period, though Cyrus overthrew the Babylonians in 539. (3) Even if one supposes Ezekiel had in mind the end of the Babylonian captivity (which seems likely), it is difficult to square his 40 years with the 70 years predicted in the book of Jeremiah (cf. Jer 25:11-12; 29:10). We would likely be better off to understand Ezekiel (and Jeremiah) to have meant that all those in Babylon would remain captive the rest of their lives, as Samaria had remained subject to Assyria. In fact, Ezekiel 4–5 does not mention an end to the exile, but paints instead a portrait of its hardship.

Ezekiel 12:1-20 depicts the prophet playing the role of someone going into exile with the baggage one would take for such a trip. It would actually make a great deal of sense to see this as an act performed by Ezekiel in Jerusalem before the first deportation, but there is no hint in the rest of the book that Ezekiel had played a prophetic role prior to 597. In any case, its meaning was clear to inhabitants of Jerusalem: they were facing exile. A third act is mentioned in 24:15-27, where the prophet is instructed not to mourn the death of his wife. Further, the people are told to take an object lesson from his behavior and not mourn the profanation of Jerusalem by the Babylonians.

A third genre used with great skill in Ezekiel is the allegory, which appears in 15:1-8; 16:1-63; 17:1-21; 23:1-49; 24:1-14; and 31:1-18. Of these, two stand out. Ezekiel 16:1-63 allegorizes Israel as a foundling God rescued from certain death (in Egypt) and reared to be God's spouse, only to see her turn into a prostitute (i.e., worship other gods). Ruin (the exile) would follow, but God would restore the fortunes not only of Judah but also of Israel (called Samaria) and Edom (called Sodom). Similarly, in 23:1-49 the allegory of the sisters Oholah (Samaria/Israel) and Oholibah (Jerusalem/ Judah) portray the two as unfaithful to God by virtue of making political alliances with other countries instead of trusting God.

The next two genres may be paired. The prophecy of disaster appears in chs. 14, 20, 21, 22, most of 25–32, and 35. This last-mentioned chapter condemns Edom as part of its portrayal of the future good God has in store for Judah. The prophecy of salvation appears mostly in chs. 33–48, which depict a time in the future when God would reverse the fortunes of Judah. Another example of this genre appears in 28:24-26, where it concludes the first half of Ezekiel's prophecies of doom against foreign nations. These verses highlight the difference between the future of Judah and that of the nations.

Ezekiel also uses a sixth genre, the lament, to good effect in 19:1-9, 10-14; 27:1-36; 28:11-19; 32:1-16. Laments normally express contrition over unfortunate events and perhaps even include complaints to God about things that have gone wrong. The last three listed laments, however, purport to bewail the misfortune that had befallen Tyre and Egypt, but are actually used ironically, even sarcastically, since it is unlikely either the prophet or his audience was saddened at punishment falling on those two countries.

A Special Feature of the Book

Much of the book of Ezekiel is written in the first person singular. That is unusual in the prophetic corpus, where even single accounts are rare. In Isaiah 1–39, for example, only the report of Isaiah's commission (Isa 6:1-13) and the narrative in Isaiah 8 could be considered autobiographical. Isaiah

5:1-7 employs the first person for the female speaker with which the passage opens and for God, who speaks in vv. 5-6. Even the account of the prophet's audience with Ahaz in Isaiah 7 and the narrative of the invasion of Sennacherib in chs. 36–39 speak of Isaiah in the third person. The book of Jeremiah contains much narrative about the prophet, but nothing autobiographical. Only one of the two accounts of Hosea's marriage uses the first person, and that for only three verses (Hos 3:1-3). Daniel 7–12 uses the first person singular, with Daniel as the "I." Daniel 4, however, also employs the first person, but purports to contain the words of Nebuchadnezzar, not Daniel.

Daniel 4, though later than the book of Ezekiel, points to a typical feature of first person writing in the ancient world: usually the subject of such accounts is a royal figure. Odell reminds us that royal inscriptions typically include three parts: a king's self-introduction, an account of his past deeds, and a list of laws or an announcement of a king's plans (e.g., building plans). She also notes that the structure of Ezekiel follows that general pattern, with an introductory vision of YHWH (chs. 1–3), a report of God's efforts to establish rulership over Judah (chs. 4–39), and an account of restoring the temple, the land, and the people of Israel (chs. 40–48).[9] That is not to say, of course, that Ezekiel had royal aspirations, only that royal inscriptions would have been well known to him in Babylonia and might have contributed to his choice of the first person.

Introduction to the Prophet

Ezekiel, whose name means "God strengthens," introduces himself as one of the exiles living along the River Chebar. An editor filled out that introduction by identifying the date given in v. 1 ("thirtieth year") with the fifth year of the exile of King Jehoiachin and by giving the prophet's name, his father's name, and the fact that he was a priest. If the reference to the "thirtieth year" in v. 1 is an indication of the prophet's age, he was about 25 when he was taken to Babylonia. His public career lasted at least until 571, the twenty-seventh year of his exile to Babylonia (29:17) and the latest date provided in the book. It could, of course, have lasted longer, since many of the chapters are undated.

9. Odell, *Ezekiel,* 15.

In addition, we know that Ezekiel was married, but that his wife died in Babylonia (24:15-27). The prophet did not mourn publicly, however, under what he took to be divine instruction. Rather, God told him to tell the people who came to visit him that God was about to destroy Jerusalem, but that they were not to mourn that calamity. They were, instead, to recognize the power of God. The passage also mentions (vv. 25-27) that on the day Jerusalem fell someone would bring him that news. Those verses anticipate 33:21-22, which says that one who escaped the destruction delivered the news of Jerusalem's fall. God loosened Ezekiel's tongue to prophesy to the man, as God promised in 24:27. Both of these verses echo 3:25-27 and point toward deliberate editing designed to tie the book together.

Finally, mention should be made of Ezekiel's psychological state. It is probably not possible, and I am not qualified in any case, to examine Ezekiel's mental stability.[10] (The difficulty of such an examination lies, among other things, in the fact that the account of his actions and words are conveyed through other hands. That is, we see Ezekiel through the eyes of at least one editor.) Even so, one is permitted to observe that a man who describes turbulent visions of God (chs. 1–3), who sets up a model of a besieged city and lies beside it 390+40 days or any serious fraction thereof (chs. 4–5), who reports being carried by the hair of his head from Babylonia to Jerusalem (8:3), and who refuses to mourn the death of his wife (24:15-27) is acting peculiarly. I would not be likely to hear him preach, and if I did I would not likely take him seriously. I fear, however, that I would thereby fail to hear what God had to say.

Basic Emphases in Ezekiel

Ezekiel features five basic emphases. The first, Ezekiel's prophetic call, has already been mentioned and may be dealt with fairly quickly. His vision of God (1:4-28) is followed by God's commissioning the prophet to preach to the rebellious people of Judah. Ezekiel 3 tells of God's extending a scroll to the prophet and commanding Ezekiel to eat it, thus ingesting the word of

---

10. For such a study, see D. J. Halperin, who speaks of Ezekiel's unconscious but overwhelming anger against women and a deeply buried rage against males due to physical abuse during his childhood; *Seeking Ezekiel: Text and Psychology* (University Park: Pennsylvania State University Press, 1993) 207-8.

God. The prophet notes that the scroll had writing on it on the front and back. In other words, it was complete; it held all God wanted the prophet to say. Its contents could be summarized as "lamentation, mourning, and woe." It is no wonder, then, that God told Ezekiel to anticipate resistance. Who — hundreds of miles from home and in need of being cheered up — would want to hear such a message? God construed this impending reaction, however, as pure hardheadedness. Consequently, God had made the prophet's forehead "as hard as flint." He could go "head-to-head" with his audience without backing down.

The Fall of Jerusalem

The second basic theme of Ezekiel is its prediction of the fall of Jerusalem. The gist of Ezekiel's early message is that Jerusalem would fall to the Babylonians. As mentioned above, Ezekiel 4–5 relates a prophetic action in which Ezekiel was to lie before a brick with toy figures of siege weapons around it to symbolize the siege of Jerusalem by Nebuchadnezzar. The vision in chs. 8–11 explains why that would happen. In that vision Ezekiel describes a clairvoyant visit in which he moves from an outer gate of the temple to its entrance, seeing the various sins being committed there. Next (ch. 9), he sees God send "a man dressed in linen" through the city of Jerusalem to mark the forehead of any who repented over the sins of Jerusalem, and six more "men" slaughter those without a mark.[11] Then (10:1-8), God tells the "man in linen" to scatter burning coals over the city, signaling the city's imminent ruin. Finally, (10:18-19) God leaves the sanctuary of the temple and stops on the mount east of the city (11:22-23), leaving it unprotected against the Babylonian army, which destroys it. Ezekiel 20 continues the theme by reminding the people of Judah of their history of worshipping other gods and predicting an end to their worship in Jerusalem (cf. chs. 21, 22, and 24). There were no "good old days" in Israel's past; its people had sinned from day one. Chapter 20 does include, however, the positive note that after punishing Jerusalem God would restore the people in a new "exodus" (vv. 33-38).

In addition to the allegories of Judah's infidelity to God in chs. 16 and

11. The "man in linen" and the six "men" are clearly angels. Ezekiel did not mean literally, however, that angels would destroy Jerusalem; that fell to the Babylonians.

23, other allegories add to the discussion of the fall of Jerusalem. Ezekiel 15:1-5 offers the "allegory of the vine." There the prophet draws a lesson from the uselessness of vines pruned from a vinestock. Such vines cannot even be used for fuel, and Judah is just as useless. Ezekiel 17:1-10 depicts a great eagle (= Nebuchadnezzar) that comes to Lebanon (= Judah) and cuts off the top of its cedar tree (= the Davidic king), indeed its topmost shoot (= Jehoiachin). Nebuchadnezzar then transplants the shoot to a "city of merchants" (= Babylon) in a "land of trade" (= Babylonia). In place of the top shoot (vv. 5-6), the eagle plants another seed (= Zedekiah) in "Lebanon," where the vine would begin to grow. Another great eagle (= Psammetichus II, ruler of Egypt 594-588) would lead the new seed/vine in revolt against Nebuchadnezzar (vv. 7-8). Its end is predictable: the east wind (= Nebuchadnezzar) would destroy the new seed/vine (v. 10).

Individual Accountability

Third, the thinking exhibited in the allegories obviously depends on a notion of collective responsibility. Kings sinned and received punishment, but other people, perhaps some of them innocent, died in siege warfare or went into exile with the kings. What is more, Ezekiel and his contemporaries were aware that sometimes the behavior of the head of a household had disastrous effects on the whole family. Conversely, it was also true that men inherited their property and — most likely — learned their trade from their fathers. Thus to a degree far beyond what most moderns experience, individuals might well reap the rewards or failures of their fathers and even earlier ancestors. In their context it was easy to blame one's forebears for one's lot in life. That blaming could extend to the moral sphere too, and both Jeremiah and Ezekiel had to deal with such excuses. Both encountered a proverb used by their contemporaries to excuse blame for the exile: "The parents [lit., 'fathers'] have eaten sour grapes, so the children's [lit., 'sons'] teeth are set on edge" (Ezek 18:2; Jer 31:29).

In refuting this application of the old proverb, Ezekiel develops a thoroughgoing hypothetical example (18:1-32). Suppose, he says, a man lived a righteous life (vv. 5-9). Would that man enjoy a lengthy life? Ezekiel answers that he would. If that man had an unrighteous son, however, one who lived a life of wickedness and violence, would the righteousness of the father atone for his wickedness? Ezekiel claims it would not, and that the son would die with his own blood upon himself (vv. 10-13). The prophet extends the example one more generation, hypothesizing for the wicked man an upright son. Would the wickedness of the third man's father be visited upon him? "No," says Ezekiel. Each person, each generation is responsible for its own behavior (vv. 14-18).

Ezekiel, however, anticipated positive answers to his questions. That is, he expected his audience to counter that children would and *should* suffer for the sins of their parents and benefit from the righteousness of their fathers. Nor were Ezekiel's contemporaries alone in the OT in their thinking, as a glance at a few other texts will demonstrate. A confessional statement that appears in both Exod 34:7 and Num 14:18 says that God would bless the descendants of those who maintained covenant fidelity with YHWH for a thousand generations, but punish the descendants of those who broke the covenant "to the third and fourth generation." That confession limits the effects of sins, but affirms the view of Ezekiel's opponents that children might well bear the results of their parents' behavior. Additionally, some proverbs clearly suggest that righteous behavior results in God's blessing (cf. Prov 10:3, 6; 11:17-18, 21), and the friends of Job clearly thought so (Eliphaz in Job 4:7; Bildad in 8:20; Zophar in 11:13-20). Deuteronomy 7:9-10, however, uses the language of Exodus (and Numbers), but specifically disagrees with punishment stretching to the third and fourth generations, saying instead that God would punish directly ("in their own person") those who sinned. This author and Jeremiah and Ezekiel, three voices from around the time of the fall of Jerusalem,[12] argued that divine punishment for sin did not cross generations, regardless of mundane repercussions for one's actions.

Ezekiel, however, carried his hypothetical example in a more complex direction by considering what effect a change in a person's behavior might have on retribution. If a sinner turns away from his sin, will God then bless him? Ezekiel answers with a resounding "Yes." Conversely, if a righteous man turns unrighteous, would he die? "Yes" is Ezekiel's answer again. So change — for better or worse — is possible.[13] This thinking marks a significant movement in the direction of individual retribution, but it does not

---

12. Critical scholars do not accept the tradition that Moses wrote the entire Pentateuch, and consider Deuteronomy a product from as late as the seventh century.

13. We probably should note that Ezekiel's argument deals with punishment in this life, not heaven and hell.

deal with the sticky issue of what to think when bad things happen to good people.

The Ethics of Exile

The fourth basic theme is that of Ezekiel's ethics. Ethical decision-making does not occur in a vacuum, and it is at least possible that what might be permissible in one context would not be in another. (For example, people who would not commit murder might well kill another person in self-defense.) In addressing the issue of Ezekiel's ethics, Andrew Mein divides Ezekiel's concerns into two categories: political and personal.[14] He notes that Ezekiel and the Jerusalemites in exile with him had likely been upper-class citizens or their retainers. Before the exile, they may well have belonged to the power structure in Judah. Not surprisingly, then, Ezekiel shows an interest in foreign policy, especially in his allegories. There Ezekiel blames the exile on the failures of the upper-class Judeans with him in Babylon. In particular he condemns them not for their failures in orthopraxy (i.e., their failures to stamp out the practices of peasant farmers), but for their failure to keep the official cult in Jerusalem within the confines of orthodoxy. Specifically, in his vision in chs. 8–11 he charges them with worshipping the gods of other peoples, and even names one of the offenders (8:11).

In terms of personal morality, Ezekiel addressed a group whose scope of action was considerably reduced when compared with their life in Jerusalem. Only in matters of family, business, and their own community were they able to act as moral agents. As a priest he thought in terms of uncleanliness and pollution, categories primarily associated with the cultus, but now pressed for use in other domains. Thus idolatry in the exile was concerned with "idolatry in the heart" (14:7), not with offering sacrifices incorrectly at the temple in Jerusalem. If such concerns are seen as "majoring on minors," they nevertheless may have been the only way Ezekiel was able to think about conditions Judeans were facing. Such thinking, moreover, might have been the best way to preserve cultic laws until a return to Jerusalem was possible.

14. See Andrew Mein, *Ezekiel and the Ethics of Exile* (Oxford: Oxford University Press, 2001) 257-63.

Hope for the Future

Fifth, 33:1–48:35 paints a picture of the future as the reversal of the past. The future would be a time when the wrongs of the past would be made right. The following list offers an overview of those reversals.

- 34:1-31 In the past Israel's kings had generally been bad shepherds (vv. 1-10); in the future God would be their Good Shepherd (vv. 11-22) and set up a new "prince" from David's line. (The word "king" is not used here, though it is in 37:15-28.)
- 36:1-38 In contrast with the future punishment of Edom, God will bless Judah, not because Judah deserves blessing but because God is a great God. The implication is that to be self-consistent God will bless God's people.
- 37:1-14 The exiles are now as "dead" as a valley of dry bones, but God will "resurrect" them by sending them home.[15]
- 37:15-28 In the past the monarchy had divided, leaving the tiny states of Israel and Judah; in the future they would be reunited, with a new Davidic "king."
- 38:1–39:20 In the past conquerors great and small had attacked Israel and Judah, reducing both of them to mere shells. Gog of Magog seems to symbolize any and every would-be future conqueror. In the future he (they) will be stopped by God.
- 40:1–42:20 In the mid-sixth century, Solomon's temple lay in ruins; Ezekiel gives a floor plan for a new one.
- 43:1-9 In 11:22-23 Ezekiel depicted God's departing the temple and Jerusalem, leaving them defenseless before Nebuchadnezzar. Here God returns to the new temple to make it his throne upon earth and to rule the world from it.
- 44:9 In the past foreigners had attacked and destroyed the temple; in the future none would enter it.
- 44:10-31 In the past, Levites had been allowed to offer sacrifice, but no more. In the future that role would be limited to the Zadokite priesthood.

15. The interpretation of the vision focuses on national resurrection, but the image is one of physical resurrection. It would be claiming too much to say Ezekiel proclaimed the resurrection of the individual, but this chapter constitutes a giant step toward that doctrine in the Hebrew Bible.

- 45:1-9 In the past provisions for the temple had come from the king, giving the monarchy control over the temple. In the future the priests would have their own land to farm. So also would the king, who would therefore not need to tax the people for his upkeep.[16]
- 47:1-12 In the past water was often a serious problem for farmers in Palestine, and famines were frequent. In the future water would flow from under the temple (the throne of God and source of all blessing) and supply the whole land, even turning the Dead Sea into fresh water (except for marshes and swamps which would remain for evaporating to obtain salt).
- 47:13–48:35 In the past tribal boundaries had been drawn inequitably and were the source of friction. In the future every allocation would be equal and sufficient.[17]

Of these texts, we should note, chs. 40–42 plus 43:1-9; 44:9; 44:10-31; 45:1-9; and 47:1-12 portray the new Jerusalem as the "navel of the earth," the source of God's blessing on the land. Ezekiel 40:2 emphasizes the height of the mountain, and 48:15 makes clear that Jerusalem will lie at the center of the land, two motifs common to the depiction of the navel.

These five themes do not exhaust the teachings of the book of Ezekiel, but they do point to the serious and necessary work of the exiled prophet to address the new situation in which he and his fellow Judeans found themselves. It was his task to reinvent himself and his work, to represent God among the people, and to make the old religion designed with a temple at its center into a new religion capable of directing communal life and preserving hope for a renewed national and cultic life in Jerusalem. He had no illusions about the difficulty of that task, as chs. 1–3 make clear. The book that bears his name is the final tribute to the man and his effectiveness.

16. Ezekiel seems to perceive a king with truncated power, responsible for civic issues perhaps, but not cultic matters.

17. See Paul L. Redditt, "The Vitality of the Apocalyptic Vision," in *Passion, Vitality, and Foment: The Dynamics of Second Temple Judaism*, ed. Lamontte M. Luker (Harrisburg: Trinity Press International, 2001) 92-94.

Problems Raised by a Study of Ezekiel

Two problems arise from a study of Ezekiel. The first is moral/theological. In 20:25-26 God says that God had given Israel statutes that were not good. Specifically, the passage says that God had commanded the Israelites to sacrifice the firstborn offspring of both children and animals. What is more, God did so to horrify the Israelites so they would not obey God. The closest such laws in the Pentateuch are Exod 13:2 and 22:29b-30, which command the Israelites to "consecrate" the firstborn of animals and humans. Exodus 13:12-13 permits the substitution of a donkey with a sheep, and 34:19-20 permits the same substitution and requires making a substitute for a human child. Ezekiel perhaps knew the first pair of pentateuchal laws and was himself horrified by them. He perhaps knew the second pair and used them as his basis for condemning such sacrifices in Ezek 16:17-21; 20:30-31; and 23:37-39. The theological issue may be stated like this: What kind of a God would actually demand that parents sacrifice their children? Would such a God be worthy of worship? Ezekiel's solution seems to be that God made the demand as a way of driving the people away from him, not because God really desired human sacrifice.

The second issue raised in Ezekiel is encountered in the book of Jeremiah as well: namely, the relationship between prophets and priests in the OT. Both Jeremiah and Ezekiel are explicitly called priests (Jer 1:1; Ezek 1:3) and prophets: Jeremiah in 1:5 and at least 31 more times, and Ezekiel in 2:5 and 33:33. Jeremiah is called a prophet frequently in the third person narratives about him, indicating that his biographer saw him as such. Ezekiel is called a prophet both times by God in the phrase "they [the exiles] shall know that there has been/is a prophet among them" (Ezek 2:5; 33:33).

Several different ways of speaking seem to be at work here. Both Ezekiel and Jeremiah were born into priestly families. Jeremiah's family, however, descended from Abiathar, whose banishment from Jerusalem under Solomon is carefully documented (1 Kgs 2:26-27). The family lived in Anathoth in the southern part of Israel and may have been out of favor and out of the power structure. Ezekiel, of course, was an exile in Babylonia and outside of the power structure there as well as in Jerusalem. Even within these limits it was still appropriate to speak of both men as priests, and both might have had a hearing in certain quarters because of their family connections.

It is pretty clear that neither man was seen as a prophet connected to the temple in Jerusalem. Their role as prophets seems to be something attributed to them by their followers. Their audience would have been larger than that group of followers, and they seem to have spent their "careers" as prophets trying to persuade people of the correctness of their perspective. That they proved correct about the fall of Jerusalem may have had much to do with their recognition as prophets. In Jeremiah's case, it appears likely that he was recognized as a prophet late in life or even after he died, though he and a small group around him might have thought of him as a prophet during his own lifetime. In Ezekiel's case, the designation "prophet" is infrequent in the book and is never presented as a self-designation. Thus, he may have thought of himself as a priest or as a spokesman for God in some sense other than as a prophet. We just do not know. What we do know is that either during his life in exile or later other exiles began to hear him as an intermediary of God, i.e., as a prophet.

Modern readers typically do not think about this issue. They know that Ezekiel and Jeremiah are prophets because their books are in the part of the Bible called Prophets. Their location, however, is a result of scribal reflection. In the process of the canonization of the Hebrew Bible, Law became identified with priests, specifically with Moses and the "sons of Aaron."[18] Ezekiel knows nothing of that identification and speaks neither of Aaron nor Aaronites. The allocation of books to the category of *Nebiim* (Prophets) in the MT was problematic enough that the LXX created two categories. Its "books of history" include not only the Former Prophets from the *Nebiim*, but also Ruth, 1 and 2 Chronicles, Ezra, Nehemiah, and Esther from the *Kethubim* (Writings) of the MT. That division obscures the role of "prophets" in the Former Prophets, but sets apart the Major and Minor Prophets more clearly. Even Daniel, the hero of the only apocalypse in the Hebrew Bible, came to be considered a prophet in the LXX, where the book bearing his name stands among the Major Prophets. The designation "Daniel the prophet" also appears in Matt 24:15 (cf. Mark 13:14) and in Josephus (*Ant.* 10.267).

So, the term "prophet" turns out to be multivalent. It behooves the Bible student to be careful to note the different shades of meaning. In the book of Ezekiel itself, the hero was born a priest and remained a priest, even after he was carried away to Babylonia. He continued to be concerned about priestly affairs, the pollution and future sanctification of the temple,

---

18. For an intriguing history of that postexilic development, see Gabriele Boccaccini, *Roots of Rabbinic Judaism* (Grand Rapids: Wm. B. Eerdmans, 2002).

and even the relative responsibilities and powers of priests and monarchs, though an early editor called him a "prophet" in 2:5 and 33:33 in view of his role as a "religious intermediar[y] who functioned at the national level."[19]

Summary

The book of Ezekiel portrays a Jerusalemite priest exiled to Babylonia whose work came to be considered that of a prophet. His message to his fellow exiles primarily included discussions of the fall of Jerusalem and an articulation of hope for a future restitution, though not one to be experienced personally by members of his audience. This message was mediated partly through visions, partly through allegories, and partly through genres such as prophecies of disaster and salvation. It was permeated by an ethic of exile that applied old laws and genres to a new situation.

Questions for Reflection

1. What difference would it make — if any — and why if Ezekiel was suffering from some sort of mental illness that influenced or shaped his visions and message?
2. How do you reconcile Ezekiel's view of retribution with natural and other calamities that befall people who appear to be kind and godly? Were such calamities even at issue in the book of Ezekiel? Why or why not?
3. How do you understand Ezekiel's view of the future? Does it anticipate current events in modern Israel? Why or why not?
4. Do you think God is the kind of God who would make morally repulsive demands of people? Why or why not? Could such commands, if given, be morally justified? Why or why not?

For Further Reading

Allen, Leslie C. *Ezekiel 1–19; Ezekiel 20–48.* WBC 28-29. Waco: Word, 1994, 1990. A study of Ezekiel offering technical notes on the text plus interpretations based on the form, structure, and setting of each passage.

19. Thomas W. Overholt, "Prophet, Prophecy," *EDB*, 1086.

Block, Daniel I. *The Book of Ezekiel.* 2 vols. NICOT. Grand Rapids: Wm. B. Eerdmans, 1997-98. A thorough study of Ezekiel, offering a discussion of the Hebrew text and the author's translation, a study of the date, purpose, structure, genres, and theology of the book.

Eichrodt, Walther. *Ezekiel.* OTL. Philadelphia: Westminster, 1970. A commentary featuring careful notes on the Hebrew text, a study of the historical background, genres, and theology of each pericope of Ezekiel.

Mein, Andrew. *Ezekiel and the Ethics of Exile.* OTM. Oxford: Oxford University Press, 2001. A study of ethics of the book of Ezekiel informed by what moderns can know about being an exile in Babylonia.

Odell, Margaret S. *Ezekiel.* SHBC. Macon: Smyth & Helwys, 2005. A study of Ezekiel featuring commentary (analysis of the text, the history and literary forms reflected in it) and connections (theology and applications).

Zimmerli, Walter. *Ezekiel 1; Ezekiel 2.* Hermeneia. Philadelphia: Fortress, 1979-1983. A meticulous and scholarly commentary on the Hebrew text, with careful attention to the genres, background, authenticity, and aim of the book.

CHAPTER 8

Daniel

The book of Daniel, technically speaking, is not a book of prophecy but an apocalypse. To be sure, Matt 24:15 refers to "Daniel the prophet" (cf. Mark 13:14; Luke 21:20), but the book bearing his name never calls him by that title.[1] Instead, it portrays him as a master of wisdom and understanding (Dan 1:20) and the revealer of end-time secrets to those who are wise (12:3-4, 10). What, then, is the relationship between a book of prophecy and an apocalypse? How should recognition of the book's genre shape our expectations about what we shall find and how to understand it?

Introduction to Apocalyptic Literature

The place to begin our study is with a definition of the terms "apocalypse," "apocalyptic eschatology," and "apocalyptic literature." Next will come a discussion of the characteristics of apocalypses and of the relationship of such literature to prophetic and other literature. Then we will turn to the book itself.

---

1. Interestingly enough, those NT passages appear in chapters belonging to the so-called "Synoptic Apocalypse" (Matt 24:4-36//Mark 13:5-37//Luke 21:8-36), so named because of the resemblance of those verses to apocalyptic literature.

"Apocalypse," "Apocalyptic Eschatology," and "Apocalyptic Literature"

An apocalypse may be defined as "a genre of revelatory literature with a narrative framework, in which a revelation is mediated by an otherworldly being to a human recipient, disclosing a transcendent reality which is both temporal, insofar as it envisages eschatological salvation, and spatial insofar as it involves another, supernatural world."[2] Continuing, apocalypses are "intended to interpret present, earthly circumstances in light of the supernatural world and of the future, and to influence both the understanding and the behavior of the audience by means of divine authority."[3] Apocalypses generally fall under two types. In one type they offer a review of history, presented from the perspective of an early seer who "predicts" the events of history. In the other type, the seer sees a vision of the heavens (and even hells). This second type may combine the vision with (1) a review of history, (2) a cosmic and/or political eschatology, or (3) a personal eschatology.[4] The book of Daniel belongs to the first type, apocalypses that offer a historical preview with no otherworldly journey. Closely related to "apocalypse" is the derived term "apocalyptic eschatology." That term should be reserved for the eschatology found in apocalypses or recognized by analogy with them.[5] Finally, "apocalyptic literature" designates any literature taking the form of an apocalypse or sharing the thought world of apocalypses.

Characteristics of Apocalypses

Apocalypses typically exhibit several (though not necessarily all) of the following literary characteristics. They often contain visions and auditions; they may reveal secret knowledge and narrate the actions of a celes-

---

2. John J. Collins, "Introduction: Towards the Morphology of a Genre," in *Apocalypse: The Morphology of a Genre. Semeia* 14 (Missoula: Scholars, 1979) 9.

3. Adela Yarbro Collins, "Introduction," in *Early Christian Apocalypticism: Genre and Social Setting. Semeia* 36 (Decatur: Scholars, 1986) 7. While this two-part definition has been challenged (see Lester L. Grabbe, "Prophetic and Apocalyptic: Time for New Definitions — and New Thinking," in *Knowing the End from the Beginning,* ed. Grabbe and Robert D. Haak, 107-33. JSPSup 46 [London: T. & T. Clark, 2003]), it still seems to me the best so far written.

4. John J. Collins, "The Jewish Apocalypses," in *Apocalypse,* 22-23.

5. Collins, "The Jewish Apocalypses," 4.

tial being, often to interpret the meaning of a vision. They are typically pseudonymous, written under a false name, usually an ancient figure.[6] Apocalypses also employ coded speech, in which numbers, animals, and odd natural occurrences take on special meanings. Over the course of time later apocalypses reuse older images so that levels of meaning are piled on top of one another. Also, apocalypses employ hortatory or parenetic material (ethical admonitions) which instructs people how to live based on the information they have received. In the book of Daniel parenesis is replaced by narratives that illustrate the preferred behavior. Such narratives may identify the seer, reveal his state of mind, his reactions to what he sees, and maybe even final instructions about preserving the revelation.

Apocalypses feature characteristic themes. First is a concern with history. Their reviews of history often periodize apocalypses according to a definite model in which the vicissitudes of life follow a set pattern. (Cf. the alternation of bright and dark waters as symbols of alternating good and bad times, faithfulness and faithlessness in 2 *Baruch*.) Regardless of how history is represented, however, the time of the actual author is depicted as the last, bitter days before a divine inbreak in which God straightens up the world. Thus, much of the "historical review" in apocalypses is really "prophecy after the fact," i.e., the known past portrayed as the future from the perspective of the ancient seer. This feature gives apocalypses the appearance of historical determinism, but they presuppose that people have the right to choose and so hold them accountable for their choices. Tours of heaven and hell portray the outcome of right and wrong choices.

Apocalyptic eschatology tends toward dualism. It envisions two aeons, this age and the age to come. This age is speeding toward its imminent finale, often accompanied by cosmic upheavals. The periodization of history often allows the seer or an interpreting angel to read the signs of the coming end. The new age will be marked by the reversal of the social order, with the righteous at last triumphing. This reversal will be brought about by God's activity, either directly or through a human medium such as the Messiah. Judgment will properly compensate both good and evil people.

---

6. Sometimes the name itself will give the reader an insight into the contents of the apocalypse. One example is Ezra in the book now called 4 *Ezra*, which utilizes the Jewish tradition that Ezra copied the whole Hebrew Bible by having him receive numerous "secret" works for the last days. Another example is 2 *Baruch*, which discusses the destruction in 70 C.E. of the Second Temple through the eyes of Jeremiah's scribe Baruch, who could be presumed to have witnessed the destruction of the First Temple in 586 B.C.E.

Sometimes the entire cosmos is renewed, and sometimes righteous people enjoy an eschatological banquet. Sometimes the nations, maybe after being purged, will be invited. The whole future scene may be populated with angels and demons.

Relationship to Prophetic and Other Literature

For decades scholars have argued about the origin of apocalyptic literature, specifically whether it derived from prophetic[7] or wisdom literature[8] and whether it was basically an inner-Jewish movement[9] or an import from surrounding cultures.[10] The truth of the matter seems to have been that apocalyptic thinking abounded in the ancient Mediterranean and Middle East in the last few centuries B.C.E. and influenced Jewish apocalyptic.[11] Moreover, any group in ancient Israel could become apocalyptic in its thinking if it understood itself as relatively deprived.[12]

For the present volume, the relationship between prophetic and apocalyptic literature is important. Paul D. Hanson suggested that the difference between them lies in their views of eschatology, with apocalyptic eschatology being an outgrowth of prophetic. The distinction is that in prophetic eschatology the "end" works out in historical realities, but in apocalyptic eschatology the future is expressed in more mythic terms.[13] Lester L. Grabbe

---

7. Perhaps the best-known scholars here are the British trio of R. H. Charles (*The Critical History of the Doctrine of a Future Life* [London: Black, 1899]), H. H. Rowley (*The Relevance of Apocalyptic* [London: Lutterworth, 1952]), and D. S. Russell (*The Method and Message of Jewish Apocalyptic, 200 B.C.-A.D. 100*. OTL [Philadelphia: Westminster, 1964]).

8. See Gerhard von Rad, *Old Testament Theology* 2 (New York: Harper & Row, 1965) 301-8.

9. See Otto Plöger, *Theocracy and Eschatology* (Richmond: John Knox, 1968).

10. See Wilhelm Bousset, *Die Religion des Judentums im neuentestamentlichen Zeitalter*, 2nd ed. (Berlin: Reuter & Reichard, 1906); and T. F. Glasson, *Greek Influences in Jewish Eschatology* (London: SPCK, 1961).

11. See George W. E. Nickelsburg, "Social Aspects of Palestinian Jewish Apocalypticism," in *Apocalypticism in the Mediterranean World and the Near East*, ed. David Hellholm (Tübingen: Mohr, 1983) 647.

12. See Robert R. Wilson, "From Prophecy to Apocalyptic: Reflections on the Shape of Israelite Religion," in *Anthropological Perspectives on Old Testament Prophecy*, ed. Robert C. Culley and Thomas W. Overholt, 79-95. Semeia 21 (Chico: Scholars, 1982).

13. Paul D. Hanson, "Apocalypses and Apocalypticism: The Genre. Introductory Overview," in *ABD*, 1:279-82.

objects that the distinction is false, because much in prophetic eschatology is otherworldly or mythic. He thinks that apocalyptic eschatology is simply a subdivision within prophetic eschatology, and he offers no new definition of apocalyptic eschatology.[14] John J. Collins thinks that both prophetic and apocalyptic writings express themselves in categories that sound like mantic wisdom, i.e., wisdom having to do with the interpreting of signs. Still, he argues that prophecy is more intermediary than is apocalypticism.[15] Scholars have not settled this issue, but the discussion may illustrate the close relationship between prophecy and apocalypticism.

Introduction to the Book and Its Times

The Place of the Book in the Canon

In English Bibles Daniel stands fifth in the Prophetic corpus, the last of the Major Prophets, following Isaiah, Jeremiah, Lamentations, and Ezekiel. In the MT the book appears near the end of the *Kethubim* or Writings (followed by Ezra, Nehemiah, and 1 and 2 Chronicles), but in the LXX it stands at the end of the Prophets, which appear in this order: first, the twelve Minor Prophets; and then Isaiah, Jeremiah, Baruch, Lamentations, the Epistle of Jeremiah, Ezekiel, and Daniel. In addition, the version of Daniel that appears in the LXX includes a long prayer in Daniel 3 and two more narratives (Susanna and Bel and the Dragon) that are not in the MT.

The Setting for the Book

The book of Daniel is set in Babylon during the exile (586-539). There are problems, however, with some of the dates and persons mentioned in the book, and they raise serious doubts about when the book was written. We shall investigate that issue here as preparation for our study of the authorship and integrity of Daniel. The opening sentence places Nebuchadnez-

14. Grabbe, "Prophetic and Apocalyptic," 109-30.

15. John J. Collins, "Prophecy, Apocalypse and Eschatology," in *Knowing the End from the Beginning,* ed. Lester L. Grabbe and Robert D. Haak. JSPSup 46 (London: T. & T. Clark, 2003) 50.

zar's attack on Jerusalem "in the third year of the reign of King Jehoiakim." Jehoiakim ascended to the throne in Jerusalem in 609, so the third year would be 606. Nebuchadnezzar did not become king in Babylon until 605, however, and did not defeat Jerusalem the first time until 598/7. The date is approximately correct, therefore, but not as exact as one might expect from a person who lived through the event. The text does not actually say that Daniel was one of those taken into exile, but certainly implies that. Still, the precise date is unimportant to the narrative, and the action of ch. 1 could have occurred at any time before the end of the Babylonian period (539).

The second problem of setting appears in chs. 5, 7, and 8, all of which are said to have occurred during the reign of "King Belshazzar." Actually, Belshazzar was the son of Nabonidus, the last king of the Neo-Babylonian Empire. Nabonidus was away from Babylon much of his reign, and Belshazzar was his viceroy. The difference, to be sure, is only technical, but technically Belshazzar was not "king."

The third problem in relation to the book's setting is much more serious. According to 5:31 someone named "Darius the Mede" succeeded Belshazzar on the throne of the Babylonian Empire. In fact, the next ruler after Nabonidus was the Persian king Cyrus.[16] What, though, does the book of Daniel say about this Darius the Mede? The most important text is 9:1, which calls him "the son of Ahasuerus." Ahasuerus, however, is usually taken to be Xerxes I, king of Persia in 486-465, not 539. It appears, therefore, as if Darius the Mede is a literary creation of one of the authors of the book of Daniel, resulting in a king of Media named Darius who conquered Babylon and whom the Danielic author considered its king. No such person, however, is known to history.[17]

Where did that author get the idea that there was a Darius the Mede? A glance at the history of the area may provide an answer. Media (located north of Assyria and the Persian Gulf) was a power that fought against the Assyrians in the ninth and eighth centuries and in the late seventh century

16. Daniel 14 in the LXX gets this information correct, even naming Astyages, who reigned from 585 to 550, as the last king of Medea.

17. A number of scholars, traditional and critical, have attempted to identify Darius the Mede with Gobryas or some other figure from the time of the transition from the Babylonian to the Persian empires. See, e.g., Klaus Koch, "Dareios, der Meder," in *The Word of the Lord Shall Go Forth: Essays in Honor of David Noel Freedman,* ed. Carol L. Meyers and M. O'Connor, 287-99 (Winona Lake: Eisenbrauns, 1983); and Gerhard F. Hasel, "The Book of Daniel: Evidences Relating to Persons and Chronology," *AUSS* 19 (1981): 45-47.

resumed the fight alongside Persia. In 550, however, the Persians, under Cyrus the Great, conquered the Medes, before capturing Babylon in 539.

How were these events depicted in Daniel? According to Daniel 8, King Belshazzar of Babylon had a vision of a ram with two horns, which conquered all the lands around it. The ram, in turn, was attacked and killed by a goat. The text specifically identifies the two horns of the ram as Media and Persia (v. 20) and the goat as Greece (v. 21). Why? Since the vision had been seen by the last Babylonian "king" Belshazzar whose defeat was implied by the comment that the ram defeated all the countries around it, and because of links through intermarriage between Media and Persia, those countries were portrayed in the vision by the ram with two horns. Since the Greek king Alexander the Great overthrew the Persians, the Greeks were understood as the goat.

This "reading" of history, however, presented the author of Daniel 8–12 with a difficulty. Before we can understand it, we need to mention a fourth error the author makes. Daniel 6 is set in the time of Darius and attributes to him the division of "the empire" into 120 satrapies. In actuality, there was a Persian king Darius I, who ruled from 522 to 486 and who divided the Persian Empire into satrapies, but only twenty of them. Here, then, was the author's quandary. On the one hand, he thought that Darius (not Cyrus) overthrew the Babylonians and divided his empire into satrapies. On the other hand, he thought that the Medes succeeded the Babylonians in power. Hence, he contrived "Darius the Mede" as the successor of Belshazzar and as succeeded by Cyrus (according to 6:28).

This interpretation of the image in Daniel 8 could hardly have been the work of a sixth-century prophet living in Babylon, and the historical inaccuracies concerning the sixth century contrast with the accuracy concerning succeeding empires. Specifically, though wrong about the end of the Babylonian Empire in 539, the author was correct about a whole series of events that took place centuries later. That series is described as the contents of visions seen by Daniel, so the ostensible setting of the date of the book remains the sixth century. The date of the book's composition, however, turns out to be much later.

Fortunately, we are in the position of knowing approximately when this four-kingdom schema of history ending with the Greeks came on the scene. The Greek historian Herodotus (484-425) developed the theory of a succession of world empires and spoke of the sequence Assyria — Media — Persia. Soon after the conquest of Persia by Alexander (331), Demetrius of Phalerum added the Greeks to the series. From the second century B.C.E. on, the theory is widely attested in both Greek and Roman writers.[18] The author(s) of Daniel modified it by substituting Babylon (the setting of Daniel) for Assyria.[19] Otherwise, the schema stood pretty much as the Greeks developed it. In their view, history led up to them. This line of reasoning would lead us to a date for Daniel 8 no earlier than late fourth or early third century. However, the reference to someone identified as the "little horn" in 8:9 will allow us to date that chapter as it now stands after 167. The "little horn" is said to have taken the regular burnt offering away from God and to have overthrown the place of God's sanctuary (8:11). The Danielic author calls this act the "transgression that makes desolate," which is a technical term for the defiling of the sanctuary by Antiochus IV Epiphanes in December 167 (cf. 1 Macc 1:41-64).

We can be quite precise also about Daniel 10–11, which also knows of the abomination that makes desolate (11:31). It shows remarkable familiarity with the battles between two of the Greek successor states, those of the Seleucids (rulers in Mesopotamia) and the Ptolemies (rulers of Egypt).[20] The interpretation in ch. 11 begins with the Persian Empire, predicting its

---

18. Paul Niskanen, *The Human and the Divine in History: Herodotus and the Book of Daniel.* JSOTSup 396 (London: T. & T. Clark, 2004) 7-8. Niskanen suggests that Daniel was the first non-Greek work to appropriate and transform this Greek view of history. The dream reported in Daniel 2 very likely originally referred not to a succession of kingdoms but only to Babylonian kings, with Nebuchadnezzar as its golden head and the subsequent members of his dynasty as the inferior metals. It probably derived from Babylon (contra Niskanen, 27-28, who follows Arnaldo Momigliano, "Biblical Studies and Classical Studies," in *Essays on Ancient and Modern Judaism* [Chicago: University of Chicago Press, 1994] 3-9). Daniel 7 has kingdoms in view, but it is later. Niskanen is correct in his insistence that Daniel took history seriously.

19. As long ago as 1953, Martin Noth (repr. as "The Understanding of History in Old Testament Apocalyptic," in *The Laws in the Pentateuch and Other Studies* [London: SCM Press, 1984] 198-209) suggested that the schema arose outside of Babylon and originally intended Assyria as the first kingdom.

20. Alexander the Great stormed out of Greece, conquering his way through Egypt, Mesopotamia, and Persia en route to India. His men refused to go further than the Indus Valley, and Alexander died in Babylon in 323 at the age of thirty-two. His half-brother Philip became the nominal ruler for seven years, but then his generals divided his empire among themselves. First there were five, then four (the number alluded to in 11:3-4). Those four were Ptolemy in Egypt, Seleucus in Babylon and Phrygia, Lysimachus in Thrace and Bithynia, and Cassander in Greece and Macedonia. They were soon reduced to three, but the two that are important in the book of Daniel were Ptolemy in Egypt and Seleucus in Mesopotamia.

overthrow by the kingdom of Greece (vv. 3-4). That kingdom would be divided into four kingdoms, two of which receive further mention in the account. Clearly, the kings of the south are the Ptolemaic kings of Egypt, and the kings of the north are the Seleucid rulers of Mesopotamia. Verses 5-20 recount in increasing detail the battles between the two, and vv. 21-39 recount in great detail events in Palestine during the reign of Antiochus IV Epiphanes (175-164), including his polluting the altar at the temple in Jerusalem (v. 31; cf. 1 Macc 1:20-61). It seems likely, therefore, that the author of Dan 8:1–11:45 lived and wrote during the time of Antiochus IV Epiphanes.

After 38 verses that discuss history in remarkable accuracy from the Persian period down to the desecration of the temple, 11:40-45 then predicts the death of the evil king (= Antiochus IV) in Canaan after a final battle against the king of the south (= Ptolemy VI). Actually, Antiochus died mysteriously in 164, but in Persia and without the aforementioned final battle against Egypt. Critical scholars conclude, therefore, that Daniel 10–11 reached its shape between the defiling of the temple in 167 and Antiochus's death in 164. Indeed, the book as a whole must have been redacted soon thereafter. We shall trace that redaction in the next section of this chapter.

The Structure, Integrity, and Authorship of the Book

A look at the structure of Daniel yields surprising results. For starters, Daniel 1–6 contains narratives that follow two basic plots. One plot (found in chs. 1, 2, 4, and 5) deals with contests at court, while the other (in chs. 3 and 6) narrates conflicts at court in which the hero(s) is (are) in danger. One may call these two "broken martyr stories," a term to which some scholars have objected, but one which makes clear the stakes in the narratives.[21] Daniel 7–12 is more uniform, consisting of reports of visions and their interpretation by a mediary.

It seems quite likely that the book grew in stages. Collins thinks that the first stage consisted of the three narratives found in chs. 4–6. He notes that the Old Greek version of these three chapters varies markedly from other Greek texts and from the MT. Those differences point to an earlier compilation of narratives, containing just those three chapters.[22]

21. Wilson, "From Prophecy to Apocalyptic," p. 89.
22. John J. Collins, *Daniel.* Hermeneia (Minneapolis: Fortress, 1993) 37.

The second stage perhaps consisted at least of chs. 2–7. This suggestion is based on two pieces of evidence. (1) These chapters are written in the Aramaic language, whereas the rest of the book is in Hebrew. (2) These chapters exhibit a clear structure.

2:4b-49   A dream about four world kingdoms replaced by a fifth

    3:1-30[23]   Three friends in the fiery furnace

        4:1-37   Daniel interprets a dream for Nebuchadnezzar

        5:1-31   Daniel interprets the handwriting on the wall for Belshazzar

    6:1-28   Daniel in the lions' den

7:1-28   A vision about four world kingdoms replaced by a fifth

It is likely that this recension opened with a narrative (in Aramaic) about the coming of Daniel and his friends to Babylon, perhaps a short version of the narrative now found in 1:1–2:4a.

The third stage probably added much or all of the remaining book, but the narratives were written in Hebrew. The hypothesized, Aramaic-language introduction to stage 2 was possibly incorporated into 1:1–2:4a, translated into Hebrew, and maybe even enlarged. Daniel 8–12 was written in Hebrew and forms the latest part of the book. The Hebrew of 1:1–2:4a, however, differs somewhat from that of chs. 8–12, suggesting different authors.[24] Further, only Daniel 8–12 reveals an acquaintance with the pollution of the temple in 167, indicating that those chapters originated after that event. They perhaps arose in response to it and related events.

Given this information, we can also attempt to date stage two. Daniel 1:1–2:4a took its present shape earlier than 164, but it is difficult to say how much earlier. The same is true for ch. 7, but one factor helps. Both chs. 7 and 8 refer to a "little horn," who in 8:9-13 disrupts sacrifices at the temple in Jerusalem. As we have seen, the "little horn" is Antiochus IV Epiphanes in those verses. Surely the "little horn" in 7:8 is as well, for he is said to have "changed the seasons and the law"(v. 25). He is not charged, however, with disrupting the sacrifices in the temple. Thus ch. 7, and by implication the

---

23. The longer version in the LXX inserts a lengthy passage including narrative, the "Song of Azariah," and the "Song of the Three Friends" between vv. 23 and 24 as vv. 24-90.

24. Collins, *Daniel,* 23.

redaction of the second stage, should be dated during the reign of Antiochus IV, so after 175, but before the defiling of the altar in 167.[25]

These observations have far-reaching implications concerning the integrity and authorship of the book. For one thing, it is quite clear that the sixth-century wise man Daniel was not the author of the book. Rather, he is the hero of the book. To be sure, beginning with 7:2 the book is written in the first person singular, so the last half of the book could be considered pseudonymous. (By contrast, chs. 1–6, except for 4:1-17, take the third person limited point of view.) In determining authorship, one might ask: which is more likely, that a person would write of himself in the third person or that an author might write in the first person as if by the hero? In any case, the historical difficulties associated with the book's handling of the Babylonian period make it unlikely that the book was written in the sixth century by anyone. Finally, if the use of the first person singular settles the issue, then one would have to conclude that Daniel 4 was written by Nebuchadnezzar.

The version of Daniel in the LXX contains later material, resulting in at least one more stage. The first addition, appearing as 3:24-90, consists of a song ascribed to Abednego under his Hebrew name Azariah (vv. 26-45), a second song ascribed to the three friends (vv. 51-90a), and enough narrative (vv. 24-25, 46-51, and 90b) to tie the songs to each other and to their context. Those songs confess the sins of the near-martyrs, beg God's mercy to spare them, and praise God for doing so. The other two additions consist of narratives designed to illustrate further the wisdom of Daniel. In ch. 13 the hero defends a married woman accused of making sexual advances on two men who actually had attempted to seduce her. In ch. 14 Daniel traps people at the Babylonian court who were taking food put out for the Babylonian gods, revealing thereby that the gods that supposedly ate the food were not real.

Main Genres in the Book

The discussion of the structure of Daniel above necessarily involved the issue of genres, so this discussion will be brief. As mentioned earlier, chs. 1, 2, 4, and 5 are narratives of court contests (as is Susanna, ch. 14 in the LXX),

25. See Paul L. Redditt, *Daniel*. NCBC (Sheffield: Sheffield Academic, 1999) 26-33.

while chs. 3 and 6 are narratives of court conflicts, also called "tales of deliverance" or "broken martyr stories," in which the hero(s) escape(s) from danger.[26] One scholar, Lawrence M. Wills, thinks all the narratives should simply be called "court narratives," which he describes as "a legend of a revered figure set in the royal court, which has the wisdom of the protagonist as a principal motif."[27] The narratives in chs. 7–12 are apocalyptic visions. These observations make clear that longer apocalypses may well include shorter genres, here court narratives and visions. Consequently, Klaus Koch called such an apocalypse a *Rahmengattung,* an "overarching genre." The smaller genres (such as the court narratives in Daniel) then are called *Gliedgattungen,* "member genres or subgenres."[28] In the LXX, ch. 13 (Bel and the Dragon) is set in a private home and narrates events of deception and discovery.

A Special Feature Connected with the Study of the Book

One remarkable feature of the book of Daniel is that it is written in two different languages, Hebrew and Aramaic.[29] (Even the additions in the LXX seem to have been composed in Hebrew or Aramaic, though they survive only in Greek.) The book begins in Hebrew, but switches to Aramaic in 2:4 and continues in that language through ch. 7. Hebrew resumes in 8:1 for the remainder of the book. (The only other lengthy Aramaic passage in the MT is Ezra 4:8–6:18.) The type of Aramaic in Ezra and in the famous manuscripts found at Elephantine in Egypt seems to continue down to 200 B.C.E.

26. See Wilson, "From Prophecy to Apocalyptic," 89; also W. Lee Humphreys, "A Lifestyle for Diaspora," *JBL* 92 (1973) 211-13; Philip R. Davies, "Eschatology in the Book of Daniel," *JSOT* (1980) 40-41; and Collins, *Daniel,* 45.

27. Lawrence M. Wills, *The Jew in the Court of the Foreign King: Ancient Jewish Court Legends.* HDR 26 (Minneapolis: Fortress, 1990) 37.

28. Cf. Klaus Koch, *Was ist Formgeschichte?* (Neukirchen-Vluyn: Neukirchener, 1964) 26-30.

29. Aramaic is a Northwest Semitic language (or group of languages) closely related to Hebrew, but not identical. It came from a group of people called Arameans, who were merchants in Mesopotamia. The language was used in trade, and it became the official language of commerce during the Assyrian, Babylonian, and Persian periods. It even served as the official language of the Persian Empire, but was replaced by Greek during the Hellenistic period. Jews continued to use Aramaic into the Common Era. See William S. LaSor, "Aramaic," *ISBE,* 1:229-31.

or later, so efforts to prove that Daniel was written in the sixth century based on the Aramaic of the book are not convincing to critical scholars.[30]

The use of the two languages is important in understanding the book. As shown above, the Hebrew narratives in chs. 1, 8-12 came into the book in the third stage of its growth. Also, 9:27 and 11:31 refer to the desecration of the altar at the temple in Jerusalem in 167, placing the final compilation of the work during the troubled days of the Maccabean Revolt. It is worth hypothesizing, therefore, that the switch to Hebrew signaled changes in the self-understanding of the community behind the third edition of the book. The change from Aramaic, the language of captivity, to Hebrew, the traditional language of the homeland, may have been part of the group's rethinking its identity. Scholars have often remarked on the poor quality of the Hebrew in comparison with the Aramaic, so the change was probably made for political and/or theological reasons, not for ease in composition by the author(s) or comprehension by the readers.[31]

Introduction to the Seer

The name of the seer in the book is Daniel, which means "God (El) is my judge." The same name appears in Ezek 14:14, 20; 28:3, where the prophet mentions three ancient worthies: Noah, Daniel, and Job. All these names, of course, appear elsewhere in the Hebrew Bible, but whether Ezekiel knew a version of the biblical narratives associated with these names is unclear. Some scholars, moreover, point to another candidate for Daniel's namesake, a Phoenician ruler named Danel, known today from an ancient text scholars call the "Ugaritic Legend of Aqht." Who knows whether the sixth-century exiles knew of that text or person? What can be said about the names in Ezekiel is that he thought of the three people as paragons of virtue. It could be, therefore, that the name Daniel was chosen simply because of his reputation. Anyway, the Hebrew name of the hero was Daniel.

He also had a Babylonian name, Belteshazzar (1:7; 2:26; 4:8; 5:12), which means "protect his life."[32] It is not possible to know whether the

---

30. Collins, *Daniel,* 13-15.

31. Redditt, *Daniel,* 134. It is not possible to say how many authors might have had a hand in this work. I shall continue to speak of the author(s).

32. See "Belteshazzar," *ISBE,* 1:456.

two names are evidence of two different sources for the traditions connected to Daniel. More important may be the significance of two names for people in exile or under subjugation. To rename someone is to claim far-reaching power over that person. Such renaming is the prerogative of kings, slave owners, and other persons of power.[33] Daniel's three friends Hananiah, Mishael, and Azariah also receive Babylonian names: Shadrach, Meshach, and Abednego (1:7; ch. 3). The name Belteshazzar receives further treatment in 4:8, where Nebuchadnezzar says the syllable "Bel" was taken from the name of his god. Scholars have speculated about the names of the three friends. They suggest that "nego" (from Abednego) is a corruption of the name of the Babylonian god Nebo. Meshach may reflect the name of the Babylonian god Misaak, and both Shadrach and Meshach may include the name of the god Ak(u).[34]

Since Daniel is the hero of the book and not its author, we can learn little directly[35] about the author(s) of the book. We can, however, and even should, examine the life of the hero as disclosed in the book. Daniel 1 introduces Daniel and his friends as members of Judean society taken into captivity by Nebuchadnezzar. In Babylon they are selected for service to the king, but refuse to defile themselves by eating Babylonian food (cf. the demands to eat pork during the reign of Antiochus IV as reported in 4 Maccabees). God intervenes and allows Daniel and his friends to receive royal favor (Dan 1:9). Fidelity to God allows the four to

---

33. Interestingly, 1:7 says Ashpenaz, the palace master for King Nebuchadnezzar, renamed Daniel (and his friends), whereas 4:8 and 5:12 say Nebuchadnezzar renamed him. Daniel 2:26 does not say how Daniel got his new name. Daniel 1:7 looks redactional, apparently an attempt to explain the names that will appear later.

34. Douglas K. Stuart, "Meshach," *ISBE*, 3:328; and "Shadrach," *ISBE*, 4:441.

35. I have argued ("Daniel 11 and the Sociohistorical Setting of the Book of Daniel," *CBQ* 60 [1998] 463-74) on indirect grounds that the group behind Daniel was likely a group of scribes, hence the portrayal of Daniel as a wise man whose revelations the "wise" (11:33, 35; 12:3, 10) would understand. These scribes possibly moved to Judah after 200 (when the Seleucids seized it from the Ptolemies) and experienced years of royal favor when Antiochus III was attempting to court the favor of Judeans by means of reduced taxes. They may have hoped that fidelity to their religion and God would help them advance in their service of the Seleucid overlords. The persecutions under Antiochus IV may have "burst their balloon." When persecution broke out under Antiochus IV, it probably affected them adversely. The author(s) saw the Maccabees as being of little help in the cosmic war being waged over Judah. The articulation of their hopes for God's rectification of their situation took the form of the book of Daniel.

outperform those who have not withstood temptation, and Daniel maintains a position as advisor to the king until the first year of King Cyrus (539). What might this portrait say, however, about the group that told this story? It seems clear that Daniel was the model for getting along in a Hellenistic environment.

This same conclusion holds for the rest of the book as well. In chs. 2 and 4, God enables Daniel to decipher Nebuchadnezzar's dream when no one else in the court could do so. In ch. 3 the three youths survive the fiery furnace by refusing to worship a statue of the king (cf. the refusal of loyal Judeans to worship the image set up in the temple by Antiochus IV). In ch. 5, God enables Daniel to decipher handwriting on the wall that no one else could read. In ch. 6 God rescues Daniel from the lions' den. In chs. 7–12, however, the hero sees visions so complex not even he can discern them, but God provides an interpreting angel to explain them to Daniel. In every case Daniel (or his friends) succeeds by remaining faithful to Israel's God and God's commandments. The lesson was clear: success in the Gentile world was possible for Judeans only through fidelity to their own God. Capitulation to threats and violence would bring failure, not success.

Basic Emphases in Daniel

It is clear that the narrator weaves a number of emphases into his stories. We shall examine six of them, beginning with what we have just seen was the most important to the author(s).

Fidelity to God

What did fidelity to God look like to the author(s) of Daniel? In ch. 1 it means avoiding the food at the foreign court. Daniel requests that the guard feed them no meat at all, only seeds (v. 12). Nowhere does the Torah require such a strict diet; it only prohibits eating certain kinds of animals including pigs, camels, badgers, and several other species of land, air, and water animals (see Leviticus 11). Not surprisingly, English Bibles often read "vegetables" for "seeds," but the MT reads the latter. It may be that the author(s) had in mind "seed-bearing plants," but it is also possible that the author(s) meant to say "seeds" to accentuate the severity of the diet of the four friends.[36] The message to the readership might have been this: if Daniel and his friends could pare down their diet this far to keep from violating dietary regulations, the readers could do without the meat the law prohibited.

Other chapters add to this picture of fidelity. In Daniel 3 and 6 fidelity means refusing to worship or pray to a foreign king. In his prayer of confession in 9:5-6, Daniel mentions sinning by turning aside from God's laws and not heeding God's prophets. "All Israel" has transgressed God's law (v. 11), so a curse has come upon them (presumably in the form of the Seleucid ruler and his army). Daniel's intercessory prayer turns out to be efficacious, and Daniel receives assurance that the end of Greek hegemony is near. The narrative certainly advocates repentance and obedience; it may have intended to promote similar prayers within the community or by its leaders. Finally, the text promises that the "wise" in Israel would be rewarded for their fidelity, even after death if necessary (12:2-3).

Honor and Shame

A second theme in Daniel is the interaction between honor and shame. Several scholars influenced by social science criticism have focused on the importance of honor in the Mediterranean world and its interplay with its opposite, shame. They argue that "Honor is ascribed by birth, replicated by blood and by name, and owned collectively by the group to which one belongs. . . ."[37] Thus, the honor and reputation of one's group must be protected before the general public. In Daniel, the honor to be protected was ostensibly that of captives in exile in the sixth century, but in actuality it was the honor of the second-century group to which the author(s) of Daniel belonged that had to be defended, lest they lose face in their own eyes and succumb to the values of Greek culture. We should remember that there was much in that culture that Judeans of the second century found alluring, and much that sounded compatible — or could be made to sound compatible — with torah and Judean values. The trick was to ac-

36. Some ancient Chinese Taoists thought they should abstain from meat, wine, strong-smelling plants and vegetables and live off of herbs and minerals. See Max Kaltenmark, *Lao Tzu and Taoism* (Stanford: Stanford University Press, 1969) 124.

37. Shane Kirkpatrick, *Competing for Honor: A Social-Scientific Reading of Daniel 1–6* (Leiden: Brill, 2005) 29.

commodate without capitulating. The "wise" were those who, among other things, could show the community what to adopt and what to eschew and still be faithful to Israel's God and ways.

Generally speaking, the narratives in chs. 1–7, 14 deal with the honor of Jewish culture (and religion) with regard to Greek culture, with Daniel and his friends exemplifying appropriate respect for their own traditions. Their fidelity came at greater or lesser threat to themselves. Daniel 13:1-64 (in the LXX) gives another perspective on honor. There the honor is that of the virtuous wife Susanna, who is charged with making improper sexual advances by two men. When she properly rejects them and cries out for help (cf. Deut 22:24, which requires that a woman being attacked in the city should attract attention by crying out), they immediately try to cover their shame by accusing her. Daniel defends her in court, getting the two men to contradict each other in their testimony.

World Kingdoms and God's Kingdom

The schema of four world kingdoms was mentioned above in connection with "Darius the Mede" (see *The Setting for the Book*). The book of Daniel identifies the kingdoms as Babylon, Media, Persia, and Greece. Such reinterpretations of symbols are fairly common in apocalyptic literature.

What is important for our consideration here, however, is the view of world kingdoms in Daniel. In ch. 2 the metals representing the four kingdoms begin with gold, suggesting that the author(s) may have seen much in Gentile kingdoms worth cultivating. Those kingdoms, nevertheless, decline in worth, from gold to silver to bronze to iron, which was eventually mixed with clay making it brittle and worthless. In ch. 7 the menacing last animal/kingdom declines into an arrogant "little horn" (v. 8) that one "like a son of a man" (i.e., Israel or the saints among the Israelites) would put down (vv. 13-14). In ch. 8 the Medes and Persians would give way to Greece, which in turn would be overthrown. The victor is not stated, but the use of the passive voice in contexts like these was often, even typically, a way to signal to the reader that God would play the major role. In chs. 10–11, the king of the north (Antiochus IV) would die in Canaan "with no one to help him" (11:45), again (implied) at the hands of God.

The uniformity of these presentations suggests that the author(s) of Daniel thought history was going downhill, that the period of foreign con-

trol over Israel was limited, and that God would rescue God's people —
and soon. Moreover, the old system of world kingdoms succeeding one another would be replaced by a new one, God's kingdom, which would include first and foremost Israel or the elect within it.

Good from the Hands of Gentiles

Not all the narratives, however, are so pessimistic about living among
Gentiles. Daniel 1 certainly indicates that Judeans could flourish among
Gentiles and reap rewards from them, provided, of course, that they did
not abandon their faith and practices in favor of Gentile ways. Daniel 4
(the madness of Nebuchadnezzar) and Daniel 5 (the interpretation of the
handwriting on the wall) also depict the wise and pious Daniel succeeding
in the Babylonian court. Even chs. 2 and 7 show Daniel excelling at the
court, despite the dangers of his task, which was to interpret a dream and a
sign that bode ill for the Babylonians. Daniel 3 (the three young men in the
fiery furnace) and Daniel 6 (Daniel in the lions' den) reveal the threat inherent in life at the foreign court, but at the same time continue to demonstrate that fidelity to God is the only hope for receiving good from the
Gentiles. The idea seems to be that even Gentiles recognize the advantages
to keeping wise, pious Judeans among their advisors. If Gentiles failed to
do so, God would protect the faithful. To prove that assurance, the last five
chapters indicate that God would bless those faithful to God, even if that
blessing lay beyond death (12:1-4).

The Future of the "Wise"

One need only read 1 Macc 1–5 to gain an appreciation for the difficulties
some Judeans felt under the Seleucids, especially Antiochus IV Epiphanes.
Persecution was common, and the benefits of the Greek lifestyle were reinforced by official actions. It would have appeared, therefore, that the way to
succeed among the Seleucids was to capitulate whenever Greece endorsed
what Torah forbade. Greek thinking was especially attractive to intellectu-
ally inclined Judeans. Yet sometimes when Judeans dissented, they were
pressured to capitulate, especially in matters that seemed important to
government. A group that understood itself as the "wise" was particularly

vulnerable, and especially if they also worked for the Seleucids.[38] Some of the narratives themselves suggest a hope for acceptance by and cooperation with the Seleucids that other narratives suggest had reached an impasse. When some Judeans took up arms, the "wise" saw those actions as futile. Instead, they seem to have advocated letting God do the fighting and waiting for God's new day. Many interpreters see the reference to receiving a "little help" in the time of persecution (11:34) as a tip of the hat to the Maccabees in their rebellion against the Seleucids.[39] The "wise" were to place no faith in such armed resistance, apparently, but were to persevere in nonviolent resistance. Evil would increase, and the author of Daniel 11 admits that some of them would "fall" until the time of the end (11:35).

At that time, however, the "wise" would be delivered by God. They would "shine like the brightness of the sky." If they were martyred, God would resurrect them to "everlasting life"; their persecutors would be raised to "everlasting contempt." Resurrection is mentioned in only one verse (12:2), but it is the clearest prediction of resurrection in the Hebrew Bible. Isaiah 26:19 might predict a resurrection for the godly, but that verse — like Ezekiel's vision of the dry bones that come back to life (Ezek 37:1-14) — is probably better read as a reference to national resurrection. In a historical situation in which the godly were not being vindicated in this life, the author of Dan 12:2 makes the leap of faith that there must be some kind of vindication beyond this life for such persons. Daniel 12:13 includes the seer himself among those to be raised by God.

---

38. See Redditt, "Daniel 11 and the Sociohistorical Setting of the Book of Daniel," 463-74. Lester L. Grabbe agrees with my view that the "wise" worked in the service of the Seleucids, but thinks they were high-ranking officials, not lower-ranking as I suggest; "A Dan(iel) for All Seasons: For Whom Was Daniel Important?" in *The Book of Daniel: Composition and Reception,* ed. John J. Collins and Peter W. Flint. VTSup 83 (Leiden: Brill, 2002) 234 n. 14. I am not sure we disagree, since I do not know how high up in the service to Seleucids a Jew could rise. In the same volume, Philip R. Davies argues that the group was directly connected to the "wise" (the *maskilim*) at Qumran; "The Scribal School of Daniel," 256-64. That is certainly an attractive suggestion that is not necessarily contradictory to my view.

39. That rebellion did not succeed in driving the Seleucids from Judah, but it did reestablish a (varying) measure of Judean control over affairs of the state. Under Judas Maccabeus Judeans regained control of the temple and installed new priests in late 164. Under Jonathan (priest from 161 to 142 and governor as well) Judea gained a measure of political freedom. Under his brother Simon the Greeks were dependent on Judeans for help in controlling the Levant. The succeeding Hasmonean Dynasty held out against the Seleucids, but came under Roman hegemony when Rome defeated the Seleucids in 63 B.C.E.

The book's description of the end-time is brief (12:2-3), giving no real details about that life. We may surmise that it would be here on earth, that the tables would be turned on the Seleucids and the Judeans who cooperated with them, and that justice and righteousness would govern human conduct. This picture corresponds well with the picture in 2:44, which promises abiding or perpetual victory for God's kingdom, and the one in 7:14, 27, which adds that the world kingdoms would serve the people, the saints of the Most High God. The brevity of these descriptions should not be surprising. For one thing, no one could know what the future kingdom would be like. But that was all right; it just had to be the opposite of what was going on at the time of the writing of Daniel. Besides, what the readers needed to know first was that Seleucid rule would soon end.

The Reuse of Scripture

Daniel 9 is noteworthy for the last feature to be discussed here, the reuse of Scripture. Verses 4-19 constitute a penitential prayer quite similar to such prayers found elsewhere in Joshua 7; Ezra 9; Nehemiah 1; and Psalm 106 and mentioned in Leviticus 26 and 1 Kings 8.[40] Verses 20-27 also contain a response to Daniel's penitential prayer. There Gabriel (cf. 8:16; in other literature identified as an archangel) interprets a prediction of Jeremiah. That prophet had anticipated that the Babylonian exile would last 70 years (Jer 25:11-12; 29:10), a figure sufficiently long to indicate that no one who had been brought to Babylon from Jerusalem would live to return. 2 Chronicles cites Jeremiah four times (2 Chr 35:25; 36:12, 21, 22), the third of them with specific reference to the seventy years.

The last half (9:24-27) of this response, however, reinterprets the time period as seventy *weeks of* years, seven times as long. Scholars have tried to make the schema fit the time frame for events known to moderns, but without much success. Stripped to its essence, this timetable envisions two "anointed ones" coming at different times. The first (probably Joshua the high priest in Jerusalem mentioned in Zechariah 3) comes after seven weeks of years. The second (probably Onias III, high priest during the reign of Seleucus IV Philopater [187-175]) is "cut off" at the beginning of

---

40. See the study by Mark J. Boda, *Praying the Tradition*. BZAW 277 (Berlin: de Gruyter, 1999).

the last week.[41] We would be well advised to see the numbers as a periodization of history built around Sabbath and Jubilee years, not a precise number of years. First, 2 Chr 36:21 restates Jeremiah's prediction (Jer 25:11, 12; 29:10) of a seventy-year exile to Babylon as ten Sabbaths. In other words, the sins of the preexilic period would require ten Sabbaths of years of rest for atonement. Second, Dan 9:24-27 says that the sins of the pre- *and postexilic* periods would take ten Jubilees[42] for atonement, seven times as long. Daniel 9 divides the time between one Jubilee (most likely, until Joshua went back to Jerusalem) and six Jubilees leading up to the end of time. The vision climaxes with the events of the last "week of years" of the last Jubilee, beginning when the second anointed one was "cut off." That "week" would be dominated throughout by fighting, and the last half by the desecration of the temple in Jerusalem by means of improper sacrifices. This "week of years," therefore, had in view the time between the end of the tenure of Onias III (somewhere between 187 and 175) and the death of Antiochus IV Epiphanes in 164.

Wilson calls attention to the perspective fueling this reuse of Jeremiah. Whatever the author of 2 Chr 36:21 thought about the timeliness of the restoration under Joshua (and Zerubbabel?), the author of Daniel 9 was not prepared to accept the conditions of the late sixth century or 165 as a fulfillment of God's promise through Jeremiah.[43] Consequently, Gabriel came to inform Daniel that the "devastation of Jerusalem" was not the same thing as the hegemony of Babylon and would last seventy weeks of years.[44] By this device the author(s) of Daniel could employ the older writings to buttress his (their) new perspective.

41. It is not clear what happened to Onias. According to 2 Macc 4:34, a king's deputy named Andronicus murdered him at Daphne, but Josephus (*J.W.* i.1.1) says Onias fled to safety in Egypt.

42. A Jubilee is forty-nine years. This way of structuring time had its roots in the Jubilee Years legislated in Leviticus 25, but it was employed in the second and first centuries B.C.E. in periodizations of history. The book of Jubilees, which perhaps dates from about 161-140, famously divides time into Jubilees, with, e.g., the period between Adam and the Exodus reckoned at 2,401 years or exactly forty-nine Jubilees. Also 11QMelch (a Dead Sea Scroll from the first century B.C.E.) looks toward a "release of the captives" mentioned in Isa 61:1 after ten Jubilees.

43. Robert R. Wilson, "Unfulfilled Prophecy and the Development of the Prophetic Tradition," a paper delivered at the Annual Meeting of the Society of Biblical Literature in 1991.

44. Paul L. Redditt, "Daniel 9: Its Structure and Meaning," *CBQ* 62 (2000) 236-49, esp. 237, 246-47.

Problems Raised by a Study of Daniel

A study of the book of Daniel raises several issues that need addressing at this point: the issue of what parts of the book belong in the Bible, the use of pseudonymity, the dating of the end time, and the problem of unfulfilled prophecy. (After all, the end has not yet come, despite the assurances of the book of Daniel that the end was rapidly approaching during its time.) We shall examine these issues in the order listed.

The Contents of the Bible

The LXX and the Roman Catholic OT contain more materials than do the MT and the Protestant OT that follows it. In the case(s) of Baruch and the Letter of Jeremiah, the difference is whether to accept other deutero-Jeremianic books than Lamentations. In Daniel, the issue is whether to accept the three ancient additions found in 3:24-90a and chs. 13–14. Obviously there is no unanimity. The answer perhaps revolves around the meaning of "canon." The term derives from the Greek word *kanon*, which means "rule" or "standard" by which something is measured, in this case conduct and belief. Used with reference to the Bible, it refers to a list of books accepted as authoritative.

Much could be said about the criteria used in selecting the contents of both Testaments, but one seems appropriate here. Books admitted into the canons of Judaism and Christianity were deemed those with the especial power to point people to God. That is, human communities selected those books that for whatever reasons rang truest as guides to faith and belief. If some people included these additions to Daniel (and Baruch and the Letter of Jeremiah) while others did not, the differences do not prove that one group is correct and the other incorrect. They are just different.

Pseudonymity

As noted above in connection with the authorship of Daniel, the last half of the book purports to have been written by Daniel, but is actually pseudonymous. That is not quite the same thing as a redactor attaching his or someone else's "updates" to a prophet's message, though the result is the same in either case: words are ascribed to someone other than the actual author. This way of stating matters, however, betrays a modern sensitivity because today it is possible for persons to earn money, maybe even a handsome income, from intellectual property. Consequently, we copyright poems, books, music, film, and art. We consider plagiarism both immoral and illegal.

Some other modern cultures do not, however, and ancient cultures seem not to have considered them as such either. To cite but one famous example from the past, many scholars of Greek philosophy think that in his early dialogues (e.g., *Apology, Crito, Meno, Phaedo,* and the *Euthyphro*) Plato tries to be faithful to what he thought Socrates had said, but in his middle dialogues (e.g., the *Republic, Symposium,* and the *Phaedrus*) he used Socrates to endorse his own positions. In view of such practices, it is dangerous, therefore, for us to superimpose our own notions about authorship on ancient literature.

What appears to have happened in the literature of the Hebrew Bible is that laws were attached to Moses, psalms to David, and proverbs and other wisdom literature to Solomon. The Prophetic literature knew a number of great figures, and much that appears secondary to many modern scholars was attached to figures like Isaiah, Jeremiah, and Ezekiel — not to mention many of the Twelve, particularly Micah and Zechariah. This practice is not plagiarism, as some modern thinkers charge, but exactly the reverse. In plagiarism a writer passes off the intellectual product of someone else as his own in an effort to take credit for the ideas. In biblical texts, later editors added their thoughts or those of other people they admired to the products of earlier thinkers in order to gain acceptance of the ideas, but not to enhance their own reputation. Nor need this activity be seen as deceitful. A later redactor modified/enlarged an earlier text to make that text address new situations. That practice was, in fact, crucial to the rise of the biblical canon, where one underlying assumption is that these old documents remain true in new contexts. In the history of the rise of the documents themselves, redactors sometimes stripped place names and dates to make a text apply to new contexts. Other times they simply hooked new sayings onto older ones with transition phrases like "on that day." The use of pseudonymity may be seen as one more step down that road.

Dating the End Time

The book of Daniel uses several phrases to date the coming end time. These include "a time, times, and a half" (7:25; 12:7), "2300 evenings and mornings" (8:14), "70 weeks of years" (9:24-27), "1290 days" (12:11), and "1335 days" (12:12). Daniel 12:7 links "a time, times, and a half" with 12:11-12, in effect interpreting the phrase to mean "a year, two years, and half a year." The phrase "2300 evenings and mornings" could refer to 2300 days or it could mean "1150 evenings and 1150 mornings," i.e., half as long. This latter interpretation would bring the time frame much closer to three and a half years, which also would correspond to the last half of the last "week of years" (9:27). One should note, however, that this time frame is superimposed on these figures. "A time, times, and a half" is remarkably indefinite, and the difference between 2300 and 1150 days is significant. Still, it is not out of the question that the author of 12:5-12 saw these figures as pointing to the same event or cluster of events.

Scholars have sometimes understood the figures 1150, 1290, and 1335 as successive projections of the end time. When the end did not come after 1150 days, the author recalculated in 12:11 and came up with 1290. When the end still did not come, he recalculated yet again, resulting in the figure 1335 in 12:12. Presumably at that point he gave up the enterprise. It is possible, however, that the author had in mind some specific event that happened on about day 1150. One possibility that suggests itself is the cleansing of the temple under Judas Maccabeus (7 December 164). That event was momentous enough to start an eschatological clock to ticking. Perhaps, then, the author of 12:5-12 expected *two more* events, 140 and 185 days later. The death of Antiochus Epiphanes might well have been the first of those two, and the expected inbreak of the end time the second.[45]

Unfulfilled or Inaccurate Prophecy

The simple fact remains, however, that the end did not come within the time frame the book of Daniel anticipated.[46] The person responsible for

---

45. See Redditt, *Daniel*, 194-99.

46. To argue otherwise requires some kind of mental gymnastics that says the writer expected his people to draw comfort from the thought that at a minimum of thousands of years later God would rescue God's people.

12:5-12 was not alone in missing his projections. One dominant character-istic of apocalypses is their insistence that the end is coming soon, and both Daniel and the Christian book of Revelation expected an imminent end (see Rev. 1:1; 22:20). The Apostle Paul appears to have expected the re-turn of Jesus during Paul's own lifetime or at least that of his readers (1 Thess 4:13-17). Do such unfulfilled (or inaccurate) predictions disqualify the message of such books? The answer lies with the reader, of course, but it is possible to suggest a few reasons why the answer should be "No."

In the first place, the lack of fulfillment did not squelch readership of the book. Despite its late date, it was accepted into both the Jewish and Christian canons. That seems to mean that both groups thought they heard the voice of God speaking in the book. What might have prompted such a reaction? Perhaps it was the book's insistence that fidelity to God is indispensable. Perhaps it was the book's insistence that in the end (when-ever that end might come) God would vindicate God's people. Perhaps it was the book's testimony to the power of faith in the presence of danger. Perhaps it was the book's depiction of success in a "foreign" or hostile con-text. Perhaps it was because in the end faith is more important than sight. Perhaps it was all of these and a number of other reasons. In any case, readership of the book flourished, despite a miscalculation of the end time in the last few verses.

Summary

The book of Daniel belongs to a genre of literature, the apocalypse, which presupposes that history is going downhill fast and that God will soon break in to rectify matters. Set in the Babylonian, the "Median," and early Persian periods, much of the book is really about life in Palestine under the Seleucid king Antiochus IV Epiphanes. Chapters 1–7 contain narratives in which fidelity to God conquers all threats, but chs. 8–12 reflect the more se-vere times following the defilement of the altar in Jerusalem (the "abomi-nation of desolation" mentioned in 1 Macc 1:54, 59) in 167 B.C.E. The book ends with a calculation of the end time and a prediction of resurrection to glorification for godly martyrs and punishment for their persecutors.

Questions for Reflection

1. If apocalyptic literature was written by and for people who perceived themselves to be deprived, what warning(s) and/or message(s) might it carry for people in middle and upper classes and/or within the power structure? Against what sorts of behaviors might the book warn such readers?
2. What in Daniel's depiction of the end is beneficial to you and why?
3. If there are historical errors in the book of Daniel, what do they suggest about the canonicity of Daniel? How might modern believers explain the presence and significance of such errors?
4. What do you think about the propriety of pseudonymity? What difference would it make to you, and why, if the Bible contains pseudonymous writings?
5. What do you think about the differences in ways worshipping communities find narratives about Daniel and his friends authoritative?

For Further Reading

Baldwin, Joyce B. *Daniel.* TOTC. Downers Grove: Inter-Varsity, 1978. Excellent, short commentary, which makes careful use of Hebrew and Aramaic.

Collins, John J. *Daniel.* Hermeneia. Minneapolis: Fortress, 1993. Thorough critical commentary that employs all major methods of study and takes cognizance of relevant ancient literature.

—————, and Peter W. Flint, eds. *The Book of Daniel: Composition and Reception.* 2 vols. VTSup 83. Leiden: Brill, 2001. Thirty-two scholarly articles covering current issues in the study of Daniel, the Near Eastern milieu of the book, the interpretation of specific passages, the book's social setting, literary context (including Qumran), reception in Judaism and Christianity, textual history, and theology.

Goldingay, John E. *Daniel.* WBC 30. Dallas: Word, 1989. Meticulous critical and insightful study. Careful attention to Hebrew and Aramaic text matched by attention to theology and relevance for modern readers.

Gowan, Donald E. *Daniel.* AOTC. Nashville: Abingdon, 2001. Brief introduction to each chapter or section of the book (key issues, literary genre, structure, character of the writings, social context), followed by exegesis and treatment of their theological/ethical significance.

Hartman, Louis F., and Alexander A. Di Lella. *The Book of Daniel.* AB 23. Garden City: Doubleday, 1978. A translation with textual notes and a full, scholarly commentary, preceded by a lengthy introduction.

Redditt, Paul L. *Daniel.* NCBC. Sheffield: Sheffield Academic, 1999. A commentary focused on the genre and structure as well as the historical and social background of each narrative of the book.

Smith-Christopher, Daniel L. "The Book of Daniel." *NIB,* 7 (1996): 17-151. Readable commentary combining the NIV and the NRSV with a study based on the Hebrew and Aramaic text. Comments include theological reflections.

The Minor Prophets

Hosea, Joel, Amos
Obadiah, Jonah, Micah
Nahum, Habakkuk, Zephaniah
Haggai, Zechariah, Malachi

The section of the English OT called the Minor Prophets (the Book of the Twelve in the Hebrew Bible) includes materials associated with twelve different prophets identified by name. Indeed, most say nothing about the prophet aside from his name, father, or hometown. Hosea contains a brief account of the prophet's marriage, which forms an integral part of his message. Amos contains one brief narrative, that of his confrontation with the priest Amaziah, in which Amos is banished from the temple at Bethel. At the other extreme, though, the collection bearing the name Jonah is really a narrative and contains only a short summary of his message. It would seem equally at home in the accounts of prophets in 1 and 2 Kings as in the Book of the Twelve. Aside from Jonah, then, the prophets named in the Twelve speak substantially out of obscurity. It was their *words* for the most part that people remembered, not the confrontations with kings or their roles in their own messages seen among the Major Prophets. They spanned roughly the same time frame as the Major Prophets, i.e., the eighth century to the Persian period, but they fill in the prophetic picture around the "major" prophets. The collection of their messages into one volume is an important part of their message, so they will be treated in what follows as twelve collections combined by a scribal editor into one volume.

CHAPTER 9

The Book of the Twelve

The Book of the Twelve presents a unique set of problems in terms of how to approach it, because it contains sayings and occasional narratives about not one, but twelve prophets, introduced in nine cases by a superscription (a heading supplying the name and perhaps other information about the author) and in three cases — Jonah, Haggai, and Zechariah — by an incipit (a sentence beginning a narrative or narrative book). At some point or points in time these sayings and narratives were collected onto one scroll, though not always in the same order.[1] The rabbis recognized the uniqueness of this compilation and called the scroll the "Book of the Twelve." In their arrangement of the Hebrew Bible, they counted four books as the Former Prophets (Joshua, Judges, Samuel, and Kings) and four more as the "Latter Prophets" (Isaiah, Jeremiah, Ezekiel, and the Twelve). Since the Twelve was reckoned as one book, the individual collections within it will be called "collections" here rather than "books."[2] Scholars have detected clues in the collections themselves concerning the process of their editorial joining. These collections, therefore, will be discussed in the order they appear in the Hebrew Bible, with attention given

---

1. The Septuagint (LXX) or Greek version of the Bible differs from the order of the MT in that it places Joel, Obadiah, and Jonah together after Hosea, Amos, and Micah and before Nahum. Other ancient lists offered varying sequences, and one of the Dead Sea Scrolls places Jonah last.

2. To be sure, the second superscription to Nahum in 1:1 refers to it as "the book of the vision of Nahum of Elkosh," but consistency dictates calling Nahum a "collection" too.

to connections between the collections and the ongoing plot of the Twelve as well as the content of the individual collections.

The Rise of the Book of the Twelve

Because of the approach adopted for this study, some introduction to reading the Twelve as one work is called for. I will begin with a hypothetical description of the rise of the Book of the Twelve. It seems to have had a series of precursors. The first we may term the "Book of the Four." Based partly on the common headings of Hosea, Amos, Micah, and Zephaniah, David Noel Freedman has suggested that the four constituted an early book.[3] James D. Nogalski accepted that conclusion and developed it in a two-volume study that focuses on redactional connections, usually repeated words or phrases at the end of one prophetic collection and the beginning of the next.[4] The Book of the Four itself may have had a precursor, a "Book of the Two" consisting of Hosea and Amos or a "Book of the Three" that also included Micah but not Zephaniah.[5] The idea of the existence of a Book of the Four edited in the early exilic period, however, seems to account best for the similarities among those collections. In the postexilic period, Haggai and Zechariah 1-8 seem to have been redacted by one hand, a conclusion affirmed by a host of scholars. Thus by the end of the sixth century two independent collections or "precursors" already existed.

It also appears that Nahum and Habakkuk underwent a redaction that pulled them together, partly by means of hymns opening Nahum and closing Habakkuk. Duane Christensen offers the following diagram:[6]

---

3. David Noel Freedman, "Headings in the Books of the Eighth-Century Prophets," in *Festschrift in Honor of Leona Glidden Running,* ed. William H. Shea, 9-26. AUSS 25 (Berrien Springs: Andrews University Press, 1987).

4. James Nogalski, *Literary Precursors to the Book of the Twelve.* BZAW 217 (Berlin: de Gruyter, 1993); *Redactional Processes in the Book of the Twelve.* BZAW 218 (Berlin: de Gruyter, 1993).

5. Aaron Schart, *Die Entstehung des Zwölfprophetenbuchs.* BZAW 260 (Berlin: de Gruyter, 1998) 151-56; Byron G. Curtis, "The Zion-Daughter Oracles: Evidence on the Identity and Ideology of the Late Redactors of the Book of the Twelve," in *Reading and Hearing the Book of the Twelve,* ed. James D. Nogalski and Marvin A. Sweeney. SBLSymS 15 (Atlanta: SBL, 2000) 171.

6. Duane Christensen, "The Book of Nahum: A History of Interpretation," in *Forming Prophetic Literature: Essays on Isaiah and the Twelve in Honor of John D. W. Watts,* ed. James W. Watts and Paul R. House. JSOTSup 235 (Sheffield: Sheffield Academic, 1996) 193.

A	Hymn of theophany	Nahum 1
B	Taunt song against Nineveh	Nahum 2–3
X	The problem of theodicy	Habakkuk 1
B′	Taunt song against the "wicked one"	Habakkuk 2
A′	Hymn of theophany	Habakkuk 3

The date for this additional "precursor" cannot be earlier than the latter days of the preexilic period, since Hab 3:16 probably has in view one or more of the Babylonian attacks against Jerusalem. How much later it came together is impossible to say, though Nogalski finds catchwords between Nahum 3 and Habakkuk 1 that he dates well into the postexilic period, when he thinks the two were drawn into the Twelve under the influence of Joel.[7] Though some scholars question the relevance of the catchwords Nogalski adduces between Nahum and Habakkuk (and between some of the other collections also), there appears to be good evidence anyway for postulating the existence of a combined Nahum-Habakkuk about the same time as the other two precursors.

Another development occurred sometime after 450 B.C.E., when the collection under the name Malachi was attached directly to Haggai-Zechariah 1–8. Nogalski argues (correctly) that Zechariah 9–14 was added later, with the superscriptions in Zech 9:1 and 12:1 imitating Mal 1:1.[8] Thus, by that point there existed three separate precursors to the Twelve: (1) the Book of the Four (Hosea, Amos, Micah, Zephaniah), (2) Nahum-Habakkuk, and (3) Haggai, Zechariah 1–8, Malachi.

This sketch leaves three more collections in the Twelve to account for: Joel, Obadiah, Jonah. In addition, the inclusion of Zechariah 9–14 requires discussion. It might be too much to claim that Joel and Obadiah formed another precursor, and no one I am aware of has made that suggestion. Still, it is clear that Obadiah is the older of the two, arising, presumably, soon after the fall of Jerusalem in 586, and that Joel 2:32 draws upon Obad 17 in predicting the restoration of Jerusalem. That Joel did the borrowing is made clear by Joel's use of the citation formula "as YHWH has said." In any case, Joel 2:32 shows that the author of Joel had Obadiah in view. Both were selected for inclusion and combined with the other precursors, bringing the total of the collections to eleven.

---

7. Nogalski, *Redactional Processes*, 150-54, 180-81.
8. Nogalski, *Redactional Processes*, 182-212.

What about Jonah and Zechariah 9–14? Jonah is an oddity in many ways, especially in the brevity of his recorded message ("Yet forty days until Nineveh is overthrown"; Jonah 3:4) versus the overall length of the narrative about him (three chapters) plus a lengthy psalm attributed to him. In fact, the Jonah narrative would be at least as much at home in 2 Kings as in the Twelve. It is easy, therefore, to see the collection as a narrative selected to bring the total of "prophets" in the book to twelve at the time the three precursors and Obadiah and Joel were combined. Thus, Zechariah 9–14 seems to have been added last as the capstone to the Twelve,[9] but without the name of a new prophet since there were already twelve.

The Sequence of the Twelve

The Book of the Twelve comes in two basic sequences, one in the MT, the other in the LXX.[10] Two columns will illustrate the differences.

Masoretic Text	Septuagint
Hosea	Hosea
Joel	Amos
Amos	Micah
Obadiah	Joel
Jonah	Obadiah
Micah	Jonah
Nahum	Nahum
Habakkuk	Habakkuk
Zephaniah	Zephaniah

9. Paul L. Redditt, "Zechariah 9–14: The Capstone of the Twelve," in *Bringing Out the Treasure: Inner Biblical Allusion in Zechariah 9–14*, ed. Mark J. Boda and Michael H. Floyd, 312-20. JSOTSup 370 (London: Sheffield Academic, 2003). Technically, Mal 4:4-6(Heb. 3:22-24) was probably added about the same time or a little later and cast a glance back over the entirety of the Torah and Nebiim.

10. Various ancient sources list the collections in differing sequences, but offer no proof of the order of the collections. Manuscripts among the Dead Sea Scrolls contain several collections in sequence, including one (4QXII[a]) that contains fragments of Zechariah and the sequence of Malachi — Jonah. On the significance of this sequence, see Barry Alan Jones, *The Formation of the Book of the Twelve: A Study in Text and Canon*. SBLDS 149 (Atlanta: Scholars, 1995) 6-7, 129-69.

Haggai   Haggai
Zechariah   Zechariah
Malachi   Malachi

The first observation to make is that both the MT and the LXX begin with the same collection, Hosea, and conclude with the same seven, Nahum through Malachi. Only collections two through six differ. The LXX places the three eighth-century collections (Hosea, Amos, and Micah) together, but leaves the other three (Joel, Obadiah, and Jonah) in the same sequence relative to each other as in the MT. Dale Schneider thinks this way of describing the differences proves that the MT was earlier. The compilers of the version of the Twelve that stands behind the LXX simply pulled the three collections from the eighth century to the beginning of the collection. Everything else remained as in the MT.[11] Marvin A. Sweeney has challenged this view, arguing that the LXX came first, with thematic factors determining the placement of other collections.[12] Clearly, chronology played a role: eighth-century collections come within the first six collections; collections concerning the fall of Assyria and threats to Jerusalem appear as collections seven through nine; and postexilic prophets conclude the Twelve. It is also clear that other factors, including themes, played a role. Still, Sweeney's argument does not have the virtue of explaining the differences in one clean stroke that Schneider's has. Consequently, this volume will proceed on the basis that the arrangement of the Twelve in the MT came first.

Diachronic and Synchronic Readings of the Twelve

Two different approaches to reading the Twelve have emerged. The typical scholarly approach is to arrange the collections chronologically, beginning with Amos, the oldest, and proceeding to Malachi, Zechariah 9–14, Jonah, or whatever a scholar thinks is the latest collection in the Twelve. That approach is facilitated by a few superscriptions that provide the dates for the

11. Dale Schneider, "The Unity of the Book of the Twelve" (Ph. D. diss., Yale, 1979) 220-21.

12. Marvin A. Sweeney, "Sequence and Interpretation in the Book of the Twelve," in Nogalski and Sweeney, *Reading and Hearing the Book of the Twelve*, 52-64. See also, Jones, *The Formation of the Book of the Twelve*, 226-34.

prophets whose words are collected: in the Book of the Four and in Haggai-Zechariah 1–8. Also the date for Jonah himself may be deduced from 2 Kgs 14:25, which mentions him as a prophet in the days of King Jeroboam II of Israel (786-746), though critical scholars typically date the collection bearing his name much later. The dates of the other prophets must be inferred from information within the collections themselves. Since this way of reading the Twelve follows the development of the Twelve *through time,* it is called a "diachronic" reading. It has the obvious advantages that it maintains the individuality of the collections (after all, the redactors retained and/or supplied the names of twelve different prophets) and it follows the development of thinking in the Twelve in historical order.

In doing so, however, this approach misses connections between the collections. One obvious example is the repetition in Amos 1:2 of the proclamation in Joel 3:16:

> YHWH roars from Zion,
> > and gives his voice from Jerusalem,
> > so that earth and heaven tremble;
> But YHWH (is) a refuge to his people,
> > a stronghold to the people of Israel.

The two occurrences are separated by a mere six verses in a consecutive reading of the Twelve, but in a chronological reading by up to ten collections. Whatever a reader might (or should) make of the repetition of the verse in so short a space in the Bible is lost in the chronological reading.

As observed in Chapter 2, more recently scholars have paid attention to the canonical structure of the OT and to reading strategies of books of the Bible that involve reading straight through without recourse to theories of composition and growth. Typically, though, that strategy is not applied to the Twelve, where, instead, scholars still study the collections in the book individually.[13] Exceptions include the commentaries on the Twelve by Sweeney and Nogalski (see For Further Reading).[14] It is possible, therefore, to adopt a canonical reading that approaches the Twelve for its

---

13. See the seminal work by Brevard S. Childs, *Introduction to the Old Testament as Scripture* (Philadelphia: Fortress, 1979) 373-498.

14. Nogalski himself is completing a commentary on the Twelve in the Smyth & Helwys commentary series.

ongoing plot. If attention is paid only to that plot, such a reading would be termed "synchronic," a term meaning *with time.*

The present volume will attempt to read the Twelve both diachronically *and* synchronically. To do that it will proceed straight through the Twelve, commenting on each collection in order.[15] (In doing so, it will join ranks with introductions to the OT like those of Walter Brueggemann and Walter Harrelson.)[16] This book will also pay heed to the development of the plot of the Twelve, discussing it as it takes up new collections, before addressing more historical issues.

Plot and Dominant Themes of the Twelve

It may seem strange to think of a plot even in one of the collections in the Twelve besides Jonah, the only real narrative, let alone the whole book. Still, prophetic speeches often had a recognizable structure, as seen in the use of form criticism. It is only one more step to see structure within a collection. Amos, for example, opens with prophecies of disaster (chs. 1–2), continues with a variety of genres employed to predict doom (chs. 3–6), then switches to visions (7:1–9:10), and concludes with a prediction of future restoration (9:11-15). While the overall tone is one of doom, the last verses give the collection a positive ending. Such a change can also be read as a plot. If one discerns such structures and changes within the Twelve, one can speak of a plot in it as well.

Plot as Comedy and Tragedy

Scholars sometimes point to classical Greek literature in speaking of plots. In doing so, they distinguish comedy from tragedy. A tragedy ends on a

15. Even apart from the reconstruction offered above, this approach still remains defensible as a canonical reading of the Book of the Twelve. It meets the insistence of Reed Lessing (review of Paul L. Redditt and Aaron Schart, *Thematic Threads in the Book of the Twelve,* in *Concordia Journal* 31 [2005] 189-90) on treating the separate collections of the Twelve as important in and of themselves.

16. Walter Brueggemann, *An Introduction to the Old Testament* (Louisville: Westminster John Knox, 2003); Walter Harrelson, *Interpreting the Old Testament* (New York: Holt, Rinehart and Winston, 1964).

downward note, with conflicts resolved unsuccessfully, perhaps even with the death of a hero or heroine. A comedy, by contrast, ends on an upward note, with the success of the hero/heroine. Difficulties are overcome; conflicts are resolved; things turn out well.[17] One need think only of the plots of *Romeo and Juliet* and *Cinderella* to see the difference.

So what is the plot of the Book of the Twelve? Paul R. House argues that the Twelve is shaped around a sequence of events seen as significant to the people of Israel: the fall of the northern kingdom of Israel in 722, of Judah in 586, and the restoration after the edict of Cyrus in 539. Another way to construe that movement is in terms of the prophetic proclamation of Israel's and its neighbors' sin (Hosea — Micah), the consequences of sin (Nah 1:1 — Zeph 3:7), and the eradication of those consequences (Zeph 3:8 — Mal 4:6.)[18] Actually, however, this plot is somewhat oversimplified. Zechariah 9–14, for example, probes the issue of why the promised upturn had not yet measured up to prophetic expectations, and Malachi is full of warnings too. Human events do not always follow a script. Thus the comedic structure in the Twelve is not clean and complete, but the religious and political situation in postexilic Judah was arguably better (even if not perfect) than conditions during the exile.

This book will suggest the following plot for the Twelve.[19] The collections of Hosea, Joel and Amos will develop the theme of *Warnings of Impending Divorce from Israel.* Hosea in particular develops the theme of divorce in the first three chapters. Obadiah, Jonah, and Micah will develop the theme of *Punishment for Judah and Others.* Here again, the plot receives a sophisticated nuance with the Jonah narrative, in which the reader learns that God does not share the prophet's (and Israel's) hope for the destruction of Nineveh, preferring instead the repentance of its inhabitants. Nahum, Habakkuk and Zephaniah develop the motif of *Punishment to Restoration,* beginning with Nahum's angry pronouncement of God's judgment on Nineveh, followed by Habakkuk's promise of the punishment of Babylon as well as Judah, and Zephaniah's idyllic picture of the

---

17. Paul R. House, *The Unity of the Twelve.* JSOTSup 97 (Sheffield: Almond, 1990) 113-14.

18. House, *The Unity of the Twelve,* 116-24.

19. This plot is modified from Gerlinde Baumann, "Die prophetische Ehemetaphorik und die Bewertung der Prophetie im Zwölfprophetenbuch," in *Thematic Threads in the Book of the Twelve,* ed. Paul L. Redditt and Aaron Schart, 214-31. BZAW 325 (Berlin: de Gruyter, 2003).

new day (Zeph 3:8-20) following widespread cataclysm (1:1–3:7). Finally, Haggai, Zechariah, and Malachi anticipate *Restoration, Renewal, and God's Eternal Love,* though not without repentance and change. Malachi also includes a return to the motif of divorce and marriage. Redactors developed this plot through the use of a number of themes, the three most important of which will be highlighted next.

The Marriage Metaphor

The previous paragraph makes clear how important this metaphor is to the Twelve. It is obviously important to the collection of Hosea, which opens with a third and first person account of his marriage, connected by an allegorization of his family life in which what happened to Hosea becomes a metaphor for the infidelity and promised restitution of Israel. Malachi 2:10-16 returns to the same theme, challenging the people of Judah for divorcing their wives and marrying prohibited women. God then announces that God hates divorce. The motif most likely carries a literal meaning in Malachi taken as a free-standing collection. At the end of the Twelve, however, one could say that the book has come almost full circle: from Hosea's divorce of Gomer for infidelity, paralleling God's divorce of Israel for idolatry, to Malachi's denunciation of the people for divorcing their wives to marry presumably idolatrous foreigners.

The Confession about YHWH

Another crucial theme is the confession about God found first on Moses' lips at Sinai (Exod 34:6-7; cf. Num 14:18 and Deut 7:9-10) and then in at least four passages in the Twelve (Joel 2:13; Jonah 4:2; Mic 7:18; Nah 1:2-3a) and possibly a fifth (Hos 1:9).[20] The passage reads as follows in Exod 34:6-7:

20. See Raymond C. Van Leeuwen, "Scribal Wisdom and Theodicy in the Book of the Twelve," in *In Search of Wisdom: Essays in Memory of John G. Gammie,* ed. Leo G. Perdue, Bernard Brandon Scott, and William Johnston Wiseman, 34-48 (Louisville: Westminster John Knox, 1993). Alan Cooper finds allusions also in Hos 14:3, 5; Joel 2:13-14; Jonah 3:8–4:2; Mic 7:18-20; and Nah 1:2-3a; "In Praise of Divine Caprice: The Significance of the Book of Jonah," in *Among the Prophets: Language, Image and Structure in the Prophetic Writings,* ed. Philip R. Davies and David J. A. Clines. JSOTSup 144 (Sheffield: JSOT, 1993) 160.

6 YHWH, YHWH, the compassionate and gracious God,
 slow in anger, abundant in covenant fidelity and faithfulness,
7 maintaining covenant fidelity to the thousands,
 forgiving wickedness, rebellion, and sin,
but not leaving unpunished those not yet punished [i.e., the guilty],
 punishing the sin of the fathers as far as their sons,
  their grandsons,
 and the third and fourth generations.

Joel 2:13 and Jonah 4:2 quote only the part about God's compassion, and Mic 7:18 paraphrases it, while Nah 1:2-3a invokes the part about God's punishment upon Nineveh. Hosea 1:9 ("you are not my people, and I am not your God") might be a paraphrase of the entire passage. Still, four or more citations of the passage in the Twelve point to a conscious agreement of the various prophets on the theology of the passage.

The Day of YHWH

The most wisely-used theme of the three was that of the "day of YHWH," which appears in Hosea, Joel, Amos, Obadiah, Nahum, Habakkuk, Zephaniah, and Malachi. It is so pervasive, in fact, that it has been identified as the most important theme in the Twelve.[21] This theme is addressed not only through specific references to "the day of YHWH," but also often by such phrases as "on that day," "days are coming," "at that time," "it shall come to pass afterwards," and "in those days and at that time."[22]

21. David L. Petersen, "A Book of the Twelve?" in Nogalski and Sweeney, *Reading and Hearing the Book of the Twelve*, 3-10.

22. Recently, Martin Beck studied the "Day of YHWH" in Amos 5:18-20; Zeph 1:2-18; 2:1-3; Joel 1:15-20; 2:1-11, 28-32; 3:14-17; Zechariah 14; and Mal 2:17–3:5; 3:13-21(Eng. 4:3); *Der "Tag YHWHs" im Dodekapropheten: Studien im Spanungsfeld von Traditions- und Redaktionsgeschichte*. BZAW 356 (Berlin: de Gruyter, 2005). He finds that the motif is an important element in all five collections, but gives no hint of a unified understanding or, therefore, redaction. Therefore, he concludes, the Twelve must be viewed as an anthology. This issue is probably not as straightforward as Beck makes it. The scholars being followed here have not argued for a single editor with a consistent theology. The present volume has made the case that there were at least five redactors and three precursors. Those redactors did not strive for overall consistency so much as they added their perspectives to an emerging volume. If "book" is the wrong word to call the Twelve because of a lack of consistency, "anthology" is

Summary

In view of research that suggests the Book of the Twelve was edited to be read straight through as a single volume, this book will attempt just such a reading in the ensuing four chapters. Not only, therefore, will it discuss the book and its times, the prophet, and the genres, themes, and times of individual collections in the Twelve, it will also follow the developing plot of the Twelve. Each chapter will present three collections.

Questions for Reflection

1. What significance, if any, should one attach to the different orders in the MT and the LXX? What significance might those differences make for the idea there is a "plot" in the Book of the Twelve?
2. How convincing is the reconstruction of the rise of the Twelve in this chapter? What are its weakest and strongest points?
3. What are the weakest and strongest points for a diachronic reading of the Twelve? For a synchronic reading?
4. Does the Twelve really have a plot? Why or why not?
5. How satisfactory theologically is the view of retribution in the confession about God in Exod 34:6-7? How does Deut 7:9-10 modify it? How satisfactory is that view? Does retribution always come in one's lifetime?

For Further Reading

Interpretation 61 (2007) 115-97 contains a guest editorial and an article on themes in the Twelve by James D. Nogalski, plus articles on themes in the Twelve, three collections per article, by Aaron Schart, Mark E. Biddle, Julia M. O'Brien, and Paul L. Redditt.

Nogalski, James D. *Literary Precursors to the Book of the Twelve.* BZAW 217. Berlin: De Gruyter, 1993; and *Redactional Processes in the Book of the*

---

the wrong word if one means thereby a group of (unrelated) works. Despite Beck's objection, the Twelve does show signs of careful editing. As will become clear in Section II of this book, the Twelve is as much a "book" as Isaiah. Perhaps the problem here is the attempt to use modern terms ("book" or "anthology") for ancient literature.

Twelve. BZAW 218. Berlin: De Gruyter, 1993. Two volumes comprising the author's dissertation laying out the case for a systematic editing of the Twelve as a unity.

Redditt, Paul L. "Recent Research on the Book of the Twelve as One Book." *CurBS* 9 (2001) 47-80. A review of the literature on the subject through 2000.

Sweeney, Marvin A. *The Twelve Prophets.* 2 vols. Berit Olam. Collegeville: Liturgical, 2000. A commentary on the Twelve, treating it as a unity.

CHAPTER 10

Hosea, Joel, Amos

Like the book of Isaiah, the prophetic collections in the Book of the Twelve include materials from the preexilic, exilic, and postexilic periods. The Twelve opens with Hosea, despite the likelihood that Hosea was not the earliest of those prophets. That distinction probably goes to Amos. Why, then, did editors put Hosea first? The answer perhaps lies in its strong emphasis on Israel's relationship to God. Amos thunders against social sins, but Hosea puts that behavior in a poignant theological context. He does so first by means of the marriage/divorce metaphor, to which we will now turn.

The Plot of the Twelve: Warnings of Impending Divorce from Israel

The Book of the Twelve opens with the issue of divorce and turns to that subject again at its end (Mal 2:13-16). In Hosea, the relationship between the prophet and his unfaithful wife Gomer is presented as an allegory of the relationship between God and northern Israel, a relationship God threatens to terminate in divorce (Hos 2:2-6). Amos, likewise an eighth-century prophet to Israel, also predicts an end to the relationship between God and Israel. While passages in these two collections in places anticipate restitution, both are aptly described as warnings of impending doom. How, then, does the plot of Hosea through Amos develop?

In Hosea 1 Hosea marries Gomer, who continues in or turns to prostitution. Hosea 2:1-23 allegorizes her relationship with Hosea in terms of the

relationship between God and Israel. God calls to two of the children of
Hosea and Gomer to plead with their mother to "put away" her adulterous
ways that led to separation from her husband. Failure to do so would lead
him to "expose" her, to divorce her and leave her without his support (v. 3).
Then (vv. 4-5) the children become the people of Israel, themselves guilty
of whoredom/adultery. Unless they repent, God would divorce them (v. 6).
The threat of an impending end of God's relationship to Israel is clear. Israel might suppose that the worship of the foreign gods of her foreign rulers is a matter of politics and expediency only, but according to Hosea God
sees things quite differently. To God, their worship of other gods is the
theological equivalent of adultery in a marriage relationship, and God
warns them to stop.

The collection concludes with a call to Israel to return to God and be
healed of their disloyalty (Hos 14:1). The concluding note (14:9) makes one
of only three references to the "wise" in the Twelve (the other two being
Obad 8 and Zech 9:2) and the only one where the wise are spoken of posi-
tively. It thus gives the appearance of being a scribal addition.

The next collection, Joel, opens (1:2) with a question for the "elders of
the land": "Has this happened in your days or in the days of your ancestors?" James D. Nogalski argues cogently that the antecedent for the word
"this" is the issue of repentance and promise in Hos 14:5-9.[1] Thus, read
consecutively Hosea calls eighth-century Israel to repentance, a call the nation did not heed, and Joel calls later Judah to lament its own sins. The second half of Joel (2:18–4:21[Heb 3:21]) depicts the promise of God's rescue
of Judah.

Joel is connected thematically to Amos, the following collection, by
means of the following verse (Joel 3:16):

> YHWH roars from Zion,
>   and gives his voice from Jerusalem,
>   so that earth and heaven tremble.
> But YHWH is a refuge to his people,
>   a stronghold to the people of Israel.

Amos 1:2 repeats the first two lines of that verse, turning the lines into a
warning of impending judgment against Mount Carmel in Israel. Amos

1. James Nogalski, *Redactional Processes in the Book of the Twelve.* BZAW 218 (Berlin: de
Gruyter, 1993) 16.

concludes (9:11-15) with the picture of a restored Judah and Davidic monarchy, widely recognized as an addition. That shift in attention to Judah not only provides a positive ending for Amos, but also prepares the way for an emphasis on Judah for most of the rest of the Twelve.[2] The motif of divorce, however, does not reappear until the end of the Twelve in Malachi. Warnings, by contrast, continue throughout the Twelve.

HOSEA
Israel the Prostitute/Divorced Wife

The motif of Israel as the prostitute/wife is characteristic of Hosea, even if it is not unique to that collection. Hosea 1 and 3 relate salient details of the prophet's marriage. In ch. 2, however, the marriage exemplifies the relationship between God and Israel. Gomer becomes the cipher for Israel. Once Israel had stood in a unique relationship with YHWH, but no more. Israel had begun dalliances with other lovers: Canaanite and Assyrian deities. God had every right, as Hosea portrays matters, to divorce her. The image is of the wronged husband expelling the guilty wife. Within the collection, however, the image is reshaped in two ways. Hosea reminds his audience that not all whores are women. God says (4:14):

> I will not punish your daughters when they commit fornication,
>   nor your daughters-in-law when they commit adultery,
> for the men go aside with whores
>   and offer sacrifices with temple-prostitutes;
> thus a people with no understanding will be thrust down.

The point, obviously, is not that God would overlook harlotry or temple prostitution, but that sexual promiscuity was no worse than religious promiscuity and the people practicing the latter would pay for their sins. Israel, the unfaithful wife, was receiving her final warning to repent. Still, Hosea portrays God as willing and ready to receive back the wayward people (cf. 11:8):

2. That shift is partially a function of the demise of Israel as an independent entity. Even so, worship of YHWH continued in the north, and the prophet Jeremiah hailed from Anathoth, a northern town.

How can I give you up, O Ephraim?
    How can I hand you over, O Israel?
How can I give you up like Admah?
    How can I make you like Zeboiim?
My heart is turned within me,
    my compassions have grown tender.

Introduction to the Collection and Its Times

The Place of the Collection in the Canon

In a canonical reading of the Twelve, the place to begin is with Hosea. Though scholars generally think that historically it followed Amos, in both the MT and the LXX Hosea comes first. In the Twelve dates seems to have been the primary, though not the only, criterion. Since the date of the career of Amos is difficult to calculate, early redactors may well have thought Hosea was older. In any case, Hosea stands first in the Twelve.

The Setting for the Collection

Determining the setting of the collection is more difficult than it might seem at first glance. One should start with the northern prophet Hosea himself, but the collection gives evidence of a long period of growth and a change in venue to Judah. Hosea addresses Israel (often by the name Ephraim, its most important tribe) and some of its cities (e.g., Mizpah and Tabor, 5:1;[3] Gibeah and Ramah, 5:8), denouncing worship in the temples in Gilgal (4:15), Bethel (4:15),[4] and Samaria (8:5). It is clear that Hosea flourished in Israel, and it is likely that his messages were first collected there. At some point, however, they underwent a southern or Judean redaction, at which time a few allusions to Judah may have been included (e.g., 1:7, 11; 4:15; 11:12), though an occasional mention of Judah may have been original (e.g., 6:4, 11; 8:14; 12:2).

---

3. Both cities were noted for temples to Baal, the most important Canaanite fertility-god.

4. Hosea 4:15 speaks of Beth-aven, "House of iniquity," but the name constitutes a wordplay on the place name Beth-el, "House of God."

The collection must date no earlier than the career of the prophet himself. That date can be deduced approximately on internal evidence. For starters, the collection opens with a superscription (1:1) that is followed by an incipit (1:2),[5] suggesting that v. 1 was penned after the narrative in 1:2-9. The superscription dates Hosea primarily during the reigns of southern kings (Uzziah, Jotham, Ahaz, and Hezekiah) and secondarily during the reign of Jeroboam II (ca. 786-746). The best explanation for the emphasis on southern kings is that the superscription was written in the south for southern readers. In any case, Jeroboam died ca. 746, thus providing the latest possible date for the beginning of Hosea's ministry (assuming the accuracy of the superscription). Hezekiah came to the throne of Judah in 725 or 715, depending on whose dating scheme one follows. Other verses offer similar results. Hosea 7:7 and 8:4 reflect turbulent times like the years between 746 and 737, when Israel went through six kings and several dynasties: "They crowned kings, but not from me; they set up princes, but I did not know them" (8:4). Also, scholars suggest that 7:11-12 reflects the vacillations in foreign policy of Israel's final king Hoshea, and 10:3 perhaps reflects the period between the death of Hoshea in 724 and the fall of Samaria in 722/21. The collection does not, however, actually mention the fall of Samaria and the northern kingdom. Though this argument involves a conclusion from silence (a shaky step logically), scholars often conclude that Hosea's recorded ministry did not continue that late. Hence, we arrive at a tentative date of approximately the third quarter of the eighth century for Hosea's ministry.

Particularly in light of the third person account of Hosea's marriage with which the collection opens, someone else seems to have been responsible for gathering and writing down the prophet's words. That person may have worked during or soon after the prophet's ministry. When Israel fell to the Assyrians as Hosea predicted, some person or group probably decided that he was a prophet to be heard. Some verses/passages in the collection, however, appear to have arisen about the time of the fall of Judah and the exile. Rainer Albertz attributes 1:1, 5, 7; 3:1bβ; 4:1 (in part), 15; 8:1b, 6a, 14; 11:5b to the hand of the redactor responsible for the Book of the Four.[6]

---

5. A superscript is a heading consisting of nouns (not sentences), which may be elaborated by adding phrases and relative clauses, while an incipit is the first sentence in a narrative that doubles as an introduction to what follows.

6. Rainer Albertz, "Exile as Purification: Reconstructing the 'Book of the Four,'" in *Thematic Threads in the Book of the Twelve,* ed. Paul L. Redditt and Aaron Schart. BZAW 325 (Berlin: de Gruyter, 2003) 247. See Chapter 9 above for a discussion of the growth of the Twelve.

Other minor revisions (e.g., the pro-Davidic addition in 3:5aβ) may come from other hands as the Four grew into the Twelve, which most likely emerged sometime during the Persian period, perhaps with additional minor touches to Hosea here and there.[7] That redaction most likely occurred in Jerusalem at the hands of scribes (cf. 14:9).

The Structure, Integrity, and Authorship of the Collection

Structurally, Hosea breaks between chs. 3 and 4, with chs. 1–3 dealing with the marriage of Hosea and chs. 4–14 further developing his message. A shift in the image for Israel also occurs at this point. In chs. 1-3 Israel is portrayed as a wife; in chs. 4–14 Israel is a son. The collection may be outlined as follows:[8]

Superscription 1:1

I. The Wife/Israel and God 1:2–3:5

A. Third person account of marriage 1:2-9

B. The Wife/Israel and Her Husband 1:10–2:23 (Allegory 2:2-23)

C. First person account of marriage 3:1-5

II. The Son/Israel and God 4:1–14:8

A. YHWH's indictment of Israel 4:1-19 and the priests 5:1-7

B. YHWH's punishment of Israel (and Judah) 5:8–6:6

C. YHWH's indictment of Israel 6:7–9:17

D. YHWH's punishment of Israel 10:1-15

E. YHWH's compassion for Israel 11:1-11

F. YHWH's indictment of Israel 11:12[Heb. 12:1]–13:16

G. YHWH's forgiveness of Israel 14:1-8

Conclusion 14:9

7. That statement seems self-evident regardless of whether there was a Book of the Four or whether the Twelve was edited to be read straight through.

8. A few elements of this structure have been borrowed from Gale A. Yee, "The Book of Hosea," *NIB*, 7 (1996) 213.

This arrangement moves twice from indictment to punishment to forgiveness. Scholars sometimes say it also may be more or less chronological, but that seems less clear. In any case, critical scholars have contested the integrity of Hosea, though the prophet himself perhaps uttered many, maybe even most of the messages.

Main Genres in the Collection

Hosea contains a variety of prophetic genres, more than we can mention here. In addition to the allegory in ch. 2 already discussed, the primary genres include autobiography and biography, trial speech, prophecy of disaster, and what we might call historical reflection. The discussion of Hosea's marriage in ch. 3 was written in the first person singular, giving it the appearance of being autobiographical; the third person account in ch. 1 is biography. There seems to be no real reason to deny the historicity of the reports, though scholars have sometimes called the entirety of chs. 1–3 allegory, since 2:2-23 clearly is. The use of the first person in 3:1-4 (v. 5 appears to be an addition) results in a greater sense of the prophet's personal pain, in contrast with the more matter-of-fact tone of ch. 1.

The combination of the first two genres (autobiography, allegory) is accomplished by means of the transition passage 1:10–2:1. In the Hebrew Bible 1:10 begins ch. 2, indicating that the persons who supplied these chapter breaks recognized the new direction. Verse 11 at least, if not v. 10 as well, looks like a later addition, perhaps after the fall of both Israel and Judah and the experience of the exile. Hosea 2:1(Heb. 2:3) forms the actual transition to the allegory. The NRSV treats 2:16-20 as prose, suggesting that those verses *might* have constituted an addition. There is, however, no reason the original author could not have combined prose and poetry. The use of the Hebrew term *Baal* ("husband") for God is surprising (2:16), since Baal was also the name of the chief fertility-god of Canaan. In a text rife with sexual imagery, in which idolatry is symbolized by adultery, the use of the word/name Baal for YHWH is at a minimum daring.

The move to the first person account in ch. 3 is abrupt, with no transition except for the word "again" in v. 1. The question is whether the woman Hosea finds in ch. 3 is Gomer; she is never identified by name. Traditionally, it has been assumed that Gomer is the woman in view in 3:1-3, and the thrust of the whole collection leans that way: just as Hosea took back Gomer, so YHWH would take back Israel.

The next genre is the familiar trial speech, modeled (apparently) on court proceedings. It appears in 4:1-3, 4-19; 5:1-7; 12:2-6. The trial speech typically contains a summons (cf. 4:1a, "Hear the word of YHWH"), an indictment (cf. 4:1b-2; 4:4-6, 12-13, 15-19; 5:1b-5), and a description of punishment the guilty people will endure (cf. 4:3; 4:9-11; 5:6-7). The explicit appeal to the Ten Commandments in 4:2, specifically commandments five through nine, is typical of a special kind of trial speech called the "covenant lawsuit" (cf. 8:1-10). A similar genre employed in Hosea is the prophecy of disaster, including 5:8–6:6; 6:7-11a; 6:11b–7:12. Like the trial speech, the prophecy of disaster describes the wrongdoing or sin of the people (cf. 5:13-14) and the punishment that will befall them (cf. 5:9-11). Characteristic of this genre is the messenger formula ("Thus says YHWH"), which, however, does not appear in Hosea. Typically, the transition between the two major sections (wrongdoing and punishment) is marked by the transition word "therefore" (cf. 5:12).

The final genre requiring mention here is what has been termed a "historical reflection," which appears most tellingly in 11:1-11.[9] In that chapter YHWH agonizes over the sinfulness of Israel, exhibited from the moment Israel set foot in Canaan and reaching its peak in the installation of the golden bull in the royal temple in Samaria (8:4-5). God called Israel out of Egypt (11:1) at the time of the exodus; the time in the wilderness was a time when God satisfied their needs (13:5-6; cf. Jer 2:2-3); but at their last stop in the wilderness at Baal-peor (Hos 9:10), if not sooner, and then again as soon as they crossed the Jordan and set foot in Canaan at Adam (cf. Josh 3:16) they indulged in sinning (Hos 6:7),[10] epitomized by the sordid events at Gibeah (9:9; cf. Judges 19–21). Yet God led Israel faithfully, like a father teaching a child how to walk (11:3).

In Hos 11:5, the mood turns abruptly. The prophet also begins to pre-

9. Marvin A. Sweeney says that the entirety of 9:1–13:16(Heb 14:1) constitutes a historical review; *The Twelve Prophets*. Berit Olam (Collegeville: Liturgical, 2000) 1:93.

10. The MT reads *ke'adam*, normally translated "like Adam," suggesting that the people of Israel had committed sin just as Adam had (Genesis 3). It is tempting, however, to read the Hebrew preposition *ke* ("like") as *be* ("at") and see in the text an allusion to the crossing of the Jordan into Canaan at Adam. *BHS*, in fact, commends that reading. *BHK*, however, prefers *ba'aram*, "at Aram." The NEB emends the noun to read Admah, which is mentioned in 11:8.

dict the future. Because of their sin, Israel would pay a price. They would not return to Egypt, whence God had called them. Rather, Assyria would be their king. Israel's vacillation between Egypt and Assyria would prove ineffective. They were attempting to apply a political fix to a theological/ moral problem, and it would not work. Israel had sinned, earning repercussions that God would not turn away. Punishment would not be God's final word, however. Beyond punishment lay restitution because God, unlike humans, would not destroy the people. Poetically, the prophet portrays YHWH as a roaring lion, whose piercing sound would reach from Jerusalem to Egypt and Assyria and call God's people home (11:10-11).

Special Features of the Collection

Commentators often note the poor condition of the text of Hosea and frequently assume that the text suffered in transmission. While that might be correct, it is also possible that the text simply contains a large number of grammatical problems compounded by a poor writing style. In any case, readers might want to compare translations of Hosea, trying not to base their own reading on one translation. (A good text to compare would be 11:3-4.) A critical edition of a modern translation may alert the reader to some of the difficulties and the emendations or changes made in the Hebrew in an attempt to read it.

A second special feature of the collection is the use of other biblical passages in Hosea. Duane A. Garrett calls attention to the use of Gen 22:17 in Hos 1:10; a reference to the creation of wild animals (Gen 1:20-25) in Hos 2:18; an allusion to the destruction of the cities of the plain (Gen 19) in Hos 11:8; a summary of the story of Jacob (Gen 25:19–35:15) in Hos 12:2-5, 12-13; references to the exodus in 9:10; 11:1-4; 12:9; 13:4-6; an appeal to the Ten Commandments in Hos 4:2; and a reference to Judges 19–21 in Hos 9:9.[11] The first two of these allusions (1:10, 2:18) appear in an allegory that is probably not from the hands of the prophet; another (9:9) may be an addition to its context, but the others may point to an acquaintance with Israelite tradition by the prophet himself.

---

11. Duane A. Garrett, *Hosea, Joel*. NAC 19A (Nashville: Broadman & Holman, 1997) 28.

Introduction to the Prophet

In contrast with the Major Prophets, whose collections often relate many events in the life of the prophet, the Twelve typically says little about the prophets. In Hosea only the opening, which deals with Hosea's marriage, talks about him. Nevertheless, it is possible to say a little about him and worth the effort to do so.

The name Hosea means something like "he has helped." It appears to be a shortened for of the name *hoshaiah,* "Yahweh has helped." The superscription (1:1) gives his father's name as Beeri, which means "my well." The details of the prophet's life are little known, aside from the few details given about his marriage. His wife is named Gomer, a name that elsewhere (Gen 10:2-3; 1 Chr 1:5-6; Ezek 38:6) refers to males. According to Hosea 1, she bears three children, though only the first is specifically said to be Hosea's. The woman in Hosea 3 seems to have been bought at a negotiated price (15 shekels[12] of silver, a *ḥomer* — approximately six and one-half bushels — and a *lethek* — approximately half a homer — of barley[13]) instead of the 30 shekels mentioned in Exod 21:32 or the 50 for which slaves might redeem themselves in eighth-century Israel (2 Kgs 15:20). If, indeed, Hosea could afford to buy a woman, he would not have been destitute.

Hosea's public career may have lasted a quarter of a century. References to the various temples might suggest he had the means to travel. It is not clear in what capacity he spoke. If he belonged to an official cult, probably he would have been at odds with other priests and prophets for his sharp denunciations of them.

Basic Emphases in Hosea

Space does not permit a verse-by-verse exegesis of Hosea any more than it does of the Major Prophets. It will be necessary, therefore, to discuss Hosea's message in terms of his major themes. We will look at six before turn-

---

12. The word *shekel* (also transliterated *sheqel*) does not appear in the Hebrew text, but is clearly implied since the price for slaves was quoted in *shekels* in the Hebrew Bible. A *shekel* was the basic measure of weight, probably about 0.4 oz or 11.4 gm. See Edward M. Cook, "Weights and Measures," *ISBE,* 4:1054.

13. The NRSV adopts the LXX.

ing to the issue of the theological problems raised by a study of Hosea's message.

Idolatry/adultery and Gomer

Hosea 1–3 employs the adultery of Gomer as a metaphor for the idolatry of the people of Israel, a metaphor that surfaced earlier in the Covenant Code (cf. Exod 34:15: "You shall not go whoring after other gods"). Hosea's indictment of Israel in 4:1-3 carries forward the same theme. He complains about a lack of faithfulness or loyalty to YHWH before charging the Israelites with swearing falsely, lying, murdering, stealing, and adultery. Like the Decalogue itself, Hosea sets such social sins or crimes in a theological context. They are not simply misdeeds; they are sins (i.e., wrongdoings) against God.

It seems strange, then, that God would tell the prophet Hosea to "Go, take for yourself a woman[14] of fornications." It is so strange, in fact, that commentators at least since the time of Jerome have felt it necessary to explain or even explain away the perceived impropriety of such a command. The context itself offers one ready explanation: the entire marriage was allegorical, not just the discussion of it in Hosea 2. There is no warrant in the text for such a reading, however, so most modern scholars do not accept it. A second possibility is that Gomer became promiscuous after the marriage; before her marriage she was a devout woman. There is no warrant for this reading either, since the word used in 1:2 is *zenunim* ("fornications"), not *na'apupim* ("adulteries" or "whoredom"), the word used in 2:4. The text may indicate, therefore, that she was a fornicator before their marriage and an adulterer afterward, though the two words are used in parallelism in 2:4. If Gomer was a prostitute before and after her marriage to Hosea, which seems to be the best understanding of the text, what kind of prostitute was she? It is possible that she was simply a promiscuous woman, but some scholars speculate that she was a cult prostitute, employed by a temple (for Baal?) for ritual sex in fertility rites. If so, the connection between adultery and idolatry would be even clearer.

---

14. The word *'ishshah* can mean either "woman" or "wife."

The Passion of God

Greek philosophy, and sometimes Christian theology too, have spoken of God as perfect and assumed that a perfect God would be unmoved by human need or deed. The technical term for such a view is "impassibility." Whatever else one might say about the presentation of God in the Hebrew, one would be hard pressed to call God impassible. In Hosea 11 in particular, God is moved to great feeling as God struggles over what to do about sinful Israel, and the compassion of God wins out. God exclaims (11:8b-9):

> My heart is turned within me,
>   my compassions have grown tender.
> I will not release my fierce anger,
>   I will not turn to destroy Ephraim;
> for I am divine and not human,
>   the Holy One in your midst,
>   so I will not come in wrath.

In other words, to destroy in anger is human; to forgive is divine. Forgiveness is part of God's character, so to be true to God's self God forgives sinners. In this case, the forgiveness comes after Israel reaps what it has sown, but it survives to be drawn back once more into God's mercy.

Like Priests (and Prophets), like People

Hosea accuses the priests of dereliction of duty. Speaking on behalf of God, he says (4:4-6):

> Yet, let no one accuse,
>   let no one rebuke;
>   for with you, O priest, is my accusation.
> You shall stumble by day;
>   and the prophet also shall stumble with you by night,
>   and I will destroy your mother.
> My people are destroyed on account of a lack of knowledge.
> Since you yourself have rejected knowledge,
>   I will reject you from being a priest before me.

And [since] you have forgotten the instruction of your God,
>   I also will forget your children.

It was the function of the priests to decide issues and give instructions or laws; it was also their duty to preserve and pass on those instructions. Hosea maintains that the priests had neglected — he says "forgotten" — to carry out those duties. Hence, God would "forget" them, thus allowing destruction to come to them. The consequences of their failure, however, led to ignorance of God's instruction *(torah)* on the part of the people, and they too would reap what they had sown (4:9): "So it shall be like people, like priests." God would hold the priests responsible for the behaviors of the people committed in ignorance.

God likewise held the prophets responsible for their failures: "the prophet also will stumble with you by night" (4:5). They had corrupted themselves as in the days of Gibeah (9:9), an allusion to the moral quagmire there described in Judges 19–21. Hosea speaks of a better day, when prophets served God faithfully. He alludes to the role of Moses, whom he terms a prophet, in leading Israel from Egypt during the exodus (Hos 12:13). Over the ensuing years God had spoken through a number of prophets to steer Israel correctly (12:10). For their efforts to correct Israel's sinfulness, they were sometimes rebuffed as fools (9:7).

The people too would be punished for their own moral failures (5:3-4).

I myself know Ephraim, yea Israel is not hidden from me,
>   for now you have played the harlot, O Ephraim;
>   Israel is defiled.
Their practices do not permit them return to their God,
>   for a spirit of fornication is in their midst,
>   and they do not know YHWH.

Blinded by the allurement of the worship of other gods (presumably the Canaanite pantheon, including Baal; cf. 13:1), they were unable to see their wrongs. Their society was full of injustice, they trusted in their own military strength, and they would reap what they had sown (10:13-15). Hosea 9:12b makes this last point with blunt force: "Woe to them when I depart from them."

The Monarchy and its Fall

Hosea also criticizes the king, and probably the institution of monarchy itself (13:10-11):

> Where[15] then is your king that he may save you in all your cities,
>   and your rulers [for] whom you said "Give me a king
>   and princes"?
> I gave you a king in my anger, and I took [him] in my wrath.[16]

The reference to God's giving a king seems to appeal to traditions like that
in 1 Samuel 8, where Israel requested a king from God. Though rebuffed
and angry at the request for its implicit rejection of the kingship of God,
God granted the request. Now (late eighth century) God would remove the
king. Monarchy had been a bad idea from the start,[17] and its demise was a
good thing. It is not clear what Hosea thought should happen next. He
probably did not intend a theocracy led by priests. Did he expect God to
rule directly? Did he think rule should revert to the tribes? Did he expect
the Assyrians to take over? Whatever his expectations, the last of these possible options came about. The Assyrians annexed Israel.

In view of Hosea's negative view of Hoshea in particular and probably
the institution of monarchy in general, it is surprising to read the phrase
"and David their king" in 3:5aβ. Perhaps Hosea only opposed the northern
monarchy. Since 3:4-5 probably came from the hand of the Redactor of the
Four (see note 6 above) as part of his "exile as purification" motif, however,

---

15. I am following the suggested reading in *BHS*. The Hebrew actually reads "and I will
be" or perhaps "and I want to be" (cf. John Joseph Owens, *Analytical Key to the Old Testament* [Grand Rapids: Baker, 1989] 4:785). A very minor emendation, however, results in the
word for "where."

16. One might argue that the reference here is to specific kings. That is clearly the case
for the reference to the removal of the final king, Hoshea; the first clause seems, however, to
look back to the founding of the monarchy under Saul.

17. While this view of monarchy is attested several places in the OT, it is not the only
view. The Psalter depicts YHWH as the real king of Israel, but the Davidic king as the one
through whom YHWH exercised that kingship. Also in Samuel and Kings, the Davidic monarchy was approved (cf. 2 Samuel 7) and the split of the northern kingdom from Jerusalem
and Judah as well (1 Kgs 11:9-13). To be sure, the historian responsible for Samuel and Kings
thought little else Jeroboam I did was theologically defensible, especially not his support of
the sanctuaries in Dan and Bethel.

it appears more likely that it was a touch added by a Judean editor, perhaps in the early postexilic period when hope for a new Davidic king blossomed in Haggai and Zechariah 1–8.

Insincere Repentance

One of the more enigmatic texts in Hosea is 6:1-6. It begins (vv. 1-3) with Israel's apparent repentance: "Come, let us return to YHWH" (v. 1). Their rationale is simple: YHWH "has torn, and will heal us, has smitten us and will bind us up" (v. 1). Thus far, their theology seems correct. Next, they anticipate that God will act quickly: "He will revive us after two days; on the third day he will raise us up that we may live before him" (v. 2). Confident of their standing before God and God's certain response, they liken that response to a gentle rain: YHWH "will come to us like the rain, like the spring rains that water the earth" (v. 3).

Though this prayer sounds good, it is flawed in some way. We know this because it is met by apparent exasperation on God's part, who complains that the love of Ephraim (and Judah) for God is "like a cloud of the morning, like the dew, which rising early goes away" (v. 4). In other words, their confession and prayer are shallow and insincere, not reflecting the depth of their sinfulness. They think they could say the right words and offer the right sacrifices and God would have to take them back. What God really desires (v. 6) is covenant fidelity, not simply sacrifices. The way back to God requires a more complete commitment on their part than they imagined.

The Fidelity of God

Despite its insincerity, God would be faithful to Israel and would keep the divine side of the bargain. There seems to be little cause for God to do so from Hosea's perspective. He describes Israel as a luxuriant vine, loaded with fruit, bent on turning to other gods, building altars to them (10:1), and sacrificing to them (11:2). When Israel really repents and turns back to God, God promises (14:4-5):

> I will heal their turning away; I will love them freely;
> for my wrath turns from them.

I will be like the dew upon Israel;
   he will sprout as the lily;
and he will thrust his roots as the [cedars of] Lebanon.

Problems Raised by a Study of Hosea

Our study of Hosea has uncovered several problematic features that we need to address before we move on to Joel. The first, dealing with the presentation of Israel as a whore, invites attention from the perspective of ideological criticism. The second, dealing with the nature and severity of God's punishment of Israel, invites investigation of Hosea's view of God. The third, dealing with the allusion to the exodus in Hosea 11, invites a look at how that text is used in the NT.

Whores and Hosea's View of Women

Hosea employs the image of a whore as a metaphor for Israel's sinfulness in chs. 1–3. It may be that the metaphor simply grew out of Hosea's experience with his wife and implies no antifeminine bias. Still, Israel is compared to a whore, not to a pimp. Further, the metaphor arose in the context of a male-dominated society, where such terms may well have embodied the society's own view of the (moral) inferiority of women to men. To be sure, Hosea makes clear that the "real" whores were the men running the country, but the use of the pejorative term perhaps put down women of the biblical age and certainly disturbs some readers today, both male and female. Of course, in Hosea 4–14 references to the people are decidedly masculine, and the metaphor changes to that of the disobedient (11:1-2) and unwise (13:13) son, so the metaphors are not exclusively feminine.

Natural Calamity and God's Punishment of Israel

A more theological[18] issue is the portrayal of God's punishment. I have in mind here passages like 9:11-14 which threaten Israelites with barrenness,

---

18. "Theological" in the more restrictive sense of "the doctrine of God."

miscarriage, and the death of their children (cf. 10:14). Other passages predict famine (2:9a; 8:7) and other natural calamities (2:9b; 4:3). As punishment for their wickedness and injustice, Israel would experience war, destruction, and the killing of their babies (10:14).

What can one say about the portrayal of God that would include such actions? First, and most obviously, God takes sin seriously and punishes it. Still, killing babies for the sins of their parents is not moral. Neither is destroying the land because of the behaviors of its inhabitants. In fact, in other places the Bible anticipates a future in which harmony is restored in nature (e.g., Isa 11:6-9). Second, perhaps looking at a different text will help. In Ps 137:9, the psalmist reaches his bitter conclusion with the wish-statement addressed literarily to the Babylonians, who had long held Judeans in exile and otherwise mistreated them: "O the happiness of those seizing and dashing your infants against the rock." A reader can agree that Babylonian hegemony was sinful and that God needed to end it. A reader can understand and appreciate the anger that welled up in the exiles toward their captors. A reader should also understand, however, that the expression of such wishes laid no obligation on God to carry out the deserved punishment in such a fashion. By the same token, we can understand a prophet speaking in terms he and his audience have experienced, anticipating that God will act in the ways people act when they conquer, punish, or take revenge. We can agree that sinners need to be stopped and punished; we do not have to expect God to use such all-too-human means.

Out of Egypt I called my son

As we saw earlier, the opening verse of Hosea 11 makes a historical allusion to the exodus:

> When Israel was a child I loved him,
>   and out of Egypt I called my son.

Remarkably, the NT Gospel of Matthew treats the verse as a passage fulfilled during the life of Jesus, specifically when his parents took him back to Palestine after the death of Herod: "This was to fulfill what had been spoken by the Lord through the prophet, 'Out of Egypt I have called my son'" (Matt 2:15 NRSV). Clearly, the prophet Hosea did not have Jesus in mind. Indeed, Hos 11:1 does not predict anything; it looks back to the exodus, which lay hundreds of years in the past. How, then, might a modern reader understand the text in Matthew? It is worth noting that Matthew does not say that Hosea predicted Jesus; rather, he says that the passage is fulfilled by this event in the infancy or childhood of Jesus.[19] Second Isaiah utilizes the exodus as the once and future constitutive event (cf. Isa 43:1-7; 52:1-10). What God had done once, God could do again. The evangelist carries forward this theme with respect to the person of Jesus.

JOEL
A Vision of the New Nation

The collection named after the prophet Joel is perhaps best known to Christians from Peter's sermon on Pentecost, where he quotes several verses from Joel about God's pouring out the spirit on all classes of people (sons and daughters, old and young, slaves and free[implied]), and says the verses came true on the day of Pentecost (Acts 2:17-21). It is also well known for its apocalyptic imagery and for its talk of locust invasions. We shall return to those topics shortly, but first we need to familiarize ourselves better with the collection itself.

Introduction to the Collection and Its Times

The Place of the Collection in the Canon

Joel always appears in the first half of the Book of the Twelve, but in different places in the MT and the LXX. In the MT (which appears to preserve the original structure),[20] Joel follows Hosea, though in the LXX it comes

19. Sometimes scholars have said that the flight to Egypt did not occur; instead the event was constructed by the evangelist from the OT text. Either way, the issue here remains the same: how one should understand a historical allusion as something fulfilled later.

20. See James D. Nogalski, "Joel as 'Literary Anchor' for the Book of the Twelve," in *Reading and Hearing the Book of the Twelve,* ed. James D. Nogalski and Marvin A. Sweeney. SBLSymS 15 (Atlanta: SBL, 2000) 91-109. Nogalski argues that Joel was the literary anchor around which the Twelve were finally assembled. In that same volume, co-editor Marvin A.

fourth, following Micah: Hosea, Amos, Micah, Joel. Nogalski argues convincingly that Joel 1:2 ("Have such things happened in your day?") looks back to something previous, not forward to something coming later. Those "things" include the flourishing predicted in Hosea 14. Such conditions contrast with those described in Joel 1:1–2:17. Likewise, Herbert Marks argues that the call to Israel to repent in Hos 14:1 is repeated in Joel 2:12,[21] though it must be noted in anticipation of what will be said shortly that the Hebrew word *shub* in v. 12 can mean simply "turn" and need not imply the need to "return" or "repent." Thus, Joel may simply have been calling the people to turn to God for help, not to repent of their sinful ways.[22] Either way, the first half of Joel seems to have in view the call of the prophet Hosea in 14:1 for Israel to (re)turn to God and in 14:4-7 to experience God's blessing.

Continuing the issue of the relationship of Joel to the collections surrounding it, we note that almost at the end of Joel (3:16a) stand these lines:

> YHWH roars from Zion,
> and from Jerusalem lifts his voice.

Only seven verses later in a canonical reading of the Twelve, Amos 1:2a repeats these words as part of what is typically called the "motto" of the collection named after Amos. Actually, however, calling that verse a "motto" simply highlights its lack of any further connection to its literary context — except for Joel 3:16a.

Sweeney argues that the LXX preserved the original sequence; "Sequence and Interpretation in the Book of the Twelve," 49-64. In Chapter 9, I argued that the placements of Joel and Obadiah, plus the inclusion of Jonah, were used to combine three precursors into the Twelve (with Zechariah 9–14 added later). The connections among Hosea, Joel, and Amos convince me that Nogalski is correct. Sweeney further points out that Hosea, Amos, and Micah all discuss the fall of Israel as a warning to Judah; *The Twelve Prophets,* 148. Hence, he argues, the three belonged together originally. One may agree that they, along with Zephaniah, constituted a Book of the Four, but the connections to Hosea and Amos suggest that Joel found its place between those two early, only to have the older sequence restored in the LXX where the connections to Hosea and Amos are much less easily explained.

21. Herbert Marks, "The Twelve Prophets," in *The Literary Guide to the Bible,* ed. Robert Alter and Frank Kermode (Cambridge, MA: Harvard University Press, 1987) 208.

22. On the point that Joel does not accuse Judah, see James L. Crenshaw, "Joel's Silence and Interpreters' Readiness to Indict the Innocent," in *Lasset uns Brücken bauen,* ed. Klaus-Dietrich Schunk and Matthias Augustin, 255-59 (Frankfurt: Lang, 1998). Repr. in Crenshaw, *Prophets, Sages, & Poets* (St. Louis: Chalice, 2006) 163-66.

Joel also seems to have been written with the little collection named for Obadiah in view. Joel 2:32 quotes Obad 17 (a verse that looks back on and explains the fall of Jerusalem to the Babylonians) as a note of assurance for the future. Joel 3:10 also reverses the command to beat swords into plowshares and spears into pruning hooks that appears in Mic 4:3 (and Isa 2:4), though it also puts those words on the lips of foreign commanders.

Another important connection with other collections in the Twelve is the confession about God found first on Moses' lips at Sinai (Exod 34:6-7; cf. Num 14:18 and Deut 7:10) and then in at least four passages in the Twelve (Joel 2:13; Jonah 4:2; Mic 7:18; Nah 1:2-3a) and possibly a fifth (Hos 1:9).[23] The passage reads as follows in Exod 34:

> 6 YHWH, YHWH, the compassionate and gracious God,
>   slow in anger, abundant in covenant fidelity and faithfulness,
> 7 maintaining covenant fidelity to the thousands,
>   forgiving wickedness, rebellion, and sin,
> but not leaving unpunished those not yet punished [i.e., the guilty],
>   punishing the sin of the fathers as far as their sons,
>   their grandsons,
>   and the third and fourth generations.

Joel 2:13 and Jonah 4:2 quote only the part about God's compassion, and Mic 7:18 paraphrases it, while Nah 1:2-3a invokes the part about God's punishment upon Nineveh. Hosea 1:9 ("you are not my people, and I am not your God") might be a paraphrase of the entire passage. These observations constitute part of the proof that Joel came to its place relatively late in the growth of the Twelve, and that it is best read as a collection in dialogue with at least six other collections: Hosea, Amos, Micah, Jonah, Obadiah, and Nahum.

---

23. Raymond C. Van Leeuwen, "Scribal Wisdom and Theodicy in the Book of the Twelve," in *In Search of Wisdom: Essays in Memory of John G. Gammie*, ed. Leo G. Perdue, Bernard Brandon Scott, and William Johnston Wiseman, 34-48 (Louisville: Westminster John Knox, 1993). See Alan Cooper, who finds allusions also in Hos 14:3, 5; Joel 2:13-14; Jonah 3:8–4:2; Mic 7:18-20; and Nah 1:2-3a; "In Praise of Divine Caprice: The Significance of the Book of Jonah," in *Among the Prophets: Language, Image and Structure in the Prophetic Writings*, ed. Philip R. Davies and David J. A. Clines. JSOTSup 144 (Sheffield: JSOT, 1993) 160.

The Setting for the Collection

The superscription supplies only the name of the prophet: Joel. It says nothing about where he flourished or when he lived. Even so, the collection's concentration on Jerusalem and the temple makes it clear that the prophet worked in Jerusalem. The same observations lead to the further conclusion that the collection probably took literary shape there or nearby. Determining the date of Joel's career or that of the collection, however, is trickier. Since the collection presupposes a functioning temple, the exilic period is excluded. Joel 3:4-8 provides some information for determining a date. A reference to Greeks (v. 6) probably points to a postexilic date, and the allusion to exilic Obad 17 in Joel 2:32 certainly does. Joel 3:4-8 presupposes the viability of both Tyre and Sidon, but the former fell to Artaxerxes III Ochus in 343 and the latter to Alexander the Great in 332. The warning about the Sabeans (a caravanning people from the area of modern-day Yemen) presupposes that they are a power to be feared. That warning probably pushes the latest possible date for the collection to the fifth century, since Sabean strength declined severely after 450. Hence, a date somewhere between the completion of the second temple in Jerusalem ca. 515 and the coming of Nehemiah in 445 seems to fit the conditions described in the collection.[24] Its inclusion in the Twelve would have occurred among scribes in Jerusalem some time later.

The Structure, Integrity, and Authorship of the Collection

James L. Crenshaw offers the following analysis of the structure of Joel.

> Superscription 1:1
> I. Calamity in Judah and Its Reversal 1:2–2:27
>> A. An infestation of locusts and an appeal to fast and pray 1:2-20

---

24. Some scholars think that the reference to "the walls" in 2:9 refers to Jerusalem, thus requiring a date after Nehemiah's rebuilding of the wall. The context, however, is the action of locusts, who "run upon the walls." Jerusalem is to be warned about the behavior of the "locusts," but nothing in the text speaks of the city wall of Jerusalem. As will become clear shortly, I think the locusts are a symbol for invading armies, but that interpretation is irrelevant to this discussion.

B. YHWH's efficient army at work 2:1-11

C. A prophetic call to turn to YHWH 2:12-17

D. The restoration of Judah and divine judgment
   on foreigners 2:18-27

II. Signs and Portents 2:28-32[Heb 3:1-5]

III. Judgment of Foreign Nations 3:1-21[4:1-21]

   A. YHWH's reasons for judging specific nations 3:1-3[4:1-3]

   B. Special instance of divine recompense 3:4-8[4:4-8]

   C. YHWH's judgment against foreign peoples 3:9-17[4:9-17]

   D. Judah's security 3:18-21[4:18-21][25]

A radical shift in God's attitude toward Israel and in the tone of the collection occurs between 2:17 and 2:18. In fact, 2:18-27 goes to great lengths to reverse the catastrophes predicted primarily in 1:5-20.

2:19a	reverses 1:10b (Grain, wine, and oil fail)
2:19b	reverses 2:17 (Make not thy heritage a reproach)
2:20	reverses the fortunes of Israel, but has no clear antecedent
2:22a	reverses 1:18 (Beasts groan, are perplexed and dismayed)
2:22b	reverses 1:7 (Fig tree and vine are destroyed)
2:23	reverses 1:20a (Water is dried up)
2:24	reverses 1:10b (Grain, wine and oil fail)
2:25	reverses 1:4 and perhaps alludes to 1:5-7 and 2:11
2:25	reverses 1:16 (Food is cut off)
2:26-27	reverses 2:17b (Israel is a reproach)[26]

It is difficult to avoid the conclusion that 2:18-27 was written with 1:5-20 (if not 1:2–2:17) in hand.

In the first half of the twentieth century scholars routinely denied the integrity of the collection, assuming that the obvious change in mood between 2:17 and 2:18 indicated a change in authors. The first half of the collection was assigned to the prophet, the second half to a later disciple.

25. James L. Crenshaw, *Joel.* AB 24C (New York: Doubleday, 1995) 12-13.
26. Paul L. Redditt, "The Book of Joel and Peripheral Prophecy," *CBQ* 48 (1986) 228.

Arvid S. Kapelrud disagreed, arguing instead for a unified collection that built up over time, following the form of the liturgical psalm of lament, in which God answers the complaint of the petitioner.[27] Hans Walter Wolff also argued for a unified collection, though not for one single author: he excluded 4:4-8 and 2:26b.[28] Neither scholar, however, denied the obvious change in tone beginning in 2:18. The issue seems to be, therefore, what holds the little collection together, given the obvious change beginning in 2:18. Structurally, Kapelrud seems to be on the right track in speaking of a lament: the first half (1:1–2:17) is the prophet's cry to God; the second half (2:18 on) is primarily God's response. It is also possible to posit a sociological unity. I have argued elsewhere that the continuity is formed by the followers of the prophet, a group originally part of the temple structure, but who found themselves over time shoved further and further to the periphery of their society. What emerges in the last half of the collection, then, is their picture of a better tomorrow.[29]

Main Genres in the Collection

As the discussion of the basic themes of Joel will show, the lament is the primary genre within the collection. Calls to communal lamentation appear in 1:5-14 and 2:15-17. As the name implies, these passages summon the people to attend a communal gathering where cult officials intercede with God on behalf of the people that are experiencing some sort of calamity. A lament proper, or at least a fragment of one, appears in 1:15-20. Wolff calls 2:12-14 a "call to repentance,"[30] but as we shall see, it is not clear that Joel charges the people with sinning or needing to repent. Perhaps the designation "call to communal lamentation" fits those verses better. Other summons also appear (in 1:2-3 and 3:9-14), but more important are the assurance oracles in 2:18-27 and 3:15-17, which respond to the laments in the collection. Finally, prophecies of disaster upon foreign nations appear in 3:1-3 and 3:4-8.

27. Arvid S. Kapelrud, *Joel Studies.* UUÅ 1948/4 (Uppsala: Almqvist & Wiksells, 1948) 1-9.
28. Hans Walter Wolff, *Joel and Amos.* Hermeneia (Philadelphia: Fortress, 1977) 8.
29. Redditt, "The Book of Joel and Peripheral Prophecy," 227-38.
30. Wolff, *Joel and Amos,* 40.

A Special Feature of the Collection

Joel refers twice (1:4; 2:25) to locusts explicitly, and a third text (2:3-9) is often understood as describing a locust invasion, though the insect is not mentioned. Joel 1:4 refers to the stages in the life of locusts. It is followed by a figurative description of an invasion, in which the invaders are compared to lions (v. 6) and the invaders' destructiveness to a locust attack (v. 7). The invaders themselves are called a nation (1:6), a term that could refer to locusts but certainly did not need to. A number of scholars, in fact, conclude that it did not. Joel 2:25 also mentions the stages of life and also says God will repay Judah for the damage done by swarming locusts. It does so, however, in the context of promising to rid Judah of foreign armies (v. 20). Most interpreters have understood the text to speak of a locust invasion that delivered the punishment of God. I have argued, however, that the text is better understood as having used the devastation of a locust invasion as a symbol of the havoc caused by invading armies.[31]

Introduction to the Prophet

The name Joel is a compound. The syllable *Jo* is a shortened form of the name YHWH, and the syllable *el* is the name of the Canaanite high god and a word meaning "god." Hence, the name means "YHWH is God," quite appropriate for a prophet. Nothing is known about Joel's private life, not even the name of his father. The messenger hides behind the message. For that matter, the collection divulges nothing else overtly about the prophet than his name, but it is perhaps possible to make a couple of inferences about him from its contents.

Twice in the collection (1:14; 2:15-17) Joel addresses the priests, exhorting them to call the people together for a solemn (or lament) ceremony. Various types of persons, of course, might have called upon priests to do that, but the explicit directions in the second exhortation suggest someone with precise information about such festivals. Also, they perhaps have an air of authority about them. Scholars quite often infer, therefore, that Joel was connected with the temple. If so, he might have been either a priest or a temple prophet.

31. Redditt, "The Book of Joel and Peripheral Prophecy," 239-40.

The second half of the collection differs significantly in two ways from the first. One difference is that the second half hypothesizes God's becoming jealous or protective on behalf of Judah instead of being silent in the face of calamity. The second difference lies in the nature of that reversal on God's part. In 2:28-32, God sends God's spirit or charisma on "all flesh." The three pairs ("sons and daughters," "old men [or elders] and young men," and "male and female slaves") include young and old, male and female, slaves and free — the entire Judean population. Such inclusiveness tends to form part of the vision of people outside the circle of power; people in power might be expected to reserve power for themselves. Hence, I hypothesize that at least the group behind the collection, and possibly even Joel himself, found itself excluded from the center of power in the temple and expressed the hope for a more inclusive future than they were experiencing.[32]

Basic Emphases in Joel

Regardless of the authorship of the collection and the status of the group responsible for the preservation of its contents, the collection features lamentation and restoration. Its hope for the future rests on this combination.

Lamentation before God

The first half of the collection (1:1–2:17) calls on its audience to "lament like a virgin dressed in sackcloth"[33] (1:8) and to "turn" to YHWH whole-

---

32. Stephen L. Cook specifically rejects my argument on the grounds that 2:1-11 is closely connected thematically with the last half of the collection and derives from a priestly circle; *Prophecy and Apocalypticism: The Postexilic Social Setting* (Minneapolis: Fortress, 1995) 170-71. On the one hand, I quite agree that 2:1-11 derives from someone connected with the temple, whether priest or prophet. On the other hand, it seems to me that the last half of the collection, especially 2:28-32, differs. I agree that the two halves are connected thematically, but it seems to me that the second half has a much more inclusive vision of the recipients of God's charisma than anything a member of the central cult is likely to have envisioned and hoped for.

33. The wearing of sackcloth was a sign of mourning, in this comparison perhaps over the death of her beloved before the marriage was consummated.

heartedly (2:12-13). If the Hebrew word *shub* means "repent" here, Joel is strangely silent about what the people have done to necessitate repentance. If they had sinned, the sin could have been either moral or ritual. In light of that fact, we should note that Joel complains that "offering and libation are withheld from the house of your God" (1:13). The word for "offering" is *minhah*, which designated either an animal or a grain sacrifice; the word for "libation" is *nasek*, which designated a liquid poured out as an offering. Perhaps the problem was that a drought (see 1:11-12) made such gifts impossible, or perhaps the problem was (from Joel's perspective) that the drought was the punishment for withholding the offerings, i.e., committing ritual sin. In either case the drought was the cause for lamenting, and Joel cries to God for relief (vv. 16-20) and to the priests to declare a fast and a ceremony of lamentation (v. 14).

Joel also thought, however, that the drought portended the day of YHWH, the day when ancient Israelites believed God would punish God's enemies and bring salvation to God's people. For Joel, as for Amos before him (Amos 5:18-20), the day would *not* be a day of blessing for Judah. He anticipates, rather, that it would come from YHWH in the form of destruction (Joel 1:15). The text reads:

> Alas, the day;
>   for near [is] the day of YHWH
>   and it comes as/like destruction from Shaddai.[34]

Perhaps Joel thought the people were deep in sin, so deep that their sinfulness was self-evident and did not need mentioning.[35] We have already seen, however, that the text does not accuse Judah of sin. Perhaps instead, Joel simply ascribed the conditions he was seeing to God, because Joel did not have any other idea of whom to blame. The text does not say that either; there is no notion here that Joel thought of Judah as innocent sufferers. Where, then, does that leave us? It leaves us with these options. At a

---

34. The last line can be translated as follows: "and it comes as destruction from the destroyer," showing the pun between the word "destruction" (Heb. *shod*) and the name of God (*Shaddai*).

35. Another possibility is that a later editor deleted the sins against which Joel inveighed because they were so specific to a particular timeframe, thus making the text relevant to other, more numerous situations. I will leave such speculation aside in order to concentrate on the text as we have it.

minimum, Joel expressed the fear that God would leave Judah in the lurch instead of rescuing the people "on that day." At a maximum he feared God had turned against Judah. Either way, he called the whole congregation, even the bride and groom on their wedding night, to implore God to act on the people's behalf.

In light of this discussion, it would be useful to remember Joel's placement in the Twelve. Hosea opens the Twelve with a warning of an impending divorce. Joel looks back on that collection, notes that the hypothesized better days that would come if Israel returned (Hosea 14) had not come to fruition (Joel 1:2), and calls his contemporaries to (re)turn to God and promises (2:18–3:21) God's turning to them.

Restoration by God

The second half of the collection (2:18–3:21) speaks of God's becoming jealous for God's people, presumably in response to the prayer for intervention. In the former days, foreign invaders had exiled God's people, parceled out their land, traded boys for prostitutes, and sold girls for alcohol (3:1-3). In the restoration God would repulse foreign invaders (2:20, 26b; 3:1-17, 19-20), renew the people's crops (2:19, 22-26a; 3:18), and take revenge for the spilling of Israelite blood (3:21). In the middle of this section (3:9-16), a voice (presumably God's) directs messengers to issue a proclamation to the nations commanding them to prepare for war and summoning the people of Judah to equip themselves for and conduct battle under the protection of God. The place for this battle is called the "valley of Jehoshaphat," a place name that means "YHWH will judge." The name is probably a cipher, a theological rather than a geographical name.[36] In this second half of the collection, moreover, the day of YHWH would involve the vindication of the people of Judah, the ones threatened in the first half. The Zion that had been in danger in the first half (2:1) hears God's promise to dwell therein once more in the second half (2:23; 3:17).

The hope for restoration involved the charisma of God falling on all categories of people: young and old, male and female, servant and master.

---

36. James L. Crenshaw, "Freeing the Imagination: The Conclusion to the Book of Joel," in *Prophecy and Prophets: The Diversity of Contemporary Issues in Scholarship*, ed. Yehoshua Gitay. SBLSemS (Atlanta: Scholars, 1997) 140.

The hope is expressed further in terms that sound apocalyptic, especially 2:30-32 where God says:

> 30 I will send wonders in heaven and earth; blood and fire and billows of smoke. 31 The sun shall turn to darkness and the moon to blood before the great and dreadful day of YHWH comes. 32 And then all who call on the name of YHWH shall be saved, for on Mount Zion and in Jerusalem there shall be those who are delivered, just as YHWH said; and among the survivors shall be those whom YHWH calls.

"Wonders" or "portents" were events brought about by God's power that would point beyond themselves to the God that performed them. Consequently, anyone who saw the events correctly (i.e., as portents) and called upon God would be saved.

Whether such thinking can properly be called "apocalyptic" depends on one's view of what constitutes apocalyptic thinking. (On that issue, see the introduction to apocalyptic literature in Chapter 8 on Daniel.) Let it be said here, however, that at most the language appears to be what scholars often call "protoapocalyptic." That term designates sections of the OT that employ (1) exaggerated literary images like those in Joel 2 or (2) ways of viewing the future that (tend to) envision a future dramatically improved from the present by the direct intervention of God. In both senses Joel seems "protoapocalyptic." Nothing in the collection, however, speaks of the end of time in the sense of the coming of the Messiah, the end of the world, judgment, heaven and hell.

Readers of the NT will recognize that in Acts 2:17-21 the Apostle Peter quotes this text in his explanation of the events of the day of Pentecost. Peter does not apply it to the end of the world, but focuses on the pouring out of the spirit, claiming that the day of Pentecost, when the Holy Spirit came upon the church collectively and individually, was God's fulfillment of Joel's prediction. In other words, for Peter in Acts the day of Pentecost ushered in the "last days," but did so through prophetic inspiration, not through world cataclysm.

To return to Joel, it is time to see how the collection functions to tie Hosea and Amos together and to speak to subsequent generations. It takes its place between collections attributed to two eighth-century prophets who address the north, though it is itself a collection aimed at Jerusalem/ Zion. It addresses them in the light of the fall of the northern kingdom Israel. It calls on them to fast and lament before God's house. Perhaps the placement of Joel between Hosea and Amos was meant to suggest that had the people of northern Israel fasted and repented before God, their fall to foreign armies could have been avoided. Perhaps, further, the collection was a reminder to postexilic Judah that it too had fallen, in its case to Babylon, a tragedy that could have been prevented if Judah had repented. Regardless, it remained a call to all those who worshipped at the second temple that they must continue to fast, lament, and implore God's favor.

A Problem Raised by a Study of Joel

One problem raised by our study of Joel is how to understand personal and collective calamity. If the situation Joel is facing is crop failure and economic downturn, is it necessarily the case that those reversals have moral causes? The observation that Joel (in contrast with Hosea) cites no such causes suggests that the Book of the Twelve has moved ahead to a new issue here not considered by Hosea. That new issue comes close to the issue of theodicy (the defense of God's goodness), but does not posit God's goodness. Indeed, one may suggest that the question raised by Joel 1:1–2:17 is whether God is good in the sense of being faithful to Israel. The answer in the second half of the collection is affirmative. Still, one can push the issue a step further. Is it necessarily proof of the lack of goodness on God's part (through either indifference or hostility) if crops fail or foreign armies invade? Perhaps Joel thought a failure to redeem Judah would reflect negatively on God. Even if he did, however, *we* are not bound to that conclusion. We might want to argue that God helps God's people through such events when they come, though God might not prevent or rescue people from them. Most captives died in the Holocaust, regardless of whether they believed in God.

AMOS
Warnings of Destruction

If the collection named for Hosea warns of impending divorce between God and Israel, and if Joel cries out to Judah to fast and lament, the collection named for Amos returns to the theme of divine judgment. Only the last five verses of the collection, verses almost certainly added by the hand of a later redactor, express any hope, and that hope is not for preexilic Israel or Judah, but for the fallen Davidic dynasty. Before examining that hope, however, we shall consider Amos's warnings of destruction to Israel.

Introduction to the Collection and Its Times

The Place of the Collection in the Canon

As mentioned in connection with Joel, the LXX differs from the MT in the sequence of the first three collections in the Book of the Twelve. In the LXX Amos follows directly upon Hosea, thus breaking up the close connection in the MT between Joel 3:16a and Amos 1:2a. A consecutive reading of the Twelve in the MT, however, forces attention on that connection. Remarkably, Amos 1:2a turns what was a word of assurance in Joel 3:16a into a warning, followed by ominous threats to pasturelands and hilltops. Let there be no mistake, the verse warns the reader, the two collections bear witness to the same God, but Amos was a different prophet than Joel and had a different message. The end of Amos also seems to figure in the later development of the Twelve. Following Aaron Schart, Albertz argues that Amos 9:7-10 derived from the hand of the redactor of the Book of the Four, who thought that the exile would be purificatory (cf. Hos 1:1, 5, 7; 3:1bβ; 4:1 (in part), 15; 8:1b, 6a, 14; 11:5b).[37] He also notes that Amos 9:11-15, which is clearly exilic or postexilic because it looks back on the fall of the Davidic dynasty (see the phrase "the booth of David that is fallen" in v. 11), derives from a later hand than the redactor of the Four. I would add that it resonates nicely with the hope for the restoration of the Davidic dynasty in Haggai and Zechariah. Hence, the beginning and the end of Amos exhibit editing to bring the collection into agreement with other parts of the Twelve.

The Setting for the Collection

What can be said, then, about the setting or settings of the collection? The superscription dates the prophet himself "in the days of King Uzziah of Judah and in the days of King Jeroboam son of Joash, (during) two years be-

37. Albertz, "Exile as Purification," 243.

fore the earthquake" (1:1). Uzziah ruled in Judah from 783 to 742, and Jeroboam II in Israel from 786 to 746, a lengthy period of diminished demands by the Assyrians. During that period the upper class in Israel seems to have prospered, and at the expense of the poor — at least as Amos saw things. A time toward the middle of their co-reigns cannot be far off. So scholars usually date Amos around 760. As for the place of his ministry, the conflict with Amaziah shows that he spoke in Bethel and may well have spoken in nearby Samaria.

Nothing in the collection prior to 9:11-15 requires a date earlier than the exilic period, though Albertz thinks 9:7-10 fits there (see above). Nothing or little else in the collection betrays a southern orientation,[38] so the collection perhaps received less revision in the transmission process than did Hosea. It was edited into the Book of the Four by means of 9:7-10 and 1:1 (compare the superscriptions of Hosea, Micah, and Zephaniah with Amos 1:1) during the exile, and it was elaborated in 9:11-15 around 520 or later. Editing almost surely took place in or around Jerusalem.

The Structure, Integrity, and Authorship of the Collection

It is clear from the preceding paragraph that Amos was not the author of 9:11-15, since those verses look back on the fall of the Davidic dynasty in 586 and Amos flourished in the mid-eighth century. Other secondary touches included the superscription and (possibly) 9:7-10. Does it follow, then, that Amos himself wrote down the rest of the messages attributed to him? That is possible, but not really likely. Few people in ancient Israel were literate, let alone capable of writing down prophetic messages, short or long. Amos, therefore, like most other "writing prophets" probably delivered his messages orally, and then someone else wrote them down. In Jeremiah's case, of course, we know the name of the scribe: Baruch. In Amos's case we do not. It seems clear from the narrative of Amos's banishment from the temple in Bethel (7:10-17) that he was not well received. Perhaps he was considered a troublemaker or at least a crank.

What, then, would have led to the recording of his message? The an-

---

38. Aaron Schart argues that Amos 9:5-6 is Jerusalemite in origin, and he may be correct; "The Fifth Vision of Amos in Context," in Redditt and Schart, *Thematic Threads in the Book of the Twelve*, 56-58. The verses constitute a hymn fragment, so the temple in Jerusalem is certainly a possibility, though not the only one.

swer is not hard to guess: Amos turned out to be correct about the fall of Israel, just as Hosea was. Once he was proven correct, people may have been more willing to listen. Perhaps he dictated the messages again, as Jeremiah did (Jer 36:1-32), or perhaps someone remembered them or collected them from people who did, wrote them down, and preserved them. If he had positive things to say about the faithful in northern Israel, no one bothered to collect them. His preaching explained to the faithful why the northern kingdom had fallen to foreign, pagan rulers: their own upper crust had betrayed God's covenant. Eventually, Amos's messages moved south to Judah to reprise the dual role of warning/explanation in the face of the Babylonian threat in 597/586. Soon thereafter they were joined to the messages of Hosea, Micah, and Zephaniah by an editor.

The structure of Amos is fairly simple, consisting of a superscription (1:1), a motto (1:2), three clusters of sayings, plus an epilogue (9:7-15). The first cluster of sayings (chs. 1 and 2) contains prophecies of disaster against two groups (the cities of Damascus, Gaza, and Tyre and the areas of Edom, Ammon, Moab, and Judah) and culminates in a more lengthy condemnation of Israel. The sayings are held together by a common introduction: "For three transgressions of . . . , yea for four. . . ." This introduction borrows from the "numerical proverb" (cf. Prov 30:18-19, 24-28, 29-31). One would expect Amos to list four[39] sins for each city or nation chastised, but he lists only one for the first six groups. For Israel, however, he names the anticipated four ways they sinned: (1) by abusing the poor (2:6-7a), (2) by participating in fertility cults with cult prostitutes (2:7b), (3) by using personal property taken as security for a debt (2:8), and (4) by causing prophets and Nazirites to violate their reason for existence (2:11-12). It would appear that the first six prophecies of disaster serve mainly to set up what Amos had to say about Israel.[40] The second cluster of sayings (chs. 3–6) groups a variety of messages designed to condemn Israel, at least its leadership, for sin. The third collection contains five visions (7:1-9; 8:1–9:6), predicting God's punishment of Israel. In the first two, Amos intercedes as a

---

39. Usually a numerical proverb states a general heading: e.g., things small but wise, things stately in their stride, things not understood. Then it lists four examples. Things not understood (Prov 30:18-19) include the way of an eagle in the sky, a serpent on a rock, a ship at sea, and a man with a maiden.

40. In passing we should note that Amos, the earliest "writing prophet," employs the prophetic practice of prophesying about foreign nations. Isaiah, Jeremiah, Ezekiel, Obadiah, Jonah, Nahum, Habakkuk, Zephaniah, and Zechariah 9–14 do likewise.

prophet might; but in the last three he does not intercede, and God does not turn from his stated intention of punishing Israel. The biographical piece in 7:10-17, detailing Amos's banishment from the royal temple at Bethel, connects thematically with the mention of King Jeroboam in 7:9.

Main Genres in the Collection

The discussion of structure above referred to the variety of genres employed in the collection named for Amos. Prophecies of disaster dominate, of course, but Amos employs a couple of other genres which envision the same outcome. Both the trial speech (cf. 3:1-15; 4:1-3) and the woe oracle (cf. 5:18-20; 6:1; 6:4-7) anticipate God's punishment. The trial speech begins with a summons to a trial, as a listener, witness, or defendant. It proceeds with an indictment and punishment. The woe oracle employs the Hebrew word *hoi*, best translated "alas" or "ah," but translated "woe" in the RSV, from which English-speaking scholars derived the name of this genre.[41] The single word *hoi* replaces the anticipated disaster or punishment, and the description or wrongdoing/indictment is indicated by the preposition *le* ("to") and one or more infinitives indicating the ones who offended God: e.g., woe to fornicators, to killers, to robbers. Another genre to Amos's liking is the admonition, which either commands or prohibits given behaviors: e.g. "seek YHWH that you may live" (5:14).

One Special Feature of the Collection

Either Amos or someone involved in the transmission of his messages employed three hymn fragments (4:13; 5:8-9; 9:5-6), which have been the subject of much scholarly attention. Within the Twelve, they stand closest to the theophanies (appearances of God) in Nahum 1 and Habakkuk 3. Erhard S. Gerstenberger has advanced the suggestion that they stem not from the hand of Amos but of later tradition-bearers who were influenced by and bearers of psalms.[42] These hymn fragments build to their climax in

---

41. The word for "woe" in the lament is *'oi*, as in the phrase "woe is me" (Isa 24:16).

42. Erhard S. Gerstenberger, "Psalms in the Book of the Twelve: How Misplaced Are They?" in Redditt and Schart, *Thematic Threads in the Book of the Twelve*, 72-89.

the phrase "YHWH of hosts (is) his name." The same God that created the heavens and earth (4:13; 5:8-9) and is powerful enough to torch it as well (9:5-6) was ready to act with regard to Israel.

Introduction to the Prophet

The name Amos derives from a Hebrew root meaning "to load" or "to carry a load." The superscription (1:1) says that he was from Tekoa, a town on a hill within view of Bethlehem, which was located about six miles to Tekoa's north. Amos is said to be "among the shepherds of Tekoa." The Hebrew word used for "shepherd" in v. 1 is a plural form of the word *noqed,* which designates someone who raised, sold, or tended sheep. 2 Kgs 3:4 is the only other place in the OT that the word appears. There the word describes King Mesha of Moab and is translated "breeder of sheep." Scholars sometimes speculate about the status the term might imply for Amos, if its use in 2 Kings is of a king. It would seem, however, that it does not necessarily follow that simply because one breeder (Mesha) was wealthy all were. In Amos 7:14 Amos calls himself a *boqer,* a word meaning "herdsman." The noun from which it derives *(baqar)* is a general word for "cattle" or "herd" that designates large animals like oxen. Some scholars have suggested that *boqer* is a mistaken reading, and that the text actually should read *noqed* ("shepherd"), as in 1:1.[43] If so, Amos worked only with sheep. If *boqer* ("herdsman") is correct in 7:14, however, we can view him as someone who tended large animals. The tension between these two ways of describing Amos's occupation, however, may be only apparent. It is possible that the phrase "among the shepherds of Tekoa" was a traditional phrase that might have been used fairly loosely of people from that area who worked with domesticated animals, even of someone who actually worked with larger animals than sheep.

The other phrase Amos uses of his occupation is "caretaker of fig trees" (7:14). The precise meaning of the word translated "caretaker" is unknown, since the word appears nowhere else in the OT. The term apparently designates something one did to figs, whether to pick them or otherwise handle them to make them more palatable. In terms of the private life

---

43. The words are really much closer in Hebrew than they appear to be in English. The first letters "b" (ב) and "n" (נ) are similar in Hebrew, as are the last letters "r" (ר) and "d" (ד).

of the prophet, therefore, we know only that he lived in Tekoa and worked in agriculture, with sheep and/or oxen and with figs.

His public career lasted no more than two years (1:1) and was spent in northern Israel rather than in his own kingdom of Judah. He may have preached in several northern sanctuaries, for he is portrayed as condemning worshippers in more than one, even including Jerusalem (6:1). The collection named after him relates what was presumably his culminating experience in the royal temple in Bethel (7:10-17). Amaziah, the main priest at Bethel, reported to King Jeroboam II that Amos was conspiring against the king by warning his audiences that the king would die by the sword and the people would go into exile (in Assyria, no doubt). Then Amaziah banished Amos from the temple in Bethel and commanded him to leave the country. Despite Amos's response that he was not a (professional) prophet or even the son of a prophet (an apprentice prophet) his career seems to have been over. He could perhaps have continued to preach from the sidelines, but no longer in temples.

Basic Emphases in Amos

The overall tone of Amos's messages is doom, particularly for the upper class. In Hosea that doom is mitigated by compassion and hope for eventual repentance and return to YHWH, but not in Amos. The only positive passage is the final one (Amos 9:11-15), and that is from the hand of a later redactor. We shall examine the message of Amos under five headings: God's punishment of foreign nations, the demand for social justice, the day of YHWH, the monarchy, and exile and restoration.

God's Punishment of Foreign Nations

As mentioned earlier, the collection opens (Amos 1:3–2:3) with predictions of disaster on six surrounding cities and nations: Damascus (1:3-5), Gaza (1:6-8), Tyre (1:9-10), Edom (1:11-12), Ammon (1:13-15), and Moab (2:1-3). In the first five cases the offending party is charged with an act of aggression against Israel, the sixth (Moab) of aggression against Edom. (By contrast the charges against Judah and Israel are for sins against their own people.) The predicted punishment would fall on the defenses and/or the kings of the guilty — presumably by means of an invading army, though that is not stated.

The Demand for Social Justice

Amos demands social justice. He denounces moneylenders for selling people into indentured servanthood for a trifling debt (2:6-7a; 5:11; 8:6). In one of his more notorious messages, he addresses the wives of the leading citizens of the capital city of Samaria, accusing them of pushing their husbands to make more money. These people thought that their sacrifices and their fasts would absolve them of any blame before God, but Amos thought otherwise. In a stunning passage (5:21-24) God tells them to abandon such sacrifices, possibly because they were done as a means of buying off God and not as an expression of contrition for their sins. Consequently, God commands them to "let justice flow like water, and righteousness like a river" (5:24). In other words, sacrifice without justice is meaningless.

Is it any wonder, then, that Amos has often been a hero of the Bible among persons advocating liberation theology? Whether those audiences are disadvantaged Americans or persons in the third world, Amos's message that God would punish those who take advantage of weaker humans is great news. Sometimes people in power defend their actions by saying that they are doing nothing illegal. Amos might respond that what the laws made by the wealthy allow the wealthy to do is beside the point. For Amos, the issue is morality, not legality. He holds God's people to a higher standard than mere legality.

The Day of YHWH

Like Joel, Amos speaks of a coming day of YHWH, a day when God would punish God's enemies (Amos 5:18-20).

> 18 Woe to the ones desiring the day of YHWH!
>   What is the day of YHWH to you?
>   It is (a day of) darkness, not light.
> 19 It will be as if a man flees from the lion, (only) to be met
>   by the bear.

Or he makes it into his house and rests his hand upon the wall,
    (only) to be bitten by the snake.
20 Is not the day of YHWH darkness and not light?
    Is it not gloomy with no brightness in it?

If the people of Israel who were Amos's targets thought they would escape from YHWH on the day of punishment, they were like the hapless person described in v. 19. Amos condemns them for conspicuous consumption in the face of poverty (6:4-6) and promises that the unscrupulous wealthy would go into exile (6:7). The best the collection promises Israel and Samaria is the rescue of a fraction of the population (3:12): "As the shepherd rescues a pair of legs or a piece of an ear from the mouth of a lion, so shall the children of Israel, the ones living in Samaria, be rescued along with the corner of a bed and the _____ [44] of a divan." The reversal the day of YHWH would bring to Israel was the demise of the selfishly successful.

The Monarchy

The king is mentioned seldom in Amos. The superscript mentions King Uzziah and King Jeroboam (II), but only to situate Amos in time. Amos 1:15 predicts exile for the king of Ammon. In 7:9 God says to Amos that God would rise up against the house of Jeroboam with the sword. That prediction introduces the narrative of the confrontation between Amos and Amaziah, in which the king must have played a crucial role. Interestingly, Jeroboam is never quoted; he remains off stage, as it were. We read that Amaziah reported Amos's actions to Jeroboam (7:10-11). Then Amaziah tells Amos to leave the sanctuary. One can only assume he did so at the directive of the king, but the reader must supply that information.

    The only other place the monarchy is mentioned is in 9:11, which refers to "the booth of David that is fallen." As we have already seen, that verse seems to have derived from a much later hand, perhaps one from the time of Haggai and Zechariah 1–8, both of which have strong hopes for a restored Davidic monarchy. Otherwise those who collected the words of Amos seem to have gone out of their way not to mention the northern

---

44. The Hebrew word appears to be the name of the city Damascus, but how does that fit the context? The required meaning would seem to be some small part of a bed.

king. By that time, perhaps, that dynasty had been dead so long it was no longer worth mentioning.

Exile and Restoration

At the end of the collection we find two apparent additions: 9:7-10 and 11-15. The first predicts exile, and it is not the only passage to do so (cf. 5:5, 27; 7:11; 9:4). The new note struck here, however, is that captivity would be therapeutic. According to 9:4, the people simply will die in captivity at the hands of their captors. Amos 9:8, however, repeats the threat, but qualifies it: "except that I will not totally destroy the house of Jacob." Many among God's people would die by the sword, even though they did not believe that God would punish them. The nation would be cleansed, and a few would survive the exile. The final passage (9:11-15) is even more optimistic. It looks unblinkingly toward the restoration of the Davidic dynasty, thus closing the otherwise pessimistic collection on a happy note.

One Problem Raised by a Study of Amos

Like Hosea, Amos also foresaw God's sending natural calamity on Israel (Amos 4:6-10). We might once again want to question the morality of God's destroying nature. In this case, however, a more nuanced reading is possible. Amos reviews a series of natural "crises": famine (4:6), drought (4:7-8), excess moisture (4:9a), locusts (4:9b), and diseases affecting people and animals (4:10). It is not clear, however, that any of these conditions constitutes the divine punishment of Israel; instead they are all natural conditions that adversely affect people. It is possible, therefore, to suggest that Amos construed these natural events (sent directly or indirectly by the Creator) as warnings to Israel: warnings that the people were dependent upon God and God's world, and not free to (mis)behave as they wished. The Israelites, however, had refused to heed the warning from nature and would reap the recompense from God for their sin and folly.

Summary

The messages of Hosea, Joel, and Amos sound the theme of the impending divorce of God from Israel. The Israelite prophet Hosea saw the divorce as the result of infidelity on the part of Israel in its relationship to God. The postexilic prophet Joel thought the divorce necessitated Israel's turning or returning to God and called the people to YHWH. He promised that if Israel did turn to God, God would turn to them. The Judean shepherd Amos, filtered through and added to by later scribes, denounced Israel for social injustice and warned that the divorce, though not irrevocable, carried a heavy price. The final addition proclaimed that restitution was possible, however, including the restitution of the Davidic monarchy.

Questions for Reflection

1. How would you defend and refute the view that Hosea's portrayal of women is sexist? that his view of a punishing God is flawed?

2. Based on Hosea 11, is God impassible? Does God change? (In answering this question, please consult Mal 3:6.) What difference does one's view of the nature of God make?

3. What are the implications of Joel 2:28-29 for religious communities, Jewish or Christian?

4. How would you deal with the issue of individual or collective calamity raised in the section "A Problem Raised by a Study of Joel"? If religion does not "pay," why be religious? (You might want to think about what counts as "pay.")

5. What do you think of Amos's demand for social justice? Is that a proper concern for religion? Is it ever permissible (or necessary) for religious leaders to oppose political leaders in a time of national danger?

6. Does Amos strike you as a preacher you would want to hear every week of the year? Why or why not?

7. What do you think of the proposed canonical reading among these collections? Does it make sense to read them this way? Is it legitimate? Can you think of a better or an additional reading?

For Further Reading

Crenshaw, James L. *Joel.* AB 24C. New York: Doubleday, 1995. New translation, introduction, and commentary on the Hebrew text of Joel.

Davies, G. I. *Hosea.* NCBC. Grand Rapids: Wm. B. Eerdmans, 1992. Stresses Hosea's reinterpretation of biblical traditions and the treatment of Hosea's sayings in ancient Israel, the Dead Sea Scrolls, and the New Testament.

Jeremias, Jörg. *The Book of Amos.* OTL. Louisville: Westminster John Knox, 1998. A form- and redaction-critical study of Amos that also deals with the text in its canonical form. Translation of ATD 24/2.

————. "The Interrelationship Between Amos and Hosea." In *Forming Prophetic Literature*, ed. James W. Watts and Paul R. House, 171-86. JSOTSup 235. Sheffield: Sheffield Academic, 1996. Argues that the disciples of Amos and Hosea edited the two collections together, thus beginning what became the Book of the Twelve.

Nogalski, James D. "Joel as 'Literary Anchor' for the Book of the Twelve." In *Reading and Hearing the Book of the Twelve*, ed. Nogalski and Marvin A. Sweeney, 91-109. SBLSymS 15. Atlanta: Society of Biblical Literature, 2000. Argues that Joel was created to anchor the assembling of the Twelve from its precursors.

Paul, Shalom M. *Amos.* Hermeneia. Minneapolis: Fortress, 1991. Thorough, scholarly commentary on the Hebrew text of Amos.

Simundson, Daniel J. *Hosea, Joel, Amos, Obadiah, Jonah, Micah.* AOTC. Nashville: Abingdon, 2005. Brief introduction of each collection or section of a collection (key issues, literary genre, structure, character of the writings, and social context) followed by exegesis and a treatment of the theological/ethical significance.

Sweeney, Marvin A. *The Twelve Prophets.* 2 vols. Berit Olam. Collegeville: Liturgical, 2000. Written to interpret the Twelve as a unity intended to be read straight through.

Wolff, Hans Walter. *Hosea.* Hermeneia. Philadelphia: Fortress, 1974. Thorough commentary on the Hebrew text of Hosea. Translation of BKAT XIV/1.

————. *Joel and Amos.* Hermeneia. Philadelphia: Fortress, 1977. Thorough commentary on the Hebrew text of Joel and Amos. Translation of BKAT XIV/2.

CHAPTER 11

Obadiah, Jonah, Micah

The next three collections in the Twelve are named for the prophets Obadiah, Jonah, and Micah. Obadiah is a brief (one-chapter) denunciation of Edom for its role in the destruction of Jerusalem by the Babylonians in 586 B.C.E. Jonah is a narrative about a recalcitrant, eighth-century prophet who attempts to flee from God rather than obey the divine command to preach to the hated Ninevites. Micah contains the preaching of an eighth-century contemporary of Hosea and Amos in the north and Isaiah in the south. Its superscription is sufficiently like those of Hosea and Amos to warrant the suggestion that the three were combined with the later collection named for the prophet Zephaniah into a Book of the Four. A canonical reading of Micah, therefore, will be complicated by its connections to other works than the ones immediately before and after it. Still, we shall begin with a discussion of the plot of the Twelve as it unfurls in Obadiah, Jonah, and Micah.

The Plot of the Twelve: Punishment for Judah and Others

The exilic collection named for Obadiah looks back on the fall of Jerusalem, reminding the postexilic reader of the Twelve that Judah fell because it did not repent. Obadiah also anticipates the day of God's punishment of Edom for its role in the fall of Jerusalem and Judah. Jonah and Micah, like Hosea and Amos, are set in the eighth century.[1] Jonah ponders the possible

1. Modern scholars who date Jonah in the postexilic period sometimes seem to forget that Jonah was set in the eighth century and treat it simply as a postexilic work.

salvation of Assyria, while Micah anticipates its fall. Micah also emphasizes the fall of Judah. So these collections anticipate God's punishment of Edom, Assyria, and Judah.

OBADIAH
Punishment of Edom Deserved

Obadiah is the shortest collection in the Book of the Twelve, encompassing only twenty-one verses. It proclaims doom upon Edom for its participation in the fall of Jerusalem at the hands of the Babylonians in 586. Then (vv. 17-21) it envisions a new day for northern Israel and for Jerusalem, when the fortunes of both would reverse and their exiles would return home.

Introduction to the Collection and Its Times

The Place of the Collection in the Canon

James D. Nogalski notes the repetition of the words "Edom" and "nations" from Amos 9:12 in Obad 1.[2] That is, Obadiah opens with words that look back to Amos 9:12, which comes just four verses before it in the canonical sequence. Obadiah ends (vv. 17 and 21) with the promise that "the saved ones" on Mount Zion would escape the day of YHWH. Nogalski also points to a couple of catchwords between Obadiah and the following narrative of Jonah, including the odd use of the phrase "cast lots" in Obad 11, which appears in Jonah 1:7.[3] Thus, Obadiah seems to be tied by catchwords to the collections immediately before and after it. It also employs (Obad 15) the theme of the "day of YHWH," used in Joel as well. In the LXX also, despite its different sequence of the collections than in the MT (LXX: Hosea, Amos, Micah, Joel, Obadiah, Jonah), Obadiah precedes Jonah,[4] so a

---

2. James D. Nogalski, *Literary Precursors to the Book of the Twelve.* BZAW 217 (Berlin: de Gruyter, 1993) 28-29.

3. Nogalski, *Literary Precursors to the Book of the Twelve,* 33-34.

4. This sequence holds in most manuscripts and lists. The exceptions are the list in the *Martyrdom and Ascension of Isaiah* 4:22, which reverses the order, and a fragment among the Dead Sea Scrolls (4QXII^a), which places Jonah after Malachi.

consecutive reading of those two is warranted based on either version of the OT.

The Setting for the Collection

Obadiah is set in Jerusalem, some time after the destruction of the city in 586 (v. 16).[5] It anticipates (v. 20) the return of exiles and the recovery of land by *Israelites* (called "the house of Joseph," v. 18) from the area of Edom and the Philistine territory in the south. The recovered land would extend as far north as Zarephath, a town in southern Phoenicia. Also, exiles from Jerusalem living in Sepharad (location unknown, but possibly in Media) would inherit the southern region of Judah called the Negeb. Mount Zion would become holy once more (v. 17), perhaps implying that Jerusalem and its temple would be rebuilt. Nothing in the collection actually reflects the return of exiles, however, despite the anticipation of such movement. Hence, in its canonical form the collection appears to be exilic.

The Structure, Integrity, and Authorship of the Collection

Whatever the collection as a whole might owe to its place in the Twelve, Obad 2-7 draws strongly on Jer 49:7-22. Three parallels between the two passages stand out: Obad 2 // Jer 49:15 (God would make Edom the least of all the nations); Obad 3-4 // Jer 49:16 (a comparison of Edomite cities with an eagle's eyrie, from which God would bring down the inhabitants); and Obad 5 // Jer 49:9 (a comparison of future punishment with plunderers and grape-gatherers). A fourth parallel follows in Obad 8 // Jer 49:7, which speaks of the elimination of the wise from Edom, but the language is not as

---

5. Marvin A. Sweeney notes that the text does not say Jerusalem fell and thinks that the prophet Obadiah might have been a ninth-century prophet concerned with a much earlier attack on Jerusalem than the one by Babylon that ended in the city's destruction in 586; *The Twelve Prophets*. Berit Olam (Collegeville: Liturgical, 2000) 1:280-85. Sweeney concludes, however, that the *present* text of Obadiah, dependent as it is on Jeremiah, is a reworking of a much older prophecy against enemies of the northern kingdom, turning the whole collection into a reflection on Jerusalem. For our purposes it will be sufficient to read the collection as a reflection on the fall of Jerusalem in 586.

close as with the previous examples.[6] It would appear, therefore, that the beginning of the message (at least vv. 3-7) was composed in dialogue with Jer 49:7-22.

Obadiah 8-18 appears to be a self-contained oracle against Edom. The verses excoriate its inhabitants for offenses against Jerusalem at the time of the city's destruction. Obadiah 19-21 is an expansion exploring the theme of the reversal of the fortunes of Edom and Judah introduced in vv. 15-17. Joel 2:32 seems to have Obad 17 and probably Obad 21 as well in view, so vv. 8-21 appear to have been combined earlier than the production of Joel (probably 515-450). At least vv. 8-18 derived from one hand. Since Obad 1-7 draws upon Jeremiah 49, it — like vv. 18-21 — arose in the exilic or early postexilic period as the prefix for vv. 8-18.

L. F. Bliese points to a chiasmic structure for the collection, which preserves these basic divisions in the growth of the text.

> A   1-4   God will humble Edom.
>   B   5-7   Edom will be attacked and abandoned by its allies.
>   C   8-11   Edom is judged for remaining passive during the slaughter of Judah.
>   C′ 12-14   Edom should not have rejoiced at or benefited from Judah's misfortunes.
>   B′ 15-18   God's people will return to rule on Mount Zion.
> A′ 19-21   God will save God's people.[7]

Genres in the Collection

The first prophecy of destruction uttered against Edom is introduced in v. 1 as a herald's report, but it contains a description of the punishment about to fall on Edom in vv. 2 and 4, with v. 3 offering the description of Edom's

---

6. Other scholars point to even broader connections between Obadiah and Jeremiah 49. Samuel Pagán, e.g., cites as parallels Obad 1a and Jer 49:7, Obad 1b-4 and Jer 49:14-16, Obad 5-6 and Jer 49:9-10a and similarities between Obad 8 and Jer 49:7, Obad 9 and Jer 49:22, and Obad 16 and Jer 49:12; "Obadiah," *NIB*, 7 (1996) 440. I have chosen to focus on passages where borrowing appears to be word for word or close.

7. L. F. Bliese, "Chiasmatic and Homogeneous Metrical Structure Enhanced by Word Patterns in Obadiah," unpublished United Bible Societies paper, 1991, cited by Pagán, "Obadiah," 439.

wrongdoing. The series of prophecies of destruction that come next (vv. 6-16) are introduced by rhetorical questions (v. 5) that gloat over Edom's future demise and are tied together by two uses of the temporal phrase "on that day" (vv. 8, 11) and a reference to the "day of YHWH" (v. 15). The collection concludes with a prophecy of salvation for Israel and Judah.

A Special Issue Connected with the Collection

The charges against Edom in Obad 11-14 are presented as a series of prohibitions. Edom had failed to act as an ally when Jerusalem was attacked, so the prophet repeats in apodictic[8] form what he thought were the covenant obligations to Judah that Edom had violated. Following the statement that Edom "stood aside" when Jerusalem was attacked, the prophet lists eight prohibitions broken by Edom. "Do not look on" (v. 11) when foreigners carry off the city's wealth. "Do not rejoice" on the day of Judah's distress (v. 12). "Do not make great" (or boast) on the day of Jerusalem's misfortune (v. 12). "Do not enter the gates of Jerusalem" at the time of its calamity (v. 13). "Do not gaze favorably" (i.e., gloat) on the day of the city's destruction (v. 13).[9] "Do not lay hands on" the property of its inhabitants (v. 13). "Do not stand in the crossings"[10] to cut off escapees (v. 14). Finally, "do not deliver up" the city's survivors on the day of its distress (v. 14).

What is not clear, however, is the nature of Edom's participation in this attack upon Jerusalem. Did Edomites participate in the looting of the city (v. 13) or just stand by? Did they perhaps even turn over escapees to the Babylonians (v. 14)? Marvin A. Sweeney points to a number of texts he thinks show that Edom did take part in the pillaging: Psalm 137, esp. v. 7; Isa 34:5-17; 63:1-6; Jer 49:7-22; Ezek 25:12-14; 35:2-15; Mal 1:2-5; Lam 4:21-22.[11] While it is true that these texts envision God's punishment on Edom, sometimes to an extreme, only two actually specify what Edom did wrong. Ezekiel 25:12-14 blames Edom for taking vengeance on Judah, and Ezek 35:2-15 condemns Edom for cherishing enmity against Judah (v. 5) and "bad-mouthing" Judah at the time of its demise (vv. 13, 15). What is clear is

---

8. Apodictic laws are commands and prohibitions.

9. The word used for "calamity" was *'edam,* a pun on the name *'Edom.*

10. NRSV. The meaning of the word translated "crossings" is uncertain.

11. Sweeney, *The Twelve Prophets,* 1:281.

that Obad 8-16 likewise expresses Judah's bad feelings toward Edom from the time of the fall of Jerusalem on. (See below "A Problem Raised by a Study of Obadiah.")

Introduction to the Prophet

The name of the prophet Obadiah is a compound of the Hebrew word meaning "one who serves" with YH, the shortened form of the divine name. Hence, the name means "one who serves (or 'servant of') YHWH." It is relatively common in the OT and not limited to any particular time period. Other than the prophet's name, we know nothing about him. Even his date is unclear if Sweeney is correct that vv. 8-18 (authentic to the prophet) fit the preexilic period of tension between Judah and Edom from the last half of the ninth century into the eighth.[12] If Sweeney is not correct, Obadiah flourished some time (shortly?) after the sack of Jerusalem by Babylon in 586. Regardless, the text as we have it derives from the exilic period.

Basic Emphasis in Obadiah

Like Joel and Amos, Obadiah employs the theme of the day of YHWH, using the phrase "the day of YHWH" in v. 15 and the phrase "on that day" to refer to the coming day of punishment on Edom in v. 8. That concept clearly presupposed the view that God would at least step into human affairs to punish those guilty of egregious misconduct. Mostly, though, the collection brims with the sense that Edom had behaved treacherously and would soon receive retributive punishment from God as a means of restoring justice. This restoration would also benefit Judah, the "victim" of whatever Edom had done wrong. This point needs further attention.

A Problem Raised by a Study of Obadiah

The problem with this twofold message, of course, is that Edom was not the real culprit in the sacking of Jerusalem. That culprit was Babylonia. If

---

12. Sweeney, *The Twelve Prophets*, 1:280.

anyone deserved to be punished severely for what happened to Jerusalem, it was Babylon. To predict the destruction of Edom for whatever minor role it had in the fall of Jerusalem was to ascribe to that role far more guilt than the circumstances might seem to us to warrant. A more measured, and in that sense perhaps more appropriate, revenge might have been for Judah to stand by and watch — and perhaps occasionally help itself — when one or more foreign nations overran Edom. Obadiah 16 seems to envision such a situation. The text does not limit itself to such recompense, however. Obadiah 18 envisions (albeit metaphorically) the Israelites' consuming Edom as a fire, and vv. 19-20 envision "Israelites" (re)possessing the towns of the Negeb, land south of Judah that Edom perhaps captured during the Babylonian period. The "day of YHWH" mentioned in v. 15, a day when Edom would receive what it deserved from others, has become in vv. 18-21 a day of disproportionate retribution, if not annihilation. Where is the justice in that?

It is clear that more was going on between Judah (or Israel) and Edom than meets the eye. In Genesis, Esau (the progenitor of Edom) and Jacob/Israel were twin brothers. They parted not on the best of terms (cf. Gen 27:39-41), but later in Genesis the two men seem to make up (33:1-17) and are last seen together burying their father (35:29). Deuteronomy 23:7 even commands Israel *not* to hate the Edomites, for they are brothers. Amos 1:11-12, however, condemns Edom; it is widely considered secondary, perhaps even based on Obadiah. It appears, then, that despite some tension between the two nations, the breakdown in relations did not take shape until the exile. Why, though, did the anti-Edomite sentiment in Obadiah emerge and become so strong? The answer may lie in failed expectations. People expect more from friends and family than from enemies. Slights by those we expect much of loom large; such slights are seen as betrayal. No animosity is stronger, and no wars more bitter, than those between "brothers," as a look at the American Civil War will show. This sentiment against Edom appears again in Mal 1:2b-3a in the famous statement placed on the lips of God: "for I have loved Jacob, but Esau I have hated."

This view of "us" versus "them" recurs in the OT. It is especially prominent in Nahum, which pits Israel versus Nineveh and subjects versus sovereigns. That same opposition appears in Jonah too, but there the author gives that opposition an ironic twist.

JONAH
Punishment of Assyria Averted Temporarily

In the narrative of Jonah, the hero — when he eventually agrees to go to Nineveh — takes the same "us" versus "them" approach to international relations. The gist of his sermon is this: "[There are] yet forty days before Nineveh is overthrown" (Jonah 3:4). The city, in response, repents with such gusto that even the animals are made to fast (3:8), but Jonah is not pleased. Jonah remains to see what would happen, and things turn out as he had expected all along: God forgives the penitent sinners and spares the city. That is not the way things were "supposed" to happen, as Jonah sees it. God was supposed to be for "us" and against "them." This aspect of God's behavior dismays God's spokesman.[13] In the plot of the Twelve, moreover, the punishment of Assyria — however richly deserved — is averted temporarily. Its fall would be predicted again in Mic 5:5b-6.

Introduction to the Collection and Its Times

The Place of the Collection in the Canon

As just observed, the narrative of Jonah moves the time frame of the Twelve back to the eighth century. In the LXX Jonah still follows Obadiah, but immediately precedes Nahum (Hosea, Amos, Micah, Joel, Obadiah, Jonah, Nahum), with its emphasis on the fall of Nineveh. In the MT, though, Jonah precedes Micah, with Nahum following Micah. This sequence was probably the result of the putative date of Jonah's activity during the reign of Jeroboam II (786-746). The superscription of Micah then places that prophet in the reigns of Jotham, Ahaz, and Hezekiah, i.e., after the reign of Jeroboam II. The sequence in the MT seems, therefore, to be determined by chronology determined from the superscriptions and incipits. The repentance of Assyria in Jonah is followed by the prediction of its fall in Nahum, a sequence that caught the attention of a few rabbis and other ancient interpreters, thus showing that some people in antiquity

---

13. One interesting feature of this narrative is that it never calls Jonah a prophet, though 2 Kgs 14:25 says he prophesied. In fact, in the Twelve only Habakkuk, Haggai, Zechariah (all in superscriptions), and Elijah (in Mal 4:5-6) are called prophets, though reference is sometimes made to "former prophets" or false prophets.

read the Twelve straight through. They adopted three reading strategies to deal with the apparent inconsistency. (1) Two (Tob 14:4, 8; and Josephus, *Ant.* 9.214) ignored the references to the repentance of the people of Nineveh. (2) Two others (*Tg. Ps.-J. Nah* 1:1; *Pirqe R. El.* 43) assumed that the people of Nineveh lapsed and return to sinning. (3) The last two (*y. Ta'an.* 1, 65d; *Pesiq. Rab Kah.* 24.11) interpreted the repentance of the Ninevites as hypocritical and superficial.[14]

Like Joel 2:13, Jonah 4:2 contains a quotation from Exod 34:6-7, though here it is shortened. Jonah pouts when God spares the city, and God calls his hand. In response, Jonah says that he knew from the first time God called him to go to Nineveh that God "was a gracious and merciful God, slow to anger and abundant in covenant mercy." Jonah 4:2 then adds a phrase appropriate to the theology of the narrator: "and penitent with respect to doing harm." The passage in Exodus 34 concludes with a portrayal of God as one who forgives the penitent and punishes those not yet forgiven (i.e., the impenitent guilty).

Finally, Jonah 3:9-10 seems to answer affirmatively the question of whether God ever changes God's mind about punishment. The question looms large in Jer 18:7-10; 26:3; and Joel 2:14. The latter reads: "Who knows [if YHWH] will turn and repent [of the evil YHWH intended to do] and leave behind a blessing after himself?" The answer of the Jonah narrative (though not of Jonah himself) is that God will spare anyone who repents, even the enemy Assyrians.

The Setting for the Collection

The setting for the Jonah narrative is, broadly speaking, the Assyrian Empire in the eighth century. The date is to be deduced from Jonah 1:1, which names the hero of the narrative as "Jonah son of Amittai." The name derives from 2 Kgs 14:25, which speaks of a prophet by that name during the reign of Jeroboam II (786-746). Otherwise, the narrative could be set any time during the Assyrian period. The narrative opens with Jonah some-

---

14. Beate Ego, "The Repentance of Nineveh in the Story of Jonah and Nahum's Prophecy of the City's Destruction — A Coherent Reading of the Book of the Twelve as Reflected in the Aggada," in *Thematic Threads in the Book of the Twelve,* ed. Paul L. Redditt and Aaron Schart. BZAW 325 (Berlin: de Gruyter, 2003) 163-64.

where in Israel, follows him to Joppa to catch a ship to Tarshish, relates his misadventures at sea, and notes his subsequent journey to Nineveh (3:3), where the remainder of the action takes place.

Nineveh was located near the Tigris River opposite the modern city of Mosul, about 220 miles northwest of Baghdad. It was a great city with huge palaces, temples, and statuary. The city covered two hills, and its wall ran about eight miles in circumference (three miles by one and one-half miles) and enclosed about 1800 acres.[15] Jonah 3:3 exaggerates its size by saying it took three days to walk across it. The presence of the king in Nineveh, however, suggests that the narrator thought of Nineveh as the capital city of Assyria, which it did not become until the reign of Sennacherib (704-681), at least four decades later than a prophet that flourished during Jeroboam's reign.

The date of the biblical version of the narrative, then, is an open and difficult matter to determine. Scholars have dated it from the late preexilic period to the Greek period (after 332). This last suggestion is based on the existence of Hellenistic parallels to the sea episode, but it has been challenged seriously by Hans Walter Wolff, who produces parallels to Jonah from the Greek singer Arion (flourished ca 620 B.C.E.).[16] It seems more likely that the narrative took its present form sometime in the latter half of the Persian period (after the date of Malachi), perhaps when it was included as the twelfth "prophet" among the Twelve.[17]

The Structure, Integrity, and Authorship of the Collection

As shown in Chapter 2 above, the structure of Jonah employs a narrative program (God, the subject, tries to conjoin Jonah to his will) and its opposite, an anti-program narrative (Jonah, the anti-subject, refusing the role of subject).[18] Following this structure, in the narrative program God di-

---

15. Charles T. Fritsch, "Nineveh," *ISBE*, 3:538.

16. Hans Walter Wolff, *Obadiah and Jonah*. CC (Minneapolis: Augsburg, 1986) 110.

17. Jack M. Sasson offers an excellent overview of the issue of the date of Jonah, concluding that a date in the postexilic period seems best, but noting that dating the collection helps little if at all in understanding it; *Jonah*. AB 24B (New York: Doubleday, 1990) 20-28.

18. Centre pour l'Analyse du Discourse Religieux, "An Approach to the Book of Jonah," in *Perspectives on Old Testament Narrative,* ed. Robert C. Culley. Semeia 15 (Missoula: Scholars, 1979) 85.

rects Jonah to go east to Nineveh to preach to its inhabitants. In the anti-program, Jonah refuses, and goes west to Tarshish instead. Jonah has mis-construed YHWH as the land-bound God of Israel only; YHWH also turns out to be God of the sea as well. Jonah's misadventures at sea ensue, and the fish spews Jonah out on dry land.

In the narrative program, Jonah travels to Nineveh, where he delivers God's message (3:4): "[There are] yet forty days before Nineveh is over-thrown." The people of Nineveh repent with such gusto that even the king repents in sackcloth and the animals are made to fast. In the anti-program, however, Jonah is incensed that the people have repented, that God has forgiven them, and has decided not to destroy them. Jonah even explains/complains to God (and the reader) that he knows that the nature of God is to forgive and wants no part in the salvation of the city; hence his flight to Tarshish. Perhaps he was even annoyed because his prediction did not come true, casting doubt on his future-telling abilities.[19]

In the anti-program, Jonah settles down to await God's punishment of the city. In the narrative program, God makes a plant grow overnight to shade the angry man. Then the next night God makes a worm to de-stroy the plant God had just made. In the anti-program Jonah sulks at this final insult. In the program narrative, however, God confronts Jo-nah. Is Jonah justified in being angry about the demise of the plant, which he had neither planted nor tended? He insists he is justified. The collection ends on a question, the final note in the program narrative: is God not, therefore, justified in God's concern for the great city Nineveh, which God had made? The reader is left to answer the question and in so doing to choose between the program narrative and the anti-program narrative.

Lawrence Boadt offers a simpler version of these reverses.

Chapter 1: The prophet is *disobedient* and refuses God,
Chapter 2: so he *praises* God in the fish for God's mercy;
Chapter 3: the prophet *obeys* the word of God and preaches,
Chapter 4: so he *complains* that God offers any mercy at all.[20]

---

19. Probably a reader would not be wrong in seeing this part of the anti-program as co-medic, even farcical.

20. Lawrence Boadt, *Reading the Old Testament* (New York: Paulist, 1984) 468.

James Limburg, however, profitably divides the narrative into seven scenes. Scene I relates Jonah's call and reaction (1:1-3). Scene II takes place on board ship in the midst of a storm (1:4-16). The setting for Scene III, remarkably, is inside a fish (1:17–2:10), while Scene IV records Jonah's second call (3:1-3a). Scene V takes place in Nineveh and records a brief version of his message (3:3b-10). Scene VI relates Jonah's prayer of anger over God's sparing of Nineveh (4:1-3), and the final scene takes place outside the city, where God and Jonah dialogue (4:4-11).[21] These three analyses of the structure of Jonah all focus on different issues, and all have their own advantages. There is no reason to try to choose the best one among them.

Determining the authorship of this narrative is impossible. In addition, its integrity is questionable in at least two places. First, Jonah's prayer from the belly of the fish (2:3-9) is a song of thanksgiving that presupposes someone who has gone through danger (vv. 3-7), prayed for God's help (v. 2), and survived to thank God by means of a personal testimony and a sacrifice at a (the?) temple (vv. 8-9). While its opening lines (esp. v. 3) would fit someone in Jonah's predicament, probably the reason it was chosen, its closing lines presuppose that the danger is past. This conclusion, however, need not imply that someone added the prayer after the narrative was committed to writing. Some kind of prayer was clearly in order, and the narrator perhaps used one he knew. Second, the recitation of Exod 34:6 in the prayer at 4:2 might be the result of editing since the second, fifth, sixth, and seventh collections of the Twelve recite it.[22]

Main Genres in the Collection

Basically, of course, the work is a narrative, which might be called a prophetic biography like those found in 1 and 2 Kings about Elijah and Elisha (but see the next paragraph). Other genres also appear within the narrative. Mention has already been made of the use of a song of thanksgiving in Jonah 2:2-9. Such songs appear rather frequently in the book of Psalms. In them, believers mention a past difficult situation, God's rescue of believers from that situation, and then give thanks to God for that deliverance.

---

21. James Limburg, *Jonah*. OTL (Louisville: Westminster/John Knox, 1993) 28.

22. Alternatively, the use of Exod 34:6-7 might have arisen independently in the collections, in which case it might have been a common theme leading to their combination.

Sometimes the believers speak of a vow they had made, and occasionally — as here — refer to a sacrifice to accompany the thanksgiving. The decree of the king of Assyria in Jonah 3:7-9 is typical of royal pronouncements. The confession of faith from Exod 34:6 in Jonah 4:2 is also a recognizable genre included in the narrative. Finally, the synopsis of Jonah's message (3:4) is a warning like one might expect in a prophecy of disaster.

The real issue literarily is whether the narrative is history or fiction, an account of a real event or a short story. Historiography typically concerns itself with natural rather than divine causality and operates with the so-called "principle of analogy." That principle states roughly: "If something can not happen now, it did not happen then." By those two standards, a narrative about a fish made by God for the purpose of swallowing but not digesting a human and eventually vomiting him up on dry land will hardly pass muster. Whether the event happened anyway is perhaps an issue of the reader's faith more than an issue of the classification of a narrative. On the basis of faith, however, some readers leap to the reference to "the sign of Jonah" placed on the lips of Jesus in Matt 12:39-40; 16:1-4; and Luke 11:29-30. That reference, however, probably proves less than such people claim. It is a reference to the Jonah narrative, but does not speak to the issue of the historicity of that narrative. Someone today could allude to a well-known quotation from a character in a play by Shakespeare, but such a citation would not turn the drama into a historical narrative. Regardless of how interpreters settle the issue, they might want to remember that generations of readers have believed they have heard the authentic voice of God in the narrative.

A Special Feature of the Collection

Mark Twain is reputed to have said that the Bible is the longest book in the world without a shred of humor. If, indeed, the humorist made such a statement, it would say more about him than about the Bible. In particular the Jonah narrative employs humor. Three examples will suffice. There is a bit of humor (in the form of irony) at Jonah's expense when he thinks he can escape God by leaving Israel and going to sea only to be cast overboard because of a wind sent by God and to end up being rescued by a great fish made by God. There is certainly humor (in the form of exaggeration) in the depiction of the king of Assyria repenting to such an extent that he commands that even the livestock fast and wear sackcloth (3:8). Finally, there is humor (in the form of satire) in the depiction of a "prophet" upset over the repentance of his audience (4:1-4). The narrator satirizes his hero to expose the moral failure of his readers, who themselves held exclusivist sentiments.

Introduction to the Prophet

The name Jonah means "dove." Steven L. McKenzie points out irony even there, noting that the name indicates someone who is "flighty" or "unstable." By contrast, the prophet's father is named Amittai, which comes from a Hebrew root meaning "truth" or "faithfulness." Thus, while the father was called "faithfulness," the prophet-son was called "flighty".[23] 2 Kings 14:25 says that King Jeroboam II restored the (Solomonic) borders of Israel from Lebo-hamath[24] (an old Hittite city on the Orontes River north of Damascus) to the Sea of the Arabah (usually understood as the Dead Sea), this restoration being a fulfillment of a prophecy by Jonah son of Amittai from Gath-hepher (a place located about three miles northeast of Nazareth). Nothing else is known of the prophet outside of the narrative bearing his name. Even that narrative speaks of only a short ministry in Nineveh (forty days), though 2 Kgs 14:25 suggests a longer ministry for the prophet.

Basic Emphases in Jonah

God's Rulership over Land and Sea

Though the list of possible emphases might be longer, we will focus on three. The first emphasis is made powerfully, though indirectly in the narrative through God's actions: YHWH is God over land and sea. That emphasis seems self-evident today, but it was hard won in the OT. Narratives of early epiphanies (appearances of God) are set (1) in the wilder-

---

23. Steven L. McKenzie, *How to Read the Bible* (Oxford: Oxford University Press, 2005) 3.
24. "Lebo" means "entrance of" or even "approaches to." Israel gained territory near the city, but never captured it.

ness in the form of a burning bush (cf. Exod 3:2), (2) in the wilderness in the form of a cloud and fire (Exod 13:21), and (3) on top of Mount Sinai (cf. Exod 19:16-18). In the narrative of Elijah's retreat to Sinai, the element of fire — and also the natural phenomena of earthquake and wind — is downplayed (1 Kgs 19:9b-18), but even there the setting is Mount Sinai. Ancient Israelites, moreover, seemed to have been suspicious of the sea. They did, however, think of God's victory over the sea in the exodus (Exodus 14), and the creation account in Gen 1:1–2:4a speaks of God's dividing the waters above the sea from those below it. Similarly, the Isaiah Apocalypse contains an allusion (Isa 27:1) to a mythic battle between divinities where one god defeats another, in particular the sea-god. In the dialogue with Job, God reminds Job that God set the boundaries for the sea (Job 38:8-11).

Jonah draws the full implications of those sentiments. Not only did YHWH create the world and its seas, God also controls them and the people who sail upon them. (Cf. Ps 139:9-10, where the psalmist confesses that even if he flees to the farthest limits of the sea God's hand will still lead him. Even if Jonah had made it to the end of the earth, he would not have escaped from God.) God works worldwide because God created the whole world and all the people in it.

God's Mercy for Penitent Sinners, Even Gentiles

The Jonah narrative draws upon the confession of faith in Exod 34:6 that God "was a gracious and merciful God, slow to anger and abundant in covenant mercy," even adding that God was "penitent with respect to doing harm" (4:2). God forgives sinners because that is the nature of a gracious God. No external power forces forgiveness on God; it wells up, as it were, from God's own being. Jonah himself explicitly acknowledges that mercy extends to the hated Ninevites; it is not exclusively for Israel. Interestingly, Jonah claims to have known that about God from the very beginning. To preclude the divine forgiveness, Jonah fled west, away from the city.[25] Even

---

25. Rüdiger Lux, from whom much in these emphases is taken, notes that God was not dependent on the prophet for getting God's work done: building a worldwide theocracy; *Jona: Prophet zwischen "Verweigerung" und 'Gehorsam'.* FRLANT 162 (Göttingen: Vandenhoeck & Ruprecht, 1994) 212. Such a theocracy, of course, could benefit Israel via Gentiles.

after all he had been through, the prophet was still angry that God would forgive the Assyrians. It might be one thing to forgive penitent Israelites. It was a different matter entirely to forgive penitent pagans, especially pagans who had held hegemony over God's people for centuries. Jonah just would not have it!

The narrative carries that sentiment to the end. Jonah sits, pouts, and waits for the destruction of the city and its 120,000 inhabitants. (Not much mercy there.) What transpires, instead, is the concluding conversation between God and Jonah. God reminds Jonah that Jonah pitied a little bush that grew overnight and died the next. The conversation (and the narrative) then ends with a question by God to Jonah: "So, as for me, should I not pity the great city of Nineveh?" Like Jonah, readers too must answer the question for themselves, but it is obvious which way the narrator (as opposed to Jonah) thinks God answers it.

The Conditional Nature of Prophetic Predictions

Most of us are conditioned to think that God's words are irreversible; once spoken, they are set forever. That understanding might apply to some, perhaps many, biblical texts, but not to all. From time to time the prophets delivered what we might call "conditional" predictions. Two visions of Amos (7:1-3, 4-6) indicate that at times a prophet might intercede for someone and gain concessions from God. Perhaps the most famous OT narrative of intercessory negotiations is Abraham's bargaining on behalf of the city of Sodom (Gen 18:16-33). Another clearly conditional warning is Jeremiah's famous Temple Sermon (Jer 7:1-15 and 26:1-9). Jeremiah predicts the destruction of the temple and the exile of people from Judah. Right in the middle of the sermon, however, Jeremiah gives the people an out. If they will truly repent, God will forgive them and continue to allow the people to dwell in Judah; indeed, God would continue to dwell there with them (Jer 7:5-7).[26]

Jonah's message is not so nuanced; the people had forty days until the city would be overthrown. Still, that message appears to fall under the category of warning, even though nothing explicitly says the punishment is

---

26. In Jer 7:16 God tells Jeremiah not to intercede any longer. Apparently the people had had their chance and blown it.

conditional. Still, giving Nineveh forty days notice is a way of inviting repentance, an action the city embarked on with astounding robustness. In view of this likely provisional prediction of Jonah, we are faced with a further question. Are readers (ancient or modern) permitted to read other prophetic messages as conditional, at least those that are not explicitly final?

A Problem Raised by a Study of Jonah

This study raised the issue of the attitude of Jonah versus that of the author. We are accustomed to assuming that the hero of a work speaks for the author, but that assumption is not always correct. In the Jonah narrative, we find a serious disjuncture between the two, and the effect is glaring. Many, perhaps most, Israelite readers, including those from the postexilic period, probably would have agreed with Jonah that Nineveh deserved all the punishment God would dump on them. If — as some scholars contend — Nineveh was a cipher for the capital of the Persian Empire (Persepolis, Susa, Ecbatana, or Babylon), many readers in the Persian period probably would have yearned for God's punishment on their Mesopotamian overlords. Even if Nineveh was not a cipher for a later capital, the Ninevites were foreigners, and it was by no means clear to people in postexilic Judah that all *Israelites* belonged to God, let alone foreigners. The author/narrator of Jonah, therefore, took his place beside the so-called Third Isaiah (cf. Isa 56:1-8) and probably the book of Ruth that YHWH was the God of the nations and not simply the God of Israel. It might be stretching the point to say the author advocated a Gentile mission, but he certainly laid the theological basis for such a movement: YHWH, the God of all creation, was the God of all nations — at least of those that repented of their sins and came to God for mercy.

The narrative of Jonah answers the question of "us" versus "them" in theological terms. From Genesis 12 on, the OT has faced this issue. If God "chose" Abraham and his offspring to be God's special people, where does that leave the rest of humanity? The Genesis narrative itself recognizes the issue. It responds (Gen 12:3) that God will bless the nations that bless Israel and curse those that curse Israel. Much in the OT can be read in that light. Other times, however, OT writers simply condemn other people regardless of their attitude toward Israel. An example of the latter is the command attributed directly to God for Israel to execute all humans Israel would find living in Canaan (Deut 20:16-18). In this case it is Canaanite sinfulness that justifies such action. The Jonah narrative seems to envision a different way of thinking about "them," a way toward a more humane treatment offered on the basis of a more compassionate God, a God the man Jonah knew all along would forgive "them" if they repented.

MICAH
Punishment of the Divine Daughter

Micah protests the sinfulness of the daughter Zion in Mic 1:13 and predicts her exile in 4:10.[27] In brief, those two verses represent the message of Micah against Jerusalem, the capital of Judah, though the collection itself contains many passages of hope beyond punishment. Micah or (more likely) the redactor of the Book of the Four seems to equate the cities of Jerusalem and Samaria with the sins of Judah and Israel, *perhaps* based on the power of such cities over their citizens. With these verses, the collection named for Micah brings to the forefront again the situation of the eighth century. Not only did Samaria fall to the Assyrians — bringing more strongly into focus the issue of God's forgiveness of Assyria — but Judah stood in danger of falling too. That she escaped destruction for the time being made it all the clearer that her future depended on her obedience to YHWH. Continued sinfulness led ultimately to Judah's punishment, just as Micah warned.

Introduction to the Collection and Its Times

The Place of the Collection in the Canon

Micah stands sixth in the Twelve in the MT, but third in the LXX (and in the hypothetical Book of the Four). The arrangement of the LXX (and the Four) is actually easier to account for than that of the MT; Micah came

27. Interestingly, references to daughter Zion in Mic 4:8 and 13 anticipate a new day for Zion, and most likely derived from a later hand. The phrase is often translated as a possessive in English ("daughter of Zion"), but the Hebrew language forms appositives by means of a grammatical device called the construct state ("daughter Zion"). The context here makes it clear that the reference is to the city, not to a particular woman or daughter in Jerusalem.

third because it derived from the eighth century. Its superscription (Mic 1:1) names Kings Jotham, Ahaz, and Hezekiah of Judah, whereas the superscript of Amos names only Uzziah among Judean kings and the superscription of Hosea mentions Uzziah, Jotham, Ahaz, and Hezekiah. In other words, by not mentioning Uzziah, the redactor of the Four placed Micah chronologically after Amos and Hosea.

Micah's place in the MT highlights differences in editorial activity in the LXX and the MT. Marvin A. Sweeney argues that the arrangement in the LXX is based on "a concern to demonstrate that the experience of the northern kingdom of Israel in the Assyrian period provides the paradigm for the experience of Jerusalem and Judah in the Babylonian period and beyond."[28] The order of the prior Book of the Four does just that; Hosea and Amos addressed to the north, followed by Micah and Zephaniah addressed to the south. The question, then, is whether in the assembling the precursors into the *original* form of the Twelve the order of the Four was disturbed. As we have seen in the previous two chapters, James D. Nogalski and Aaron Schart argue that it was;[29] Sweeney argues that it was not and that the LXX order is primary, the MT order secondary. Both arrangements result in meaningful readings, but two factors tilt the decision in favor of the priority of the MT. First, the order in the LXX destroys the obvious connection between Joel 3:16 and Amos 1:2 on the one hand and the fruitful reading of Joel that comes from its juxtaposition with Hosea on the other. Second, the explanation that the order in the LXX can be achieved simply by pulling the three collections from the eighth century to the beginning of the collection accounts for the differences in one clean stroke.

Micah shares the style of its superscription with Hosea, Amos, and Zephaniah. In Mic 5:2-5a it also shows affinity with Haggai/Zechariah 1–8 in its hopes for a Davidic king. Like Joel 2:13; Jonah 4:2; and Nah 1:2-3a, Mic 7:18 employs the confession of faith about YHWH from Exod 34:6-7. Micah 4:1-3 also shares a prophecy of salvation with Isa 2:2-4, a point dealt with in the discussion of Isaiah in Chapter 3 above. Those passages predict

28. Marvin A. Sweeney, "Sequence and Interpretation in the Book of the Twelve," in *Reading and Hearing the Book of the Twelve*, ed. James D. Nogalski and Marvin A. Sweeney. SBLSymS 15 (Atlanta: SBL, 2000) 49-64. See also Sweeney, *The Twelve Prophets*, 1:xxvii-xxxv.

29. James D. Nogalski, *Redactional Processes in the Book of the Twelve*. BZAW 218 (Berlin: de Gruyter, 1993) 1-57; Aaron Schart, *Die Entstehung des Zwölfprophetenbuchs*. BZAW 260 (Berlin: de Gruyter, 1998) 261-82.

that in the future soldiers will turn their weapons of war (swords and spears) into agricultural implements (plowshares and pruning hooks).[30]

The Setting for the Collection

The setting for Micah is Judah in the eighth century B.C.E. In places (e.g., 1:2-5a, 9) the collection presupposes a functioning Israel and Judah, i.e., a date before 722. In other places (e.g., 7:8-20) it presupposes a fallen Judah, i.e., the time after 586. Rainer Albertz thinks 1:5b-7 and 5:10-14 reflect the theology of the redactor of the Book of the Four, for whom the exile functioned to cleanse Israel and Judah.[31] Quite possibly Mic 5:2-5a arose after the exile, in or around 520, agreeing in general with the pro-Davidic sentiments of Haggai and Zechariah. If so, the materials collected in Micah grew over a period of two centuries from before 722 until 520 or later.

The Structure, Integrity, and Authorship of the Collection

This conclusion means, of course, that the collection derived from a series of hands. Besides the prophet, at least two other identifiable persons had their hands in the product, both mentioned in the previous chapter: the redactor responsible for the Book of the Four and the person responsible for adding pro-Davidic sentiments in Hos 3:5ab and Amos 9:11-15.

As the product of a series of writers, the structure of Micah is not always simple and clear. Scholars usually see an alternation between doom and hope. A typical analysis reveals the following:

1–3	Invectives and threats against Israel and Judah (except 2:12-13)
4–5	Promises to Israel and Judah (except 4:10a, 5:1)
6:1–7:7	Exhortation, invectives, and threats
7:8-20	Promises

30. Later, Joel 3:10 turns that saying around and places it on the lips of Judah's enemies as they summoned their soldiers to war against Judah.

31. Rainer Albertz, "Exile as Purification: Reconstructing the 'Book of the Four,'" in *Thematic Threads in the Book of the Twelve*, ed. Paul L. Redditt and Aaron Schart. BZAW 325 (Berlin: de Gruyter, 2003) 238-40.

One advantage to this arrangement is that it makes clear the alternation between passages of doom and hope. The obvious shortcoming is that both of the first two sections have passages that contrast with their contexts and thus may be seen as composites themselves.

Perhaps a better analysis of the structure is that of Kenneth H. Cuffey, who sees a different fourfold arrangement. In each case he specifies a theme (revised somewhat here) explicated by a passage of doom followed by a passage of hope. In each, the passage of hope contains a promise.

> THEME: 1:2–2:13 Honesty and justice among the people
>> DOOM: 1:2–2:11 Punishment for social sins committed by the wealthy
>> HOPE: 2:12-13 Promise: God will gather a remnant
> THEME: 3:1–4:8 Honesty and justice among the leaders
>> DOOM: 3:1-12 Punishment against rulers, prophets, and priests
>> HOPE: 4:1-8 Promise in 4:6-7: God will gather a remnant
> THEME: 4:9–5:15 Punishment and redemption of Jerusalem
>> DOOM: 4:9–5:1 Punishment against Jerusalem
>> HOPE: 5:2-15 Promise in 5:7-8: God will reign over Zion
> THEME: 6:1–7:20 Sin and righteousness before God
>> DOOM: 6:1–7:6 Punishment for injustice and idolatry
>> HOPE: 7:7-20 Promise in 7:18: God will pardon a remnant[32]

Main Genres in the Collection

Possibly the most forceful passages in the collection are the trial speeches, in which Micah reports God's calling upon witnesses (not just humans, but even the earth or the mountains; cf. 1:2; 6:1)[33] to hear evidence or even

---

32. Kenneth H. Cuffey, "Remnant, Redactor, and Biblical Theologian," in Nogalski and Sweeney, *Reading and Hearing the Book of the Twelve*, 187-97. Cuffey, however, did not write the "Themes" as they appear above; they reflect my reading of Micah.

33. Scholars sometimes argue that 6:1-5 belongs to a separate genre best called a "covenant lawsuit," but it seems better to treat such passages as belonging to an identifiable subgenre of trial speeches, just as call visions are a particular type of vision, not a separate genre.

to testify against Judah, stating the charges in the form of an indictment, and then pronouncing the judgment. (The mountains presumably concur.) Modern Americans might cringe at the thought of a prosecuting attorney doubling as the judge, but Micah (and other prophets as well) did not even blush at the prospect. After all, who else but God is qualified to hear a case brought by God? Even the mountains are God's creation. Besides, in the trial speeches God lays out the charge(s) and the punishment for all to see. The prophet at least expects the reader to agree that the punishment fits the crime.[34] The opening trial speech contains a description of a theophany (an appearance by God), which depicts God in full power (1:3-4). Micah also employs the disputation speech in 3:1-4. He begins with a proposition he believes his opponents will agree with (the rulers should know and maintain justice), accuses them of violating the principle, and adduces evidence in support of his thesis.

Other genres of prophetic speech also appear in Micah. First is the woe oracle, in 2:1-11 combined with a prophecy of disaster. The lament in 7:1-7 shows pain at the behaviors criticized. By contrast, the collection includes prophecies of salvation (cf. 2:12-13 and 4:1-8; 5:2-15 and 7:8-20), which many scholars consider exilic because they presuppose the fall of Jerusalem (7:8-20). If so, they would express hope for those who had experienced the fall of Jerusalem and the exile. Another genre is the entrance liturgy in 6:6-8. In these liturgies (cf. Psalm 15 and 24), the worshippers approach the temple asking who can approach God and/or what to offer God. In Mic 6:6-7 the worshippers start with customary offerings, but fearful of God's rejection they keep upping the offer until they ask whether they should offer the most precious things they have: their children. The answer comes in the form of a priestly torah, which asks for justice, kindness, and humility instead of animal and human sacrifices. The collection concludes with a liturgy (7:8-20), in which again (as in the entrance liturgy in 6:6-8) two voices speak: a priest in vv. 11-13, the people in the rest. Verses 14-17 read like a prayer, as does v. 18a (which quotes part of Exod 34:6-7). Also, vv. 18-20 sound like a hymn in praise of God's forgiveness and mercy toward Judah. The overall effect, however, is to proclaim a new day for Ju-

---

34. Daniel J. Simundson, *Hosea, Joel, Amos, Obadiah, Jonah, Micah*. AOTC (Nashville: Abingdon, 2005) 308. The prophets probably had the same expectation when they gave the causes for prophecies of disaster, at least those that specified the wrongdoings. In other cases, they may have thought the sins were so evident they did not require enumerating.

dah. All in all, therefore, the collection manifests a rich treasury of genres used with great rhetorical and theological effect.

Special Features of the Collection

Three special features of Micah deserve attention here: the relationship of Micah to Isaiah, the mention of the prophet Micah in the book of Jeremiah, and the difficulty of understanding the pun-laden passage 1:10-15. The relationship of Micah to Isaiah comes front and center in Mic 4:1-3, which appears almost word for word in Isa 2:2-4. The verses depict what might be called a messianic period, a time of peace and tranquility but without a messiah (a king). Further, Mic 4:5 resonates with Isa 2:5, though the verses are not identical. It would appear, therefore, that some borrowing took place. The relationship is further complicated by the similarity between Mic 4:4 and Zech 3:10, which itself reads like an addition to its context. It would appear that Mic 4:1-5 was composed by borrowing Isa 2:2-5 and adding Zech 3:10 between Mic 4:3 and 5. Isaiah 2:5 then seems to have been slightly modified as well. The exact relationship between the two prophetic corpora is part of the larger issue of the relationship between Isaiah and the Twelve and must remain unexamined here due to a lack of space.

The second special feature is the fact that the man Micah is mentioned in Jer 26:18. This is the only place in the Latter Prophets that one prophet is definitely mentioned in another prophet's work.[35] Jeremiah 26 epitomizes the prophet's famous Temple Sermon and describes the violent reaction to it. Jeremiah was mobbed for what he said, then arrested. During the impromptu trial that followed, some of the elders cited the example of Micah, who also threatened Jerusalem by saying:

> Zion shall be a plowed field,
>> and Jerusalem heaps of rubble,
>> and the mountain of the house [= temple] wooded ridges.
>>>>> (Mic 3:12)

Of interest here is that the elders in Jeremiah's day (ca. 605) said Micah also had prophesied by threatening the city with destruction, but their

---

35. To be sure, Ezek 14:14 and 20 mention a man named Daniel. It is likely but not certain that the Daniel in question was the hero of the book of Daniel.

eighth-century predecessors had repented, thus forestalling God's punishment. The narrative in Jeremiah supplies information found in Isaiah (chs. 36–39) but not in Micah to explain what happened. King Hezekiah had repented, and God spared the city. The collection named for Micah, however, dedicates the remainder of chs. 4 and 5 to dealing with Jerusalem *after* Micah's prediction could be said to have come true and the city had fallen to the Babylonians. Those verses discuss Jerusalem's future restitution by God.

The third special feature is a lament announcing God's punishment of Samaria and Israel as the paradigm for the punishment of Jerusalem and Judah.[36] The text of Mic 1:10-15 is difficult to translate into English because it is laden with puns. Clyde T. Francisco is credited with the following translation (left column), which attempts to capture the force of the puns.[37] The translation in the NRSV (right column) may render the meaning more clear, but loses the artistry.

Francisco	NRSV

10 Tell it not in Gath,
    in Weepville, do not weep.
In Duston,
    roll in the dust.
	10 Tell it not in Gath,
	    weep not at all;
	in Beth-leaphrah
	    roll yourselves in the dust.

11 Pass over Beautytown
 	
    in nakedness and shame;
the people of Rescueville
    have not rescued;
the lamentation of Helpvillehouse
    has taken from you its help.
	11 Pass on your way,
	    inhabitants of Shaphir,
	    in nakedness and shame;
	the inhabitants of Zaanan
	    do not come forth;
	Beth-ezel is wailing
	    and shall remove its support
	        from you.

12 The people of Bittertown
    are longing for sweet,
for evil from Yahweh has come
 	
    to the gate of Jerusalem.
	12 For the inhabitants of Maroth
	    wait anxiously for good,
	yet disaster has come down from
	    the LORD
	    to the gate of Jerusalem.

36. Sweeney, *The Twelve Prophets,* 2:347.
37. Translation by Clyde T. Francisco for a graduate seminar at The Southern Baptist Theological Seminary, Louisville; quoted in Robert L. Cate, *An Introduction to the Old Testament and Its Study* (Nashville: Broadman, 1987) 345-46.

13 Hitch your chariots to a *reckesh* (horse), people of Lachish.	13 Harness the steeds to the chariots, inhabitants of Lachish;
The beginning of sin to the daughter Zion,	it was the beginning of sin to the daughter Zion,
for in you has been found the apostasy of Israel.	for in you were found the transgressions of Israel.
14 Therefore you shall give a parting dowry to Bridesburg.	14 Therefore you shall give parting gifts to Moresheth-gath;
The houses of Snaretown are a snare to the kings of Israel.	the houses of Achzib shall be a deception to the kings of Israel.
15 Therefore the owner has come to you, Ownapolis.	15 I will again bring a conqueror upon you, inhabitants of Mareshah;
The glory of Israel shall go into oblivion.	the glory of Israel shall come to Adullam.

The clearest of these puns play upon the names of towns mentioned, all in the Shephelah (the area between the coastal plain and the mountains of Judah). The sound of the cities' names reminds one of words that describe the approaching disaster: e.g., Beth-leaphrah sounds like "house of dust"; Zaanan sounds like "go out"; Maroth reminds one of *mar,* the word for "bitter"; and Lachish sounds like *reckesh,* the word for a "team of horses."[38] The larger passage (1:8-16) anticipates God's punishment falling upon the people of Judah and Jerusalem for their sinfulness. The use of puns on the names of the towns makes obvious the appropriateness of that punishment, which fit the deeds well.

Introduction to the Prophet

The name Micah is probably to be understood as a shortened form of the Hebrew word *micayah:* "who" *(mi)* "like" *(ca)* "YH" *(yah):* "who is like YHWH?" He was remembered as a prophet in the narrative in Jer 26:16-19, but information about him is scarce in the collection named for him. Two relevant texts speak in the first person singular. Micah 2:6-11 contains a disputation speech, in which Micah upbraids members of his audience as fol-

---

38. Simundson, *Hosea, Joel, Amos, Obadiah, Jonah, Micah,* 301.

lows: "Don't you [pl.] preach, these ones are preaching, don't you [pl.] preach about these [things]" (v. 6). The Hebrew word for "preach" used here three times is not *nb'*, the usual word for "prophesy," but *ntp*, a word literally meaning "drop" or "drip" but used figuratively of preaching. Micah's opponents perhaps do not recognize that what he is doing is prophesying and want him to stop his speaking. Micah himself can be read similarly in 3:6-8, where he distinguishes himself from prophets, seers, and diviners and claims that he was filled with the power and spirit (or charisma) of YHWH to declare to Israel its transgression. It is possible, of course, that Micah intended simply to brand their perspectives as false prophecy and his as genuine, but he can be read as denying that he was a prophet at all.

Only one thing is known of Micah's private life: he was from the small town of Moresheth-gath, which lay in the Shephelah about six miles northeast of Lachish. Micah appears to have addressed people in Jerusalem (cf. 3:1-12) and perhaps Samaria (1:4-5), though that is less obvious since the verses might stem from a later hand.[39] If we should imagine Micah traveling from Moresheth to Jerusalem with any frequency, that might suggest he was at least a man of a little means. On the other hand, Sweeney's suggestion may be correct that Micah fled his home town during the siege of nearby Lachish in 701 and waited out that conflict in Jerusalem, experiencing hardship at the hands of city dwellers.[40] Regardless, Micah determined to do battle against Jerusalem and its lords on behalf of the poor there and in Judah in general. Judging by Micah 3, he thought the urban leadership, including rulers, prophets, and even priests, was corrupt, on the take for bribes (3:11).

To help position Micah in his culture, we can construct a typology of prophets, distinguishing central prophets from peripheral prophets like Micah or Amos.[41] For a representation of the typology in table form, see page 275. To be sure, this typology is only that: a typology. It is not a description of any given society, not even Israel. There, for example, the issue of gender is not fully illuminated by it. The prophet Isaiah seems to be a central prophet functioning at the temple in Jerusalem, but he also seems

---

39. Albertz, "Exile as Purification," 238-40.

40. Sweeney, *The Twelve Prophets*, 2:394.

41. This typology combines distinctions made by I. M. Lewis (*Ecstatic Religion* [Baltimore: Penguin, 1971] 25-26) with elements from the traditional church-sect typology.

	Central Prophets	Peripheral Prophets
Basis of Authority	From their office	From ecstatic experiences
Social Class	Upper class elite	Lower class
Gender	Always male	Male or female
Occupation	Work at a sanctuary	Derive income from other work
Duties	Support the status quo	Revitalization
Followers	Whole nation (in theory; in reality perhaps the upper class)	Small group excluded from the power structure

to have had visions[42] — though not necessarily in ecstatic trances. He conceived a child through a "prophetess" (Isa 8:3), presumably his wife, though the text does not actually say so. She and Hulda (2 Kgs 22:14) seem to have been regarded prophetesses in Jerusalem, suggesting that a few women enjoyed official recognition. This typology does, however, reflect several realities of ancient Israel: (1) there were only two classes; (2) priests and prophets at the royal sanctuaries were part of the urban elite; and (3) they might thereby have a stake in the status quo (even if they criticized it as Isaiah did). Certainly Micah paints both priests and prophets as supportive of the status quo; he perhaps does not include himself in their number, as we have already seen. He appears, instead, to have been someone from outside Jerusalem and outside the power structure condemning corruption he saw among the elite.

Delbert R. Hillers lists five elements of Micah's program of revitalization: (1) the removal of foreign hegemony, (2) the birth pangs of the new age, (3) the reversal of social classes, (4) the rise of a righteous, peaceable ruler, and (5) a new age in which Judah triumphs over its enemies.[43] The revitalization he longed for included social justice, which will be the first topic to be discussed among the basic emphases of the collection.

42. Cf. Ezekiel, who was a displaced Zadokite priest, and Zechariah, who advocated the rebuilding of the temple in Jerusalem.
43. Delbert R. Hillers, *Micah*. Hermeneia (Philadelphia: Fortress, 1984) 6-7.

Basic Emphases in Micah

We have already seen several themes in the collection named after Micah (e.g., its critique of rulers, prophets, and priests and its view that God's punishment would fit the people's sins), but here we will focus on four others in particular: the demand for social justice, the failure of the monarchs, the hope for a new David, and the idea of a righteous remnant.

The Demand for Social Justice

As we have seen in connection with other prophets, one concept of justice in Israel had to do with the treatment of widows, orphans, poor people, and resident aliens. Isaiah, for example, called upon Israel to "seek justice," explaining that to do so they should "rescue the oppressed, defend the orphan, and plead for the widow" (Isa 1:17). Jeremiah added the alien, i.e., the stranger living within the country and not just visiting (Jer 7:6). All of these people would likely share the common feature of poverty, whatever other inequities they might suffer from. So, Jeremiah condemned King Jehoiakim as unjust, by contrasting his behavior of conscripting laborers to work for nothing with his father Josiah's practice of judging rightly the cause of the needy and the poor (Jer 22:16). The book of Psalms also concurs with the view that justice for strangers, orphans, and widows lay especially close to God's heart (Ps 68:5; 146:9; cf. 89:14).

Micah subscribed to this same view of justice for the poor. In Mic 6:9-12, he specifically objects to the acts by which merchants cheated their customers.[44] The phrase "scant measure" (v. 10) refers to underfilling the customer's container, and the reference to "dishonest weights" (v. 11) condemns using weights favoring the merchant. There being no Bureau of Weights and Measures to set standards and enforce their use, the buyer could do little to combat the avarice of the merchant — except, perhaps, to seek out another (also possibly dishonest) seller. Micah imagines a trial of the guilty before God, in which God makes clear that what God requires of

44. A number of scholars consider Micah 6 secondary, but there is nothing in it that requires a late date, not even the reference to Moses, Aaron, and Miriam (said to appear together first in the pentateuchal P source) or the fact that the chapter is composed of a variety of genres. The chapter has a single-minded focus on the topic of justice and refers to no event later than the ninth-century reigns of Omri and Ahab.

God's people is "to do justice, to love kindness, and to walk humbly with
. . . God" (v. 8). The punishment for the guilty would be food that did not
fill their stomachs and fields and orchards that did not produce fruit.

The Failure of the Monarchs

The monarchs were implicated in the social injustice if for no other reason
than that it was their responsibility to insure that justice prevailed, a responsibility thought to have been assumed already by David (2 Sam 8:15).[45]
Micah, however, does not actually draw that inference. He does, however,
speak of the king in Mic 4:9-10aα in the form of two questions: "Is there
lacking to you a king?" The continuing line reads: "Has your counselor
perished?"[46] (Verses 9-10aα read as if they might have originally concluded
the prophetic denunciation of the leaders of Jerusalem in Micah 3, though
there is no way to prove that suggestion.) Assuming, then, that these questions are authentic, they reflect sarcasm about the failure of the king to
protect the city, possibly against Sennacherib in 701.[47] Then they were
elaborated later in the light of the exile of Jews to Babylon in 597 and 586.

The Hope for a New David

It is useful to read Micah 4–5 against the backdrop of Micah's implied criticism of and sarcasm toward the ineffectual king in 4:9-10aα. In the re-

45. Micah does charge the "rulers" of Judah with injustice. The Hebrew term translated
"rulers" in 3:1 and 9, however, is *qetsinim,* a word that could designate commanders in war,
dictators, or rulers (men in authority). It is used both times in parallelism with *rashim,*
"heads" of something, such as a household. The word for "king" *(melek)* is not used.

46. Even the authenticity of this short saying is not beyond challenge, since Hillers thinks
it possible that this passage as it stands derived from the time of Jeremiah; *Micah,* 59. Furthermore, Francis I. Andersen and David Noel Freedman translate the first question as follows:
"Thou didst not have a king, didst thou?"; *Micah.* AB 24E (New York: Doubleday, 2000) 441.
They argue that the context exudes deeper pathos than mere sarcasm, and their translation
mandates a time after the fall of the Davidic dynasty in 586. Still, there is nothing in this short
passage that is incompatible with a late-eighth-century date. The following explicit reference
to Babylon, however, raises a different issue and should be attributed to a later hand.

47. If so, they reflect a very different view of Hezekiah than that reflected in Isaiah 36–
39 // 2 Kgs 18:13–20:21.

mainder of these two chapters, hope for the future, including a new David, is a dominant theme. Eventually, the time would come when God would teach and judge people with the result that war would end (4:2-3). Then God would restore Jerusalem and reign over the "sovereign" city (4:6-8). God would arm Jerusalem to attack the nations that had been guilty of profaning Jerusalem (4:11-13). Hope for a new David emerges in 5:2-5a, a text related in sentiment to the predictions of Haggai and Zechariah about the restitution of the monarchy under Zerubbabel. It takes the form of an apostrophe spoken by God: "And as for you, O Bethlehem Ephratha, [though] you are insignificant among the clans of Judah, from you he shall go out to be ruler over Israel for me. His origin is from old, from bygone days." To be sure, the word for "king" *(melek)* does not appear here, but the word for "ruler" *(moshel)* found here does in places refer to kings.[48] What is more, the reference to David's hometown and clan make it clear the "ruler" in question here is the Davidic ruler.

Hope for this new David builds upon the demise of the old David (i.e., the Davidic dynasty), which already had been overthrown and would languish for a time (5:3). When it flourished again, the people of Israel would return home (5:3b), which sounds like a promise the exile would end and the expatriates would come home. Like a shepherd he would feed his flock, standing and acting in the strength and majesty of YHWH (5:4). Under this new king, the people would be safe.

The ensuing verses (5:5b-9) are at least curious if not enigmatic. They deal with the possibility of the "Assyrians" coming into the land. The text reads: "As for Assyria, if it comes into our borders, and if it walks in our palaces, then we [Israel] will raise against it seven shepherds, yea eight leaders of a man" (5:5b). At a minimum this verse predicts that Israel would have its own "homegrown" rulers in the future. Those Israelite kings, moreover, would turn the tables on Assyria and conquer it. The remnant Jacob would rely on God, not on mortals, and defeat the nations that dared to attack it (5:6). While these verses appear to derive from a later

---

48. Verses using *moshel* to designate a king include Isa 49:7; Jer 30:21; and Ps 105:20[MT 21], where the word is used in parallelism with "kings" and/or "princes"; Jer 33:26, which speaks of the descendants of David as rulers; Ezek 19:11, which seems to refer to Zedekiah; and Isa 14:5, which seems to refer to foreign kings. On this issue, see Paul L. Redditt, "The King in the Book of the Twelve," in *Tradition in Transition,* ed. Mark J. Boda and Michael H. Floyd. LHB/OTS (London: T. & T. Clark, forthcoming).

hand than Micah, the one adding them spoke of Assyria as Micah would have done, since Assyria was the foe during Micah's time.

This mixture of threat and promise in Micah 4–5 requires a little more attention. The situation seems to be that the earliest written version of this passage anticipated (4:9-10aα) the punishment of Judah during the reign of Hezekiah, a threat that seems to have been averted. 2 Kings 18–21 and Isaiah 36–39 explain the turn of events by telling of Hezekiah's turning to God, an event also mentioned in Jeremiah 26. In 586, though, the disaster came. Micah's old warning presumably took on new relevance. In the exilic period then, his message was updated by several passages, themselves possibly from different hands, so that Micah was made to look beyond the disaster of 586 to restoration.

I have used historical and source criticism on Micah 4–5, attempting to assign differing messages to differing time periods. This procedure results in a sensible explanation for conflict within the text. A reader critic might well chafe at the attribution of verses to differing writers and ask "What is the meaning of the text *as it stands?*" Such a critic, however, might assume a postexilic date for the current text of Micah and argue that the text means something like what I said in the previous paragraph. Diverse reading strategies do not always have to end in disagreement.

The Idea of a Righteous Remnant

Not only does the collection anticipate an ideal future king, it also predicts a righteous remnant. Four passages deal with it: 2:12-13; 4:6-7; 5:7-8; and 7:18.[49] The first text (2:12-13) presupposes the fall of Jerusalem and the scattering of Israel, and it predicts the return of the survivors. It depicts the remnant as sheep, safe in a fold and fed in safe surroundings, with God as their shepherd. The second text (4:6-7) likewise presupposes the exile and predicts its end, calling exiles the "lame" and those "driven away." Once again, God would bring them home and rule directly in this restored community, restoring dominion to Jerusalem in the process (v. 8). The third text (5:7-8) portrays the remnant as "surrounded by many peoples," but not as sheep needing protection. Instead, the remnant would be like a lion among (weaker) enemies or a young lion among sheep. These verses in

---

49. Cuffey, "Remnant, Redactor, and Biblical Theologian," 187.

particular reflect harsh treatment at the hands of the nations, a treatment that needed to be recompensed. Again, however, these verses do not predict a future king to lead them into battle.

The fourth mention of the remnant appears in the abbreviated quotation of Exod 34:6-7 found in Mic 7:18. The verse begins with a play on the full name of the prophet (Micayah) in the question "Who is a God like you?" It continues with the phrase about God's pardoning iniquity and passing over transgression. Instead of referring to the number of generations to whom that pardon extends ("the thousandth generation,"as does Exod 34:7), however, v. 18 speaks of God extending pardon to the "*remnant* of your [God's] possession." In doing so, this voice claims that exile did not mean that God had abandoned all of God's people; instead, at least a remnant would survive. There is no explicit claim here that the people constituting the remnant were righteous, though that might be implied. What is said (in 7:19) is that God would tread their iniquities under foot and cast their sins into the sea. Again, there is no mention of a king. The future lay in God's hands, and the future looked bright.

A Problem Raised by a Study of Micah

One problem raised by the study of Micah is the identity of the new David foreseen in 5:2-5a but not invoked as the leader of the remnant. As mentioned above, this text seems in sympathy with the hopes for Zerubbabel expressed in Haggai and Zechariah, but that does not prove Mic 5:2-5a necessarily had Zerubbabel in view. Regardless, it anticipates someone from the line of David, a hope that continued on in the minds and hopes of some. As time passed and no new David appeared, many in Israel seem to have abandoned hope in a future king and focused on getting along with foreign kings. Others looked directly to God for help. At the dawn of the Common Era, all of these views had their followers.

The NT writers, of course, believed that in some way Jesus was that new David, though his death at the hands of the Romans forced them to revise their understanding of Messiah in light of the circumstances of his death. The focus on the humble origin of the new David and the view that he would emerge in a time of travail made this passage an obvious text for Christian apologetics. Still, the insistence that the new David would work in the strength and majesty of the Lord was problematic, forcing the NT to look elsewhere (particularly Isa 52:13–53:12) for a satisfactory explanation of the death of the new David at the hands of his enemies, the Romans.

Summary

In this chapter, we have studied three collections that emphasize the theme of punishment. Obadiah looks back on the fall of Jerusalem in the sixth century, reminding the reader that Jerusalem had not repented of its sins any more than had the northern kingdom. Obadiah anticipates the day of God's punishment of Edom for its role in the fall of Jerusalem. Obadiah also anticipates the restoration of Judah. The narrative about Jonah moves the time of the action back to the eighth century and tells about a recalcitrant spokesman for God. In the process it ponders the possible salvation of Assyria — and by implication of other Gentile world powers. Eighth-century Micah also emphasizes the fall of Judah as just deserts for the action of its lay and religious leaders, but additions to his message focus on a time to come — after the exile — when a remnant in Judah would be restored. One voice (in Mic 5:2-5a) even anticipates the restitution of the monarchy.

The next three collections in the Twelve, Nahum, Habakkuk, and Zephaniah, explore the tumultuous days of the last quarter of the seventh century. The Assyrians fell before the Babylonians, but no new day came to fruition. Nahum announces that fall, indeed takes glee in it. Habakkuk views the tactics of the Babylonians and sees in them no improvement over the Assyrians. Zephaniah sees a whole world order in need of replacement. In all three the prophets take hope in the power of God to right wrongs.

Questions for Reflection

1. Reflecting on Obadiah's view of the punishment of Edom, does God's own nature restrict God to proportionate punishment?
2. Reflecting on the narrative of Jonah, what conditions — if any — do you think would cause God to change God's mind?
3. Do you think the Jonah narrative is fiction or nonfiction, and why? What are the implications of the conclusion that the collection is fictional?

4. Is it permissible to read prophetic predictions as conditional, i.e., both as warnings to repent and predictions of what would happen if people do not?

5. Since at times the collection attributed to Micah threatens Israel and sometimes promises restoration, how were/are readers of Micah to sort out what is promise and what is threat to them?

6. Is hope for world peace something for believers to work toward, or should they wait for God to bring it in?

For Further Reading

Andersen, Francis I., and David Noel Freedman. *Micah*. AB 24E. New York: Doubleday, 2000. New translation, introduction, and commentary on the Hebrew text of Micah.

Hillers, Delbert R. *Micah*. Hermeneia. Philadelphia: Fortress, 1984. Thorough commentary on the Hebrew text of Micah.

Limburg, James. *Jonah*. OTL. Louisville: Westminster John Knox, 1993. In addition to textual issues, pays particular attention to artists, musicians, painters, and sculptors who may have been among the best interpreters of Jonah.

Mays, James Luther. *Micah*. OTL. Philadelphia: Westminster, 1976. Argues that Micah emerged in a series of stages, each shaped as a message to its own time. Also pays particular attention to the formation of each collection and to its canonical shape.

Raabe, Paul R. *Obadiah*. AB 24D. New York: Doubleday, 1996. New translation, introduction, and commentary on the Hebrew text of Obadiah.

Sasson, Jack M. *Jonah*. AB 24B. New York: Doubleday, 1990. New translation, introduction, and commentary on the Hebrew text of Jonah.

Simundson, Daniel J. *Hosea, Joel, Amos, Obadiah, Jonah, Micah*. AOTC. Nashville: Abingdon, 2005. Brief introduction to each collection or section of a collection (key issues, literary genre, structure, character of the writings, social context) followed by exegesis and treatment of theological/ethical significance.

Smith, Ralph L. *Micah-Malachi*. WBC 32. Waco: Word, 1984. Interprets the collections from the perspective of historical, form-critical, and exegetical investigation.

Stansell, Gary. *Micah and Isaiah: A Form and Tradition Historical Comparison*. SBLDS 85. Atlanta: Scholars, 1988. A doctoral dissertation on the similarities in language and content between Isaiah and Micah. Reviews the research and shows how Micah diverged from Isaiah.

Sweeney, Marvin A. *The Twelve Prophets.* 2 vols. Berit Olam. Collegeville: Liturgical, 2000. Written to interpret the Twelve as a unity intended to be read straight through.

CHAPTER 12

Nahum, Habakkuk, Zephaniah

The third group of prophetic collections in the Book of the Twelve is the trio of Nahum, Habakkuk, and Zephaniah. Nahum addresses Judah, condemning the hated enemy Assyria. Habakkuk and Zephaniah, though, have Babylon in view. Habakkuk deplores sin in Jerusalem and Judah and anticipates the coming of Babylon. Zephaniah calls upon Jerusalem and Judah to repent, thereby avoiding the punishment they deserved. We shall investigate this plot more thoroughly.

The Plot of the Twelve: Punishment to Restoration

Micah ends on an upbeat. Much of the collection threatens Judah with punishment for the sins of its leaders, but Mic 7:8-20 foresees a new day. The enemies of God and Judah would fall because God is peerless, pardoning iniquity and forgiving transgressions (7:18; cf. Exod 34:6-7). Nahum opens (Nah 1:2) on the note that YHWH is a jealous and avenging God, followed (v. 3a) by citations from and allusions to the same Exodus passage with the comments that God is "slow to anger" but great in power, one who will "by no means clear the guilty." These verses link Micah and Nahum by means of applications of God's self-description to Moses on Mount Sinai. Micah speaks of the Assyrian threat in his own day (e.g., in 701), a threat which came to pass, but which the concluding verses (Mic 7:8-20) promise God would overcome. This same God would act again. Nahum, Habakkuk, and Zephaniah develop the motif of *Punishment to*

Restoration, beginning with Nahum's angry pronouncement of God's judgment on Nineveh, followed by Habakkuk's promise of the punishment of Babylon as well as Judah, and Zephaniah's depiction of widespread cataclysm (Zeph 1:2–3:7). The plot of these three collections does not stop there either, however, but ends with an idyllic picture of a new day (Zeph 3:8-20).

NAHUM
Punishment of Assyria Accomplished

Nahum is vindictive. No doubt he thought he had cause to be, but he is vindictive. He describes with glee the future destruction of Nineveh, the capital city of Assyria, and portrays it as a woman, whose skirt God would lift over her head so that nations could see her nakedness and at whom God would throw filth. What would cause a prophet to use such intemperate language? The short answer is "hundreds of years of subjection to Assyria." Our study of Nahum will explain these dynamics further.

Introduction to the Collection and Its Times

The Place of the Collection in the Canon

Nahum is the seventh collection in the Book of the Twelve. In the MT Nahum follows Micah, and — as already shown — begins where Micah left off: with YHWH's self-description to Moses on Mount Sinai. That juxtaposition is nearly as obvious as the repetition of Joel 3:16 seven verses later in Amos 1:2. It appears then that during the growth of the Twelve someone tied Micah and Nahum together with quotations from Exod 34:6-7.[1]

In the LXX, however, Nahum follows Joel, Obadiah, and Jonah.[2] That

---

1. James D. Nogalski, *Literary Precursors to the Book of the Twelve.* BZAW 217 (Berlin: de Gruyter, 1993) 37-40, argues for a series of catchwords between Mic 7:8-20 and Nah 1:1-8. He may be correct, but the connection based on Exod 34:6-7 seems as clear or clearer.

2. The sequence in the LXX is first the eighth-century prophets Hosea, Amos, Micah; then Joel, Obadiah, and Jonah. Both versions end with the same six collections (Nahum through Malachi) in the same order.

placement has the advantage of juxtaposing two collections dealing with the fall of Nineveh (Jonah then Nahum) and makes starker the difference in perspective between the two. In Jonah, the prophet preaches to Nineveh at God's behest, and the inhabitants of the city repent. In Nahum, the prophet inveighs against the city and portrays God's defiling it. Like Mic 7:18, Jonah 4:2 also contains a reference to Exod 34:6-7.

What can we say about this sequence? Marvin A. Sweeney argues that the LXX places back to back four collections (Joel, Obadiah, Jonah, and Nahum) that deal with the nations, while Hosea, Amos, and Micah concern themselves with Israel and Judah.[3] While that observation is basically correct, the differences are not absolute: Amos begins with six prophecies of disaster against surrounding countries (1:3–2:3), Joel deals extensively with Judah, and Obadiah depicts a new day for Jerusalem (Obad 17-21). Finally, the closest parallels between Joel and Nahum come at the end of Nahum in the mention of locusts (Nah 3:15). Nahum, however, does not develop the theme to the degree Joel does. Sweeney's argument fails to convince because the previously-mentioned connection between the end of Joel and the beginning of Amos anchors Joel to a position right before Amos, not Obadiah. (See the discussion of Joel in Chapter 10 above.) It also seems that Jonah was added last to the Twelve (except for Zechariah 9–14) to bring the number of "prophets" to Twelve. (See the discussion of the rise of the Book of the Twelve in Chapter 9 above.) In what follows, therefore, I will work with the conclusion that the MT preserves the original sequence in the Twelve.

The Setting for the Collection

The superscription says that Nahum was from Elkosh, but its location is unknown. It is difficult to say anything definite about Nahum's circumstances except that he appears to have lived in Judah.[4] Neither the time nor

---

3. Marvin A. Sweeney, "Sequence and Interpretation in the Book of the Twelve," in *Reading and Hearing the Book of the Twelve*, ed. James D. Nogalski and Sweeney. SBLSymS 15 (Atlanta: SBL, 2000) 57.

4. Nahum 1:15 commands Judah to celebrate its festivals, since it would never again be cut off. That verse, however, seems to look back on the fall of Jerusalem and perhaps even its restitution after the exile. It opens with a reference to the feet of one bringing good tidings that sounds like Isa 52:7.

the place Nahum flourished is specified in the collection, only the name of the city he inveighed against — Nineveh (2:8; 3:7)[5] — and the nation — Assyria (3:18). It is possible, however, to deduce the approximate time and general location for the prophet. The depiction of Assyria is one of the nation in full strength, with a walled capital city (2:5-6) bursting with war booty from all over (3:1). Nahum looks back on the fall of the Egyptian city Thebes to Assyria in 663 and anticipates the fall of Nineveh, which occurred in 612 at the hands of the Babylonians.

It is difficult to say when during those five decades Nahum flourished, but we can try. Ashurbanipal became king of Assyria in 669 and reigned until 627. He defeated Babylon and Elam by 639, after which Assyrian records become scanty. The last Assyrian king to rule in Nineveh was Sin-sar-iskun (627-612). Since Babylon rebelled soon after the ascension of Nabopolassar to the throne in 626, we might guess that Nahum flourished about then, as apparently did Jeremiah and Zephaniah. If so, Nahum may have sensed the coming change and ascribed it to the work of YHWH.

The Structure, Integrity, and Authorship of the Collection

James D. Nogalski distinguishes several layers in the present collection, but nevertheless finds an overarching chiastic structure that is convincing. He argues that the initial verses (which many scholars think constitute a partial acrostic) were added to an earlier collection after the exile. The structure would look like this:

Introduction: 1:1-8 Semi-acrostic theophany hymn

Transition: 1:9-10 Postexilic redactional connection to older text

A[1] 1:11-12a The numerical strength of Nineveh will not deliver it from destruction

A[2] 1:14 The preparation of the grave of the king of Assyria

　B 2:4-14 (Eng. 2:3-13) First description of Nineveh's destruction

　B′ 3:1-15 Second description of Nineveh's destruction

---

5. See the discussion of Nineveh in Chapter 11 above, under the heading *The Setting for the Collection* in the section on Jonah.

A^1 3:16-17 The numerical strength of Nineveh will not deliver it
from destruction

A^2 3:18-19 Mocking funeral dirge at the grave of the king of Assyria

Nogalski notes that later "accretions" (1:12b, 13; 2:1-3[Eng. 1:15–2:2]) "blend
allusions and quotes from Isaiah 52 as promises to Zion and Judah."[6]

The issue of integrity has already been addressed by Nogalski's analysis. A late preexilic text (presumably originating during or shortly after the
career of Nahum) underwent later redaction, in which it received an introduction (1:2-8), a transition to the older compilation, and the later "accretions" mentioned by Nogalski. One piece of evidence for this dual
recension is the dual superscription. The older core of the text may have
circulated simply under the heading "An oracle (Heb. *massa'*) concerning
Nineveh." To that a later scribe saw fit to add the name of the prophet:
Nahum of Elkosh. The second superscript also designated the work as a
"book" or "writing," suggesting that the redactor acquired it in written
form.

The issue of authorship is therefore muddy. It appears as if someone
(the prophet or someone else) wrote down the prophet's sayings concerning Nineveh. Then a later scribe collected them into a burgeoning precursor to the Twelve. Either that scribe or someone else connected it to Micah.

Main Genres in the Collection

Much of Nahum takes the form of prophecies of disaster and prophecies
of salvation. Two other genres warrant attention. First, mention has already made of the semi-acrostic theophanic hymn with which the collection begins (1:2-8). Hymns celebrate the mighty deeds of YHWH, usually
in retrospect. This one does so too (vv. 3b-5), but in this case in view of
mighty acts by God in the future. The hymn also draws upon images of
God in a whirlwind and storm and an earthquake (*contra* 1 Kgs 19:11). Its
subject matter is the appearance of God before God's people — a theophany. Second, Nahum's prophecies of disaster include at least one taunt

---

6. James D. Nogalski, "The Redactional Shaping of Nahum 1 for the Book of the
Twelve," in *Among the Prophets: Language, Image and Structure in the Prophetic Writings*, ed.
Philip R. Davies and David J. A. Clines. JSOTSup 144 (Sheffield: JSOT, 1993) 198.

(2:11-13) and possibly a second (3:18-19). A taunt is a sarcastic insult designed to belittle its object. The great city of Nineveh, symbolized by a den of lions (2:11-12), would itself fall prey to One greater than the king of Assyria. Its protectors were asleep on the job (3:18-19).

Special Feature of the Collection

As already mentioned, it is widely held that the collection opens (1:2-8) with half an alphabetical acrostic (through the Hebrew letter *kaph*). It must be noted, however, that the superscription stands outside the acrostic, and two lines intervene (vv. 2b-3a) between *'aleph* and *beth*. The line that should open with a *daleth* (the fourth letter) opens instead with another *'aleph*. In addition, a preposition stands before the word beginning with a *zayin* (the seventh letter in the Hebrew alphabet). Nor do the beginnings or the Masoretic divisions within v. 8 correspond with the alphabet. Still, eight to ten verses more or less follow an alphabetical acrostic. Some scholars have been so certain that an original acrostic underlay ch. 1 that they have reconstructed one.[7] Such reconstructions are not convincing, however. Hence, it seems better to suppose that someone used the first half of an acrostic, taking liberties with it to make it say what the new author wanted it to say. Perhaps the text also suffered somewhat in transmission as well. In any case, Nogalski calls 1:2-8 a "semi-acrostic theophanic hymn," a description that seems to do justice to the text as it stands.[8]

It seems self-evident that no one writes an alphabetical acrostic by accident. It is possible that someone might author half or so of an acrostic and stop, but generally speaking not. Hence, it seems safe to conclude (as above) that a redactor used roughly the first half of an existing acrostic, a half that helped make his point(s) while the rest did not. That redactor

---

7. BHK extends the acrostic through *samekh*, the fifteenth letter, though it omits the *nun*, the fourteenth letter. In addition, the *mem* (the thirteenth letter) and the *lamedh* (the twelfth) are reversed. Herman Gunkel ("Nahum 1," *ZAW* 11 [1893] 223-44) and W. R. Arnold ("The Composition of Nahum 1-2:3," *ZAW* 21 [1901] 225-65) tried to reconstruct the entire acrostic. Michael H. Floyd ("The Chimerical Acrostic of Nahum 1:2-10," *JBL* 113 [1994] 421-37) showed the implausibility of such attempts, arguing that the acrostic is more apparent than real.

8. James D. Nogalski, *Redactional Processes in the Book of the Twelve*. BZAW 218 (Berlin: de Gruyter, 1993) 101-11.

presumably was responsible also for 1:9-10, which ties the half-acrostic to the predictions of the overthrow of Nineveh.

The poem/hymn itself opens (v. 2) on a note of vengeance:

> A God ['*el* — the first letter is an '*aleph*] jealous and avenging
>   is YHWH;
>   avenging is YHWH and full of wrath.
> YHWH[9] is about to avenge his foe;
>   and he maintains [his wrath] against his foes.

Verse 3a then picks up Exod 34:6-7.

> YHWH [is] slow of anger, but great in power;
>   YHWH does not just acquit [the guilty].

In other words, the two-line interruption (2b-3a) in the half-acrostic is a theological addition, making clear who is about to do the punishing in what follows: YHWH, the God of Israel. Verse 3 makes it clear also that though God's justice may be delayed, it is inevitable. The anger and justice of God having been emphasized, v. 7 mentions the goodness of YHWH. The original hymn, thus, appears to have pointed both to the wrath (v. 2a) and the forgiveness (v. 7) of God. The redactor includes v. 7 en route to his own addition beginning in v. 9, which drives home the point that plotting against YHWH is futile. Whatever else the acrostic might have contained, the redactor was finished with it. He had used it to set the tone for Nahum's message.

Introduction to the Prophet

It became clear in the discussion of structure, integrity, and authorship that it will be difficult, if not impossible, to say much about the prophet. Even if more were known, that still would not tell us anything about the redactor(s)/scribe(s) who collected and edited the sayings. Such is the state of contemporary scholarship. We shall do our best to describe the prophet.

The name of the prophet means "comfort," but he brings comfort only

---

9. This line should be the *beth* (or "b") line in an alphabetical acrostic, but it is not. It begins with the letter *nun* (n).

to Judah. Nothing is known about his life, private or public. Judging by what he said, he seems to have flourished during the late sixth century, perhaps around 626. (See the discussion of the setting of the collection above.) The duration of his career can not be discerned from the text at all. Nahum is sometimes called a "false" prophet because he predicts only good for Judah, while a genuine prophet predicts doom, based on Jer 28:8. That is too facile a reading of Jeremiah, however. Nahum's focus was single-minded, to be sure, and there are problems with his vindictive spirit, but he was right to see that Assyria needed punishment. Nahum has also been called a "cult" prophet. The assumption behind this view is that he supported the temple and the king, the "system" in other words. Perhaps that is correct. What is clear from the text, however, is that he foresaw God's striking down Assyria for its sins.

Basic Emphasis in Nahum

The basic emphasis of the collection is the punishment of Nineveh. In vivid language Nahum has God promise that the numerical strength and weapons of Assyria would be no match for God (1:12a),[10] who would de-throne and prepare the grave of the king of Assyria and demolish the im-ages of the Assyrian gods (1:14).[11] Nahum 2:3-13 describes the coming at-tack on Nineveh, whose walls and soldiers would be unable to prevent the fall of the city. Lest anyone should miss the point, 3:1-15 offers a second de-scription of the defeat of Nineveh. Verses 16-17 emphasize that neither Nineveh's economic (cf. the reference to the merchants) nor military might would protect the city. Indeed, her leaders and king were asleep on the job (vv. 18-19).

---

10. Verse 13, which Nogalski ascribes to the later "accretions," has God vow specifically to break the yoke of the king from someone's neck, presumably Judah's.

11. Following Floyd ("The Chimerical Acrostic of Nahum 1:2-10"), Julia O'Brien argues that feminine singular pronouns in 1:11-14 refer to Judah, while masculine pronouns (in vv. 13, 14) refer to the Assyrians; *Nahum, Habakkuk, Zephaniah, Haggai, Zechariah, Malachi.* AOTC (Nashville: Abingdon, 2004) 41-42. Cf. Marvin A. Sweeney, *The Twelve Prophets.* Berit Olam (Collegeville: Liturgical, 2000) 2:431-32.

A Problem Raised by a Study of Nahum

We have already noted Nahum's vindictive spirit. It is all the more obvious if we contrast it with the view of the author of Jonah. That author left the reader with the question God put to Jonah: should not God who made the great city of Nineveh care about its salvation? Jonah the character in the narrative, as opposed to its author, had not thought so, and neither did Nahum. It is easy to understand why. The Assyrians had ruled Judah more or less cruelly for three hundred years. Most likely, there was little love for Assyria in Judah in Nahum's time. Concern for and compassion toward that enemy would have seemed out of touch with reality in late-seventh-century Judah. We can understand that. We can also see, though, at least through the lens of the author of Jonah, that God still felt compassion toward Nineveh. We should probably conclude, therefore, that when Nahum depicted God's lifting the skirt of mother Nineveh, exposing her nakedness for all to see, and God's throwing filth at her we are really reading the prophet's understandable hatred for his people's enemy.[12]

That sentiment, however, did not go unchecked in the Twelve. In its canonical arrangement, we see a truth in Jonah that Nahum did not mention and perhaps did not and could not see. That truth is that God's mercy extended to Assyria. If *subsequently* Nineveh sinned and was destroyed (as Micah and Nahum anticipated), that was the city's own fault, not God's. We should also note Nahum's sexist depiction of Nineveh as a woman demeaned and shamed by God. Yet that motif is less developed in Nahum than the lengthy description of the disaster that would fall upon the male soldiers. The greater problem in this collection is Nahum's vindictiveness.

HABAKKUK
Punishment of Babylon Deserved

Nahum turned out to be correct about Assyria. Its capital city Nineveh fell to the Babylonians in 612, and the kingdom itself in 605. The Babylonian

---

12. J. J. M. Roberts says of Nahum's portrayal of God: "One cannot offend God with impunity. He has a violent temper"); *Nahum, Habakkuk, and Zephaniah.* OTL (Louisville: Westminster John Knox, 1991) 49-50. Still, Roberts sees such language as "metaphorical," language which "must be held in tension with other biblical metaphors that stress God's love" (50).

Empire replaced it and soon turned out to be cruel also. Whereas the Assyrians had typically exacted tribute and placed a ruler favorable to them on the throne, the Babylonians also developed the practice of taking captives to Babylon. That fate befell Jerusalem and Judah three times: in 597 (2 Kgs 24:10-16; 2 Chr 36:6-7; Jer 52:28), in 586 (2 Kgs 25:1-21; 2 Chr 36:17-21; Jer 52:29), and in 582 (Jer 52:30). The prophet Habakkuk anticipated that fall and depicted the cruelty and idolatry of the Babylonians, showing that they deserved to be punished too.

Introduction to the Collection and Its Times

The Place of the Collection in the Canon

Habakkuk stands eighth in both the MT and the LXX, right behind Nahum, with which it may well have formed a precursor to the Twelve. In their superscripts, the two collections are each called a *massa'* (a prophetic pronouncement explaining what God is about to do),[13] and each follows that word with a form derived from a Hebrew root meaning "to see." No other collections in the Twelve use that combination in their superscriptions. In addition, Duane Christensen describes the structure of the two collections together as a chiasmus, arranged as follows.

A	Hymn of theophany	Nahum 1
B	Taunt song against Nineveh	Nahum 2–3
X	The problem of theodicy	Hab 1:1–2:5
B'	Taunt song against the wicked	Hab 2:6-20
A'	Hymn of theophany	Habakkuk 3[14]

This structure is fully compatible with Nogalski's view of Nahum's structure, which also distinguishes a theophanic hymn in Nahum 1 from taunts

---

13. The word appears also in Isa 13:1; 14:28; 15:1; 17:1; and 19:1, in view of which Ralph L. Smith suggests that the word introduces oracles on foreign nations; *Micah-Malachi.* WBC 32 (Waco: Word, 1984) 98. That suggestion might fit Zech 9:1 too, but does not fit Zech 12:1 and Mal 1:1, both of which open with the word but are directed to Israel specifically.

14. Duane Christensen, "The Book of Nahum: A History of Interpretation," in *Forming Prophetic Literature: Essays on Isaiah and the Twelve in Honor of John D. W. Watts*, ed. James W. Watts and Paul R. House. JSOTSup 235 (Sheffield: Sheffield Academic, 1996) 193.

against Nineveh in Nahum 2–3.[15] Christensen spotted the reversal of those two elements (first the taunt, then a theophonic hymn) in Hab 2:6-20 and Habakkuk 3. Seeing the two collections as a redacted precursor places the problem of theodicy squarely in the center (Hab 1:1–2:5) of the redacted work. It will be the crucial issue, therefore, in the collection named for Habakkuk. (See "Problems Raised by a Study of Habakkuk" below.)

The Setting for the Collection

The setting for the collection is Judah, and the use of the Hebrew word *selah*[16] in 3:3, 9, and 13 ties the prayer/song in that chapter to the temple, since the word appears elsewhere only in the Psalter. The earliest possible time for the collection may be inferred from the mention of the Chaldeans (or Babylonians) in 1:6. The Chaldeans were a tribe in southern Babylonia that seized control of the whole area under Nabopolassar in 626. They captured Nineveh in 612 and overthrew the Assyrian Empire in 605. Thus, the beginnings of the collection most likely fall some time after 612. It is not clear who "the wicked" are against whom Habakkuk complains in 1:4. They could have been Judean leaders who raised the ire of the prophets, or they could have been the Babylonians, or both. The "enemy" mentioned in 1:15 could well be Babylon. Nothing in the text, however, refers unmistakably to the fall of Jerusalem to Babylon. Hence, it is best to see Habakkuk 1–2 as late preexilic, from shortly after 612 to near 586. The hymn in Habakkuk 3 is undatable. The reference to the "anointed" in 3:13 seems to have the king in view, so the hymn might have preceded the fall of the monarchy in 586.

---

15. The catchwords Nogalski identifies between Nahum and Habakkuk are fairly common terms and are spread throughout the two chapters; cf. *Literary Precursors to the Book of the Twelve*, 40-45. Christensen's analysis makes the stronger case for a redacted relationship between these two collections.

16. The meaning of *selah* is obscure. BDB derives it from *salal*, a Hebrew verb meaning "lift up, cast up," and suggests that it was used to indicate places where benedictions would be said. Another suggestion, however, based on an Arabic word, is that it meant for worshippers to bow down. The word *shigionoth* (apparently a type of song; 3:1) appears elsewhere only in Ps 7:1 and in the singular, but it is dangerous to draw conclusions from such slender evidence.

The Structure, Integrity, and Authorship of the Collection

The structure of the collection was given above:

> The problem of theodicy: Hab 1:1–2:5
> Taunt song against the wicked one: Hab 2:6-20
> Hymn of theophany: Habakkuk 3.

This view of the structure is not without dissenters. The division between the dialogue in 1:1–2:5 and the woe oracles (2:6-20) has been contested. Frances I. Andersen, for example, argues that the woe oracles continue the speech by God begun in the dialogue in 2:2. The gist of his argument is that 2:6b, 8a offer God's answer to the protest against plundering; 2:9 answers the protest against greed in 1:4; 2:12 answers the protest against murder in 1:17; 2:15 answers the protest in 2:5 against drunkenness; and 2:18 answers the protest against idolatry in 1:16.[17] The first problem with this analysis is that in 1:6 God is speaking, not Habakkuk. It is already an answer to Habakkuk's complaint in 1:2-4. Second, in all five pairings, the prophet's complaints and the responses are quite general, with no necessary connection between them. Even the mention of human bloodshed and building a city by violence in 2:17 is not really a response to a complaint against destroying nations, though both require killing and might have been carried out by the same people — the Babylonians, for instance.

The view that 2:6 continues God's response begun in 2:2 also suffers from the vagueness concerning the identity of the speaker in 2:6a, which reads: "Shall not these — all of them — lift up a taunt against him and [lift up] scorns against him with ridicule, and say. . . ." Not only is the speaker unspecified, but so is the identity of those who he thinks will do the taunting. If the redactor wanted to signify that God continues speaking in 2:6, he did a poor job! It would seem, instead, that the woe oracles are redactionally attached to the dialogue by 2:6a. The "speaker" in 2:6a, then, is the redactor. One might also note that the oracles never use the first person and refer to God three times (2:13, 14, 16) in the third person, an unusual (though not impossible) phenomenon if we are to read the verses as continuing God's speech.

At the conclusion (2:20) of the woe oracles, moreover, is another

---

17. Francis I. Andersen, *Habakkuk*. AB 25 (New York: Doubleday, 2001) 14-19.

redactional transition, this one to the hymn in Habakkuk 3. It invokes the temple, about which 1:2–2:19 says nothing, but where 3:3-15 would have been at home. The second issue, then, is the relationship of chs. 1–2 to ch. 3. The first thing to note is that ch. 3 has its own superscription, identifying it as "a prayer of the prophet Habakkuk." By contrast, 1:1 introduces the first two chapters as a *massa'*. In addition, ch. 3 is not included in the commentary on Habakkuk among the Dead Sea Scrolls. J. J. M. Roberts argues, however, that headings, conclusions, and use of the term *selah* aside, the text (beginning with 3:2) fits very well after 2:20, which ends by affirming that God is still in God's holy temple (heavenly or earthly?).[18] Roberts notes that such headings and terms are routinely regarded as secondary in the Psalms and should be in Hab 3:1 as well. He continues that 3:3-15 serves as God's response to 3:2, which Roberts takes as à statement by Habakkuk like 1:2-4 and 2:1-5, and the prophet responds in 3:16-19. Roberts contends, therefore, that there is no reason to set aside Habakkuk 3 as independent or for denying its attribution to Habakkuk.

There is truth in what Roberts says. The chapter as a whole does fit Habakkuk better than scholars often say. There is also, however, perfectly good evidence for arguing that Habakkuk 3 is not of one piece. A historical and redactional critical argument to that effect might run like this. Habakkuk 3 contains a hymn (vv. 3-15) similar to those sung in the temple. That hymn opens and closes with references to the wilderness and the exodus (vv. 3-8, 15), includes a reference to Sinai (v. 3), the plagues in Egypt (v. 5), the wandering in the wilderness (v. 7), and to God's past rescue of the king (v. 13). It does not, however, refer to the fall of Jerusalem or the events Habakkuk is concerned with. The hymn is bracketed with comments (in 3:2, 16-19) and introduced with its own superscription (3:1). The structure of Habakkuk 3 may be diagrammed as follows.

Superscription (v. 1)
Prophetic petition (v. 2)
Theophany (vv. 3-15)
Prophetic response (vv. 16-19a)
Subscription (v. 19b)

---

18. Roberts, *Nahum, Habakkuk, and Zephaniah,* 148-49. Of course, Roberts's argument for the authenticity of Habakkuk 3 would lose more of its cogency if — as seems likely — 2:20 derived from the redactor who put together 1:1–2:18 and 3:1-19.

Thus Habakkuk 3, a redacted piece, fits well as the culmination of the collection, but the hymn itself bears no obvious connection to the events the prophet bewailed.

The term *selah* (in vv. 3, 9, 13), furthermore, seems to have been favored during a relatively short period of the development of the psalter, specifically during the Persian period. It appears seventy times in the first three "books" of the Psalms (1–89), but only four times afterwards (140:3, 5, 8; 143:6).[19] It appears likely, then, that the word was added to Hab 3:3-15 during the Persian period, with the psalm itself perhaps dating between the late preexilic and the early postexilic period.[20] If so, the hymn and its context then quite possibly were added to Habakkuk at the time of the collection's redaction with Nahum (which began with a redacted semi-acrostic, theophanic hymn).

Nogalski points, furthermore, to themes in Joel taken up in Hab 3:17. Fig trees, vines, olives and other agricultural crops figure prominently in Joel 1–2 especially.[21] Whether those connections are redactional may remain open, but what is clear is that Habakkuk ends on a note of nervous expectation for calamity, followed in Zephaniah 1 with the prediction of worldwide calamity. The fact that the speaker in Hab 3:16-19 expresses faith that God will protect him does nothing to break the flow from Habakkuk to Zephaniah.

Another feature of the structure of Habakkuk is the layering of meaning in some of the individual passages. They begin as if directed at local Judeans for their sinfulness but then seem to take on broader application. An excellent example is 2:6b-8, which begins as an attack on local citizens for demanding/keeping items as security for loans, behavior prohibited in Torah (Deut 24:12-13, 17) and condemned in the prophets (e.g., Isa 5:8-10). Verse 8, however, condemns someone (Babylon?) for plundering nations. The next woe (Hab 2:9-11) begins with a critique of an individual but shifts in v. 10b to a political critique of someone for "cutting off many peoples." Another (2:15-17) begins as a recrimination for sexual misconduct but turns into a condemnation of violence against Lebanon.[22] Finally, the last woe (2:18-19) is widely considered an addition, at

---

19. Nogalski, *Redactional Processes in the Book of the Twelve*, 156, n. 70.

20. Nogalski, *Redactional Processes in the Book of the Twelve*, 180. Nogalski says the hymn arose in the exilic or postexilic period, but it is possible that it was preexilic.

21. Nogalski, *Redactional Processes in the Book of the Twelve*, 176-77.

22. Nogalski, *Redactional Processes in the Book of the Twelve*, 130-33.

least in part because it sounds like Second Isaiah's mocking of idols, idol-making, and idol worship.

This analysis leads to the following reconstruction of the redaction of Habakkuk. The dialogue (1:2–2:5) and at least some of the woe oracles (2:6b-17 or 19) formed two early collections. They seem to have undergone some revision in light of the Babylonian destruction of Judah (see next paragraph). The heart of the hymn (3:3-15) perhaps belonged to the temple, but not necessarily. At the time of the redaction of Nahum-Habakkuk, the redactor pieced together these three components by means of two superscriptions (1:1 and 3:1), transitional insertions (2:6a, 20 and 3:2), the subscription (3:19b), and perhaps all or part of 2:18-19. These components were arranged in their order with an eye on the chiasmic structure being formed with Nahum.

Main Genres in the Collection

Aside from the hymn in Habakkuk 3, the collection contains five woe oracles (2:6-8, 9-11, 12-14, 15-17, and 18-20) and a dialogue (1:2–2:1). In the dialogue, the prophet raises two complaints (1:2-4 and 1:12–2:1), and God responds to each (1:5-11 and 2:2-5). Even so, there is tension within the dialogue. Like the woe oracles, it seems to have undergone a second recension, turning moral accusations into political ones. The prophet's first complaint (1:2-4) opens (vv. 2-3a) with Habakkuk complaining about the personal suffering of the prophet, but concludes (vv. 3b-4) by complaining about what appears to have been widespread destruction by "the wicked," who are not identified. God's first response (1:5-11) begins (v. 5) with the command for the prophet to be astounded that God is about to send the Chaldeans (Babylonians). What for? Are they to punish "the wicked" (1:4), or is their appearance unexplained? The first option makes sense, but Sweeney thinks the wicked are the Babylonians all the way through.[23] Regardless, the description of the Chaldeans extends six more verses (1:6-11), and the description of their behavior culminates with a charge against their idolatry ("whose might is his god"). These verses seem

---

23. Sweeney, *The Twelve Prophets*, 2:455. In that case, 1:5-11 does not describe what God is going to do to punish the wicked and the prophet's complaint is ignored. Sweeney thinks 2:13 also has Babylon in view, so there is no expansion in 2:15-17.

so to ignore the prophet's complaint that Robert Haak has argued that the prophet resumes speaking in 1:6.[24] The tension is relieved, however, if the "wicked" in 1:4 are understood as Judeans, whom God was sending the Babylonians to punish.[25]

In the second exchange, the prophet begins his complaint (1:12–2:1) by paying his respects to God but then repeats his charge that God is ignoring the actions of the wicked (1:13), adding that "the enemy" (1:15) is destroying nations without mercy (1:17). That objection seems to have the Babylonians in view, not just avaricious Judeans, suggesting at least that three verses (1:15-17) were added in a second recension. If so, the dialogue is a composite, written originally about local Judeans, but expanded to refer to the Babylonians. This same expansion appears in some of the woe oracles as well, as we have already seen.

A Special Issue Connected with the Collection

The use of the hymn in Habakkuk 3 deserves further attention. One may surely ask how a hymn associated with Israel/Judah's past got pressed into service in a chapter of a prophetic collection dealing with Judah's future. One answer might be simply that the prophet put it there. That answer, though, leaves open the question of why: why would a prophet attach a hymn? Is it comparable to a preacher's reading a hymn during a sermon? Perhaps, but Erhard S. Gerstenberger argues that if the hymn entered during the redactional process, its inclusion possibly intimates more about the redactor of Habakkuk than the author. Gerstenberger points to the doxologies in Amos and to other songs in the Twelve as evidence that the Twelve passed through the hands of communities that brought together the prophetic traditions and who responded to prophetic doom by singing hymns or staging lament services.[26] In other words, Nahum-Habakkuk, like other parts of the Twelve, was redacted at one level by people who edited with an

---

24. Robert Haak, *Habakkuk*. VTSup 44 (Leiden: Brill, 1992) 14.

25. Mária Eszenyei Széles agrees, however, that the "wicked" in 1:4 appear to be Judeans; *Wrath and Mercy: A Commentary on the Books of Habakkuk and Zephaniah*. ITC (Grand Rapids: Wm. B. Eerdmans, 1987) 19.

26. Erhard S. Gerstenberger, "Psalms in the Book of the Twelve: How Misplaced Are They?" in *Thematic Threads in the Book of the Twelve*, ed. Paul L. Redditt and Aaron Schart, 72-89. BZAW 325 (Berlin: de Gruyter, 2003), esp. 83-84.

eye to the postexilic community reading and trying to appropriate the texts spiritually for themselves.

Introduction to the Prophet

Even though more than one hand probably stands behind the collection named for Habakkuk, it is useful to keep in mind that an editor named him twice in the collection's superscriptions. It is appropriate, then, to say what little we can about him. BDB derives the name Habakkuk from a root meaning "clasp, embrace," but some modern scholars think the name was an Akkadian word for a garden plant. He is identified as a prophet *(nabi')* in both superscriptions. It is impossible to tell how long his ministry lasted. Habakkuk 2:20 follows the five woe oracles (in 2:6b-19) with the invitation "For YHWH is in his holy temple, let the whole earth keep silent before him." The first phrase resembles Ps 11:4, and the second resembles Zeph 1:7 and Zech 2:13. It is likely that the verse stems from the hand of the redactor who put together 1:1–2:19 and 3:1-19, but it might suggest a cultic background for Habakkuk himself.[27] We saw earlier that Habakkuk's reference to the Chaldeans makes a date after 612 likely for his ministry. The absence of any mention of the fall of the temple is compatible with a date down to 586, though an argument from silence is always shaky. So, Habakkuk probably flourished sometime between 612 and 586. The redaction of the collection, however, seems to have occurred later, during the Persian period.[28]

Basic Emphases in Habakkuk

Two emphases stand out in the collection named for Habakkuk. The first is God's punishment of sinners, action the prophet eagerly awaited. The second emphasis is simply the reverse side of God's punishment of sinners, God's insistence to the prophet that the righteous would live by their faith.

---

27. For more, see Smith, *Micah-Malachi,* 93.

28. Contrast that conclusion with Andersen's (*Habakkuk,* 27) that nothing in the collection is incompatible with the dates of 605 (when the Babylonians ended the Assyrian Empire at the battle of Carchemish) and 575.

God's Punishment of Sinners

Habakkuk awaits God's punishment of the wicked. In doing so he employs the concept of *lex talionis* (law of retaliation) in Hab 2:6b-8. The classic statement of such laws in the Bible appears in Exod 21:23-24, which limits revenge to the damage suffered: "If there is any harm, then you shall give life for life, eye for eye, tooth for tooth, hand for hand, foot for foot, burn for burn, wound for wound, stripe for stripe" (see also Lev 24:19-20). Habakkuk seems to expect the same retribution from God. Those who take pledges from the poor will lose their possessions to someone else (Hab 2:6-7). The nation (presumably Babylon) that plunders others will itself be plundered (2:8). Those who abuse their neighbors will themselves be similarly abused (2:15-16). The one who practices violence against Lebanon will suffer violence at the hands of someone else (2:17). What could be fairer? Interestingly enough, the prophet records no response of God agreeing.

The Righteous Will Survive through Their Faith

God's last comment to the dialogue appears in Hab 2:2-5. God's answer to Habakkuk promises no action against Babylon or anyone else. Instead, God tells Habakkuk that "the righteous one shall live by his faith" (2:4b).[29] In other words, "keep the faith; do not quit." When Jeremiah complained about the troubles his preaching caused him, God's answer was the same: hang on (cf. Jer 15:19-21). Such talk is tough to swallow when one feels oppressed. It may not always be God's answer to difficulties, but sometimes it is the only viable response to problems. The poor and powerless often understand that better than do the rich and powerful.

Problems Raised by a Study of Habakkuk

A study of Habakkuk raises two problems requiring further attention. The first is the theological issue of theodicy, which may be articulated as follows: if God is good and in charge of the world, why do evil things happen?

---

29. Andersen points to this verse as the crux of Habakkuk; *Habakkuk*, 11.

Is God unwilling to prevent them? Unable? Is there some reason or explanation for bad things happening even to good people? The second problem is the exegetical issue of the identity of the "anointed one" in 3:13.

The Issue of Theodicy

As Julia M. O'Brien states the issue, Habakkuk does not question the existence, or the power, but the willingness of God to act on behalf of Israel.[30] She is correct. The prophet would not protest to a god he deemed nonexistent or powerless. The issue of theodicy for Habakkuk, then, is whether God will or should act. If God simply will not act, is that because God does not care for Israel? Again, it is hard to see why the prophet would complain to a god that did not care, unless the prophet thought that god should care. His complaint (in 1:4) seems in fact to be that "justice delayed is justice denied." Whether the "wicked" are members of the Judean community or the Babylonians, the issue is the same. The prophet thinks it is high time for God to step up and be God. His confidence is based on God's divine sense of justice (1:13).

For Jeremiah, Lamentations, Ezekiel, the Second Isaiah, Zephaniah, and the so-called Deuteronomistic Historian, Jerusalem fell because of homegrown sin, i.e., because it deserved to. For them the issue of theodicy was transformed at least partially into an issue of sin and punishment. Even then sometimes they had to acknowledge that Judah was less sinful than Babylon, so that is why God would ultimately punish Babylon and rescue God's people. Habakkuk did not stand at their vantage point. Jerusalem had not fallen, and, he thought, justice would not continue to be delayed; God would act. Its delay, then, was ameliorated by the promise (2:3) that good would come to those who awaited it. The prophet says nothing, however, to explain (away) the delay. He leaves standing his complaint against God. Sometimes, that is the best one can do.[31]

---

30. O'Brien, *Nahum, Habakkuk, Zephaniah, Haggai, Zechariah, Malachi*, 73.

31. Laurence H. Kant notes that there is a long tradition in the OT of heroes debating with God, including Abraham (Gen 18:22-33). Moses (Exodus 3–4), Joshua (Josh 7:7-9), and Job (Job 13:3); "Restorative Thoughts on an Agonizing Text: Abraham's Binding of Isaac and the Horror of Mt. Moriah (Genesis 22), Part 1," *LTQ* 38/2 (2003) 79, 89; cf. James L. Crenshaw, *A Whirlpool of Torment: Israelite Traditions of God as an Oppressive Presence*. OBT 12 (Philadelphia: Fortress, 1984) 18-19.

The "Anointed One"

The second problem is the identity of the "anointed one" in Hab 3:13. The context is a hymn celebrating God's deliverance of Israel in the exodus. The hymn also praises God for trampling nations in divine fury (3:12). Verse 13 offers two sides of God's action. On the one hand, God had acted to save God's people, including God's anointed. On the other hand, God had crushed "the head of the wicked house." If that is a reference to a specific event, it is no longer possible to identify the event. It could also celebrate a characteristic behavior of God, celebrating God as one who at various times rescues God's "anointed."

Various people in the OT were anointed for a variety of offices and purposes, the king especially. The verse is often understood, therefore, as a reference to a time or to times when God had rescued the king of Judah from some other king. That explanation makes perfectly good sense and is probably correct. The next verse (3:14) seems to have in view warriors of a king. The text then returns (3:15) to the theme of the exodus. The hymn seems to say, therefore, that the God who delivered Israel in the exodus would deliver the king of Judah. If so, it has been shorn of specificity in its new context in Habakkuk. If, however, it did in fact refer to the Davidic king, that reference would place the origin of the hymn in the preexilic period.

ZEPHANIAH
Punishment and Restoration

Nahum addresses Judah, condemning the hated enemy Assyria. Habakkuk made the transition to Babylon. That collection deplores sin in Jerusalem and Judah, and anticipates the coming of the Babylonian army. Zephaniah calls upon Jerusalem and Judah to repent, thereby avoiding the punishment they deserve. The knowledgeable reader, however, is aware that Judah fell to Babylon not long after the reign of Josiah (the last king mentioned in the superscription, Zeph 1:1). The collection ends, moreover, with sentiments that sound like what someone experiencing the exile might say. Sweeney observes that the placement of Zephaniah "suggests a hermeneutical perspective that would maintain that the people of Jerusalem and Judah failed to heed t[he] prophet's call and thereby suffered the consequences as G-d brought the Babylonians upon the nation as a means to carry out the punishment threatened in Zephaniah."[32] One may also observe that especially Zeph 3:19-20, with the threat against Judah's oppressors and the promise that God would bring home the exiles, seems to anticipate and prepare for the postexilic hope of Haggai and Zechariah 1-8, which follow.

Introduction to the Collection and Its Times

The Place of the Collection in the Canon

Zephaniah stands ninth in the Book of the Twelve in both the MT and the LXX. Still, its superscription closely resembles those introducing Hosea, Amos, and Micah, prophets from the eighth century. Moreover, the superscription reaches back four generations, back in other words to the eighth century. As we shall see, Zeph 1:4-6 and 3:1-13 share the opinion of passages in Hosea, Amos, and Micah that portray the exile as a time when God purified Judah. Also, the last verses (3:14-20) connect Zephaniah to the postexilic period, thus leading the reader to Haggai/Zechariah 1–8. It seems safe to conclude, then, that redactors were busily at work on this collection.

The Setting for the Collection

The superscription places Zephaniah in the reign of Josiah (640-609). The prophet anticipates the demise of Assyria, which occurred in 605 (2:13). The closing verses (3:14-20), however, seem to presuppose the exilic period, after the Davidic monarchy had fallen, and they praise God as king and anticipate a return to the city and a new day for it. While the ostensible time for the collection is the reign of Josiah, and much of the collection may have arisen then, the date of its writing/editing runs well into the next century. The place of the entire collection is Jerusalem (1:4, 10-12; 3:1, 11-13, 14-20). Sweeney is more precise. Pointing to the specific concern with the purity of the temple as the center of creation (e.g., 1:7-8, 12-13;

---

32. Marvin A. Sweeney, *Zephaniah*. Hermeneia (Minneapolis: Fortress, 2002) 12.

3:9, 12-13, 14-20), he thinks that the temple would be a likely setting for the prophet's speech.[33]

The Structure, Integrity, and Authorship of the Collection

In his study of the structure of Zephaniah, Paul R. House focuses on shifts in person in the work's portrayal of God: it switches back and forth from first person sayings by God to third person sayings about God. Using that action to analyze the text, House argues that the collection is basically a dialogue or conversation between God and the prophet with the following structure.

Conversation Set 1: 1:2-7
YHWH: 1:2-6 ("says the Lord" in 1:2)   Prophet: 1:7
Conversation Set 2: 1:8-16
YHWH: 1:8-13 ("says the Lord" in 1:10)   Prophet: 1:14-16
Conversation Set 3: 1:17–2:7
YHWH: 1:17 (in a reference)   Prophet: 1:18–2:7
Conversation Set 4: 2:8-11
YHWH: 2:8-10 ("says the Lord" in 2:9)   Prophet: 2:11
Conversation Set 5: 2:12–3:5
YHWH: 2:12   Prophet: 2:13–3:5
Conversation Set 6: 3:6-17
YHWH: 3:6-13 ("says the Lord" in 3:8)   Prophet: 3:14-17
Conversation Set 7: 3:18-20. YHWH only[34]

In several places, however, the scheme is not as precise as House suggests. First, 1:8 opens Set 2 with a third person reference to YHWH, not God speaking in the first person. The switch occurs in mid-verse. Second, 2:5a seems to introduce a word of the Lord, which follows, possibly extending through 2:7a, all of which House attributes to the prophet. Third, another minor anomaly appears in 2:10, which concludes with a third person reference to YHWH. It is quite possible, therefore, that the prophet simply switches from speaking for YHWH to speaking about YHWH, rather than carrying on a dialogue with YHWH.

33. Sweeney, *Zephaniah*, 16.
34. Paul R. House, *Zephaniah: A Prophetic Drama.* JSOTSup 69 (Sheffield: Almond, 1988) 56-61.

Mária Eszenyei Széles offers a much simpler analysis, based on what she calls "the characteristic threefold eschatological schema to be found in the books of the great writing prophets."[35]

1:1	Superscription
1:2–2:3	Judgment on the Day of the Lord's Wrath
2:4–3:8	Announcement of judgment upon foreign nations and upon Jerusalem
3:9-20	Prophecies of universal salvation

Roberts's analysis is similar, seeing judgment against Judah and Jerusalem in 1:2–2:3 and oracles against foreign rulers in 2:4-15, but then he rightly places together two passages dealing with the judgment and deliverance of Jerusalem (3:1-20).[36]

O'Brien offers a fourth understanding of the structure, one taking note of genres and shifts in plot.[37]

1:1	Superscription
1:2-18	Coming punishment
2:1-3(4)	Call to repentance[38]
2:5-15	Judgment on the nations
3:1-13	Woe and salvation to Judah (and the nations in v. 9)
3:14-20	Promises of restoration for Judah (and the nations)

This outline helps one see the main redactional seam in Zephaniah, which falls between chs. 2 and 3. Zephaniah 2 ends with a taunt against Nineveh and the Assyrian Empire. That setting corresponds to the super-

---

35. Széles, *Wrath and Mercy,* 64. That structure is often described as (1) Doom against Judah (cf. Ezekiel 1–34); (2) Doom against Foreign Nations (cf. Ezekiel 35–39); and (3) Hope for Judah (cf. Ezekiel 40–48).

36. Roberts, *Nahum, Habakkuk, and Zephaniah,* 162-63.

37. O'Brien, *Nahum, Habakkuk, Zephaniah, Haggai, Zechariah, Malachi,* 90-91. Zephaniah 3:9 seems to speak of the conversion of the nations. If 3:14-20 has any hope for them, it appears only in v. 20, which says that God will make the nations praise Judah. That line could just as easily mean that in their defeated state they would recognize the superiority of Judah.

38. O'Brien recognizes the difference in tone between 1:2-18 and 2:1-3 that Sweeney (*The Twelve Prophets,* 496-97) points to. Sweeney, however, treats 2:1–3:20 as Zephaniah's prophetic exhortation to seek YHWH.

scription, which places the prophet during the reign of Josiah (640-609), in the waning days of the Assyrian Empire. Zephaniah 3, however, deals with Jerusalem. It anticipates the fall of Jerusalem for its sins (cf. 1:4-6, 10-13), but adds (3:10) that God will bring home the exiles. Also, it portrays the fall of Jerusalem as a cleansing process. Consequently, Rainer Albertz thinks 3:1-13 (and 1:1, 4-6 as well) were added by the redactor that pulled together the Book of the Four.[39] The conclusion of the collection (3:14-20) appears to have arisen even later. It not only presupposes the fall of Jerusalem but also looks to the return of the exiles and the restoration of the city of Jerusalem, though not the restoration of the Davidic dynasty (cf. 3:15b). It seems to fit the late exilic period, and it prepares the way for the early postexilic hopes of Haggai and Zechariah for a new temple. These prophets, however, did anticipate a new king: Zerubbabel.

This analysis suggests three stages in the growth of the collection. Stage one would have appeared sometime after, perhaps soon after, the career of Zephaniah, when his preaching was collected. That preaching would have included much or all of 1:2–2:15, minus 1:4-6. The second stage would have occurred when a redactor added 1:1 plus 1:4-6 and 3:1-13 around the theme of the exile as purification. The third stage would have consisted of 3:14-20, added either before Haggai/Zechariah 1-8 were connected to the Book of the Four or at the same time, providing a transition from the early to the late sixth century.

Main Genres in the Collection

The predominant genre is the prophecy of disaster, either against the face of the whole earth/land (1:2-3), Jerusalem (1:4-6, 8-13, 14-18; 3:1-8), or foreign nations (2:4-15). Other genres include prophecies of salvation (3:9-13, 14-20) and admonitions (1:7; 2:1-3).

A Special Issue Connected with the Collection

A unique feature of Zephaniah is the genealogy provided for the prophet. It is unique in that it traces the prophet back four generations. Most pro-

---

39. Rainer Albertz, "Exile as Purification: Reconstructing the 'Book of the Four,'" in Redditt and Schart, *Thematic Threads in the Book of the Twelve*, 241-42.

phetic genealogies name only the father: e.g., Isaiah son of Amoz (Isa 1:1). Zechariah's genealogy goes back two generations: Zechariah son of Berechiah son of Iddo. Tracing the descent two generations was perhaps necessary to distinguish Zechariah the prophet from some other Zechariah. Four generations probably points to a different cause.

Zephaniah is said to have been "the son of Cushi son of Gedaliah son of Amariah son of Hezekiah" (Zeph 1:1). The name Cushi can mean "Ethiopian" (cf. Num 12:1; 2 Sam 18:21; Jer 36:14), but the superscription to Psalm 7 mentions someone named "Cush" and specifies that he was a Benjaminite.[40] Hence, the name need not necessarily have designated Cushi as a foreigner. Since children were sometimes named for physical attributes in ancient Israel, we might surmise that an unusually dark-skinned baby might be named (or nicknamed?) "Cushi." Even so, a name like "Ethiopian" in a prophet's family tree might raise the question of whether he was properly Yahwistic. If so, the three succeeding names, all formed with the first syllable of the divine name (YH, Eng. "iah"), would have settled the issue. Cushi and three prior generations (at least) worshipped YHWH.

It is also worth noting that the fourth ancestor carried the name Hezekiah. That, of course, is the name of the eighth-century king who ruled from 725/15 to 697/87. That the Hezekiah mentioned here was the king is not said, and scholars have argued both ways. Some would say it was not necessary to mention that Hezekiah was king any more than an American would have to specify that George Washington was the President of the United States. Others object that the name was common enough that one would need to specify that this Hezekiah was indeed Hezekiah the king. The issue is probably insolvable, but we need to notice something. Hosea 1:1 and Mic 1:1 both mention Hezekiah, though there was no need to do so in the case of the northern prophet Hosea. The king of Judah was important to the redactor, not to Hosea. The similarity of the superscription of Zephaniah to those of Hosea, Amos, and Micah has caused scholars to postulate the existence of a Book of the Four compiled by a Judean redactor about the fall of Jerusalem in 587. Tracing Zephaniah's genealogy back to Hezekiah, therefore, probably had King Hezekiah in view and was probably a deliberate device used to link Zephaniah to the three eighth-century prophets. Even if the prophet were a direct descendant of Hezekiah, how-

40. Adele Berlin, *Zephaniah*. AB 25A (New York: Doubleday, 1994) 66.

ever, he would not necessarily be part of the ruling line. The superscript closes with the reference to King Josiah, who reigned during the career of Zephaniah.

Introduction to the Prophet

Unfortunately, the collection says nothing about the private life or public career of Zephaniah. We can only investigate his name. It most likely meant "YH has concealed" or "treasured," though another meaning has been proposed: "Zaphon[41] is YH." That he descended from King Hezekiah is possible, though not certain (see above). Nor is it clear what relationship he might have had to King Josiah, who is also mentioned in the superscription. We should probably remember that the redactor of the Four was interested in the kings of Judah, but Zephaniah never mentions one by name. He does have God threaten to punish "the officials and the king's sons and all who dress in foreign attire" (1:8), but that designation seems quite broad, having in view the upper-class elite substantially or entirely. The redactional passage 3:1-13 also condemns the officials, judges, prophets, and priests of Jerusalem, but does not mention the king — quite possibly because the monarchy had already fallen. The only other text to mention the king is the exilic 3:15, which designates YHWH as the king of Israel. Nor does the collection say anything about the private life or public career of the prophet.

Basic Emphases in Zephaniah

Day of YHWH

While the collection mentions the kingship of YHWH, the basic emphasis of the collection is the concept "day of YHWH." The interesting thing about Zephaniah's depiction of the day of YHWH is its comprehensiveness. The message begins with the assertion that God would "completely sweep away everything from upon the face of the ground" (1:2). To be sure,

---

41. Mount Zaphon, the abode of Baal, is also regarded as a deity in Ugaritic mythology; Herbert Neihr, "Zaphon," *DDD*, 927-29.

the Hebrew term 'adamah can mean "tilled land," "a piece of ground," or a "territory"; it could also mean "earth as material substance," "ground as earth's visible surface," or the whole inhabited earth.[42] One might have expected the prophet to condemn Jerusalem or the nations, and the collection does some of both. It is difficult, therefore, to tell against whom the opening volley (1:2-3, 7-9) was fired. Verses 2-3 might sound universal; vv. 7-9 might sound more local. The redactor of the Book of the Four was responsible for vv. 4-6, and he clearly had in mind Judah and Jerusalem, regardless of whom the other verses condemned. Read from his perspective, 1:2-9 explains the fall of Jerusalem to Babylon as God's cleansing act against Judah and its capital. After that, God would restore the cleansed community (3:1-13). Within the first passage (1:2-9), vv. 2-3 constitute an example of hyperbole, exaggeration for effect. If God actually intended to wipe humans and animals off the face of the entire earth or just Judah alone, there was no point in talking about a remnant (2:3, 7, 9). The rest of Zephaniah 1–2 is more restrained in scope, though not in fury.

We have encountered the idea of the day of YHWH before (beginning with Amos), but Zephaniah fills out the concept. The "Day" was the time when God would punish God's enemies. The conventional wisdom almost surely was that God's enemies were those that opposed Israel/Judah, but several of the prophets warned their own audiences that they too stood in danger of punishment. Zephaniah mentions the "day" explicitly in 1:7, 9, 10, 14-16, all in terms of God's punishment on Jerusalem. The temporal clause "at that time" also appears in 1:12 in the same context, so that verse too describes the "day of YHWH."

The "day" is described as a day of wrath, distress, anguish, ruin, devastation, darkness and gloom, clouds and thick darkness, and trumpet blast and battle cry (1:14-16). Zephaniah 3 also speaks of a "day," but with a somewhat different flavor.

The redactor of the Four speaks in Zeph 3:8 of the day when God would arise as a "witness." God intended to gather nations and pour out divine wrath on Jerusalem, presumably until sin was atoned for and the divine wrath was spent. Next, "at that time" God would change the speech of the nations into a pure speech so that they could call upon the name of YHWH and serve YHWH with one accord (3:9-10). What would such a reversal mean for Jerusalem? "On that day" God would remove the proud

42. BDB, 9-10.

from Judah so that the people would become humble and lowly, a people that would utter no lies and commit no deceit, but — like sheep — feed in pastures and lie down unafraid (3:12-13).

The final passage (3:14-20), perhaps added when the Four was joined to Haggai/Zechaiah 1–8 (and Malachi?), does not actually use the phrase "day of YHWH." Nevertheless, God's action was to be in the midst of the people of Judah as king (v. 15), to give victory to Judah (v. 17), to remove disaster (v. 18), and act against Judah's oppressors (v. 19). Finally, God would gather the outcast (3:19), and bring home God's people (3:20). These hopes are probably typical of "day of YHWH" thinking, but are used in a positive way here, whereas the concept is turned against Judah in 1:1–2:3.

God Is King

This final passage brings us to the second motif to consider in Zephaniah, the kingship of God over Israel. Obviously, that idea was not original with or unique to Zephaniah. Various Psalms celebrate the kingship of YHWH (e.g., Ps 10:16; 24:7-10; 44:4; 47:2, 6-8; 74:12; 84:3; 93:1, 2; 95:3; 96:10; 97:1; 99:1; 145:1). Further, God established the Israelite monarchy, a concept that met some resistance, as seen in 1 Sam 8:4-22. Hence, one should be careful how one understands Zeph 3:15: "The king of Israel, YHWH, is in your midst!" It does not have an earthly king in view as does Hag 2:20-23. Rather, it perhaps reflects the situation of the exile when no king ruled in Jerusalem and none was expected. It was easy enough for Haggai and Zechariah to kindle anew hope for a Davidic king with the arrival of Zerubbabel in Jerusalem, but that hope does not seem to be present in Zephaniah anywhere.

A Problem Raised by a Study of Zephaniah

We have seen before that prophetic collections sometimes contain violent depictions of God's destructive punishment. Sometimes God's wrath is announced on the natural world (e.g., Amos 4:1-10; 7:4), sometimes on the enemies of Israel/Judah (e.g., Nahum 2 and 3), and sometimes on Israel/Judah itself (e.g., Isa 1:2-6). The interesting thing about Zephaniah is that its discussion of the "day of YHWH" contains destruction of all three. The opening pronouncement (Zeph 1:2-6) predicts destruction on the earth, animals, birds, and fish, as well as humans. While one may well agree that humans are capable of behavior deserving punishment, it is hard to see how the mineral earth (if that is what Zephaniah means) or the animal world could deserve such treatment. Presumably, then, their destruction was foreseen as punishment for human misbehavior (cf. 2:9).

If humans scorched the earth to starve other humans, we would raise ethical objections, and as a matter of fact so does Deut 20:19-20. So then, what are we to think of the divine threat to exterminate humanity? In the discussion of the "day of YHWH" above, I suggested that the language is hyperbolic. Even so, it is violent. It is also aimed against Jerusalem and Judah in Zephaniah 1 and against the remnants of the Philistines (Gaza, Askelon, and Ekron), Moab, Ethiopia, and Assyria in ch. 2. It is one thing to predict a nation's exile (2:4), quite a different thing to predict its annihilation (2:5). Human retaliation was limited to "an eye for an eye" (cf. Exod 21:23-25; Lev 24:19-20), i.e., punishment or retaliation limited to the damage done, but talk of annihilation clearly exceeds the provocation. Does and should divine rage know no limits?

The redactor of the Four limited retaliation to specific sinners in Zeph 1:4-5, promising God would "cut off" those who trespassed. Whether that punishment specifically entailed death is not said. Also in 3:6-7 he speaks of punishment designed to correct the nations, but not to obliterate them. Perhaps the redactor deliberately modified the severity of the earlier prophet's language. In 3:14-20 as well, God "turns away" the enemy and acts against them, but is not said to eliminate them.

We do need to recognize that the OT speaks of God as One who holds people — both Israel/Judah and the nations — accountable for their actions, correcting, even punishing, sinners for their misdeeds. To do otherwise would be to wink at sin. We may wonder, however, whether the more restrained language in Zephaniah more adequately reflects how God deals with people and the world than does the most violent language.

Summary

In Nahum, Habakkuk, and Zephaniah, the Twelve moves from the last days of the Assyrian period into the Babylonian period and anticipates Babylonia's fall as well. Nahum makes the case against Assyria and revels in its imminent demise. Habakkuk incriminates the wicked in Jerusalem in terms easily morphed into recriminations against Babylon. Zephaniah warns Jerusalem and Judah against sinning and threatens the imminent day of YHWH against all who oppose its coming. Its conclusion leaves the reader in no-man's-land, between the Babylonian and Persian eras, with Jerusalem lying ruined under God's judgment, but with the promise that God is in her midst (Zeph 3:15), would remove disaster from her (3:18), destroy her enemies (3:19), and return her inhabitants (3:20). While Zephaniah makes no mention of a new Davidic king, it lays the groundwork for the restoration in the early Persian period and the hopes of Haggai/Zechariah 1–8.

Questions for Reflection

1. Are God's people allowed to hate their enemies (cf. Nahum), even if those enemies have used force in exacting their way? Why and/or why not? Do such sentiments make Nahum a "false prophet"? Why and/or why not?

2. In view of the discussion of theodicy in connection with Habakkuk, how would you respond to the old double maxim: if God is good, God is not God; if God is God, God is not good?

3. What is different about Zephaniah as compared to Nahum that almost never leads biblical scholars to call Zephaniah a "false" prophet?

For Further Reading

Andersen, Francis I. *Habakkuk*. AB 25. New York: Doubleday, 2001. New translation, introduction, and commentary on the Hebrew text of Habakkuk.

Berlin, Adele. *Zephaniah*. AB 25A. New York: Doubleday, 1994. New translation, introduction, and commentary on the Hebrew text of Zephaniah.

Floyd, Michael H. *Minor Prophets, Part 2*. FOTL 22. Grand Rapids: Wm. B. Eerdmans, 2000. Excellent study of the genres used in the last six collections of the Book of the Twelve.

House, Paul R. *Zephaniah; A Prophetic Drama*. JSOTSup 69. Sheffield: Almond, 1988. A literary analysis and reading of Zephaniah as a prophetic drama.

O'Brien, Julia M. *Nahum, Habakkuk, Zephaniah, Haggai, Zechariah, Malachi*.

AOTC. Nashville: Abingdon, 2004. Brief introduction of each collection or section of a collection (key issues, literary genre, structure, character of the writings, social context) followed by exegesis and treatment of theological/ethical significance.

Roberts, J. J. M. *Nahum, Habakkuk, and Zephaniah.* OTL. Louisville: Westminster John Knox, 1991. Attentive to the Hebrew text, the ancient Near Eastern background of the Bible, and the theological messages of these three prophets.

Smith, Ralph L. *Micah-Malachi.* WBC 32. Waco: Word, 1984. Interprets the collections from the perspective of historical, form-critical, and exegetical investigation.

Sweeney, Marvin A. *The Twelve Prophets.* Vol. 2. Berit Olam. Collegeville: Liturgical, 2000. Interprets the Twelve as a unity intended to be read straight through.

————. *Zephaniah.* Hermeneia. Minneapolis: Fortress, 2002. Thorough commentary on the Hebrew text of Zephaniah.

Széles, Mária Eszenyei. *Wrath and Mercy: A Commentary on the Books of Habakkuk and Zephaniah.* ITC. Grand Rapids: Wm. B. Eerdmans, 1987. Focuses on the issue of God's apparent absence or weakness when God's people encounter suffering at the hands of a totalitarian empire.

CHAPTER 13

Haggai, Zechariah, Malachi

The fourth group of prophetic collections in the Book of the Twelve is the trio of Haggai, Zechariah, and Malachi. Haggai and Zechariah 1-8 appear to derive from the early days of the Persian Empire. Their superscriptions are dated in the second and fourth years of King Darius of Persia (e.g., 520 and 518). Zechariah 9–14, however, opens with the simple heading: An Oracle. It appears to reflect a later time period than Zechariah 1–8, though how much later is debated. Malachi closes out the trio sometime after the second temple began flourishing. The plot of these collections covers perhaps the first century after the end of the exile (539). They also conclude the plot of the Twelve.

The Plot of the Twelve: Restoration, Renewal, and God's Abiding Love

The Twelve opens in Hosea with the threat of divorce between God and Israel; it returns to the motif of divorce (though of persons) in Malachi. The idea that God would punish Israel continues in Amos and is extended to Edom in Obadiah and to Judah in Micah. Nahum anticipates the fall of Assyria, Habakkuk the fall of Babylon, and Zephaniah the fall of Jerusalem. The ending of Zephaniah, in addition, envisions a new Judah after the exile. Haggai and Zechariah 1-8 develop that motif in terms of the restoration of the population, the temple, the priesthood, and even the monarchy in Jerusalem/Judah. Even so, the new day did not dawn, at least not completely, particularly not the restitution of the monarchy. Zechariah 9-14 and Malachi address the issue of what went wrong to delay the full restoration. So we now turn our attention to Haggai through Malachi to study the hopes and frustrations they express.

HAGGAI
The Desire for a New Temple and King

Two visible signs of the Judean restoration would be the reestablishment of the monarchy and the rebuilding of the ruined temple. The ending of 2 Kings points to the former possibility in its mention of the elevation in 560 of King Jehoiachin to eat at the table of the Babylonian King Evil-merodach. His new status meant to the exiles that if they were ever allowed to return to Judah, their king would be free to go with them. As it turned out, the exile outlasted Jehoiachin, but his grandson Zerubbabel[1] did return to Judah, probably about 521.[2]

Introduction to the Collection and Its Times

The Place of the Collection in the Canon

Haggai always stands between Zephaniah and Zechariah in ancient collections. The system of dating prophetic statement in terms of the year of the reign of King Darius of Persia is unique to Haggai and Zechariah 1–8. For this and other reasons, scholars have long held that the two collections underwent a joint redaction, at which time the dating system was added to each. It also seems plausible that Zeph 3:14-20 provided a transition from the exilic to the postexilic period, added at the time the Book of the Four

---

1. According to Hag 1:1, Zerubbabel was the son of Shealtiel, while 1 Chr 3:18-19 traces him back through Pedaiah. Either way, he was the grandson of Jehoiachin.

2. From reading Ezra 1–3, one might suppose that Zerubbabel returned to Jerusalem soon after Cyrus issued the edict allowing Judeans to return home. The text does not actually say that, however, and it makes a great deal of sense to suppose that Sheshbazzar led the first group back (Ezra 1:5-11) and began the work on the temple (5:16), but was unable to complete it (4:24). Why his work stopped is not clear, though it may have had to do with the death of his patron, Cyrus. Haggai seems to have flourished a few years later (in 521 under King Darius) and expected Zerubbabel to complete the task.

was attached to Haggai-Zechariah 1-8. Finally, we might note that Zech 9:1-10 celebrates an anticipated procession of the king into Jerusalem, a procession that never took place as far as we know. It is again possible — though by no means proved — that those verses accrued to Haggai 1–Zechariah 8 during the rush of the anticipation that Zerubbabel would become king, as promised in Hag 2:20-23 and probably implied in Zech 4:6b-10a. This common redaction of Haggai and Zechariah 1–8 formed a precursor of the Twelve (along with the "Book of the Four" and Nahum-Habakkuk).

The Setting for the Collection

The date for the first prophetic message in Haggai (1:1-15a) is the second year of King Darius (520), the sixth month (mid-August to mid September), the first day. The second message (1:15b–2:9) came in the next month on the twenty-first day, and the third (2:10-19) and fourth (2:20-23) in the ninth month on the twenty-fourth day. The place is the ruined city of Jerusalem (not specifically named but obviously intended in view of the emphasis on the temple) and its environs.

Darius was not the founding king of the Persian Empire. The founder was Cyrus the Great (550-530), who captured Babylon in 539 and authorized exiles to return to Judah in Jerusalem and to rebuild the temple. Cambyses, Cyrus's son, succeeded his father (530-522). At the end of his reign the empire was wracked with upheaval, and Cambyses died en route home from Egypt to attempt to settle things down. Darius I, one of his officers, claimed the throne and won the support of Cambyses' army in defeating a counter-claimant named Gaumata. Revolt spread, so it was not until 520 that Darius established peace. Under these auspicious circumstances Haggai and Zechariah flourished.

The Structure, Integrity, and Authorship of the Collection

Clearly, the collection is comprised of four short sayings of the prophet. The first saying is shorter than it might seem at first. The prophet's saying is reported in Hag 1:4-6, 7-11; the remainder of the pericope is a third person narrative, raising the suspicion that those verses derived from a redac-

tor. The incipits (introductory sentences) beginning the remaining three
prophetic messages are also in the third person. The opening pericope of
Zechariah (Zech 1:2-6) is also basically a third person narrative, as is Zech
7:1-3. These observations point toward the conclusion that a redactor
wrote those verses to introduce sayings from the prophets Haggai and
Zechariah.

The structure of Haggai is as follows:

1:1-15a   Message One: A Call to the People to Work on the Temple
1:15b–2:9   Message Two: The Coming Splendor of the Temple
             Versus Its Existing Appearance
2:10-19   Message Three: The Founding of the Temple as the
             Turning Point in Judah's Fortunes
2:20-23   Message Four: God's Overthrow of the Nations and Choice
             of Zerubbabel as King

Main Genres of the Collection

The opening narrative contains a disputation speech, woven into the narrative. The dispute concerns whether it is time to rebuild the temple in Jerusalem. The people say "No," but Haggai disagrees. The result is that they
fail to prosper. The rest of the narrative says that under the leadership of
Zerubbabel and Joshua, the people resume rebuilding the temple. The
second passage (1:15b–2:9) overall is probably a prophecy of salvation, but
it opens with overtones of a disputation speech, and 2:4 is an admonition.
The third passage (2:10-19) is complex, but seems to be a prophecy of salvation, in which (1) Haggai reviews the past situation in vv. 10-14,
(2) claims in vv. 15-19 that the day he addresses the people is the day Israel's fortunes would change to the future, and (3) depicts that changed
future.

A Special Feature of the Collection

A special feature of Haggai (and Zechariah 1–8) is the inclusion of third
person narrative as prophecy. That feature is not unique to Haggai-
Zechariah 1-8; it appears elsewhere in the Twelve in Amos 7:10-17; Mal 3:16-

18; and especially Jonah, and outside the Twelve in Isaiah (e.g., Isa 7:1-25) and Jeremiah (ch. 52), among other places. Still, most prophetic collections in the Latter Prophets are long on speech and short on third person narrative. Reports of visions and of symbolic acts take the form of narratives, but typically the prophet speaks in the first person (see Zechariah, where all eight visions are in the first person singular). It is possible, of course, that Haggai wrote about himself in the third person, but it seems more likely that someone else (i.e., a redactor) did the writing.

Introduction to the Prophet

The name Haggai comes from the Hebrew noun *ḥag*, which means "festival," suggesting perhaps that he was born on a festival day. The collection named for him contains no genealogy. Nor does it provide any other biographical information, public or private. It records four prophetic speeches attributed to him over a period of less than three months in the year 520. The first two concern the rebuilding of the temple and the third the issue of ritual cleanliness. The fourth, by contrast, announces that God is about to overthrow the nations and make the Davidic prince Zerubbabel "like a signet ring." Scholars often understand that promise to mean that Haggai expected the Davidic dynasty to resume (see the second basic emphasis below). Hence, the entire short collection focuses on the temple and the monarchy in Jerusalem. That Haggai flourished there seems likely.

Basic Emphases in Haggai

The Temple and Calamity

Haggai's particular perspective on rebuilding the temple ties the future prosperity of the people to that task (Hag 1:1-15a). Apparently they were experiencing bad fortune (1:6), in particular a severe drought (1:11). Haggai diagnosed the cause of that drought as the community's failure to rebuild the temple. According to Ezra 1:8, that task was assigned originally by the Persian King Cyrus to Sheshbazzar, an obscure (to us) exile. An Aramaic-language letter reports in Ezra 5:16 that Sheshbazzar began the project, but did not complete it. How long the task lay dormant is unclear, but probably from sometime in Cyrus's reign through that of Cambyses. Haggai flourished early in the reign of Darius, who — according to Ezra 6:1 — decreed that the work resume.

Life must have been difficult in the early years of the restoration, and the people most likely thought they had good reason for not working on the temple. Haggai 1:4 uses a word (Heb. *saphan*) for their houses that is often translated "paneled," indicating a degree of luxury. The term, however, could also mean "covered" or "roofed" (see REB "well-roofed," though there is no word in Hebrew for the adverb "well"). In other words, their houses may simply have been under roof. There is no real reason to suppose that the people were living in luxurious houses while the temple stood in ruins. Perhaps without further royal aid the returnees thought they were in no shape financially to do the rebuilding correctly. Regardless of which scenario (if either) is correct, Haggai would have none of it. He challenged the people to quit delaying and rebuild at once. If they would, Haggai perhaps implies a reversal and an end to the drought by means of God's blessings on the people (2:19). The result was that the people resumed the work twenty-three days later (1:14-15a).

After the work resumed, the temple's plainness in comparison to Solomon's temple was obvious to those who had seen the original (2:3). In response Haggai argues that the people's job was to build the temple. God would beautify it by "shaking" the heavens and earth, both sea and dry ground, and the nations all around with the result that wealth would pour in to beautify the building. The image calls to mind someone's turning a bag of grain or a money bag upside down and shaking it to empty it of its contents. Haggai quotes God as saying: "The silver is mine, and the gold is mine" (2:8). Haggai concludes that the second temple would be more splendid than the first. Obviously, this is not a plan for building, but a call to action.

Hope for Zerubbabel

After a third pronouncement (2:10-19) repeating the idea that the people had fared poorly at God's hand, but would be blessed in the future for beginning the work, Haggai turns to the second theme: his hope for Zerubbabel (2:20-23). Haggai expresses that hope with a figure of speech; he says God would make Zerubbabel "like a signet ring" (2:23). Most scholars think this verse constitutes a statement that God intended to make Zerubbabel the monarch in Jerusalem.[3] This act would follow God's overthrow of "the throne of the kingdoms" (2:22), i.e., the Persian Empire. It would presumably prepare the way for a "proper" government with a Davidic king and a functioning temple in Jerusalem.

A Problem Raised by a Study of Haggai

Our discussion has uncovered a problem in the form of an apparent disagreement between two prophets, Jeremiah and Haggai, about Jehoiachin and his descendants. In a prose passage, the book of Jeremiah has God declare that even if Jehoiachin were God's signet ring,[4] he would take it off and throw it away (Jer 22:24). In a subsequent poetical passage (22:30), Jeremiah declares that no "seed" of Jehoiachin would ever sit on David's throne to rule Judah. It would appear that Haggai sees the matter differently, for he says that God would make Zerubbabel God's signet ring, i.e., having God-given royal authority. Haggai calls Zerubbabel the son of Shealtiel, who was a son of Jehoiachin. Haggai apparently thought things had changed by the time of Zerubbabel. While Jehoiachin went into exile as Jeremiah had predicted, Haggai predicts that one of his descendants would again become God's signet ring. We are reminded again that prophetic predictions were subject to revision if times and circumstances warranted.

ZECHARIAH 1–8
Encouraging the Restoration

A contemporary of Haggai was Zechariah son of Berechiah son of Iddo (whom Neh 12:16 lists among the priests). It is not surprising, therefore, that Zechariah was concerned with Jerusalem (cf. Zech 1:12-17), the high

---

3. Whether Zerubbabel ever reigned in Jerusalem is unknown. Indeed, we do not even know whether Zerubbabel shared Haggai's hopes or what happened to Zerubbabel. All we have are references to his building the temple and this hope for his assumption of the throne.

4. A signet ring was a ring with one's distinctive seal on it, used to mark or "sign" documents.

priesthood (3:1-9), and the temple (4:6-10a). He was also concerned with
the monarchy, but in terms of Zerubbabel's role in rebuilding the temple
(4:6-10a; 6:9-15). His hopes for the restoration centered on the temple.

Introduction to the Collection and Its Times

The Place of the Collection in the Canon

Zechariah follows Haggai, and the prophets themselves were contemporaries. No two other prophets are linked more closely. Haggai flourished
between the sixth and ninth months of the second year of King Darius;
Zechariah's first dated message was the eighth month of that same year,
i.e., between Haggai's second and third messages. The other dates are the
twenty-fourth day of the eleventh month (1:7) of that same year and the
fourth day of the ninth month of the fourth year of Darius (7:1). The superscripts follow the same basic pattern, suggesting they were added by the
same redactor.

The Setting for the Collection

The dates given in the collection are in the years surrounding the collapse
of the Babylonian Empire (anticipated in 1:15, 21) and the rebuilding of the
temple under Zerubbabel ca. 520 (4:6-10a; 6:12-13). The obvious place in
view is Jerusalem, but Babylon comes in for attention as well.

The Structure, Integrity, and Authorship of the Collection

The collection named for Zechariah does not seem unified. Zechariah 1–8
consists mostly of visions, especially chs. 1–6, while chs. 9–14 contain none.
Moreover, the above-mentioned preoccupation with rebuilding the temple
in Zechariah 1–8 disappears in chs. 9–14. The king remains a concern, but
aside from 9:9-10 leadership is a problem, and the Davidides are said to
need cleansing (12:10) before they could assume prominence (12:8). The
need to rebuild Jerusalem takes a back seat in one place (12:7) to a concern
that Jerusalem would lord it over Judah. Given these differences between

Zechariah 1–8 and 9–14, scholars often divide the collection into two or three sections (1–8, 9–14 or 1–8, 9–11, 12–14). Consequently, this discussion will focus first on chs. 1–8.

Zechariah 1–8 is cast in the form of three prophetic addresses: 1:1-6; 1:7–6:15; and 7:1–8:23. The length of the second address suggests that it is a composite, not a record of what the prophet said on one occasion. It consists of eight visions interspersed with two exhortations. The third address is also composite, consisting of a question (7:1-7) and answer (8:18-19), which has been expanded into a lengthy question about fasting (7:1-14) and ten sayings about the future (8:1-23).

The structure of Zechariah 1–8 looks like this.

1:1-6   The First Address, admonishing listeners not to be like their ancestors

1:7–6:15 The Second Address

  1:7-17   Vision 1. Four Horsemen: God's Return to Jerusalem

  1:18-21   Vision 2. Horns and Smiths: The End of Foreign Control

  2:1-5   Vision 3. A Man Measuring Jerusalem: The Return of Prosperity

  2:6-13   Exhortation 1. To the Exiles: Return Home

  3:1-10   Vision 4. The Cleansing of Joshua

  4:1-14   Vision 5. The Lampstand and Olive Trees: God's Presence

  5:1-4   Vision 6. The Flying Scroll: The Cleansing of Jerusalem

  5:5-11   Vision 7. A Woman in a Basket: Wickedness Sent to Babylon

  6:1-8   Vision 8. Four Chariots: God at Rest

  6:9-15   Exhortation 2. To Returned Exiles: Make Crowns as a Memorial

7:1–8:23 The Third Address

  7:1-14   The Question about Fasting

  8:1-23   Ten Words about the Future

Scholars have raised the question of the unity even of Zechariah 1-8. In particular, they have questioned the originality of the fourth vision (3:1-10) concerning Joshua; the integrity of the fifth vision, in which 4:6b (following the words "He said to me") through v. 10a seems to break the connection between the question in v. 5 and the answer beginning in v. 10b; and the integrity of 6:9-15, in which v. 11b (after the word "crown," lit., "crowns") through v. 13 interrupts the flow. All of these verses, as well as 3:9, most likely have to do with Zerubbabel, who is also called "Branch."[5] (See the discussion of this issue in the "Problems" section below.) It would appear, therefore, that there were originally seven visions dealing with the exile, joined to two visions exhorting exiles to return to Judah. If so, that original collection could have been compiled anytime after Cyrus's edict allowing Jews to return to Jerusalem. The Zerubbabel additions are dated to 520/19 and were intended to justify the rebuilding program of Zerubbabel.

Once again the issue of authorship is muddled. It is likely that the text as we have it is from the hand of a redactor, whether Zechariah or someone else. The reports of visions and other materials themselves could go back to the prophet, even if someone else wrote them down.

Main Genres in the Collection

The preponderant genre is the report of a vision. There are eight, comprising most of Zech 1:7–6:8. Combined with the admonitions in 2:6-13 and 6:9-15, they appear to form a booklet designed to encourage exiles to return to Jerusalem. It is the visions that cause some commentators to remark on the difficulty of understanding Zechariah 1–8. The third address (7:1–8:23) includes a report of a dialogue between Zechariah and representatives of people from Bethel, who come with a question about mourning and fasting at the temple in remembrance of its destruction. Zechariah gives an answer, by genre a torah or priestly teaching. The original answer is probably found in 8:18-19, but as the text now stands a different answer follows directly on the question in 7:5-7. The dialogue is further expanded

---

5. Wolter H. Rose challenges this identification and argues instead that the Branch is unknowable; *Zemah and Zerubbabel*. JSOTSup 304 (Sheffield: Sheffield Academic, 2000). Rose's position has not won wide acceptance.

by admonitions (commands and prohibitions) in 7:8-14 + 8:9 and by ten prophecies of salvation in ch. 8, all introduced with the formula: "Thus says YHWH of hosts" (actually 8:3 omits the word "hosts").

A Special Feature of the Collection

The structure of the second address (1:7–6:8), with its alternation of visions and admonitions, anticipates the structure of later apocalypses, which often exhibit the same structure. Still, one need only think of Daniel 7–12 to see that apocalypses do not necessarily include hortatory sections. Similarly, John J. Collins points out that "apocalyptic eschatology could accommodate messianic expectation, but only as part of a larger, cosmic transformation,"[6] of which there is no hint in Zechariah 1–8. It seems incorrect to call Zechariah 1–8 "apocalyptic," as is sometimes done,[7] but the second address (1:7–6:15) does seem to stand in the series of precursors that bequeathed characteristics — this time literary, not theological — to the later apocalyptic movement.

Introduction to the Prophet

The name Zechariah is a compound formed from YH (the first syllable of YHWH) and the verb *zakar*, which means "remember." It may be translated "YHWH has remembered." Assuming his parents gave him that name, it is impossible to know what they had in mind that God remembered, but a couple of possibilities suggest themselves: their own state, especially if they had been childless, or perhaps the condition of the exiles. The name might also be translated "YHWH is renowned," in which case it simply honors God. According to Ezra 5:1; 6:14; and Neh 12:16, Zechariah was the son (not the grandson) of Iddo. Scholars sometimes assume that genealogy is better, but since it appears in writings that date from at least one if not two centuries later, one suspects that the second name Berechiah

6. John J. Collins, "The Eschatology of Zechariah," in *Knowing the End from the Beginning: The Prophetic, the Apocalyptic, and Their Relationships*, ed. Lester L. Grabbe and Robert D. Haak. JSPSup 46 (London: T. & T. Clark, 2003) 82.

7. See recently Stephen L. Cook, *The Apocalyptic Literature* (Nashville: Abingdon, 2003) 99-105.

(Zech 1:1) may simply have fallen out in the intervening time. Nothing is said in the collection about the prophet, either his private or public life. One might infer, however, that he had been among the exiles in Babylon, given his references to it in his message.

Basic Emphases in Zechariah 1–8

Four emphases stand out in Zechariah 1-8: (1) a call to Judah to repent, (2) a hope for the restoration of the land to the people of Israel, (3) exhortations to exiles to return to Jerusalem, and (4) advocacy for restoring the temple, the priesthood, and (in all likelihood) the monarchy under Zerubbabel.

Call to Repentance

The first address (1:1-6) issues a call to repentance. Earlier generations, especially those in Jerusalem in the late seventh and early sixth centuries, had failed to heed the call of the prophets to repent of their sin and turn to God. They died in their folly, receiving from God the punishment they deserved, but the word of God to Judah to repent lived on for Zechariah to pass to his contemporaries. Everything in the two addresses that follow depended on the people's obeying the call to repentance.

Hope for the Restoration

The second address (1:7–6:15) contains eight visions that set out Zechariah's hope for the future. The first step, upon their repentance, would be God's turning to Jerusalem with compassion (1:16). The temple would be rebuilt, and God would protect the city from future destruction. Next, the same divine forces (called "four horns") that scattered the exiles would then drive the foreign conquerors from the city (1:21). Third would come the reinhabiting of Jerusalem (2:4) and fourth the reinstitution of the high priesthood in the person of Joshua (3:1-10). Fifth, Zerubbabel would rebuild the temple (4:1-14). Sixth would come the cleansing of the land from thieves and liars (5:3-4). One might assume that these people could be nonrepentant Judeans (though that is not said explicitly) as well as Babylonians and other foreigners. Seventh, two "women" would bear "wickedness" (possibly the worship of Babylonian gods) to Babylon, its place of origin (5:11). The final vision (of four chariots with different colored horses) resembles the first (of four horses; 1:7-11), bringing a close to the series. The chariots report back to God, presumably of the fall of the Babylonian empire, and God announces that God is at rest with respect to the north country, i.e., Babylon (6:8).

Tasks for the Community

The exhortations connected to the visions specify what the readers of the visions are to do. The first task is for those living in the lands of the north (i.e., Babylon and perhaps elsewhere) to flee to Zion (2:6-7). In the process, they would loot their Babylonian masters (2:8-9), a motif reminiscent of Israel's plundering the Egyptians at the time of the exodus (Exod 12:36b). Many nations would join themselves to the returnees, just as a mixed multitude attached itself to Israel during the exodus (Exod 12:38). At least implicitly, then, Zechariah's first exhortation envisions the participation of non-Israelites in the future Zion. The repatriates were to settle in Judah and Jerusalem, both of which would be God's inheritance.

The second exhortation (Zech 6:9-15) is shrouded even more with difficulty, probably in part because it has been modified. The original exhortation (vv. 9-11a, 14-15) concerns three returnees, Heldai, Tobijah, and Jedaiah, who brought silver and gold from Babylon. Someone (Zechariah the prophet?) was to receive the metal and take it to Josiah ben Zephaniah, who was to make "crowns" of the precious metals (6:10-11a). These crowns were to be placed in the temple as a memorial. The word for "memorial" (Heb. *zikkaron*) is used of days (Exod 12:14), a memorial record in a book (Exod 17:14), inscribed stones (Exod 28:12), and stones in the Jordan (Josh 4:7). In short, all sorts of things could be memorials. In Neh 2:20 the word is connected with the building of the temple, emphasizing the people's historic right to membership in Jerusalem. This last example perhaps sheds light on the purpose of the crowns: to certify the rights of the contributors. It is quite possible that a crown was to be made for each contributor.[8] The

---

8. Alternatively there may have been three, one each for Heldai, Tobijah and Jedaiah, or

word "crowns" came in for further attention when the exhortation underwent a revision (Zech 6:11b-13) in support of Joshua the high priest and
Zerubbabel the descendant of Jehoiachin and thus David.

Advocacy of Temple, Priest, and Royalty

As mentioned earlier, the rebuilding of the temple was delayed. Haggai
urged its resumption, and so do a few verses in Zechariah 1–8. Haggai also
championed Zerubbabel as Judah's new monarch, and Haggai 1 under-
scores the role of Joshua and Zerubbabel in that rebuilding project. One
whole vision (now Zechariah 3), plus an addition to the fifth vision (4:6b-
10a), and an addition to the second exhortation (6:11b-13) champion their
roles as a further development in the advocacy of the temple.

Zechariah 3 is a vision of the divine cleansing of Joshua as high priest.
It addresses his possible ritual contamination from Babylon, which God
dismisses the moment the Satan raises the issue (see below, Problems
Raised by a Study of Zechariah 1–8). As the vision stands, however, vv. 8
and 10 do not seem to fit. Verse 8 introduces another character, called
Branch, but he is not identified in the text as it now stands.[9] Verse 10 introduces another messianic image: neighbors sitting together under the vine
and fig tree (cf. Mic 4:4). So, vv. 8 and 10 may be additions. Regardless, they
seem to have in view a Davidic figure separate from Joshua.

The next vision (Zech 4:1-14) concerns a lampstand with two olive
trees beside it. In that vision, an interpreting angel asks (4:5) whether
Zechariah understands the vision. The prophet says he does not, but the
explanation does not come until v. 10b. There the angel tells Zechariah that
the seven lamps on the stand are "the eyes of the Lord, which range
throughout the earth." He further identifies the olive trees as "two
anointed ones" standing beside God. Scholars routinely understand vv. 12-
14 as pointing to Joshua and Zerubbabel as dual messiahs, one cultic and
one royal, though that is not a necessary interpretation.[10] Verses 6b-10a in-
terrupt the vision, and they have to do with Zerubbabel's function in re-

---

four, including one for Zechariah. See Paul L. Redditt, *Haggai, Zechariah, Malachi.* NCBC
(Grand Rapids: Wm. B. Eerdmans, 1995) 77-78.

9. The same term appears also in Jer 33:15, where the Branch is identified as a future David, who would execute justice in Judah.

10. Redditt, *Haggai, Zechariah, Malachi,* 68.

building the temple. The verses insist that he had begun the work on the temple, and he would complete it.[11]

The exhortation in 6:9-15 also contains a secondary section: the discussion of the Branch in vv. 11b-13. The crowns[12] mentioned in 6:11a are placed on the head of Joshua in v. 11b, a comical scene to say the least. "Take the silver and gold and make crowns and place (. . .) on the head of the high priest Joshua. . . ." There is no pronoun in the MT where I have placed parentheses. NRSV supplies the singular pronoun "it," but one would be at least equally justified in supplying the plural pronoun "them." What is more, where the original version resumes in v. 14, the plural form of the noun resumes, though with a singular verb. The difficulty, I would suggest, was caused by a reinterpretation of the exhortation by means of vv. 11b-13. These verses proclaim the role of Zerubbabel in rebuilding the temple, and they also envision a priest at his side. The exhortation closes with a reference to those who are "far off" (presumably the exiles in Babylon) coming to help rebuild the temple.

Problems Raised by a Study of Zechariah 1–8

Given the visionary nature of Zechariah 1–8, it should not be surprising that several issues remain unsolved. Two of those issues are the identity of the Branch *(Tsemah)* and the role and fate of Zerubbabel. A third issue is the figure of the *Satan,* who appears in Zechariah 3. We will begin with him, and then turn to the other two, which are interrelated.

The Figure of the Satan

In the vision that comprises Zechariah 3, a figure called the *Satan* plays a role. He appears in v. 1, ready to accuse Joshua. Presumably he wants to deny the high priesthood in the temple to Joshua. There is no question that Joshua has been contaminated, as symbolized by the filthy clothes he is

---

11. As mentioned earlier, Ezra 5:16 credits Sheshbazzar with beginning the rebuilding process, but the work seems to have stopped.

12. In the MT the word is plural, but modern translations routinely translate the word in the singular.

wearing. Scholars usually suggest that his contamination derived from his living in Babylon before returning to Jerusalem with Zerubbabel (cf. Ezra 2:2 // Neh 7:7). God, however, will hear nothing of the Satan's objection and orders Joshua stripped of his filthy attire and clothed with festal garments. It seems likely that that this vision responded to objections concerning Joshua from people in Jerusalem who had never been in Babylon, perhaps even from people who had officiated at the temple after the fall of Jerusalem in 586.

Regardless, the point of interest here is the role of the Satan. The first thing to note is that the term is probably a title, not a name. It does, of course, carry over into the NT as the name of God's antagonist, but the Satan in Zechariah 3 does not seem to be the tempter or the personification of evil. Rather, scholars have often argued that he was a member of God's "divine council," the heavenly beings gathered around God on God's heavenly throne (cf. Ps 82:1). This argument is based on the role of the Satan in Job 1 and 2, where he appears in the divine council after patrolling the earth. He asserts the corruption of all humans, only to have God remind him of God's blameless servant Job. As the dialogue continues in heaven, the Satan presses his case, even against Job. Our interest in this text is not who was correct (obviously God was), but the role of the Satan in charging human beings with wrongdoing. He looks like a prosecuting attorney, not a tempter. The serpent in Genesis 3 does tempt Eve and Adam, but the OT does not call him the Satan. The two concepts come together and undergo considerable development in the intertestamental period, emerging as the opponent of God and the tempter even of Jesus in the NT.

The Identity of the Branch

In the discussion above, we followed the overwhelming majority of scholars that the Branch (sometimes the word is translated "Shoot"), mentioned in 3:8 and 6:12, originally had in view Zerubbabel, the named subject of 4:6, 7, 9, 10, all part of the insertion from 4:6b (following the first phrase) through 4:10a. The word Branch (Hebrew *Tsemah*) derives from a verb meaning "sprout, spring up," but in Jer 23:5 and 33:15 it refers to a future ruler, a "branch" or "shoot" off the old king. In Zech 3:8 the Branch seems to be someone other than Joshua, and v. 10 employs a possibly messianic image of fertility. The fourfold naming of Zerubbabel in the role of founding a temple sounds messianic.[13] The addition to Zechariah 6 employs the word *tsemah* again in v. 12. It insists that the Branch would build the temple and adds that he would "bear majesty and sit and rule upon his throne" (v. 13). The language is undeniably royal. The only problem is that 6:11a, speaking of the "crowns" to be made by Josiah ben Zephaniah, commands Zechariah to set it/them on the head of Joshua. Scholars have typically postulated that the text originally designated Zerubbabel (or some other royal figure), whose name was replaced with "Joshua" in light of the later ascendance of the priesthood in Jerusalem. Complicating this issue is the fact that Zerubbabel's fate is not mentioned in Zechariah or elsewhere in the OT, making certainty about the identities in v. 13 impossible.[14]

The Role and Fate of Zerubbabel

In view of this uncertainty, scholars have hypothesized that the Persians removed the would-be new king of Judah, Zerubbabel. That hypothesis, however, assumes that Zerubbabel shared the hopes that Haggai and Zechariah seem to have held for him as a new David. While that supposition is possible, it is not necessary. Zerubbabel perhaps entertained no such views. For all we know, he came to Jerusalem to partake in the rebuilding of the temple, did so, and returned home to Babylon. (We should note that his name means "Begotten in Babylon"; he may have had little interest in living in Jerusalem.) Or he perhaps remained in Judah, but died of natural causes without taking up the task the two prophets had in mind for him. What does seem clear from Zechariah 4 is that he conducted the religious ceremonies that constituted "founding" a temple to be rebuilt on the site of an older one.

---

13. Scholars often point to Zech 4:14, where the phrase *bene-hayyitshar* (lit., "sons of the oil") is often translated "anointed ones," but *yitshar* nowhere else in the OT refers to anointing; rather it designates "fresh oil, as product of land, in [its] unmanufactured state" (BDB, 844). As such it is an agricultural product that signifies God's blessing. It seems preferable, therefore, not to use it in defense of a messianic interpretation of v. 14. The references to Zerubbabel, by contrast, do carry messianic overtones in view of Zerubbabel's work in founding the temple, a royal act.

14. Recently, Mark J. Boda has argued that only two crowns were made, one for Joshua and one for Zerubbabel, who was not yet in Jerusalem; *Haggai, Zechariah*. NIVAC (Grand Rapids: Zondervan, 2004) 334-43.

ZECHARIAH 9–14
Criticizing the Restoration

Zechariah 9–14 opens depicting the arrival of Judah's hoped-for king (9:1-10) and promising release from captivity (9:11-17), but the mood turns negative, sometimes bitter, thereafter, with only intermittent passages of hope. Before the monarchy could be restored, the Davidides would have to repent and be cleansed (12:10-13:1). The same held true for the priests (12:13-14) and the prophets (13:3-6). While many exiles had returned, they could be "scattered" again (13:7-9). Though God had overthrown the Babylonians, other enemies would attack in the future (12:1-6; 14:1-5, 12). The north and the south would not reunite (11:7-11), at least not as long as the current leaders (the "shepherds" of 10:1-3a; 11:4-17; 13:7-9) remained in control and unrepentant. It appears, then, as if the prophet responsible for the final form of these chapters thought the restoration had not lived up to its billing. It appears as if he repeats inherited hopes for restoration, only to explain why they had not come about or to qualify them in some way. If so, his is a later voice than Zechariah's, though not necessarily significantly later.[15]

Introduction to the Collection and Its Times

The Place of the Collection in the Canon

If one is convinced of the break between chs. 8 and 9, the similarities between the opening of chs. 9, 12 and Malachi 1 invite seeing Zechariah 9–11, 12–14, and Malachi as a threefold addition to Zechariah 1–8. All three begin with the same three words: *massa'* ("oracle") *dabar-* ("the word of") YHWH. The similarities, however, are more apparent than real. In Zech 9:1, the word *massa'* is the superscript. It is followed by an incipit that runs as follows: "The word of YHWH [is] against the land of Hadrach, and Da-

---

15. Byron G. Curtis (*Up the Steep and Stony Road: The Book of Zechariah in Social Location Trajectory Analysis.* SBL Academia Biblica 25 [Atlanta: SBL, 2006] 164-86) argues carefully that Zechariah 9 (indeed Zechariah 9–14; cf. Curtis, 277) derives from the early Persian period, sometime between 515 and 475. My own work, on quite different grounds, suggests a date prior to Nehemiah (cf. Paul L. Redditt, "Nehemiah's First Mission and the Date of Zechariah 9–14," *CBQ* 56 [1994] 664-78), but Zechariah 9 in particular seems earlier and fits admirably well with the hopes surrounding Zerubbabel in Haggai and Zechariah 1–8.

mascus [is] its resting place." Zechariah 12:1 opens with a double super-script: "Oracle. The word of YHWH concerning Israel." Then follows yet another superscript: "A saying of YHWH, the one who stretched out the heavens, and founded the earth, and formed the human spirit within . . ." Malachi opens with a third variation: "Oracle. The word of YHWH to Israel by the hand of Malachi," which is rather similar to the superscription of other prophetic collections. The beginnings turn out to be quite different, therefore, and probably not the work of a single redactor.

Why, then, treat Zechariah 9–14 as a unit, especially since many scholars do not? The answer is that chs. 9–11 and 12–14 seem to have been sewn together by one motif that appears in both Zechariah 9–11 and 12–14, that of the "shepherd." It appears in 10:1-3; 11:4-17; and 13:7-9, constituting twenty of the ninety verses in Zechariah 9–14. It is the linchpin of the criticism of the restoration, calling attention to that criticism throughout the six chapters. I have long argued that criticism of the restoration is the connecting theme for these six chapters.[16] They entertain a number of other themes, including the restoration of the land of Canaan to Israel (9:1-8), the restitution of the monarchy (9:9-10), the return of all the exiles (9:11-12), the overthrow of foreign enemies (9:13-16), the reunion of northern and southern Israel (10:6-7), and the defense of Jerusalem from foreign enemies (12:1-6; 14:1-21). These hopes would not be realized, however, unless the leadership of the nation repented (12:10–13:6). The "shepherd" passages function to prove their guilt.

The Setting for the Collection

The date of this collection is tenuous. It can hardly be earlier than Zechariah 1–8, though a few scholars have argued that it was. It mentions Assyria (10:11), but that seems hardly definitive, since the context appears to be God's returning the exiles (both Israel and Judah) to Israel. In addition, 11:7-14 builds on the exilic Ezek 37:15-28, reversing it. How much later Zechariah 9–14 originated is difficult to say. The mention of Greece (Heb. *yawan*) in 9:13 causes many scholars to suggest the Hellenistic period (after 332-141). Greece is mentioned as early as Ezek 27:13, however, so its mention is not definitive for a fourth/third-century date. Some scholars, how-

---

16. See Paul L. Redditt, "Israel's Shepherds: Hope and Pessimism in Zechariah 9–14," *CBQ* 51 (1989) 631-42.

ever, go so far as to suggest that the list of cities in 9:1-8 follows the route that Alexander followed in 332, which it does not. After the battle of Issus, at which he defeated the Persians under Darius III in 333, Alexander marched down the seacoast to Egypt, besieging Tyre and Gaza along the way. He rested in Egypt during the winter of 332/1 and then returned north along the coast to Tyre, where he turned inland.

There being no good reason to place the chapters in the Greek period, a date during the Persian period seems best. The opening verses (9:1-13 at least) may have arisen by about 500. One possible indicator of the date appears in the latest part of the collection. It is the allusion in 14:10-11 to the Benjamin and the Corner Gates, two gates not mentioned as repaired by Nehemiah. Such a description is understandable as the projection of a prophet who flourished while the gates were in ruins, but not of one who flourished after they were replaced by others.[17] Consequently, a time in the fifth century prior to the career of Nehemiah might best fit Zechariah 14 and the redaction of the six chapters.

The Structure, Integrity, and Authorship of the Collection

The structure of Zechariah 9–14 is fairly straightforward, and may be outlined as follows.

9:1-17	The Davidic Empire Restored
10:1-12	The Reunion of the Homeland
11:1-17	The Treachery of the Shepherds
12:1-9	The War against Jerusalem, Version I
12:10–13:9	The Cleansing of Jerusalem
14:1-21	The War against Jerusalem, Version II[18]

This structure reveals internal inconsistency over the restitution of the monarchy and the status of Jerusalem, with one whole section (12:10–13:9) calling for wholesale repentance by the leading families, including the Davidides and the priests.

17. Redditt, "Nehemiah's First Mission and the Date of Zechariah 9-14," 664-78. Cf. Redditt, *Haggai, Zechariah, Malachi*, 99.
18. Redditt, *Haggai, Zechariah, Malachi*, 105.

From what has been said already, it should be clear that Zechariah 9–14 as a whole did not derive from the same hand as Zechariah 1–8. The opening verses (particularly 9:9-13), however, do conceive of Jerusalem as sparsely populated, with many of its inhabitants in exile. They also share the excitement of Haggai and Zechariah 1–8 about a coming king. So those verses may have arisen soon after Haggai-Zechariah 1–8 and share their optimism. That hope is perhaps abandoned in the last chapter, which explicitly substitutes God for the king (esp. 14:17). Pro-Jerusalem verses in 12:1-5, 8-9, moreover, show no interest in exiles or the size of Jerusalem, suggesting a time and/or a group in which such concerns have died down. The opposition to Jerusalem that emerges in 12:7 and 12:10–13:9, as well as the limited hopes for David, suggest a different hand than that (or those) in 12:1-5, 8-9 and 14:1-21. The number and identity of the different authors responsible for these verses are no longer discernable.

The final redactor paid attention to the "house of David" in his own way. He inherited a tradition that ran as follows: "On that day YHWH will shield the inhabitants of Jerusalem so that those among them that stumble on that day will be like David; and the house of David will be like God, like the messenger [or angel] of God before them" (12:8). According to this tradition, the king would lead the army of Judah, which would be invincible before its foes. The redactor was less optimistic. He offered the following limitations. (1) The glory of the house of David and of Jerusalem would not outshine Judah (12:7). (2) The house of David had "pierced" someone (identity unspecified), a deed for which they would one day mourn (12:10). Indeed, the Davidides (i.e., the whole royal family), as well as the houses of Nathan and Levi plus the Shimeites[19] and other families, needed to mourn (12:11-14) and be cleansed (13:1). Only after such repentance, apparently, would the promised future materialize for Jerusalem.

Main Genres in the Collection

Zechariah 9–14 exhibits a mixture of genres, due somewhat to its reuse of other texts. The two dominant genres are prophecies of disaster (9:1-7a) and of salvation (9:7b-8, 11-13, 14-17; 10:3b-12; 14:6-11, 16, 20-21). The two

---

19. The reference to the Shimeites most likely had in view a Levitical family, though 1 Chr 3:19 mentions a man named Shimei as a brother of Zerubbabel.

are also mixed together in 12:1-9 and 14:1-5, 12-15, 17-19. Likewise, 12:10-13:9 is a rich composite of various genres. An admonition appears in 10:1-2 and a taunt song in 11:1-3. The most remarkable text, however, is 11:4-17. It has been classified as an allegory, a parable, a vision, or a report of a symbolic act. The verses certainly remind one of the last of these genres. However, it would have been impossible for the prophet to carry out the command to become the "shepherd" of the people. Thus, the report seems to have been a literary device and not a report of something the prophet actually did. In addition, the passage looks like an allegory, in which the sheep represent the people of Judah and the shepherd some figure or group. Thus, 11:4-17 seems to combine at least some elements of the report of a symbolic act and the allegory.

A Special Issue Connected with the Collection

Nicholas Ho Fai Tai has argued convincingly that Zech 9:1–11:3 borrows heavily from Jer 5:20-25; 25:34-38, and chs. 21-23 and 31; Zech 11:4-17 from Ezekiel 34 and 37; Zech 11:4–13:9 more broadly from Ezekiel 34–39; and Zechariah 14 from Joel 3 and Amos 5:15.[20] Katrina J. A. Larkin also thinks the components drew on a variety of other OT passages and concludes that Zechariah 9–13 was an anthology of "mantological wisdom."[21] Her study points to numerous examples of reused texts. This feature opens rich treasures of intertextuality to the reader. It also leads to the conclusion that Zechariah 9-14 was likely a literary production from the beginning. In other words, its messages were probably not originally delivered orally, though the chapters may have been written to be read aloud.

---

20. Nicholas Ho Fai Tai, *Prophetie als Schriftauslegung in Sacharja 9–14* (Stuttgart: Calwer, 1996) 280-90.

21. Katrina J. A. Larkin, *The Eschatology of Second Zechariah: A Study of the Formation of a Mantological Wisdom Anthology* (Kampen: Kok Pharos, 1994) 53-179. She thinks Zechariah 14 fell outside that schema and is best viewed as an epilogue comparable to Amos 9 and Zechariah 7–8 (Larkin, 180-220, 252). The term "mantological" or "divinatory" designates wisdom texts dealing with the reading of signs or the discovery of that which is hidden or obscure, whether in the present or the future. Such texts fall under two broad categories: (1) dreams, visions, and omens, and (2) oracles consisting of auditory material whose meaning was originally self-explanatory but over time became obscure (Larkin, 31).

Introduction to the Prophet

The superscriptions in 9:1 and 12:1 give no names. The only name associated with these chapters is that of Zechariah, and even that is by implication, because the last actual mention of Zechariah is in 7:1, the last of three superscriptions (the other two appearing in 1:1 and 1:7). Thus, Zechariah 9-14 is either anonymous or pseudonymous. If anonymous, however, the collection became pseudonymous, since it was attached to the messages bearing Zechariah's name. Since the author is otherwise unknown, little can be said about him. A few conjectures, however, might be in order. He was likely a scribe familiar with a great deal of the emerging prophetic corpus. If Larkin is correct, he drew upon all five books of the Torah and on Job as well. His overwhelming focus on Jerusalem suggests that he lived there, but his view of the city's leaders shows him to be their critic, even as he shared the hope for a better future and attempted to explain its delay. He does not advocate their overthrow, only their cleansing.

Basic Emphases in Zechariah 9–14

Zechariah 9–14 has three basic emphases that merit further explication: the lowly messiah, the need for cleansing, and the status of Jerusalem.

The Lowly Messiah

The opening verses, 9:1-13, express hope for the Messiah. Verses 1-8 describe YHWH's defeat of the surrounding nations from Hadrach in northern Syria to Damascus, from the north Syrian city of Hamath to Tyre and Sidon on the Phoenician coast and to the Philistine cities of Ashkelon, Gaza, Ekron, and Ashdod further south. Then God encamps before the temple to prevent any future overthrow of it. Verses 9-13 address Jerusalem itself, promising a return of the king to the city (vv. 9-10) and God's repopulation of the city by prisoners (vv. 11-13), presumably exiles. Within the promise, God says to the people that God will restore them double what they lost, probably an allusion to Isa 40:2, which says that Jerusalem had paid double for her sins. In the restoration, therefore, the city would receive back twice as much as it lost. The king is described (Zech 9:9b) as one coming to Jerusalem "upright" (or "just" or "vindicated") and "saved" (or "liberated"), "humble" (or "afflicted" or "poor") and "mounted on a donkey, yea upon a colt, the foal of a jenny." He is not a conquering messiah; he is one being restored to his rightful place by God. In v. 10, the MT text reads:

> I [God] will cut off the chariot from Ephraim
>   and the horse from Jerusalem;
> so that the bow of battle will be cut off,
>   and he [the king] shall speak peace to the nations.

The LXX reads the first verb as a third masculine singular ("he [the king] will cut off"), making both main verbs ("cut" and "speak") agree in number. Either way, the future king will be a peacemaker.

This description follows canonically in the wake of Haggai's and Zechariah's hope for Zerubbabel as the next king but names no one. The verses that follow in 9:14-17 speak of God's actions in the third person and make no mention of a king. In v. 15, God's people will "eat and trample the slingstones, and they will drink, they will roar as with wine; they will be full like the bowl, like corners of an altar." The reference to slingstones is obscure but perhaps compares the stones to grapes to be trampled in the making of wine. Consequently, scholars sometimes emend the passage, but the overall passage employs the symbolism of harvesting, mashing, and storing wine, likely a symbol for the return of God's blessing. The verses are not nearly as bloody as the NRSV makes them sound.[22]

The Need for Cleansing

The collection returns to the topic of the king in 12:7–13:1, where it discusses the family of David. Verse 8 predicts that the house of David will become "like God" in its eminence. In the preceding verse, however, the voice of the redactor seems to break through. The glory of the house of David and that of Jerusalem would not take preeminence over the people of Judah. Verse 10 then insists that before the restoration of this king can come

---

22. The NRSV translates "they shall drink their blood like wine," but the reference to blood is taken from the LXX, not the MT, and there is no reason to suppose the LXX preserves the better text.

about the Davidides must mourn for someone they have "pierced." The identity of that person is not recoverable, though it was presumably known to the redactor and persons for whom he wrote.[23] Nor were the Davidides the only Jerusalemites needing to repent; the redactor adds a whole list that includes the entire city (12:12-14). Insofar as these thoughts are compatible, the idea seems to be that the future David would be peaceable and would come only after the city and the royal family were ready to receive such a king.

The City of Jerusalem

Two texts in particular depict the future Jerusalem as a city under attack. In 12:1-9, the nations will gather against Jerusalem, but it will remain unscathed. Instead, the attackers will reel before it (v. 2) or fail in a way like someone's hurting himself trying to lift a large stone (v. 3). The last verse (v. 9) returns to the theme of God's defending Jerusalem, rounding off the passage. Verses 4-5 are connected by means of the phrase "on that day," which is often redactional and probably is here. Verse 4 says that God will strike the horses of the enemy with panic and the riders with madness, then says God would strike the horses with blindness. The odds of success for such an army are not very good. The verses also say that God will keep an eye (whether for good or evil is not said) on the people of Judah, who will recognize God's protection of Jerusalem.

The ensuing three verses (12:6-8) sound like two different voices arguing about the future of Jerusalem. One voice (in v. 8) champions the future of the city and the Davidic king.

> On that day, YHWH will shield the inhabitants of Jerusalem, and it will come to pass that the ones among them who are stumbling shall be like

---

23. Interestingly, the Hebrew of 12:10 actually uses a first person singular pronoun, in which case the one pierced would be God (in some symbolic sense, obviously). It is possible to repoint the Hebrew, arriving at a reading that would support the NRSV translation, "the one." Many Christians have understood the reference to be to Jesus, but that would mean no one before the time of Jesus could understand it. Some scholars have suggested that the text had in view the Messiah, the shepherd in 11:4-17, or Onias III (a priest in Jerusalem in the second century B.C.E. who fled for his life to Egypt). Others suggest the verse had in view Jewish martyrs or a group of priests who fell out of power.

David on that day, and the house of David shall be like *elohim* ("God" or "gods"), like a messenger of YHWH before them.

A second voice (v. 7) insists that YHWH would give victory to "the tents of Judah" first and that the glory of the inhabitants of Jerusalem would not outshine those of Judah. Verse 6 promises Judean victory and the resettlement of Jerusalem.

The second passage about the city under attack is 14:1-21. It opens (vv. 1-2) with the prediction the city would be plundered and looted. The remainder of the chapter then describes the restored city, against whom the impious would do battle at their own peril. There is no mention of a Davidic king, however. Verse 5 announces the coming of God to the city, v. 9 God's assuming kingship, and vv. 16-17 the nations worshipping or not worshipping "the king, YHWH of hosts." The city will become so holy that its sanctity would spread to Judah (vv. 20-21).

Problems Raised by a Study of Zechariah 9–14

Contemporary readings of Zechariah 9–14 have raised two quite distinct issues yet to be addressed. The first is the new question by reader critics about the legitimacy, or at least the advisability, of reading Zechariah as two separate collections (chs. 1–8 and 9–14). The second is the relationship of those chapters to the rest of the Twelve, which the chapters appear to know well and allude to in places.

Reading Zechariah as Two Collections

Edgar W. Conrad argues that what is accessible to a contemporary reader is a literary work that appears as part of the Twelve. The prophet Zechariah is "a literary character portrayed in the text, because the literary creation of the Twelve in which he appears as a character, not Zechariah as a historical person, is accessible for study."[24] While it is true that Zechariah is known only through literature, that is true of most other persons from the past as well. Carried to its logical extreme, historiography would be a literary en-

---

24. Edgar W. Conrad, *Zechariah* (Sheffield: Sheffield Academic, 1999) 16.

terprise only, and persons of today could know precious little about persons of the past.

Both Conrad and R. David Moseman propose to read Zechariah as one collection, but both also point to the differences between Zechariah 1–8 and 9–14. Moseman, for example, comments: "Zechariah 9–14, envisioning the future differently than 1–8, uses dissonance to emphasize that 1–8 is unfulfilled prophecy."[25] In other words, chs. 9–14 were written later and look back on chs. 1–8. Nevertheless, Zechariah appears in the Twelve as one collection, and both scholars do a great service to insist that Zechariah be read as one collection. It is appropriate, therefore, to see what such a reading produces.

We shall begin with the indicators in the text.[26] The most obvious have already been mentioned: the date formulae in Zechariah 1–8 and the use of the word "oracle" in 9:1 and 12:1. The date formulae appear in 1:1, 7 and 7:1. Each marks a beginning; each refers to Darius, whom Ezra 6:1 says made a decree allowing the work on the temple to resume after a work stoppage. As mentioned earlier, Zech 1:1-6 reminds people of the "former prophets"; 1:7–6:15 contains visions and exhortations concerning the rebuilding of the temple; and 7:1–8:23 looks to the days when the temple was finished. In other words, Zechariah 1–8 creates an expectation of good days to come for Jerusalem and Judah. The "oracles" that follow seem "dissonant." Things have not panned out as expected. "But wait," the collection named for Zechariah says, "there is a reason." That reason is spelled out in two additional "oracles." Zechariah 9–11 says that the shepherds have failed, and Zechariah 12–14 says that a new day is still coming.

Such a reading epitomizes Zechariah as a whole, but it ignores other features. We shall make a different case now. Haggai also begins with an incipit dated during the reign of Darius and contains three other such notations with dates during the reign of Darius (Hag 1:15; 2:1, 20). Do not those verses beg for Haggai and Zechariah 1-8 to be read together? Further, the three words with which Zech 9:1 and 12:1 open also appear in Mal 1:1. Does that repetition not beg for Zechariah 9–Malachi 4 to be read together? The Hebrew Bible, however, makes not two but three collections of

---

25. R. David Moseman, "Reading the Two Zechariahs as One," *RevExp* 97 (2000) 494.

26. This reading is based on Conrad and Moseman, but is not exactly what either one said.

the verses and provides names for all three, even though it had to invent
the name Malachi. If, as seems likely, Zechariah 9–14 was the last addition
to the Twelve, taking its place even after the Jonah narrative was added, no
superscription was provided in order to hold the number of prophets
within the book to an even dozen.

One decides how to approach such texts on grounds that value one set
of observations over another. It is not necessary, however, to ignore the
lesser-valued set. The approach taken in this collection, moreover, is that
its placement near the end of the Twelve should also be taken into account,
one way or the other. So, for example, when Zech 1:1-6 refers to the "former
prophets" (1:4; cf. v. 6 where they are simply called "prophets"), for the
reader of the Twelve that presumably refers to Hosea through Zephaniah
(if not Haggai).

Readers like Conrad and Moseman remind all readers of Zechariah to
take seriously the literary context. Theirs is a warning that is needed. Modern scholars have sometimes assumed that the only "context" for reading a
text is its reconstructed "setting in life," a setting reconstructed by the
scholars themselves. While the attempt to recover that setting may be done
carefully and profitably, other readings may also be valuable.

Reading Zechariah 9–14 as the Capstone of the Twelve

As mentioned earlier, Zechariah 9–14 utilizes verses from Jeremiah,
Ezekiel, Joel, and Amos, among other books. It also borrows from Malachi,
however. Two verses in particular will illustrate that borrowing. Zechariah
14:9 reads:

> And YHWH shall be [or become] king over all the earth,
>   On that day it will come to pass that YHWH will be one and
>   his name one.

That verse draws upon several verses from Malachi. The first, dealing with
the kingship of God, is Mal 1:14, where God proclaims: "for I am a great
king, says YHWH of hosts, and my name is dreaded in the nations." The
kingship of God appears in the Twelve only at the end of Zechariah (14:9
and 17), the beginning of Malachi (1:14) — and the end of Zephaniah (3:15).
The Zephaniah verse was part of an addition (3:14-20), probably written to

tie Zephaniah to Haggai + Zechariah 1–8 + Malachi.[27] It appears to represent a postexilic conclusion that the monarchy was not necessary and/or possible for Judeans living in the Persian Empire. The second passage from which Zech 14:9 borrows is Mal 2:10-16, which insists on the oneness of God as the father and creator.[28] Nowhere else than these verses does the Twelve speak of God as father or as one, singly or together. It is reasonable to conclude, therefore, that Zech 14:9 looks ahead and pieces together the two ideas from Malachi. That few scholars make much of that connection is probably a consequence of failing to read the text canonically.

Another theme also reveals a connection between Zechariah 9–14 and Malachi, a connection pointed out by James D. Nogalski.[29] The verses also connect Zechariah 9–14 to Hosea.

Zech 13:9a
Then I will send this third into the fire to *refine* them as *silver* is *refined* and
to assay them
as *gold* is assayed

Mal 3:2b-3
For he is like a *refiner's* fire and like fuller's soap; he will sit as a *refiner* and cleanser of *silver,* and he will purify the descendants of Levi and refine them like *gold* and *silver.* . . .

Zech 13:9b
and I will say,
"They are *my people*," and he will say, "The Lord is *our God.*

Hos 2:23
And I will say to Lo-ammi,
"You are my people," and he shall say, "You are *our God.*"

Zechariah 13:9 looks redactional in its context, leading to the conclusion that it was written with both Mal 3:2b-3 and Hos 2:23 in view (compare

27. James D. Nogalski shows connections between Zechariah 1–8 and Malachi, leading to the conclusion adopted here that Malachi was attached to Zechariah 8 before Zechariah 9–14 was; *Redactional Processes in the Book of the Twelve*. BZAW 218 (Berlin: de Gruyter, 1993) 229-36. The timing of the attaching of Malachi to Haggai-Zechariah 1–8 is not precise, but it happened sometime after the writing of Malachi (often dated around 450), by which time the restoration of the monarchy — so important a theme in Haggai-Zechariah 1–8 — was probably a dead issue for most Judeans.

28. It is possible to understand the reference to "one father" as Abraham, but parallelism in Mal 2:10 suggests otherwise and marriage permeates the whole passage. Besides, Mal 1:6 has already called God "father." References to the oneness of God are rarer than a person might suppose. Deuteronomy 6:4 is the best known, with Second Isaiah close behind.

29. Nogalski, *Redactional Processes in the Book of the Twelve*, 235; "Zechariah 13:7-9 as a Transitional Text," in *Bringing Out the Treasure: Inner Biblical Allusion in Zechariah 9–14,* ed. Mark J. Boda and Michael H. Floyd. JSOTSup 370 (London: Sheffield Academic, 2003) 302-3.

also Zech 10:10 with Hos 11:5). If so, that would mean Zechariah 9-14 took its place in the Twelve after the Book of the Four (which began with Hosea) was merged with Haggai + Zechariah 1–8 + Malachi, probably as the last major addition.[30] That addition allowed the redactor who made it (whether the redactor of Zechariah 9–14 or someone later) to stamp the Twelve with this word of caution: the promised restoration cannot come about until the leadership in Jerusalem repents and changes its ways.

MALACHI
Renewing the Restoration and God's Abiding Love

Whereas Haggai and Zechariah 1–8/9–14 deal with priests and Davidides, with north and south, and with Persia and the nations, Malachi focuses on the temple only as the medium of the restoration. The basis of the restoration would be God's abiding love for Israel, which Israel needed to recognize through proper worship. Arising as the collection did in the middle of the fifth century B.C.E. (see below), the fate of the monarchy seems to have been a dead issue, at least for the author. The priesthood, purity, sacrifices, and tithes, therefore, appear as major concerns in the collection.

Introduction to the Collection and Its Times

The Place of the Collection in the Canon

Clearly the place of Malachi at the end of the Twelve is important. While Zechariah 9–14 was arguably the capstone of the Twelve, Malachi gets to offer the final word. Malachi probably linked first with just Haggai-Zechariah 1–8. If Zechariah 3 is concerned with the high priest and Zech 4:6-10a with the rebuilding of the temple, Malachi was interested in ritual (Mal 1:6–2:9), the moral purity (2:13-16; 3:2b-5) of the priesthood, and the sufficiency of the sacrifices (3:8-10).

The opening verses of the collection ground the restoration in God's love for Jacob/Israel (Mal 1:2-5). That grounding reaches all the way back

---

30. See the discussion under the heading "The Rise of the Book of the Twelve" in Chapter 9 above.

to the book of Genesis. In addition, several verses in Malachi refer to other pentateuchal persons (Esau in 1:2; Levi in 2:4-6; Moses in 4:4) and even to the early prophet Elijah (4:5-6). Thus, in the MT Malachi's motif of God's love for Israel/Jacob rounds off the first two sections of the Hebrew Bible, Torah and Nebiim, the "Law and the Prophets." In the LXX and versions based on its sequence (e.g., English-language Bibles), moreover, the motif of God's love for Israel rounds off the entire Testament since the books of Wisdom are placed between the Law and the Prophets.

Continuing, the last three verses in Malachi cast a glance backward in time. Malachi 4:4 advocates "remembering" the teachings of Moses that God revealed to him at Horeb. This verse seems to have drawn from 3:16, which says that God will remember and record in a book the names of those who revere God. Further, 4:5-6 promises that God would send the prophet Elijah. Interestingly, Moses is mentioned elsewhere in the Twelve only in Mic 6:4; and Elijah is mentioned nowhere else in the Twelve. Consequently, a number of scholars have argued that Mal 4:4-6 were added to Malachi after it reached its place in the Twelve and after the Twelve was attached to Torah (where Moses was the first lawgiver) and the Former Prophets (where Elijah was one of the great early prophets).

The Setting for the Collection

The provenance of Malachi can scarcely have been anywhere but Jerusalem and its environs because it records several disputes between Malachi and people at the temple, both priests and laity. Scholars typically date Malachi after the fall of the monarchy (the chief ruler in Jerusalem is called a "governor," not a "king" in 1:8) and after the rebuilding of the temple (which is clearly functioning) between 520 and 515. The latest possible date is unclear, but many scholars point to the problem of divorce in Ezra-Nehemiah as evidence for a mid-fifth century date. In any case, the date is not likely to have been much earlier.[31]

---

31. Julia M. O'Brien argues that the date must have been earlier, between 605 and 550, on the grounds that Edom fell during that time frame and its hope for restitution could not have lasted long; *Priest and Levite in Malachi*. SBLDS 121 (Atlanta: Scholars, 1990) 113-33. Actually, O'Brien's dates for Malachi are limited to 605-586, when the temple fell as well as the monarchy. While no one knows when Edom fell (there being no Babylonian or Persian account of such), there is little reason to suppose it preceded the fall of Judah. Hence, the

The Structure, Integrity, and Authorship of the Collection

The structure of Malachi is quite simple and may be outlined as follows:

1:1	Superscription
1:2-5	God's Love for Israel
1:6–2:9	Pollution by the Priesthood
2:10-16	Unfaithfulness within the Community
2:17–3:5	Cleansing of the Community
3:6-12	Paying for Cultic Worship
3:13–4:3	Hope for the Community
4:4-6	Living in the Community

Perhaps a majority of scholars hold to the unity of the collection, but it should already be clear from the comments above about 4:4-6 that the question bears investigating. A couple of other rough spots suggest the possibility of more than one edition, whether by one hand or more. The longest section, a dispute between Malachi and the priests (1:6–2:9) looks composite, with the question-and-answer format that dominates the collection giving way in 2:1-9 to a warning and prophecy of disaster. Even 1:6-14 may divide after v. 10, as suggested by Karl Elliger.[32] If so, 1:6–2:9 may have been composed from three separate sayings gathered around the general theme of the "name of the Lord."[33] The next passage (2:10-16) appears as well to combine two separate issues: polluting the altar through improper sacrifices and polluting the community through improper marriages. Continuing, Bruce V. Malchow argues that 3:1b-4 was an addition to 2:17–3:5, with 2:17–3:1a+5 forming the original dispute. This suggestion addresses several anomalies. (1) The question asked in 2:17 was not really addressed until 3:5. (2) Verse 3:1b suddenly addresses an audience that sought the Lord of the temple or his messenger. That audience can hardly be the one addressed in 2:17 and threatened in 3:5. Finally, those who sought the

---

collection of Malachi must be dated later than 515, not between 605 and 550. The question, then, is how much later. Few would date it later than the fifth century, since the Greek writer Diodorus Siculus (*Bibliotheca Historica* 19:94-97) indicates that another group, the Nabateans, occupied Edom by 313.

32. Karl Elliger, *Das Buch der zwölf kleinen Propheten 2.* ATD 25 (Göttingen: Vandenhoeck & Ruprecht, 1982) 189, 195.

33. Redditt, *Haggai, Zechariah, Malachi,* 153.

Lord are addressed again in Mal 3:13–4:3, another dispute that looks composite. These and other considerations lead to the following possibility: a redactor combined two strands of thought (1:6–2:9, [11?], 13-16 castigating priests, and 2:17–3:1a+5; 1:2-5; 3:8-12; 3:13-15 addressed to the laity) to compile the collection named for Malachi.[34]

Main Genres in the Collection

The collection as it now stands consists of six disputation speeches between God or the prophet and the members of the community, both priests and laity. These disputes share a common, basic structure: (1) The prophet makes a claim through a statement or a rhetorical question. (2) His audience disagrees. (3) The prophet offers evidence in support of his claim. Scholars debate whether the structure rests upon and reflects actual encounters between the prophet and his opponents,[35] reproduces only the essence of such a debate,[36] or was a literary device.[37] The last two options seem better than the first, with the third fitting best the argument about authorship laid out above.

A Special Issue Connected with the Study of the Collection

The collection has much to say about the priesthood, and it draws upon various passages of Scripture to make its points. Scholars are generally agreed that the author/redactor knew Deuteronomy. The most obvious evidence is the use of the terms "Horeb," "all Israel," and "law of Moses" in Mal 4:4. The word for divorce in 2:16 is the same as in Deuteronomy. The emphasis on Levi and Levites is characteristic of Deuteronomy.

It is more debatable whether Malachi knew the Priestly Code of the

---

34. Redditt, *Haggai, Zechariah, Malachi,* 154-55; cf. "The Book of Malachi in Its Social Setting," *CBQ* 56 (1994): 244-49.

35. Gerhard Wallis, "Wesen und Struktur der Botschaft Maleachis," in *Das ferne und nähe Wort: Festschrift Leonhard Rost,* ed. Fritz Maass. BZAW 105 (Berlin: Töpelmann, 1967) 232.

36. Wilhelm Rudolph, *Haggai — Sacharja 1–8 — Sacharja 9–14 — Maleachi.* KAT XIII/4 (Gütersloh: Gerd Mohn, 1976) 250.

37. Robert C. Dentan, "The Book of Malachi: Introduction and Exegesis," *IB,* 6:1119.

Pentateuch.[38] The two use many of the same technical terms associated with sacrifice, but both might simply draw on cultic language. More definitively, however, Beth Glazier-McDonald points to the parallels between Mal 2:4-5 and Num 25:12-13 as clear evidence of the dependence of Malachi on P.[39]

Malachi 2	Numbers 25
4b [M]y covenant with Levi shall always abide, says YHWH of hosts. 5 My covenant was with him, life and peace I gave him.	12 Behold I am giving him my covenant of peace. 13 It shall be for him and for his seed after him an abiding covenant of priesthood.

To be sure, the wording is only similar, but the thinking is the same in both texts. God had made a covenant of perpetual priesthood with someone, Levi in Malachi, Aaron or Phinehas in Numbers. That difference, however, perhaps reflects the friction between Malachi and the priests of his day. As Malachi perhaps saw things, some of the roles assigned to all the Levites had been preempted by one group of priests and read into Numbers. In any case, Malachi made its appeal to an ideal Levi. O'Brien is probably correct, therefore, to conclude that "Malachi employs the language and ideas of both sources . . . ," but "feels compelled to replicate neither P's technical terminology nor its language for priests."[40]

Introduction to the Prophet

The word "Malachi" (1:1) actually means "My Messenger" (or even "My Angel") and is so translated in the LXX and the Targum. It would seem an odd name for parents to give a child, though not impossible. The term appears again in 3:1: "Behold, I am about to send my messenger." Thus, it seems more likely that the term was lifted from that verse for use in 1:1 as well. If so, it is a

38. Critical scholars typically speak of a number of sources that underlie the Pentateuch. One of those alleged sources contains much material concerning priests, the tabernacle, and laws concerning sacrifice. Other materials in the Pentateuch tell narratives from a priestly point of view.

39. Beth Glazier-McDonald, *Malachi: The Divine Messenger.* SBLDS 98 (Atlanta: Scholars, 1987) 79.

40. O'Brien, *Priest and Levite,* 106-7. O'Brien, however, might not be comfortable with the suggestion above that Malachi modified the language of Num 25:12-13 for polemical reasons.

title, not a name. Strictly speaking, then, the collection is anonymous. Moreover, it is impossible to say anything much about the life of the prophet. Given the collection's defense of Levites and disputes with priests, one might speculate that the collection was prepared by one or more Levites.

Basic Emphases in Malachi

The confrontational nature of the collection generated pointed emphases in this short collection. Four stand out above all others: images of God (as father, master, king, refiner), priestly contempt for sacrifice, the full tithe, and hope for the future.

Images of God as Father, Master, King, and Refiner

Malachi offers rich metaphors for God, characterizing the divinity in terms of authority figures. The first such metaphor (in 1:6) is "father." The dispute begins with a pair of assertions the prophet expects his audience to accept: a son honors a father and servants honor their masters. Honor was part of the fabric of that society, and one's livelihood depended on staying in the good graces of one's father (who would teach the son the father's trade and at or before death pass on property to him) or master (who provided upkeep for the worker). A fatherless son or a masterless servant could well be destitute.

Next, God charges the son/servant Judah with failure to honor/respect God. This charge is lodged against the priests, who disagree: "How have we despised God?" God's answer is they had offered polluted food on the altar. Again the priests protest, only to be charged with offering blind, lame, or sick animals (1:8, 13). The law prohibited offering blind or lame animals as sacrifices (cf. Deut 15:21), but not sick ones. If the priests wish to plead innocent, therefore, the prophet challenges them to give their governor a sick animal and see if he will be impressed. Obviously he is not, and neither is God.

In the same context, the prophet has God proclaim that God is a great king, whose name is reverenced among the nations (Mal 1:14). That assertion links this second periscope to the first (1:2-5), which proclaims that God is great beyond the borders of Judah. God reigns over Judah (cf. Zeph

3:15), to be sure, but also far beyond its borders (cf. Ps. 24; 47:2, 7; 98:6). The idea that God is king has replaced the hope for a human king.

Malachi also presents God as a refiner of precious metals (3:3). Here too the flow of the verses is not smooth. The passage begins (3:2b) by saying that God is like a refiner's fire and a fuller's soap. The emphasis in both images is on cleansing or purifying that which has become dirty or impure. The prophet develops the image further by comparing God to a "refiner and purifier" of silver, whose fire burns away the dross — not a soothing image. Verse 3 applies the image to the descendents of Levi, whom God will purify like silver and gold. The result would be that they would again — like the idealized Levi of old (2:4-7) — present offerings to God in purity (3:3).

Priestly Contempt for Sacrifices

The second emphasis generated in the disputes between the prophet and the priests is the latter's contempt for the sacrifice. God says, "You say 'Behold, what a weariness' and snort at me" (1:13).[41] The picture is that of priests too indifferent to bother with their service to the people. When professionals treat their *raison d'être* with contempt, they commit the professional "unpardonable sin." Next, God pronounces a curse on anyone who substitutes a blemished animal for an unblemished one. Indirectly that statement too is a condemnation of the priests, who should have refused to offer such a sacrifice. The pericope ends by returning to the topic of God's kingship.

The Full Tithe

A third emphasis is on the "full tithe" (3:10). The phrase suggests that the people claim to be tithing, but the prophet disagrees, contending they are giving less. He also insists that the tithes are to be brought to the "storehouse." One might surmise that the dispute at least partly concerns the portion of the tithe intended for the priests and Levites. Deuteronomy 26:12-15 required that the tithe of the third year be given to the Levites,

---

41. The MT reads "at it," but scribes corrected the text (it is one of the so-called *tiqqune sopherim,* "corrections of the scribes") to read "at me."

aliens, orphans, and widows in one's own town. Should the people also tithe at the temple that year? One can easily imagine people's reluctance to do so,[42] but the prophet may have wanted them to do so. Malachi's view here seems to agree instead with the Priestly Code (Lev 27:30-33), which required that all the tithes be given to the priests and Levites. Nehemiah 12:44 seems to support such as interpretation. It reports that men were appointed (by whom?) to gather "portions" for the Levites and the priests in storage facilities in Jerusalem in fulfillment of the law.

The phrase "priests and Levites" is a postexilic phrase, recognizing a distinction that did not exist in the preexilic period. After the exile, one group of priests — called Zadokites after one of the priests of David in Jerusalem — gained ascendancy. Priests then were either Zadokites or non-Zadokites. Other priests associated themselves with the name Aaron, the brother of Moses, and claimed preeminence. The books of Ezra and Nehemiah make only a few references to Aaron (Ezra 7:5; Neh 10:38; 12:47). Of these, the first calls Aaron the "chief priest," and the latter two speak of his descendants. Similarly, the Priestly Code seems to limit authority to Aaron and his descendants. It would appear, therefore, that during the fifth century the priesthood was in flux, with Zadokite priests being challenged sooner or later by Aaronic priests.[43]

Malachi resists such distinctions, extolling Levi and using the words "priests" and "Levites" interchangeably. His condemnation of the priests in the temple and his holding them to stricter rules than they followed perhaps also reveals his standing *outside* the power structure. Nehemiah 10:38-39 makes clear that it was the responsibility of the Levites to collect and bring the tithes to the temple. It would seem possible, therefore, maybe even likely, that Malachi was a Levite. If so, he may well have been the spokesman for a group of non-Zadokite Levites.

Hope for the Future

While not as focused on the future as Zechariah 1–8 and 9–14, Malachi nevertheless contains some such thinking. It looks ahead to God's abiding

---

42. Eugene E. Carpenter, "Tithe," *ISBE*, 4:862.

43. Taken from Gabriele Boccaccini, *Roots of Rabbinic Judaism* (Grand Rapids: Wm. B. Eerdmans, 2002) 49-66.

punishment on Edom (1:4), the punishment of his contemporary priests (2:3, 9), and the coming of God's messenger to purify the descendents of Levi (3:3). The most obvious expression of hope concerns "those who revere the Lord and think on his name" (3:16–4:3). The persons would be named in "a book of remembrance," written before the Lord. What is more, 4:3 even promises them victory over the wicked (the priests?), who would be like ashes under the soles of the feet of those who revere the name of God. Those righteous ones clearly constituted a "remnant" in the mind of the author of those verses.

Problems Raised by a Study of Malachi

Divorce

Malachi raises two problems that need further attention. The first is the issue of divorce, about which the Hebrew Bible has remarkably little to say. Generally speaking, men were permitted to divorce their wives if they had cause, however slight. Remarriage was also permitted, except that priests should not marry divorcees (or other women who presumably had had sexual relations with another man; cf. Lev 21:14). When divorcing a woman, a man had to present her with a bill of divorce (Deut 24:1, 3), which would prove to other men that she was free to remarry. If a divorced woman married another man, she could not subsequently remarry a husband.

It is a little surprising, therefore, to read of God's declaring in Mal 2:16 that God hates divorce. Not a few scholars, therefore, argue that the passage really is condemning idolatry. We have seen earlier that the context mixes the profanation of the altar by unfit sacrifices with whatever the prophet means by "divorce." The phrase "faithless to the wife of one's youth," however, can hardly refer to anyone but someone's wife. Malachi 2:15 insists that God made her, implying that divorce is an insult to her status before God. Also, calling her one's companion and wife by covenant sounds like references to human wives. How, then, should one understand this situation?

It may be that the books of Ezra and Nehemiah will help provide an answer. Both Ezra 9:1-15 and Neh 10:28-30; 13:3, 23-30 narrate the divorce of Jewish people from persons not of "proper" descent. These divorces include priests and others and represent a new restriction in possible marriage partners not made in older laws. Perhaps Malachi spoke from the other side of the issue and opposed the mandated divorces or at least the thinking that led to those divorces.

A Loving and Hating God

The second problem concerns the collection's portrayal of God. Malachi 1:2b-3a reads: "Jacob I have loved, but Esau I have hated." Scholars have tried to soften or explain away this contrast by translating "prefer/not prefer" or "elect/reject." Others have suggested that (1) the main emphasis is on God's freedom to act as God chooses, (2) the verbs reflect a relationship in which Jacob remained in union with God and Esau/Edom did not, or (3) the reader should simply emphasize God's love for Jacob and downplay the hatred for Esau.

At least this much may be said in light of the last two suggestions: the text does emphasize that God had remained and would remain faithful to Jacob. But what about God's "hatred" for Edom? Two points may be made in that regard. (1) The text maintains that God had punished Edom for its sins against Judah (presumably in 586, in connection with the destruction of Jerusalem by Babylon). (2) The contention that God "hates" Edom perhaps is better seen as the author's projecting his own feelings on God.[44]

Summary

As we have seen, Haggai and Zechariah 1–8 develop the motif of a new Judah in terms of the restoration of the population, the temple, the priesthood, and the monarchy. Even so, the new day did not dawn, at least not completely, particularly not the restitution of the monarchy. Zechariah 9–14 and Malachi address the issue of what went wrong to delay the full restoration. For Zechariah 9–14 the problem lies with the "shepherds," the priests, the Davidides, and perhaps even the prophets. For Malachi, the monarchy seems to have been a dead issue, but the need for priests to change was ever sharper.

44. See Paul L. Redditt, "The God Who Loves and Hates," in *Shall Not the Judge of All the Earth Do What Is Right? Studies on the Nature of God in Tribute to James L. Crenshaw*, ed. David Penchansky and Paul L. Redditt (Winona Lake: Eisenbrauns, 2000) 176-79.

Questions for Reflection

1. Are hopes for God's kingdom tied to any political group, office, or state, even modern Israel? Why do you answer as you do?
2. Compare and contrast the expectations of the king as presented in Isaiah 9 and 11 with the charges against the Davidides in Zech 12:10-12 and 13:1. Does the author of those four verses long for or expect a new Davidic king? Why do you answer as you do?
3. Does God hate people? Why do you answer as you do?

For Further Reading

Baldwin, Joyce G. *Haggai, Zechariah, Malachi*. TOTC. Downers Grove: InterVarsity, 1972. Excellent, short, traditional commentary, making careful use of Hebrew.

Boda, Mark J. *Haggai, Zechariah*. NIVAC. Grand Rapids: Zondervan, 2004. A careful study of Haggai and Zechariah that includes a discussion of the meaning of the text for modern life.

Conrad, Edgar W. *Zechariah*. Sheffield: Sheffield Academic, 1999. A study of Zechariah from the perspective of reader criticism, understanding Zechariah as the implied author of the entire work.

Floyd, Michael H. *Minor Prophets, Part 2*. FOTL 22. Grand Rapids: Wm. B. Eerdmans, 2000. Excellent study of the genres used in the last six collections of the Book of the Twelve.

Hill, Andrew E. *Malachi*. AB 25D. New York: Doubleday, 1998. Translation and extensive scholarly notes, preceded by a lengthy introduction to Malachi.

Kessler, John. *The Book of Haggai: Prophecy and Society in Early Persian Yehud*. VTSup 91. Leiden: Brill, 2002. Not a commentary, but a study of the perceptions reflected in Haggai of the social, political, and religious institutions in early Persian Judah.

Meyers, Carol L., and Eric M. Meyers. *Haggai, Zechariah 1–8*. AB 25B. Garden City: Doubleday, 1987. A translation with textual notes and a full, scholarly commentary, preceded by a lengthy introduction to Haggai-Zechariah 1–8.

————. *Zechariah 9–14*. AB 25C. New York: Doubleday, 1993. A translation with textual notes and a full, scholarly commentary, preceded by a lengthy introduction to Zechariah 9–14.

O'Brien, Julia M. *Nahum, Habakkuk, Zephaniah, Haggai, Zechariah, Malachi.* AOTC. Nashville: Abingdon, 2005. Brief introduction to each collection or section of a collection (key issues, literary genre, structure, character of the writings, social context) followed by exegesis and treatment of their theological/ethical significance.

Petersen, David L. *Haggai and Zechariah 1–8.* OTL. Philadelphia: Westminster, 1984. A scholarly treatment of Haggai as an activist concerned with rebuilding the temple and Zechariah as a visionary who gave advice.

————. *Zechariah 9–14 and Malachi.* OTL. Louisville: Westminster John Knox, 1995. A scholarly commentary, treating Zechariah 9–11, 12–14 and Malachi as separate collections. Each is carefully placed in its social and historical context.

Redditt, Paul L. *Haggai, Zechariah, Malachi.* NCBC. Grand Rapids: Wm. B. Eerdmans, 1995. Commentary based on the social settings and editorial shaping of each section.

Smith, Ralph L. *Micah-Malachi.* WBC 32. Waco: Word, 1984. Interprets the collections from the perspective of historical, form-critical, and exegetical investigation.

Stuhlmueller, Carroll. *Rebuilding with Hope: A Commentary on the Books of Haggai and Zechariah.* ITC. Grand Rapids: Wm. B. Eerdmans, 1988. Presents these two collections as bridges between the traditions of older Israelite religion and the changes necessary to preserve the late-sixth-century community.

Sweeney, Marvin A. *The Twelve Prophets.* Vol. 2. Berit Olam. Collegeville: Liturgical, 2000. Written to interpret the Twelve as a unity intended to be read straight through.

Taylor, Richard A., and E. Ray Clendenen. *Haggai, Malachi.* NAC 21A. Nashville: Broadman & Holman, 2004. An avowedly inerrantist commentary that deals carefully with the Hebrew text, the genres of the literature, and the theological meaning of the two prophets.

Wolff, Hans Walter. *Haggai.* Minneapolis: Augsburg, 1988. A presentation of Haggai as a model of effective proclamation, leading a discouraged people to a new hope by means of questions and admonitions.

Conclusion

We have been on a journey through the thinking of a number of prophets, who flourished over hundreds of years. We have seen them struggle with God, their people, and their own doubts. We have seen them disagree with each other in places; we have assuredly seen them address a variety of issues. It is certainly not clear that there is one overall center around which the prophets rally or to which they all point. Rather, they address a series of themes from different perspectives. Of those themes eight seem most important: God's election of Israel, the oneness of God, the worship of God, Israel's fidelity to its God, social responsibility, punishment for sin, God's fidelity to Israel, and eschatology. Hence, the first task in this conclusion is to survey these themes. Then we will deal with two more issues: the canonization of the Major and Minor Prophets and strategies of reading them in use around the beginning of the Common Era.

Eight Themes in the Major and Minor Prophets

God's Election of Israel

God's election of Israel is articulated in the Torah, especially in the covenants with the Patriarchs (beginning with Abraham in Genesis 12), the call of Moses in Exodus 3–6, and the announcement of God's choice of Israel as a function of God's love in Deut 7:6-11. The Former Prophets also repeat this theme of election, particularly but not only in Josh 24:2-13.[1] It also plays a role in the Latter Prophets. It appears in the exilic thinking of Second Isaiah, where God calls Israel "my servant, Jacob, whom I have chosen" (Isa 41:8-9; cf. 43:10; 44:1-2; 45:4), and the postexilic thinking of Third Isaiah, where God promises that the elect will inherit the Holy Land (65:8-10). The promised rescue from Babylon would make God Israel's savior (Isa 43:3; 45:15, 21; 49:26; cf. 60:16 and 63:8 in Third Isaiah). This election of Israel had been ratified by a covenant, which Israel had broken (Jer 7:8-9; Ezek 16:59; 44:7; Hos 8:1), but which God would renew (Jer 31:31-34; cf. Ezek 16:60-62). The prophets could speak of this election/covenant in family terms, in which God was Israel's father (Isa 63:16; 64:8; Jer 31:9; Mal 1:6) or even husband (Isa 54:5; Hos 2:19-20).

The Oneness of God

This second theme might seem self-evident. Did not the Jews give us monotheism, the Greeks democracy, and the Romans law, as the old saying goes? The answer to the first part of the question is "Yes, the Jews did give us monotheism," but not everything in the OT is monotheistic. In Genesis 12 God calls Abraham out of a polytheistic background. The Ten Commandments call on Israel to have no other gods than YHWH (Exod 20:3), and Joshua instructs the people to choose which god(s) they would serve: the gods of Mesopotamia, the gods of Canaan, or the God who was giving them the land of Canaan (Josh 24:15). Belief in and worship of one God among many is called monolatry. Monotheism is the belief in and worship of one God, combined with the denial of the existence of all other gods. As we saw earlier, belief in monotheism first appears in Jer 2:11 and then comes to the forefront in Isa 40:12-31; 44:6; 45:5-8; and 46:1-13. These verses make it clear that images of nonexistent gods were laughable. They could not move themselves about; still less could they support or defend their worshippers. By contrast, Israel's God had created everything, cared for Israel, and would defeat the Babylonians, rescue the exiles, and restore Jerusalem.

---

1. The texts cited in this discussion have been selected for their clarity in presenting the concepts under discussion. They are, however, only a representative sampling of the texts possible.

The Worship of God

Israel's God deserved Israel's exclusive worship. Israel's prophets, from Isaiah to Malachi, therefore, address the worship of God. One fundamental act of worship was the offering of sacrifices. The opening chapter of Isaiah denounces worship that amounts to sacrifice without compassion for humans or the confession of sins (Isa 1:10-17; cf. Amos 4:4-5; 5:21-27), and Malachi complains about priests who are contemptuous of the sacrificial system they administer (Mal 1:13) and about laity who try to shortchange God and to hold back part of the tithe (3:8-12). Half-hearted worship marked by insincere praise recited from rote is an affront to God (Isa 29:13-14). Micah insists that true worship consists of doing justice, loving kindness, and walking humbly with God (Mic 6:8). A passage of indeterminable age, and possibly not authentic to Isaiah, envisions three temples in the future for the worship of God: one in Egypt and another in Assyria, in addition to the one in Jerusalem (Isa 19:16-25). Jeremiah excoriates his audience for breaking every commandment God had given them and still thinking they are worshiping God (Jer 7:8-15). His sermon stands as the explanation in the book of Jeremiah for the destruction of the temple, as does Ezekiel's vision of sin in the very precincts of the temple (Ezekiel 8–11). After the exile, Haggai and Zechariah advocate the rebuilding of the temple destroyed by the Babylonians. There true worship could begin again (Hag 1:7-11; Zech 4:6b-10a) with a purified priesthood (Zech 3). Their contemporary, the so-called Third Isaiah, insists that the temple should be a house of prayer for all peoples (Isa 56:3-8; cf. Zech 14:16-21). Second Zechariah calls for the repentance of the Levites and the removal of idols from the land before the new day could dawn (Zech 12:13 and 13:2). Joel calls on the people of his day to repent (Joel 2:12-14) and to hold a public lamentation to express their contrition and their hope that God would respond affirmatively (Joel 1:8-14; 2:15-17).

Israel's Fidelity to God

How loyal was Israel to this covenant? The answer has already been hinted at in the topic above. Jeremiah and Ezekiel blame the exiles for worshipping other gods instead of worshipping YHWH only (Jeremiah 2; Ezek 16; 20:27-29). Instead they worshipped idols "on every hill" (Ezek 6:13). Even some not guilty of worshipping other gods openly had committed idolatry in their hearts (Ezek 14:3). Hosea equates such behavior with adultery (Hos 1:2), and Habakkuk ridicules the worship of idols (Hab 2:18-19) in language like that in Second Isaiah (Isa 44:9-17). Zephaniah also rails against those who took oaths in God's name but also in the name of Milcom[2] (Zeph 1:4-6).

Social Responsibility

Social responsibility centers on the concept of justice. In the opening verses of Isaiah (Isa 1:16b-17), we read the following:

> Cease doing evil; learn to do good.
>> Seek justice, rescue the oppressed,
>> defend the orphan, plead for the widow.[3]

For Isaiah, the seeking of justice consists of trying to secure the benefits of society for people least able to fight for them: the oppressed, the orphan, and the widow.[4] Amos and Micah likewise are champions of the poor, criticizing crown and upper crust alike for injustice (Amos 4:1-13; 6:1-7; Mic 2:1-2; 3:11-12). Micah sounds like Isaiah when he tells the people what God requires (6:8): make justice, love covenant fidelity, and walk humbly with God. These three groups generally share the common characteristic that they have little wealth; hence they have little political clout either. Zechariah defends them too (Zech 7:8-10) in what appears to be a summary of the preexilic preaching ignored by the ancestors but still incumbent on the people of Judah (8:16-17). For him, social responsibility also includes telling the truth, giving correct rulings in court, and making peace among the people.

---

2. Manuscripts of the LXX plus the Syriac Peshitta and the Latin Vulgate read "Milcom," who was the god of the Ammonites. The MT actually reads *malkham* ("their king"). The context seems to demand the name of a god.

3. Deut 10:18 also includes the stranger that moved in and lived among the Israelites, i.e., the resident alien.

4. Psalm 72:4 seems to imply that the king was responsible for justice (cf. Jer 22:15).

Punishment for Sin

As seen elsewhere in this study, sin is a wrongdoing or wrong attitude against God that separates a person or persons from God. It also includes failure to obey God (sometimes called "sins of omission") and violating the rules of ritual. Sin may also involve harming humans or breaking human laws, but what makes a behavior a sin is that it is directed against God, knowingly or unknowingly. When the prophets accused people of sinning, therefore, they had a wide range of behaviors in view. What made abuse of the poor a sin against God was either that the poor were part of the people in covenant with God or that all people were creations of God.

To be sure, not all prophets were particularly worried about the sinfulness of other nations or with God's forgiving them. Nahum and Jonah had little concern for Assyrians, Habakkuk for Babylonians, or Obadiah and Malachi for Edomites. The books of Isaiah, Jeremiah, and Ezekiel all have sections of prophecy against the foreign nations, though those passages probably were contrived with an eye on influencing the behavior of Judah more than that of foreigners. At their best, however, the prophets thought God would forgive the sins of even the nations and receive their worship (Isa 19:19-25; 56:3-8; Zech 14:16-19).

Sins for which the prophets anticipated divine punishment include oppressing the poor, stealing, murder, adultery, swearing false oaths, idolatry, and sacrificing to gods other than YHWH (all mentioned in Jer 7:5-9). Isaiah considers Ahaz's refusal to trust God to defend Judah sinful (Isa 7:13-17), and Malachi condemns priests for their attitude toward the sacrificial system (Mal 1:12-14). Many of these behaviors are not the kinds of things which modern Westerners think of as sinful. Sin for many moderns consists only or mainly of private behaviors like adultery or murder, not attitudes toward other people, values and practices at a national level, and certainly not failure to defend the poor.

God's forgiveness of sins rests — as Jonah learned — on God's creation of all humanity. In other words, it grows out of God's own nature. More than one prophet made it clear that sacrifices did not buy off God; rather, God forgave the penitent out of compassion for them. Sacrifice, then, was the means God had provided God's people to express their contrition.

God's Fidelity to Israel

Despite Israel's recurring apostasy, God remained faithful and promised to take back the wayward nation and/or save a righteous remnant. The opening chapter of Isaiah contains a blistering attack on the people of Israel for their sinfulness, but the chapter is interrupted (Isa 1:26-28) with the anticipation of God's restoration of Jerusalem's judges and the city's repentance. Isaiah 2 begins with a passage (Isa 2:2-5) shared with Micah 4, in which God promises to elevate Zion as the highest of the mountains (i.e., as the navel of the earth once more). This interweaving of doom followed by restoration is characteristic of the rest of the book.

It is not unusual to find God calling Israel to repent in order to undergo this change of fortune. An explicit call to repentance (to turn back to God) may be found, for example, in Isa 31:6: "Turn back, O children of Israel, to the one [against] whom you have committed deep apostasy." Likewise, Second Zechariah calls for widespread mourning for sin by the leading families of Jerusalem before the promised new day can dawn (Zech 12:10–13:6). In Hos 6:1, however, the people respond to God's punishment:

> Come, let us return to YHWH,
>> For [God] has torn, but will heal us;
>> Has injured, but will bandage us.

In this particular verse, however, their repentance appears to be facile. Micah 6:6-8 makes clear what Israel must do to regain God's blessing: do justice, love kindness, and be humble before God.

Demands for repentance (or renewed obedience) do not always accompany promises of God's redemption of Israel. The new covenant foreseen in Jer 31:31-34 might be just a matter of God's grace, and the "wife" in Hosea 2 seems simply to realize that she was better off with her first husband (cf. v. 7b) and to act out of self-interest. God seems to act out of jealousy in Zech 1:14 and out of a sense of justice in the next verse. Guilty as Jerusalem might have been, the city was not as deserving of punishment as the Babylonians, who had exceeded what God had in mind for God's people (cf. Obad 17-21). In Zeph 3:1-13 we find the motif of God's purging the leadership of Judah, who were guilty of oppression, and replacing that leadership with the faithful. At still other times, demands for repentance might be implied. Regardless, our point holds: God promises to be faithful to Israel.

As indicated, God does not always promise to rescue the whole nation. Sometimes, in fact, it is clear that only a remnant will survive. The most succinct statement of that idea is found in Hab 2:4b: "the righteous shall live by its/his faithfulness." The sentence is not quite clear. Many interpreters think the antecedent of the masculine pronoun is the word "righteous" (i.e. the righteous person), but J. J. M. Roberts thinks the antecedent is the vision alluded to in v. 2.[5] Either way, the righteous person or people constitute the remnant.

This concept shows up first in Isaiah. In Isa 1:9 (cf. 10:20-22; 37:4) the remnant is simply the few who survive the coming punishment. In Isa 11:11 and 16 (cf. 46:3) the term refers to Israelites in exile outside Palestine, but in those texts God promises to rescue them and bring them home. The late passage in Jer 23:3 uses the term the same way, and combines it with a promise for a new David (vv. 5-6). Joel 2:32 quotes Obad 17, but defines those who escape as the survivors whom YHWH calls. Micah 4:7 promises the restitution of those "cast off." Micah 7:18 praises God for pardoning the iniquity of the remnant of God's possession. The book of Daniel does not use the term "remnant," but the concept appears in Daniel's concluding vision of the escape of God's righteous people in the end time (Daniel 12; cf. the "people, the saints of the most high" in 7:27).

Eschatology

Finally, we come to the topic of eschatology, the doctrine of the end. In the NT the term typically refers to events at the end of time: the second coming of Jesus, the resurrection of the dead, judgment, and heaven/hell. In that sense there is little or no eschatology in the Hebrew Bible. Daniel 12 might constitute the only example. Hence, scholars of the Hebrew Bible use the term in a broader sense to designate a future which is radically improved. Ezekiel 34–48 envisions a future in which the exiles go home, the temple is rebuilt and the priests control it, the king minds his limited business, the land is equitably divided and safe from foreign invasion, and resources such as water are sufficient.

5. J. J. M. Roberts, *Nahum, Habakkuk, and Zephaniah.* OTL. Louisville: Westminster John Knox, 1991) 111.

Donald E. Gowan is correct that eschatology in the OT does have a center, however, and that center is Jerusalem. Much/most eschatology develops during the exile and afterwards. In it three motifs develop around Jerusalem. The first is the transformation of human society, comprised of restoration to the promised land, the restoration of the righteous king, victory over the surrounding nations, and even the conversion of some of them. The second motif is the transformation of the human person, brought about by God's forgiveness, the means of re-creation (the new covenant, good health, long life, and — rarely — resurrection), and the new person or personality. The third motif is the transformation of nature, in which God restores fertility to the land, ordains a new natural order in which things do not kill each other, and renews the earth.[6]

The Process of Canonizing the Major and Minor Prophets

We turn next to the process of collecting, preserving, and canonizing the prophetic books. In these books we have seen examples of texts borrowing from each other, even though those texts arose over several centuries and with little hint that the prophets knew each other, even by reputation. That borrowing, and theme-building along with it, appears to have come at the level of editing, not at the level of oral performance or early reduction to writing. Indeed, scholars have traced some of that theme-building in different parts of the Hebrew Bible. The first such theme is the idea of Israel as the people of God and descendants of Abraham. It was introduced in Genesis 12 and ran through the narrative of the Pentateuch. The Former Prophets also speak of Abraham on occasion (Josh 24:2-3; 1 Kgs 18:36; 2 Kgs 13:23). Chronicles retells Samuel–Kings and mentions Abraham twice (2 Chr 20:7; 30:6). A second theme introduced in the Torah is God's covenant with Israel through Moses. That theme is shared by the Former Prophets, which introduce a third: the Davidic monarchy and David's city, Jerusalem. Three of the Latter Prophets mention Abraham (Isa 29:22; 41:8; 63:16; Jer 33:26; Ezek 33:24) and share the themes of covenant and David/Jerusalem. Thus the "Law and the Prophets" focus on several shared themes.[7]

---

6. Donald E. Gowan, *Eschatology in the Old Testament*. 2nd ed. (Edinburgh: T. & T. Clark, 2000) 10.

7. It should be mentioned in addition that critical scholars typically think that Genesis

I have argued in Chapter 9 above that the Book of the Twelve arose over time, as a redacted work. The work of redactors or editors presupposes the process of urbanization, which began in ancient Israel in the eighth century, when the use of writing began to spread and scribes arose to write documents and keep records. This nascent urbanization practically disappeared in Judah at the time of the fall of Jerusalem, but survived in exile, and rebounded in the postexilic period.[8] It should come as no surprise, then, that the "writing prophets" began in the eighth century, moved out of Judah in the sixth, and returned with the exiles' efforts to rebuild the temple in Jerusalem.

It is part of the work of scribes to collect, preserve, edit, and publish literature, and the postexilic period was the period for doing just that. Scribes were not, however, just copyists, but editors as well and people with a slant, a perspective. At times we can detect their own additions to the emerging texts.[9] Beyond that, they tried to make sense out of obscure passages in the texts. The process continued for centuries into the Common Era, when the Masoretes decided what vowels to read (originally only Hebrew consonants were written) and where to divide texts into sentences, verses, and chapters. It is to them that we owe the Hebrew Bible.

We ought to pause at this point and remember that the English word "Bible" comes from Greek *biblia,* which means "books." The Bible is, quite simply, a collection of books chosen by religious bodies as authoritative for them. We have already seen that Christians and Jews do not always agree on what books belong in their shared Bible, but that is not our concern here. Our concern is to observe their shaping of the Latter Prophets.

We shall begin with the observation that both Isaiah and the Twelve cover pretty much the same sweep of time, from the mid-eighth through the end of the sixth centuries B.C.E. Not all the prophetic voices in the Twelve fall in that time period (e.g., Malachi, Joel, Jonah), but the dates, where given, do. There is reason to think, though not the space here to discuss, that Isaiah and the Twelve were developed with an eye on one an-

---

through Numbers took their final shape in the postexilic period, despite their earlier subject matter.

8. F. E. Peters, *The Voice, the Word, the Books: The Sacred Scripture of the Jews, Christians, and Muslims* (Princeton: Princeton University Press, 2007) 94.

9. One example is the comment in Isa 26:19 that "my corpse" shall rise, noted in Chapter Two above.

other.[10] It also appears (to me at least) that Jeremiah and Ezekiel were redacted about the same time among exiles in Egypt and Babylonia respectively, in response to the destruction of Judah. So these four books came into being during the Persian period, and began to draw on each other in the process. Zechariah 9–14 is perhaps the clearest example of this process. We have also seen, however, that the end of Malachi casts a backward glance to Moses and Elijah, the "Law and the Prophets." Much in Malachi dialogues with the law codes in the Pentateuch, and the mention of Elijah allows Mal 4:4-6 to form a large *inclusio* around both Moses and Elijah, the Law and the Prophets, without at the same time naming the contents.

Turning briefly to the Former Prophets, we note that they also came into being in the years before and after the exile. Critical scholars often argue that a redactor or school of scribes influenced by the theology of Deuteronomy compiled the first edition of the Former Prophets during the heyday of its great hero King Josiah (640-609). His death at the hands of the Egyptian pharaoh Neco and the fall of Jerusalem to the Babylonians triggered a second edition that ended on the upbeat note that in 560 King Jehoiachin of Judah had been released from prison. The date of that edition is debated and need not concern us here. All we need to do is note that it could have come any time after the release of the Judean king. What emerged from their scribal activity was four books as well: Joshua, Judges, Samuel, and Kings.[11] It is tempting to speculate that the four Latter Prophets were selected to balance the four Former Prophets.

What is not clear is exactly how early that work was completed. The latest date would seem to be the career of Jesus ben Sira, who wrote Ecclesiasticus in Jerusalem probably before the Maccabean Revolt. Chapters 44–50 of his work "sing the praises of famous men" (Sir 44:1). They include the following, in order: Enoch, Noah, Abraham, Isaac, Jacob, and the twelve tribes (all in Genesis); Moses, Aaron, and Phinehas (in Exodus through Numbers); Joshua (in Exodus through Joshua) and Caleb (in Numbers through Joshua); "the judges"; Samuel, Nathan, David, Solomon

---

10. See Erich Bosshard-Nepustil, *Rezeption von Jesaja 1–39 im Zwölfprophetenbuch: Untersuchungen zur literarischen Verbindung von Prophetenbüchern in Babylonischer und Persicher Zeit.* OBO 154 (Freiburg: Universitätsverlag, 1997); and Odil Hannes Steck, *Der Abschluss der Prophetie im Alten Testament: Ein Versuch zur Frage des Vorgeschichte des Kanons.* Biblische-Theologische Studien 17 (Neukirchen: Neukirchener, 1991) 196-98.

11. Originally 1 and 2 Samuel were one book, as were 1 and 2 Kings.

(in the book of Samuel); Rehoboam, Jeroboam, Elijah, Elisha, Hezekiah, Isaiah, and Josiah (in Kings); Jeremiah, Ezekiel, and "the bones of the Twelve Prophets"; Zerubbabel and Jeshua (in Haggai and Zechariah as well as Ezra); and Nehemiah. In Sir 49:15-16 he mentions Joseph, the three sons of Enoch, and Adam. In this list only Nehemiah is not mentioned in the Torah and Nebiim. The only other person ben Sira mentions is his contemporary Simon, son of Onias, a priest. It is pretty clear that ben Sira had his eyes on the heroes of the first two parts of Tanak. What is more, he alludes to them in a way that shows he expects his readers to know who they are and what they did. The list of heroes of ben Sira, therefore, suggests that the Law and the Prophets had been collected and joined sometime before he wrote. How much earlier is impossible to say. That process may have begun in the exile, but in no case later than the early Persian period. In my reading, nothing in the Latter Prophets necessitates a date in the Greek period, but many scholars would disagree. Anyway, "the Law and the Prophets" came into place somewhere between 400 and 200 B.C.E.

Ben Sira, however, does not mention Daniel, and in the MT that book does not belong to the Prophets. In the LXX, however, it does. Modern scholarship has a ready explanation for its omission from ben Sira: the book was not completed until 164 or so, well after ben Sira wrote. It is not difficult to say why it was added to the LXX and to the Kethubim of the MT: Daniel the wise man was a hero in Babylon like Ezekiel; indeed, later scribes may have thought he was the "Danel" mentioned in Ezek 14:14, 20. With its emphasis on piety and its articulation of the resurrection of the godly, Daniel perhaps had an early appeal. Certainly the Jewish/Christian writers of the NT had no qualms about citing Daniel as one of the Prophets. We turn next, then, to examine briefly their reading of the prophets.

Four Connections to the Prophets Made by the New Testament

For Christians, the Hebrew Bible is the first and much longer of two collections that form their Scriptures. The typical Christian designation "Old Testament" suggests that the Hebrew Bible is in some sense incomplete *from a Christian perspective.*[12] To call that collection the "Old Testament"

---

12. This Christian perception is sometimes seen as anti-Jewish, but it certainly need not be. Rabbinic Judaism developed the Talmud, at least partly in an effort to apply laws and

presupposes that there is also another collection, a "New Testament." In the Christian Bible the two collections stand next to each other, the Old as the background for the New. The Old supplies the worldview, the view of God, the eschatology, and the ethics with which the New works. What is more, the New is acutely aware of that relationship. Its authors in fact proclaim that connection. In the next few pages we shall examine the bridge that the authors of the NT built, not from the whole of Tanak, but from the Major and Minor Prophets to the NT.[13]

The Prophets in the New Testament

The NT took over the idea that some people are prophets and labeled a number of persons within the new Christian community as such. For example, Matt 10:41 speaks of Christians receiving a prophet's reward; Acts 13:1 simply asserts that there were prophets and teachers in the church in Antioch; and in 1 Cor 14:37 Paul speaks of people in Corinth who claimed to be prophets. Of concern in these pages, however, are the numerous references to or quotations from OT prophets. In the book of Acts alone, we see appeals to the following texts as authorities. Acts 2:16 refers to Joel, 7:49 to Isa 66:1-2, 8:28-34 to Isa 53:7-8, and 13:20 to the prophet Samuel. Moreover, Acts 2:30 counts King David among the prophets, and Acts 3:22 and 7:37 apply Deut 18:15 to Jesus, calling him the "prophet like Moses." As Acts 2:30 and 3:22 make clear, for the NT authors the word "prophets" included the Latter Prophets, but was not limited to them.

The God Spoken of by the Prophets

The authors of the NT were convinced that the God and father of Jesus (Rom 15:6; cf. 2 Cor 11:31) was the God spoken of by the Major and Minor Prophets. A few examples must suffice. In Luke 1:68-71, Zechariah, the father of John the Baptist, speaks of God's announcing through the prophets

---

other teachings to their ever-changing world. In that sense, the Hebrew Bible was as incomplete for them as it was for Christians.

13. Again I am aware that other scholars might have chosen more, fewer, or different issues. These seem crucial to me.

that he would raise up a mighty savior (i.e., Jesus, so far as the author of Luke was concerned) to rescue God's people from their enemies (cf. Isa 9:2-7), before which savior John the Baptist would go as forerunner (Luke 1:68-71). Mark 1:2-3 quotes Mal 3:1 (where God is the speaker) to the same effect: that John would be God's messenger announcing Jesus' coming.[14] In Acts 2:17-21, the author has Peter apply Joel 2:28-32 to the coming of the Holy Spirit on the day of Pentecost. Finally, Revelation 4 portrays God in phrases and images taken from Ezekiel 1–3 (Rev 4:2-6a) and Isa 6:2-3 (Rev 4:8).

Prophecies Fulfilled by Jesus

In particular, however, the writers of the NT believed that Jesus fulfilled many of the prophecies of the OT. I have mentioned several such texts in earlier chapters; here I will pull together only a few representative texts. Among the Gospels, Matthew especially works on this issue as part and parcel of his contention that Jesus was the Jewish Messiah. A look at his opening two chapters will illustrate that point. He employs a truncated genealogy[15] of Jesus (Matt 1:1-16), designed to show that Jesus descended from David. Even his division into three groups of fourteen generations (Matt 1:17) points to David. The name "David" includes the Hebrew consonant D, W (for V), D. Letters also served as numbers in Hebrew, however. The letter D comes fourth in the Hebrew alphabet and represents the number four; W (or V) is sixth and is used for the number six. So, since $D(4)+W(6)+D(4) = 14$, the threefold division into fourteen generations seems to point to David.

A few verses later (Matt 1:23), the evangelist quotes Isa 7:14. In our study of Isaiah, we noted that the Hebrew text of that verse is best translated "Behold, a young woman shall conceive and bear a child." The LXX, however, translates Hebrew 'almah with the Greek word for virgin, parthenos, allowing the evangelist to make the further point that Joseph was not Jesus' physical father (Matt 1:25). Continuing, Matt 2:6 quotes Mic 5:2 (about the place of origin of David) as a prediction that the Messiah would be born in Bethlehem. Also, Matt 2:15 quotes Hos 11:1, which makes

---

14. Mark 1:2 does, however, attribute Mal 3:1 to Isaiah.

15. This genealogy was drawn from texts like 1 Chronicles 1–9, not from any prophetic text. The focus on Zerubbabel, however, brings to mind Hag 2:20-23 and Zech 4:9b-10a.

a historical allusion to the exodus from Egypt. The evangelist claims that the Holy Family's return to Palestine "fulfilled" that verse too. Next, he takes the Slaughter of the Innocents (Matt 2:16-18) to be a fulfillment of the lament over the fall of the northern kingdom of Israel (Jer 31:15). Obviously, the verse in Jeremiah is not a prediction of anything, but a response to something that already happened. The evangelist, however, seems to present the murder of infants in Bethlehem as another such tragedy deserving of great weeping.[16] Finally, in Matt 2:23 ("He will be called a Nazorean"), the evangelist alludes to a phrase from Isa 11:1, which might be translated "and a branch will go forth from his roots." The Hebrew word translated "branch" is *netser.* That word sounds similar to "Nazareth," similar enough that the evangelist seized it to help him account for why the Judean son of David grew up in the northern city of Nazareth.

In only the first two chapters, the evangelist employs three predictions (Isa 7:14; Isa 11:1; and Mic 5:2), a historical retrospection (Hos 11:1), and a lament (Jer 31:15) to proclaim that Jesus had "fulfilled" the words/intentions of those verses.[17] It is probably worth reminding ourselves here that to say Jesus "fulfilled" a passage is not the same as saying that the passage "predicted" Jesus. Rather, the evangelist (and other NT authors as well) searched the OT, seeking texts to help explain what God was up to in the man Jesus.

16. This application of Jer 31:15 to the Slaughter of the Innocents may be a stretch in another way as well. Rachel, the second wife of Jacob, was the mother of Joseph and Benjamin. If, indeed, the verse referred originally to the northern tribes, its new application in Matt 2:16-18 is to a different geographical area, Bethlehem, a town in the old southern kingdom of Judah.

17. There is no reason to belabor this point further. I will simply list other texts in Matthew that make the same point about Jesus fulfilling OT prophecies: Matt 4:15-16 quotes Isa 9:1-2; 12:18-21 quotes Isa 42:1-4, saying Jesus fulfilled the role of the servant; Matt 13:14-15 has Jesus apply Isa 6:9-10 to those listening to him preach; Matt 15:8-9 has Jesus apply Isa 29:13 to the Pharisees; Matt 21:5 has Jesus say that his entrance into Jerusalem on Palm Sunday fulfilled Zech 9:9-10; Matt 21:13 has Jesus combine Isa 56:7 with Jer 7:11 at the cleansing of the temple; Matt 24:29 echoes Ezek 32:7; Joel 2:10-11; and Zeph 1:15; Matt 26:31 has Jesus apply Zech 13:7 to himself; and Matt 26:64 has Jesus apply Dan 7:13 to himself, or at least quote it. Obviously, other NT books do the same sorts of things with some of these and with other OT texts, but these will suffice.

The Church as the New Israel

If the OT prophets were concerned with Israel as the people of God, the NT was concerned with the church (comprised of both Jews and Gentiles) as the people of God. The Apostle Paul, apparently the earliest author in the NT, lays out his case in both Galatians and Romans. In Galatians, however, Paul appeals to God's covenant with Abraham as a covenant of faith, not race. In Rom 1:17 he buttresses that argument by appealing to Hab 2:4: "the righteous one shall live by his faith." He also quotes Hos 2:23 in his argument in Rom 9:25-26: "Those who were not my people I will call 'my people,' and her who was not beloved I will call 'beloved'" (NRSV). In Hosea 2 the referent for "her" is first Gomer and then, in the allegory Hosea is weaving, the people of the northern kingdom of Israel. For Paul, the people are Christians, both Jew and Gentile, who now make up the new wife. In Rom 9:27-29 Paul cites two more texts from Isaiah: "Though the number of the children of Israel were like the sand of the sea, only a remnant of them will be saved; for the Lord will execute his sentence on the earth quickly and decisively" (NRSV; taken from Isa 10:22-23 with modification); and "If the Lord of hosts had not left survivors to us, we would have fared like Sodom and been made like Gomorrah" (NRSV; taken from Isa 1:9). Paul cites both texts (and more) as part of his argument that the church had become the true people of God, that God had brought in Gentiles before all Israel accepted Jesus as the Messiah as a means of securing their conversion. The book of Hebrews, though not itself Pauline, makes quite clear what Paul may well have had in mind when it cites Jeremiah's prediction of the new covenant (Jer 31:31-34) and claims that Jesus established that new and better covenant. The original, Hebrews says, is becoming old and obsolete.

One more text must suffice, 1 Pet 2:6, which quotes Isa 28:16:

> See, I am laying in Zion a stone, a cornerstone chosen and precious;
> and whoever believes in him will not be put to shame. (NRSV)

In Isaiah, the verse refers to God's intention to save Jerusalem. It does so by means of an image, namely that God is laying a new cornerstone for God's people. The name of the stone is the phrase "Whoever trusts will not hasten." The title is cryptic, but it possibly means that whoever trusted God would not hasten away or flee (prematurely) in fear of the Assyrians, but remain steadfast in his faith in God. In other words it offers assurance that

Israel would continue. For the author of 1 Peter, however, the cornerstone has become Jesus (2:4-5), and God would save Christians, those who believe "in him" (Jesus). The prophet Isaiah calls on his contemporaries to trust the God of Israel; 1 Peter substitutes what is for him the "real" Israel, the church, as the recipient of God's promises and care. Since the recipients of 1 Peter appear to be largely Gentiles, this use of Isa 28:16 is both evangelistic in its attempt to convert readers and polemical in its attempt to claim for Gentiles the perks Isaiah saw for Israel and Judah.

Two Other Jewish Approaches to the Prophets

The paradigm shift for Christian Jews in reading the OT was dramatic, but probably no less than for non-Christian Jews at the turn of the era. With the destruction of the temple in Jerusalem by the Romans in 70 C.E., Judaism was transformed from a religion focused on sacrifice into the religion of a people of the book. To be sure, that change did not happen all at once. The development of the synagogue, the experience of the Diaspora, and the impact of Hellenism on Palestine itself resulted in differing ways of being religious and differing ways of reading the books that eventually made up Jewish Scripture.

This is not the place to try to describe the development of Judaism, but it would be appropriate to point to ways some of those Jews appropriated the prophetic texts. To keep these remarks to a minimum, I will mention only the dissenting covenanters whose books appear among the Dead Sea Scrolls and the Hellenistically-influenced thinker Philo. To try to describe the use of the Prophets in the Talmud is too large a task for this space and would take us deeply into the first millennium of the Common Era (as would any attempt to trace the use of the Prophets further in the early church).

The Prophets among Selected Dead Sea Scrolls

The hypothesis that the Dead Sea Scrolls belonged to a group called Essenes has been challenged from time to time, but still remains the best.[18] The members of the group appear to have been a disenfranchised group

---

18. James C. VanderKam, *The Dead Sea Scrolls Today* (Grand Rapids: Wm. B. Eerdmans, 1994) 92, 97.

with aspirations to control the temple in Jerusalem. Judging by such texts as the *War Scroll, The Description of the New Jerusalem,* and others, their hopes were as apocalyptic as those in Daniel. For our purposes, however, it will be most useful to look at their treatment of prophetic texts.[19] We are in the fortunate position of having commentaries (called *pesherim*) on Isaiah, Hosea, Micah, Nahum, Habakkuk, Zephaniah, and Malachi. The most famous is the one on Habakkuk (abbreviated 1QpHab), which appears to have been written in the last century B.C.E.

The Commentary interprets the text of Habakkuk against the background of the dissenters' own experiences. Habakkuk itself opens (Hab 1:2-4) with a lament, in which the prophet complains about problems in his own, late-sixth-century context: violence and destruction abound, and justice is denied. The wicked surround the righteous. The Habakkuk Commentary, however, equates the "wicked" with a figure it calls the "Wicked Priest," most likely the Maccabean Jonathan, the successor (160-143) of Judas Maccabeus in their battle against the Seleucids. He perhaps earned the wrath of the Covenanters when he accepted from the Greek Alexander Balas priestly garments he was not qualified to wear. He was also called the Spouter of Lies, the Liar, and the Scoffer.[20] The upright man opposing the Wicked Priest was someone the Commentary calls "The Teacher of Righteousness," the founder of the Covenanters. According to the Commentary it was Jonathan's opposition to the Teacher that caused injustice to prevail. In its interpretation of Hab 1:6, God promises to rouse the Chaldeans (Babylonians) to punish the Wicked Priest and his followers, and the following verses detail their military prowess and fierceness. The Commentary identifies Chaldeans with the Kittim, the Romans, and designates them as the ones who will capture the wicked (Commentary on Hab 1:11).

These "interpretations" do two things. First, they turn the book of Habakkuk into a prediction of their own time and movement. Second, they show predictions fulfilled by the rise of the Wicked Priest Jonathan and thereby build confidence in the further predictions that the Romans would defeat him. The reader may believe what he reads because God has already brought to pass the first part of the prediction.

---

19. Commentaries and other works on texts other than those by prophets appear among the Dead Sea Scrolls. Those biblical books include Genesis, Exodus, Leviticus, Numbers, Deuteronomy, Samuel, Psalms, and Daniel.

20. Geza Vermes, *The Dead Sea Scrolls in English,* 3rd ed. (London: Penguin, 1987) 30-31.

In Hab 1:12 the lament of the prophet resumes. The remark in v. 13 that God's eyes are too pure to behold evil elicits the comment in the scroll that God had not led the evildoers to sin. The reference to those who are silent when the wicked swallow the innocent is interpreted as a reference to the "House of Absalom." Absalom, of course, was the name of one of David's rebellious sons (2 Sam 13–20), but perhaps the referent in the Commentary is an ambassador of Judas Maccabeus by that same name (mentioned in 2 Macc 11:17).[21] This Absalom did not assist the Teacher of Righteousness at the time of his reproach by the Man of Lies. As divine punishment the Kittim/Romans would enrich themselves with loot.

In Column 7 of the Commentary the author says that God told Habakkuk to write what was going to happen to the last generation (i.e., that of the author of the Commentary). The Commentary interprets the vision mentioned, but not explained, in Hab 2:2 as a reference to the teachings of the Teacher of Righteousness. None of the prophets described what would happen to that generation, but the Teacher of Righteousness could foresee their fate (a comment on 2:4). Habakkuk 2:8 foresees punishment on Babylon for its plundering its neighbor nations, but the Commentary applies it to "the last priests of Jerusalem," whose wealth will fall into the hands of the Romans. In other words, those who had persecuted the Teacher and his community would be defeated by the Romans.

The Commentary continues in this vein through the rest of Habakkuk, but this much is sufficient to show how the Community used the prophetic texts. What is also important for our purposes is to note that it claims that the Teacher of Righteousness saw further into the future than did the prophet Habakkuk himself. It is tantamount to claiming prophetic stature for the Teacher that exceeded that even of the Latter Prophets. For the Covenanters prophecy was alive and well in their community. It had not died with Malachi, but lived on in the Teacher of Righteousness.

The Prophets in Philo

Philo was an educated defender of Judaism who lived from about 20 B.C.E. to 50 C.E. in Alexandria, Egypt, the largest Jewish community outside of Palestine. Trained in Greek philosophy, especially Plato, he was an apolo-

---

21. Vermes, *The Dead Sea Scrolls in English*, 32-33.

gist for Judaism, often employing the allegorical method of interpretation. In his extant works, Philo devotes himself overwhelmingly to the Torah, whose author he identifies as Moses the prophet. He also calls Noah, Abraham, Isaac, Jacob, and every good man "prophets" (*Heir* LII.258-63). He names a number of other persons (male and female) from the Pentateuch, but the only Latter Prophet he names is Jeremiah (*Cherubim* 2, XIII.49). He nevertheless makes occasional references to prophets or prophetic books without naming them, so we shall examine those references briefly.

In a tract on Genesis (*QG* 2, 43), Philo quotes Isa 1:9, citing its author as "a certain prophet, the kinsman and friend of Moses."[22] This identification is a striking example of an anachronism, but it illustrates Philo's heavy concentration on defending Moses and the Torah. An allegorist himself, Philo quotes the allegorization of God as the husbandman of Israel in Isa 5:7 in his own work, *On Dreams* 2 (XXVI.172). He quotes Isa 48:22, which, however, is a verse reflecting on the patriarch Joseph, whom Philo considers a prophet (*Names* XXVIII.169). In discussing a warning of punishment attributed to Moses, Philo quotes Isa 54:1, which he quickly allegorizes into a saying concerning the joy of a soul restored to God after participating in a life of sin.

Philo also alludes to two verses in Jeremiah, one in Hosea, and one in Zechariah. In *Flight* XXXVI.197, he quotes Jer 2:13 with the note that God has said "somewhere" that God is the fountain of life. In defending the thesis that even wise people fight to defend virtue, he quotes Jer 15:10, in which Jeremiah complains that his career has led him to become a man of war and disquietude in the land (*Confusion* XI.44). In *Planting* XXXIII.138, Philo cites "one of the prophets" and quotes Hos 14:9, claiming it has to do with the fruit of the mind. (Cf. *Names* XXIV.139, which Philo says is "from the mouth of one of the prophets.") Finally, in *Confusion* XIII.62, he quotes Zech 6:12, calling the prophet one of the companions of Moses. Zechariah 6:12 refers to the man called "Branch," very likely Zerubbabel. The LXX translates the word for "Shoot" or "Branch" with a word meaning "rising" or "East," causing Philo to comment on how unusual the name is. That said, he allegorizes the name as another word for the soul.

For our purposes, what is most interesting here is how little significance Philo attaches to the prophets. Where he cites them at all, he does so to buttress his own interpretations of the Torah. Moses is his hero. To be sure, we do not have the whole literary production of Philo, but what we

---

22. *The Works of Philo*, trans. C. D. Yonge (Peabody: Hendrickson, 1993) 827.

have shows a preference for, if not a preoccupation with, the Torah over the Latter Prophets. This preference sets him apart from the slightly earlier Covenanters at Qumran and the slightly later followers of Jesus in the Jewish community in Palestine, both of which utilized far more of the books of the Law and the Prophets.

The End of Our Survey

We come to the end of our survey of the Major and Minor Prophets. They reveal themselves to be a collection of edited works designed to record, preserve, and make generally accessible the words of distinctive prophets in ancient Israel. Jonah and Daniel aside, these prophets were more associated with what they said than what they did. Even Jonah and Daniel are remembered as having done some preaching or speaking. The legacy of all these prophets was secured by scribes/editors and has impacted both Jews and Christians for thousands of years.

Questions for Reflection

1. What do you make of the insistence by some of the prophets that God demands justice on the part of God's people? Does that demand apply to Jews or Christians today? How well do modern democracies fare in preserving the rights and welfare of the poor?
2. Is God still faithful to the people of Israel? If so, who belongs to that people? How does the modern state of Israel fit into this picture, if at all? How does the United States fit, if at all?
3. How does the eschatology of the Old Testament compare and/or contrast with popular eschatology today?
4. Does learning about the process of canonization of the Bible make it seem any more or less inspired? Why?

For Further Reading

Gowan, Donald E. *Eschatology in the Old Testament.* 2nd ed. Edinburgh: T. & T. Clark, 2000. A canonical approach to the various presentations of eschatology in the Hebrew Bible, the Apocrypha, Pseudepigrapha, and contemporary manifestations.

Mason, Rex. *Old Testament Pictures of God*. Regent's Study Guides 2. Macon: Smyth & Helwys, 1993. A study of the terms and titles used to describe God in the Hebrew Bible.

Peters, F. E. *The Voice. The Word, the Books*. Princeton: Princeton University Press, 2007. A study of the rise of the Hebrew Bible, the New Testament, and the Quran from their earliest oral articulations through their transference to written documents, their publication as books, and their use in worship. Not written for specialists.

VanderKam, James C. *The Dead Sea Scrolls Today*. Grand Rapids: Wm. B. Eerdmans, 1994. A readable discussion of the discovery of the Dead Sea Scrolls, with a survey of the manuscripts, an identification and a discussion of the group responsible for them, and a discussion of their relationship to the OT and NT.

Glossary

Allegory A narrative containing a series of comparisons or metaphors. E.g., in Isa 5:1-7 the vineyard represents Israel, the grape plants represent the individual Israelites, and the owner represents God.

Alphabetical acrostic A literary genre in which the first word in the first line begins with the first letter of the alphabet, the first word in the second with the second letter of the alphabet, etc. Acrostics in the Bible may be complete or partial.

Apocalypse A "genre of revelatory literature with a narrative framework, in which a revelation is mediated by an otherworldly being to a human recipient, disclosing a transcendent reality which is both temporal, insofar as it envisages eschatological salvation, and spatial, insofar as it involves another, supernatural world." See John J. Collins, "Introduction: Towards the Morphology of a Genre," *Apocalypse: The Morphology of a Genre.* Semeia 14 (Missoula: Scholars, 1979) 9.

Apocalyptic Any literature taking the form of an apocalypse or sharing the thought world of apocalypses.

Apodictic A genre of laws that give commands or prohibitions.

Aramaic A Northwest Semitic language (or group of languages) closely related to Hebrew, but not identical to it. It became the official language of commerce during the Assyrian, Babylonian, and Persian periods and was used by Jews into the Common Era.

Authenticity A term indicating that a book derives from the author to whom tradition ascribed it. See also the related term "integrity."

Bible Taken from the Greek word *biblia* ("books"), the word refers to any collection of books chosen by groups as authoritative for them. For Jews the Bible is Tanak; for Christians both the Old and New Testaments.

Canon A word derived from the Greek word *kanon,* which designates a "rule" or "measure." By extension it has come to refer to an authoritative group of texts (e.g., the books in the Bible).

Chaldean Another name for the Neo-Babylonian Empire, which began in 626 B.C.E. when the Chaldean tribe in southern Babylonia took control over all of Babylonia.

Chiasmus A rhetorical structure that develops and then returns to its starting point in parallel phrases, lines, or thoughts.

Comedy A plot in which problems and difficulties are resolved to the benefit of the heroes and/or heroines.

Critical Any investigation or argument that moves forward on the basis of evaluation.

Criticism, Canonical The study of the Hebrew Bible in its final form, as a completed whole, as represented in the Masoretic Text.

Criticism, Form The attempt to uncover the earliest oral stage behind a written text and to describe its structure, the nature of its content, and its typical setting in life.

Criticism, Historical The attempt to uncover the historical background for biblical texts and sometimes to determine whether biblical narratives are historically likely.

Criticism, Ideological The study of the Hebrew Bible from a particular perspective (e.g. feminist, liberation, and third-world perspectives), searching for and evaluating the Bible's handling of those perspectives.

Criticism, Literary The effort to read the Bible mindful of its genres, structures, and literary devices. Broadly conceived it can include form, redactional, and rhetorical criticism, as well as narrative analysis. Scholars earlier than the 1970s used the term to designate what today is called source criticism.

Criticism, Narrative The effort to read biblical narratives as the reader implied by those texts.

Criticism, Poststructuralist The effort to read biblical texts from any of several recent reading approaches applied to the Bible after the rise of structural exegesis in the 1960s and 1970s. These methods include deconstructionism and ideological criticism.

Criticism, Reader An approach which recognizes that readers themselves participate in the making of meaning in texts. Reader critics note that all texts imply an author and audience. Those implied authors are the flesh-and-blood authors once removed, the authors as they attempt to portray themselves. The implied readers are the readers as the authors want them to be, seeing and buying into what the real authors want them to accept.

Criticism, Redaction The attempt to discern the theology, purposes or intentions, and perspectives of editors, particularly the main editor(s) who complied biblical books by taking account of such things as the place(s) of origin of traditions or sources, their arrangement within a larger work, and the introduction of such sources. Particular attention is given to disagreement between such editorial indicators and the traditions employed.

Criticism, Rhetorical The study of the literary artistry and effectiveness of a text.

Criticism, Social-scientific The use of the work of cultural anthropologists and sociologists to derive models by which to interpret biblical texts.

Criticism, Source The attempt to uncover and delineate written sources underlying a text.

Criticism, Structural A particular form of social-scientific criticism that focuses on interrelations or structures built on similarities and differences ranging from letters, syllables, and words to characters, plots, metaphors, and allusions to other texts.

Criticism, Text The attempt to reconstruct as far as possible the best wording for problematic biblical texts.

Cultus A site for worship, and the objects and persons associated with it.

Diaspora Judeans living outside Israel without foreign constraint forbidding a return.

Eschatology The doctrine of the end. In Christian theology, the term typically refers to the second coming of Jesus, resurrection, judgment, and the afterlife.

Scholars of the Hebrew Bible use the term to designate a radical change for the better instigated by God.

Exile   The time between 586 and 539 B.C.E. when Judeans were forced to live outside of Judah. The term also refers to the people experiencing the exile, usually in the plural (exiles).

Gliedgattung   A member genre or subgenre appearing in a larger text or *Rahmengattung*.

Hasmonean   The name of the family of priests who lived in Modein and staged the Maccabean Revolt against the Seleucids. Three brothers, Judas, Jonathan, and Simon, led the nation, one after another. Upon Simon's death, his descendants formed the Hasmonean dynasty, lasting until 63 B.C.E.

Hebrew Bible   Since Jews do not recognize the New Testament as Scripture, scholarly convention avoids calling the books recognized by Jews the "Old Testament," sometimes preferring instead the term "Hebrew Bible." Its three sections included Torah, Nebiim, and Kethubim.

Inauthenticity   A term designating that a book or section thereof did not originate with the author to whom the book is (traditionally) ascribed.

Incipit   The first sentence in a narrative that doubles as an introduction to what follows.

Inclusion   A stylistic device in which a piece returns to its starting place, making a full circle, as it were.

Integrity   A term indicating that a book is considered to derive from one hand; an alternative term is "unity." See also the related term "authenticity."

Intertextuality   The attempt to trace references in one text, such as allusions, citations, quotations, to other texts, particularly earlier texts.

Kethubim   A Hebrew word meaning "writings," it designates the third section of the Hebrew Bible, which contains in this order the books of Psalms, Job, Proverbs, Ruth, Song of Songs (or Song of Solomon), Ecclesiastes, Lamentations, Esther, Daniel, and Ezra-Nehemiah.

Levant   The countries bordering on the eastern shore of the Mediterranean Sea.

Lex talionis   A law of retaliation, as expressed in the formula "an eye for an eye, a tooth for a tooth." The idea is that revenge should be proportional to the damage received.

Mantic Wisdom derived from divination.

Mantological Anthology Wisdom collections dealing with the reading of signs or the discovery of that which is hidden or obscure, whether in the present or the future.

Masoretic Text The text of the Hebrew Bible produced by Hebrew scholars called Masoretes, who worked between 600 and 1000 C.E., and who were concerned with the accurate transmission of the Hebrew Bible. The term also refers to the system of vowels, accentuation, and other pointers for reading the consonantal text.

Megilloth A Hebrew word meaning "scrolls." The *Megilloth* are the five books Ruth, Song of Songs, Ecclesiastes, Lamentations, and Esther. See **Kethubim.**

Monolatry Belief in and the worship of one God out of all the gods. It does not deny the existence of other gods, but declines to worship them.

Monotheism Belief in and the worship of one God, combined with the denial of the existence of all other gods.

Nebiim A Hebrew word meaning "prophets," it includes both the four Former Prophets (Joshua, Judges, Samuel, and Kings — though not Ruth, which belonged to the Kethubim) and the four Latter Prophets (Isaiah, Jeremiah, Ezekiel, and the Book of the Twelve, the Minor Prophets of the Christian OT together counted as one book). The books of Lamentations and Daniel belong to the Kethubim.

Negeb The area roughly between Beer-sheba in southern Judah and Kadesh-barnea. Edom lay traditionally to its east, but seems to have gained control over the Negeb during the Babylonian period and afterward.

Parallelism The repetition of the same or similar semantic patterns, content, or words in consecutive lines of Hebrew poetry.

Pesher/Pesherim A loanword from Aramaic that means "commentary/commentaries."

Peshitta A term meaning "ordinary" or "simple," designating the Bible in Syriac.

Profane Something not dedicated to God or something holy that has been defiled or made common. Antonym of "sacred."

Pseudonym A "false" or assumed name taken by an author, to whom the author's thinking is thereby ascribed. A pen name.

Ptolemies Rulers of Egypt following the death of Alexander the Great and the subsequent breakup of the empire he had conquered. Their founder was Ptolemy I (323-285), one of Alexander's generals. The Ptolemies ruled Israel until it was taken by the Seleucids in 200-198.

Rahmengattung A German word meaning "overarching genre." It designates longer literary works (e.g., "short story" or "novel") that contain shorter *Gliedgattungen* or "member genres" (e.g., poem, joke, fairy tale).

Reading, Diachronic A reading of a text that follows its development through time, separating earlier and later strands.

Reading, Synchronic A reading of a text that follows it straight through (or *with time*), as though the text emerged in the order in which it stands in the Bible.

Sacred A special status belonging to persons, objects, and events dedicated to God.

Seleucids Rulers of Mesopotamia after the breakup of the empire conquered by Alexander the Great. Their founder was Seleucus I (312/11-280), who ruled Israel beginning in 200-198.

Septuagint A translation of the Hebrew Bible into Greek, typically abbreviated LXX.

Shephelah A name meaning "lowland" and designating the area between the coastal plain and the hill country of Judah.

Sin A wrongdoing or wrong attitude against God that separates a person or persons from God. Sin also includes failure to obey God (sometimes called "sins of omission") and violating the rules of ritual. A sin may also harm humans or break human laws, but what makes a behavior a sin is that it is directed against God, knowingly or unknowingly.

Superscription A heading consisting of nouns (not sentences), which may be elaborated by adding phrases and relative clauses. It usually supplies the name and perhaps other information about the author of a book, section of a book, or a chapter.

Talmud Ancient rabbinic writings from ca. 200-600 C.E., consisting of the Mishnah (Jewish oral law) and the Gemara (secondary writings on that law).

Tanak An acronym designating the Hebrew Bible, taken from the initial letters of its component parts, Torah, Nebiim, and Kethubim.

Teacher of Righteousness The prophetic teacher whose life and teachings are the key focus of the Habakkuk Commentary among the Dead Sea Scrolls.

Theodicy The defense of God's goodness.

Theophany A visible manifestation of a god.

Torah A Hebrew word meaning "instruction." These instructions or teachings were delivered by priests and took on the force of "law." The term also designates the first five books of the Hebrew Bible, where the preponderance of such instructions appears.

Tragedy A plot in which problems and difficulties are resolved with serious losses to the hero(es) and/or heroine(s).

Tradition History A method of biblical criticism that attempts to trace the rise of a biblical passage from its earliest oral to its final written stage, and perhaps its reuse in later books (cf. Intertextuality).

Unity A term applied to the authorship of a biblical book meaning that the book's contents derive from one author.

Vision A narrative genre describing an altered state of consciousness in which a prophet or a seer perceives extrasensory experiences.

Vulgate The Latin translation of the Bible that replaced earlier translations called "Old Latin." This translation was begun by Jerome and completed after his death.

Wicked Priest The priest, probably the Maccabean Jonathan, who opposed the Teacher of Righteousness according to the Habakkuk Commentary.

Index of Authors

Index of Names

Index of Subjects

Abomination that makes desolate, 175

Acrostic, 134, 135, 287, 288, 290, 297

Adultery, 50, 127, 137, 210, 211

Apocalypse(s), 19, 45, 55, 57, 76, 77, 87, 165, 168, 169, 170, 179, 192, 263, 325

Apocalyptic, 42, 87, 168, 169, 170, 171, 172, 179, 184, 226, 236, 325

Canon, x, 17, 19, 41, 54, 109, 117, 132, 143, 144, 148, 152, 172, 189, 190, 192, 212, 226, 238, 250, 256, 266, 285, 293, 304, 316, 322, 332, 344

Chiasmus, 39, 293

Cleansing, 191, 307, 310, 322, 323, 326, 328, 334, 337, 338, 346, 350, 369

Court narrative(s), 42, 179

Covenant, 96, 116, 240, 253, 257, 263, 348, 352, 357, 358, 360, 370; Code, 219; Davidic, 127, 139; fidelity, 160, 206, 223, 228, 359; lawsuit, 216, 269; Mosaic, 139, 127, 138, 139, 358; new, 8, 127, 128, 129, 160, 206, 223, 228, 359

Creation, 20, 86, 87, 88, 89, 92, 99, 101, 102, 105, 107, 173, 217, 263, 265, 270, 304, 340, 360, 363

Criticism: Black, 26, 49; Canonical, 26, 28, 32, 38, 40, 41, 60, 105, 202, 203, 212, 227, 247, 249, 292, 338, 343, 375; Feminist, 26, 38, 50, 119; Form, 25, 29, 31, 32, 34, 41, 43, 45, 60, 122, 136, 203, 231, 270; Historical, 25, 34, 35, 36, 47, 279, 296; Ideological, 26, 49, 51, 224; Narrative, 26, 44, 45, 46, 47; Reader, 26, 32, 44, 46, 48; Redaction, 25, 32, 33, 34, 40, 41, 81, 114, 117, 152, 176, 178, 181, 198, 206, 212, 214, 287, 288, 295, 296, 297, 298, 299, 300, 306, 309, 316, 317, 334, 339, 343; Rhetorical, 26, 38, 39, 40, 105; Social-scientific, 26, 34, 41, 183; Source, 25, 28, 31, 32, 34, 41, 51, 55, 112, 141, 181, 200, 276, 279, 348; Structural, 26, 39, 42, 43, 44, 46, 51, 150; Textual, 25, 26, 27; Third World, 26, 38, 49, 244

Day of YHWH/Lord, 206, 234, 235, 236, 243, 245, 250, 253, 254, 255, 306, 309

Divination, 2, 5

Divorce, 204, 205, 209, 210, 235, 237, 247, 315, 345, 347, 353

Election, 2, 356, 357

Eschatology, 67, 76, 83, 104, 168, 169, 170, 171, 172, 325, 356, 363, 363, 367

Ethics, 161, 367

Exile, 6, 7, 8, 10, 28, 29, 37, 55, 56, 61, 79,

Index of Selected Biblical
and Ancient Author References

400 INDEX OF SELECTED BIBLICAL AND ANCIENT AUTHOR REFERENCES

8-18 252
11 250
11-14 253
16 255
17 199, 228, 229, 252, 362
18 255
19-20 255
19-21 252

Jonah

1:2 257
1:3 40
1:17 335
2:3-7 260
2:8-9 260
3:3 258
3:4 15, 44
3:7-9 261
3:9-10 257
4:2 205, 206, 228, 257, 261, 286

Micah

1–5 271
1–3 267, 308
1:1 267, 308
1:3-4 270
1:4-5 274
1:10-15 271, 272
1:13 266
2:1-11 270
2:4 271
2:6-11 273
2:12-13 279
3:1 277
3:1-4 270
3:1-12 274
3:6-8 274
3:9 277
3:12 40, 271, 274
4–5 102, 268, 277, 279
4:1-3 63, 267, 271
4:3 228

4:4 228
4:5 63, 271, 279
4:6-7 279, 362
4:8 266
4:9-10aα 277
4:10 266
4:13 266
5:2 368, 369
5:2-5a 13, 267, 268, 280, 281
5:5b-6 256
5:7-8 279
6:1-5 269
6:1–7:7 268
6:4 345
6:6-7 270
6:6-8 361
6:8 358
6:9-12 276
7:1-7 270
7:8-20 268, 270, 284, 285
7:18 205, 206, 228, 267, 279, 280, 286, 362
7:18-20 205, 228

Nahum

1:1-8 285
1:2-3a 205, 206, 228, 267
1:2-8 288, 289
1:9-10 290
1:12a 291
1:14 291
2:3-13 291
2:11-13 289
3:1-15 291
3:16-17 291
3:18-19 289, 291

Habakkuk

1:1 296
1:1–2:5 294, 295

1:2-4 298
1:2–2:5 298
1:2–2:19 295, 296
1:5 372
1:5-11 298
1:11 372
1:12 373
1:12–2:1 299
2:2 373
2:2-5 301
2:4b 301, 362, 370
2:6-20 295
2:6b-8 297, 301
2:6b-17 296
2:6b-19 300
2:8 373
2:9-11 297
2:15-17 297
2:18-19 297, 359
2:20 300
3:1 296
3:2 296
3:3-15 296, 297
3:13 303
3:16 199
3:16-19 296, 297
3:17 297

Zephaniah

1:1 303, 307, 308
1:1–3:7 205, 285
1:2-9 310
1:2-18 306
1:2-28 206
1:2–2:15 307
1:4-5 312
1:4-6 304, 307, 359
1:10-13 307
1:14-16 310
2:1-3 306
2:1–3:20 306
3:1-13 304, 307, 310, 361
3:6-7 312
3:8 310

Index of Hebrew and Greek Words

HEBREW WORDS

'abib (ears [of grain], a month, roughly March/April), 149
'adam (Adam), 216
'edam (destruction), 253
'adamah (ground, tilled land), 310
'oi (woe), 241
'ishshah (woman, wife), 219
'el (god), 72
'el gibbor (godlike warrior), 78
'elohim (God, gods), 28, 340
'aram (Aram), 216

boqer (herdsman), 242
baqar (cattle, herd or oxen), 242
bethulah (virgin), 25, 72

dabar (word), 332

hoi (alas, woe), 241
hoshaiah (Yahweh has helped), 218

zikaron (memorial, remembrance), 327
zenunim (fornication), 219

hag (festival), 319
hozeh (seer, diviner), 16

homer (about 6.5 bushels), 218

yawan (Greece), 333
yitshar (fresh olive oil), 331
yashub (turn, return, repent), 74
Yeshayah (salvation of *yah*), 65

kethubim (the writings), 19, 165, 172
kethib (written), 27

le (to), 241
lethek (half a homer), 218

megilloth (scrolls), 133
maher-shalal-hash-baz (speedy spoil, hasty prey), 65, 67, 72
moshel (ruler), 278
micayah (Who is like Yah), 273, 280
melek (king), 277, 278
malkam (their king), 359
minhah (animal or grain sacrifice), 234
maskilim (wise men), 186
massa' (a prophetic pronouncement explaining what God is about to do), 63, 75, 296, 332

na'apupim (adulteries, whoredom), 219
nb' (root meaning prophesy), 274

GREEK WORDS